LAW AND SOCIAL CHANGE
IN
CONTEMPORARY BRITAIN

AUSTRALIA
The Law Book Co. of Australasia Pty Ltd.
Sydney : Melbourne : Brisbane

CANADA AND U.S.A.
The Carswell Company Ltd.
Toronto

INDIA AND PAKISTAN
N. M. Tripathi Ltd.
Bombay

NEW ZEALAND
Legal Publications Ltd.
Wellington

LAW AND SOCIAL CHANGE

IN

CONTEMPORARY BRITAIN

BY

W. FRIEDMANN

LL.D.(London), DR.IUR.(Berlin), LL.M.(Melbourne)
of the Middle Temple, Barrister-at-Law;
Professor of Law, University of Toronto

WITH A FOREWORD

BY

THE RIGHT HONOURABLE

SIR ALFRED DENNING

One of the Lords Justices of His Majesty's
Court of Appeal in England

LONDON

STEVENS & SONS LIMITED

1951

*First published in 1951
by Stevens & Sons Limited
of 119 & 120 Chancery Lane
London — Law Publishers
and Printed in Great Britain
by The Eastern Press Limited
of London and Reading.*

To The
University of Melbourne

CONTENTS

Foreword by the Right Hon. Sir Alfred Denning   ix

Preface   xi

Table of Statutes   xiii

Table of Cases   xvii

Abbreviations   xxiv

1. Introduction   3

PART ONE

THE COMMON LAW IN A CHANGING SOCIETY

2. The Functions of Property in Modern English Law   9

3. Changing Functions of Contract and the Common Law   34

4. Social Insurance and the Principles of Tort Liability   73

5. Public Welfare Offences and the Principles of Criminal Liability..   102

6. Freedom of Trade, Public Policy and the Courts   109

7. Trusts, Corporate Bodies and the Welfare State   ..   133

PART TWO

THE PLACE OF PUBLIC LAW IN CONTEMPORARY ENGLISH JURISPRUDENCE

8. Public Law Problems in recent English Decisions   153

9. The Legal Status and Organisation of the Public Corporation   187

10. Declaratory Judgment and Injunction as Public Law Remedies   217

Contents

PART THREE

STATUTE LAW AND THE WELFARE STATE

11. Statute Law and its Interpretation in the Modern
    State 237

12. Statute Law and the Privileges of the Crown .. 266

PART FOUR

THE WELFARE STATE AND THE RULE OF LAW

13. The Planned State and The Rule of Law 277

Suggested Readings 311

Index 315

FOREWORD

SOME of those who read Professor Friedmann's *Legal Theory* may have thought, as I did, that the first part of it was too philosophical but that the second part was of great interest and importance. My failure to appreciate the first part was due to a deep-seated distrust of abstract philosophy, a failing which is, I believe, shared by many of my fellow-countrymen. But my admiration of the second part was due to the light it threw on the practical problems which face lawyers at the present time: for in it Professor Friedmann analysed the effect of social changes on the law in a way not attempted in this country since the days of Maitland and Dicey.

In the present work Professor Friedmann has carried this analysis farther. He takes the great social revolution of our times and shows its effect on the law. He diagnoses the ills which affect the new-born welfare State and points the way to the remedies. He does this, not by vague generalisations, but by discussing the new statutes and the new cases which together make up the new law, and seeing what is the policy which prompts them, and what social purposes they fulfil. By doing this he opens up a new approach to legal problems. In former days lawyers used to think they were not concerned with the social changes which went on around them. No matter how society changed, the law never changed. The law for them was fixed and constant, never to be altered except by Parliament: and the meaning of Parliament was only to be gathered from the literal sense of the words used, not from the social purpose that lay behind the words. In this the lawyers deceived themselves. Judges and lawyers have always been influenced by the society in which they lived; and the sooner this fact is recognised the better. The great merit of Professor Friedmann's book is that it shows us the pattern of legal development against its social background: and thus enables us to know what we are about. A craftsman always works better if he not only knows how to do this or that, but also why he does it.

I cannot help thinking that one of the great advantages enjoyed by Professor Friedmann is that he is so well acquainted with the laws of many countries. The title page shows that he is a Doctor of Laws of London and Berlin, and Master of Laws of Melbourne. These are not mere honorary degrees, but degrees conferred for his learning. Brought up under a continental legal system, he afterwards came to England and studied the common law in its home surroundings. Transferred to Australia and thence to Canada, he has seen the development of the common law in the new nations of the Commonwealth. He is able to compare the legal systems of the world in a way which few others have been able to do. Thence he is able to draw the lessons which each system is able to teach the other.

At one time, imbued with native prejudice, I thought that no one could catch the spirit of the common law unless he had been bred in it. Professor Friedmann's book effectively dispels that prejudice. Here he teaches us more about ourselves and our law than we ourselves knew. He puts it all, statute-law and judge-made law, into its social setting. He fits it all into one great canvas and shows that the law is simply a means—albeit an elaborate and uncertain means—by which society works out its purposes.

A. T. DENNING.

PREFACE

THIS book attempts to apply the general approach to the study of law and society, developed in the second part of my *Legal Theory*, to some vital problems of contemporary jurisprudence. It is a comparative study, with frequent references to other common law systems and to continental law. But legal and social developments in Great Britain have furnished the starting point and most of the material used.

Some parts of the book have been published as articles, although they have all been revised and brought up to date. I should like to thank the editors of the following publications for permission to reprint, wholly or in part, articles published by them:—

The Australian Law Journal (chaps. 10, 13).
The British Journal of Sociology (chap. 2).
The Canadian Bar Review (chap. 11).
Current Legal Problems (chap. 8).
The Harvard Law Review (chap. 4).
Law and Contemporary Problems (chap. 9).
The Modern Law Review (chaps. 5, 6, 12).
The University of Toronto Law Journal (chap. 3).

I should also like to thank the Melbourne University Press for permission to use parts of my *The Planned State and the Rule of Law*, published by them in 1948 (chap. 13).

Sir Geoffrey Vickers, v.c., Professor L. C. B. Gower, and Dr. O. Kahn-Freund, of the University of London, and Professor G. W. Paton, Vice-Chancellor of the University of Melbourne, have each read some parts of the book. While none of them bears any responsibility for either the views expressed or the errors committed in this book,

I should like to thank them for their helpful and valuable criticisms. The notes on American law in chapter 4 are the work of the editors of *The Harvard Law Review*, who have kindly permitted me to use them.

Lord Justice Denning has generously consented to write a short Foreword. His active interest in legal education, and his own, judicial and extra-judicial, efforts to link legal and social problems are an inspiration to law teachers. Finally, I should like to thank Messrs. Stevens & Sons, who have, as always, been most helpful and enterprising in publishing a book of this kind.

Most of this book was written during my tenure of the Chair of Public Law in the University of Melbourne. It is dedicated to that great University.

W. F.

TORONTO,
August, 1951.

TABLE OF STATUTES

GREAT BRITAIN

Acquisition of Land (Authorisation and Procedure) Act, 1946   291
Agriculture Act, 1947   .   .   26, 57, 189, 192, 194, 200-01, 280, 290
Agricultural Wages Act, 1948   49
Air Corporations Act, 1949   .   .   .   198, 199-200, 203, 215

Bankruptcy Act, 1914   263
British North America Act, 1867   .   .   .   .   253-54, 283

Catering Wages Act, 1943   49
Cinematograph Film Order, 1943   69
Civil Aviation Act, 1949   198
Civil Defence Act, 1939   174
Coal Industry Act, 1949   .   .   .   .   .   .   58, 189, 194
Coal Industry Nationalisation Act, 1946   .   189, 194, 196, 197, 198-99, 206
Coal Mines Act, 1911   .   .   .   .   .   86, 92, 94, 290
Companies Act, 1929   248
Companies Act, 1948   136-37
Cotton Manufacturing Industry (Temporary Provisions) Act,
    1934   .   .   .   .   20, 50
Criminal Justice Act, 1925   105
Crown Proceedings Act, 1947   .   .   35, 93, 106, 158, 209, 218, 260

Defence Regulations, 1939.   .   .   .   .   157-58, 159, 167

Education Act, 1944   .   .   .   .   257-58, 263, 293-94
Electricity Act, 1947   .   .   .   189, 194, 198, 200, 206, 212, 290
Emergency Powers (Defence) Act, 1939   .   .   .   69, 171, 246

Factories Act, 1937   .   .   .   .   .   86, 92, 94, 290
Finance Act, 1910   218
Finance (No. 2) Act, 1939   263
Finance Act, 1943   262
Furnished Houses (Rent Control) Act, 1946   .   .   .   162

Gaming Act, 1845   260
Gas Act, 1948   .   .   .   .   .   .   189, 195, 196

Hire-Purchase Act, 1948   47
Housing Act, 1925   .   .   .   .   .   .   86, 160, 248
Housing Act, 1936   .   .   .   .   .   56-57, 160-61

Iron and Steel Act, 1949   .   .   59, 189, 194, 196, 197, 198, 206

Land Drainage Act, 1930 . . . . . . 175, 177
Landlord and Tenant (Rent Control) Act, 1949 . . 58
Law of Property Act, 1925 35
Law Reform (Contributory Negligence) Act, 1945 . . 260
Law Reform (Frustrated Contracts) Act, 1943 . . . 59
Law Reform (Personal Injuries) Act, 1948 . . 43, 85, 88-91
Legal Aid and Advice Act, 1949 148
Limitation Act, 1939 . . . . 182, 207

Maritime Conventions Act, 1911 245
Married Women's Property Act, 1882 263
Medical Act, 1950 148
Monopoly and Restrictive Practices (Inquiry and Control)
    Act, 1948 . . . . 17, 130, 292

National Assistance Act, 1948 . . . . 194, 207, 257, 258
National Health Service Act, 1946 . 27, 74, 87, 189, 192, 194, 200,
                   206, 207-08, 215, 257, 258
National Insurance Act, 1946 . . . . 21, 27, 87, 257, 280
National Insurance (Industrial Injuries) Act, 1946 . 21, 56, 74, 87
New Towns Act, 1946 . . . 189, 194, 198, 200, 206, 212, 290

Overseas Resources Development Act, 1948 . . . 189

Patents and Designs Act, 1949 23-24
Public Authorities Protection Act, 1893 207

Road Traffic Act, 1930 . . . . 47, 247
Road Traffic Act, 1934 137

Solicitors Act, 1932 148
State Carriages Act, 1832 263
Statute of Westminster, 1931 253
Supplies and Services Act, 1945 69

Town and Country Planning Act, 1943 162-63
Town and Country Planning Act, 1947 . 189, 192, 194, 207, 290

AUSTRALIA

COMMONWEALTH

Australian Industries Preservation Act, 1906 . . . 125
Banking Act, 1945 27
Communist Party Dissolution Act, 1950 159
Re-establishment and Employment Act, 1945 . . . 103

SOUTH AUSTRALIA

Electricity Trust of South Australia Act, 1946 . . . 215

AUSTRALIA—*continued*
VICTORIA

Landlord and Tenant Act, 1948	269
Railways Act, 1928	269

WESTERN AUSTRALIA

Crown Proceedings Act, 1947	35

CANADA
DOMINION

Income Tax Act, 1948	263
Federal Industrial Relations and Disputes Investigations Act, 1948	52
National Emergency Transitional Powers Act, 1946 . .	259
War Measures Act, 1927	263

ONTARIO

Charitable Gifts Act, 1949	139
Labour Relations Act, 1950	52
Workmen's Compensation Act, 1950	100

SASKATCHEWAN

Automobile Accident Insurance Act, 1947 . . .	100

FRANCE

Code Civil, 1805	11

GERMANY

Cartel Law, 1923	17
Civil Code, 1900	11, 68
Fundamental Tax Law, 1919	263

GREECE

Civil Code, 1946	68

SWITZERLAND

Civil Code, 1907 . . . . 11, 252, 277, 295

U.S.A.

Clayton Act, 1914	17, 292
Declaratory Judgments Act, 1934—1948	230
Labour Management Relations Act, 1947	51
National Labour Relations Act, 1935	50-51
Sherman Act, 1890	17, 292

Table of Statutes

U.S.S.R.

Civil Code, RSFSR. (1923) 23, 65, 101
Decree of Council of Ministers, April 21, 1949 . . 66

INTERNATIONAL CONVENTIONS

Brussels Convention, 1926 272

TABLE OF CASES

GREAT BRITAIN

Adams v. Naylor	93
Allen v. Flood	110, 113
Almeroth v. Chivers Limited	260
Ashbury Carriage Co. v. Riche	201
Associated Provincial Picture Houses Ltd. v. Wednesday Corp.	166
Attorney-General v. Ashborne Recreation Ground	222
Attorney-General v. Hancock	267
Attorney-General v. North Eastern Railway	224
Attorney-General v. Premier Lines	222, 225, 229
Attorney-General v. Sharp	222, 225, 229
Attorney-General v. Wimbledon House Estate Co.	224
Attorney-General for Alberta v. Attorney-General for Canada	248
Attorney-General of Australia v. Adelaide S.S. Co.	125
Attorney-General for Ontario v. Attorney-General for Canada	253
Ball v. L.C.C.	76, 96
Barcock v. Brighton Corporation	85
Barker v. Allanson	136
Barraclough v. Brown	220
Benham v. Gambling	37
Bilston Corporation v. Wolverhampton Corporation	220
Blackpool Corporation v. Locker	167, 286, 300
Bowman, Re	242
Boyce v. Paddington Borough Council	219, 221, 228
Bradford Corporation v. Pickles	22, 23
British Coal Corporation v. The King	248, 253
British Movietonews v. London & District Cinemas Ltd.	69
Brocklebank v. R.	260
Burland v. Earle	204
Caminer v. Northern & London Investment Trust Ltd.	79
Candler v. Crane, Christmas & Co.	78
Cassidy v. Minister of Health	96
Caswell v. Powell Duffryn Collieries	85
Cavalier v. Pope	35, 77, 83
Charing Cross Electricity Supply Co. v. Hydraulic Power Co.	81
Clark v. Epsom R.D.C.	220
Colonial Sugar Refining Co. v. Melbourne Harbour Trust Commissioners	242
Congreve v. Inland Revenue Commissioners	243
Conway v. Wade	116
Coomber v. Justices of the County of Berkshire	210, 298
Cooper v. Wilson	220

xvii

Crofter Harris Tweed Co. *v.* Veitch . . 42, 109, 117, 118, 131, 147
Crown Milling Company *v.* The King 127

Daniels *v.* R. White & Sons Ltd. 77
Deen *v.* Davies 83
Devonport Corporation *v.* Tozer 222
Donaldson *v.* Institute of Botano-Therapy . . . 146
Donoghue *v.* Stevenson 25, 75, 77, 78
Duncan *v.* Cammell Laird & Co. 158, 307
Dyson *v.* Attorney-General 218, 227

Ecclesiastical Persons Case 267
Edginton *v.* Swindon Corporation 174, 242
Ellerman Lines *v.* Murray 245, 248, 261
Ellis *v.* Fulham B.C. 82, 96
English Hopgrowers Ltd. *v.* Dering 127
Estate & Trust Agencies *v.* Singapore Improvement Trust . 247
Eurymedon, The 245, 261
Evans, Joseph *v.* Heathcote 123, 125, 127

Fairman *v.* Perpetual Investment Building Society . . 96
Falmouth Boat Construction Ltd. *v.* Howell . . 180
Fisher *v.* Ruislip U.D.C. 171, 185
Foss *v.* Harbottle 204
Franklin *v.* Minister of Town & Country Planning 31, 148, 170, 248, 291
Free Church of Scotland *v.* Overtoun . . . 144

General Medical Council *v.* Spackman . . . 129, 143
Glasgow Corporation *v.* Taylor 82
Grant *v.* Australian Knitting Mills 76

Haseldine *v.* C. A. Daw & Son Ltd. . . . 77, 79, 96
Heath's Garage Ltd. *v.* Hodges 83
Henson *v.* L.N.E.R. 46
Heydon's Case 240, 257, 263
Hilder *v.* Dexter 245
Hill *v.* William Hill (Park Lane) Ltd. . . . 259
Hilton *v.* Eckersley 123
Holland *v.* London Society of Compositors . . 50, 52
Holt *v.* Inland Revenue Commissioners . . . 243, 262
Horton *v.* London Graving Dock Co. . . . 78, 83, 96
Horwood *v.* Millar's Timber & Trading Co. . . 37
Howard de Walden *v.* Inland Revenue Commissioners . 243
Hughes *v.* Williams 83, 95
Hulland *v.* Sanders 50
Hutley's Legal Charge, *Re* 268
Hyams *v.* Stuart King 259

Ideal Films *v.* Richards 136
Imperial Tobacco Company *v.* Parslay . . . 128
Institute of Patent Agents *v.* Lockwood . . . 223

Jacobs *v.* L.C.C. 96
Johnson *v.* Ministry of Health 31, 148, 170, 248
Jones *v.* Green 160

Kent *v.* East Suffolk River Catchment Board . 63, 175, 184, 233
Kruse *v.* Johnson 164, 202

Latilla *v.* Inland Revenue 243
Leeds Industrial Co-operative *v.* Slack . . . 232
Lennard's Carrying Co. Ltd. *v.* Asiatic Petroleum Co. Ltd. 102
Levene *v.* Inland Revenue Commissioners 30, 242
Liesbosch Dredger *v.* Edison S.S. 36
Liversidge *v.* Anderson . . . 157, 159, 183, 246, 254, 307
Lochgelly Iron & Coal Co. *v.* M'Mullan . . . 86
London County Council *v.* Attorney-General . . . 222, 231
London County Territorial & Auxiliary Forces Association *v.*
    Nichols 268
London Graving Dock Co. *v.* Horton . . . 78, 83, 96
London Passenger Transport Board *v.* Moscrop . 220, 228, 231
Lumley *v.* Gye 113

McEllistrim *v.* Ballymacelligott Co-operative Agricultural and
    Dairy Society 123, 125
MacLean *v.* Workers' Union 129, 145
Magdalen College Case 267
Marriage *v.* East Norfolk Catchment Board . . . 177
Mason *v.* Provident Clothing Co. 21, 43
Mersey Docks Trustees *v.* Gibbs 210
Metropolitan Asylum District *v.* Hill 173, 184
Middlesex County Council *v.* Miller 165
Minister of Health *v.* Yaffe 248
Mint *v.* Good 79, 83
Mogul Steamship Company *v.* MacGregor Gow & Co.
    42, 110, 112, 117, 121, 292
Monk *v.* Warbey 25, 247
Morgan *v.* Liverpool Corporation . . . 57, 86, 160, 246
Morris *v.* Saxelby 43

Nakkuda Ali *v.* M.F. De S. Jayaratne . . 159, 170, 246
Nokes *v.* Doncaster Amalgamated Collieries . . 248, 263
Nordenfelt *v.* Maxim Nordenfelt Guns & Ammunition Co. 43
North Western Salt Co. *v.* Electrolytic Alkali Co. . 126
Northwestern Utilities Ltd. *v.* London Guarantee &
    Accident Co. 81

Oakes *v.* Minister of War Transport 174
Otto *v.* Bolton 77

Paine *v.* Colne Valley Electricity Co. 77

Parkinson (Sir Lindsay) & Co. Ltd. *v.* Commissioner of Works
    and Public Buildings 69
Powlett *v.* Attorney-General 219
Pratt *v.* British Medical Association 129
Pratt *v.* Cook 56
Province of Bombay *v.* Municipal Corporation of Bombay 268

Quinn *v.* Leathem 42, 110, 113, 114

R. *v.* Armagh 267
R. *v.* Bedwelty U.D.C., *ex parte* Price . . . 206
R. *v.* Cory Brothers 105
R. *v.* Electricity Commissioners . . . 30, 148, 169, 247, 266
R. *v.* Fulham Rent Tribunal 171
R. *v.* Halliday 307
R. *v.* I.C.R. Haulage Ltd. 105
R. *v.* International Trustee 272
R. *v.* Lewisham Union 206
R. *v.* Northumberland Comp. Appeal Tribunal . . . 171
R. *v.* Paddington & St. Marylebone Rent Tribunal . . 162, 171
R. *v.* Woodrow 107
Ransom and Luck *v.* Surbiton B.C. . . . 63, 162, 182, 184
Read *v.* Croydon Corporation 25
Read *v.* J. Lyons & Co. 80, 81, 93
Rederiaktiebolaget Amphitrite *v.* The King . . 179, 183, 272
Reilly *v.* The King 181
Reynolds *v.* Shipping Federation 117
Rickards *v.* Lothian 80
Riddell *v.* Reid 86
River Wear Commissioners *v.* Adamson . . . 245
Roberts *v.* Hopwood 164, 166, 202, 246, 247
Robertson *v.* Minister of Pensions . . . 180, 185
Robinson *v.* Minister of Town & Country Planning . 203
Robinson *v.* South Australia 307
Rose *v.* Ford 37, 245, 260
Russell *v.* Duke of Norfolk 146
Rylands *v.* Fletcher 75, 80, 81, 94

Salomon *v.* Salomon 31
Scottish Co-operative Wholesale Society *v.* Glasgow Fleshers'
    Trade Defence Association 115
Scranton's Trustees *v.* Pearse 245
Searle *v.* Wallbank 84, 95
Smeeton *v.* Attorney-General 220
Smith *v.* Baker 85
Smith *v.* River Douglas Catchment Board . . . 63, 176, 185
Sorrell *v.* Smith 110, 116, 147
Speed *v.* Swift 85
Stanton *v.* Southwick 86
Summers *v.* Salford Corporation . . 21, 57, 86, 160, 246, 247, 258

Taff Vale Railway Co. *v.* Amalgamated Society of Railway
    Servants 136
Tamlin *v.* Hannaford 192, 208, 213, 269
Taylor *v.* Brighton Corporation 30
Temperton *v.* Russell 113, 115
Thomson *v.* British Medical Association . . . 129
Thorne *v.* Motor Trade Association 42, 110, 128, 147
Turburville *v.* West Ham Corporation . . . 181, 185

United Australia Ltd. *v.* Barclays Bank 261

Vestey's (Lord) Executors *v.* I.R.C. 30, 243, 262

Walker, *Re* Decision of 165, 247
Walker *v.* Sur 136
Ware and De Frevill *v.* Motor Trade Association . . 115
Weinberger *v.* Inglis 129, 144
Western Engraving Company *v.* Film Laboratories Ltd. . 80
Westminster Corporation *v.* L.N.E.R. . . . 202
White *v.* Kuzych 147
Willon *v.* Berkeley 266
Wilsons & Clyde Coal Company *v.* English . . . 21, 84, 299
Wringe *v.* Cohen 79
Wyatt *v.* Kreglinger 38, 126

Young *v.* Canadian Northern Railway Company . . 52

AUSTRALIA

Anderson *v.* Commonwealth of Australia . . . 219
Attorney-General *v.* Gill 223, 230
Attorney-General for Victoria *v.* Commonwealth (Pharmaceu-
    tical Benefits Case) 221, 227, 231
Australian National Airways *v.* Commonwealth (Airlines Case) 302

Bank of New South Wales *v.* Commonwealth (Bank
    Nationalisation Case) 255, 256
Bertrand *v.* The King 181

Cain *v.* Doyle 102, 108
Cameron *v.* Hogan 145
Council of the Shire of Hornsby *v.* Danglade . . . 222, 226
Crouch *v.* Commonwealth 220

David Jones *v.* Leventhal 218

Electricity Trust of South Australia *v.* Lintern's Ltd. . . 214

Graham, *Ex parte*: *Re* Forestry Commission . . . 213
Grain Elevators Board (Vic.) *v.* Shire of Dunmunkle . . 212, 214

Hume *v.* Munro 218

James *v.* Commonwealth 255
Jumbunna Case 254

McKernan *v.* Fraser 110, 114, 117
Marks *v.* Forest Commission 213, 240
Minister of Works (W.A) *v.* Gulson . . . 268, 269

New South Wales *v.* Bardolph 179
N. Sydney Council *v.* Housing Commission . . . 269

Oriental Holdings Pty. Ltd., *Re* 213

Ramsay *v.* Aberfoyle Manufacturing Company . 225, 226, 229
Reid *v.* Sinderberg 256
Repatriation Commission *v.* Kirkland 213

Sydney Harbour Trust Commissioners *v.* Ryan . . . 213, 269
Sydney Municipal Council *v.* Housing Commission of N.S.W. 213

Tasmania *v.* Victoria 227
Tooth & Company Ltd. *v.* Coombes 218
Toowoomba Foundry Pty. Ltd. *v.* Commonwealth . . 221

Union Label Case 224

Victorian Chamber of Manufacturers *v.* Commonwealth
    (Industrial Lighting Case) 308
Victorian Railways Commissioners *v.* Greelish . . . 213
Victorian Railways Commissioners *v.* Herbert . . 213, 269

Yates *v.* Vegetable Seeds Commission 168

CANADA

Aris *v.* Toronto, Hamilton & Buffalo Railway Co. . . 52

Canadian Wheat Board *v.* Hallet Carey; Attorney-General of
    Canada *v.* Nolan 258

Kennedy *v.* Union Estates Ltd. 78

Nova Mink Ltd. *v.* T.C.A. 78

Wright *v.* Calgary Herald 52

UNITED STATES

Adkins *v.* Children's Hospital 20

Carbide Corporation of America *v.* American Patents
    Development Corporation 25
Colegrove *v.* Green 230
Coppage *v.* Kansas 40

Degge *v.* Hitchcock 230

Flies *v.* Fox Bros. Buick Co. 77

Galeppi Bros. Inc. *v.* Bartlett 83

Hartford-Empire Co. *v.* United States 25

J. I. Case Co. *v.* N.L.R.B. 51

Korematsu *v.* United States 256

Lochner *v.* New York 20

MacPherson *v.* Buick Motor Co. 76
Moody *v.* Model Window Glass Co. 51
Moran *v.* Pittsburgh-Des Moines Steel Co. . . . 76

Nanay *v.* Raimist 110
New York *v.* United States 211, 255

Ohio *v.* Helvering 211, 298

Pacific Fire Insurance Company *v.* Kenny Boiler & Mfg. Co. 78

Schechter Poultry Corporation *v.* United States . . 20
Schlesinger *v.* Quinto 51
Shelley *v.* Portland Tug & Barge Co. . . . 51
Slavin *v.* Francis H. Leggatt & Co. 76
Special Equipment Co. *v.* Coe 25
Steward Machine Co. *v.* Davis 20

Vegelahn *v.* Guntner 114

West Coast Hotel *v.* Parrish 20
Wilson *v.* Airline Coal Co. 51

ABBREVIATIONS

A.L.J.	.. .. ..	Australian Law Journal
A.L.R.	.. .. ..	Argus Law Reports (Australia)
C.L.R.	.. .. ..	Commonwealth Law Reports (Australia)
Cal. L.R.	.. .. ..	California Law Review
Can. Bar. Rev.	.. ..	Canadian Bar Review
Col. L.R.	.. .. ..	Columbia Law Review
D.L.R.	.. .. ..	Dominion Law Reports (Canada)
Harv. L.R.	.. ..	Harvard Law Review
Ill. L.R.	.. .. ..	Illinois Law Review
L.Q.R.	.. .. ..	Law Quarterly Review
M.L.R.	.. .. ..	Modern Law Review
Penn. L.R.	.. ..	Pennsylvania Law Review
S.R. (N.S.W.)	.. ..	New South Wales State Reports (Australia)
T.L.R.	.. .. ..	Times Law Reports
V.L.R.	.. .. ..	Victorian Law Reports (Australia)
Virg. L.R.	.. ..	Virginia Law Review

INTRODUCTION

CHAPTER 1

INTRODUCTION

IN the greater of his two classical works, Dicey traced the interconnection between law and the evolution of public opinion and social policy through the nineteenth century. He showed in particular how the Liberal State which, under the influence of Bentham and his followers, had developed the legislative machinery in order to remove the many inequalities and archaic formalities of an antiquated legal system, thereby forged the weapon which new political philosophies could use as an instrument of social reform. Thus, Dicey—who through his *Law of the Constitution* greatly retarded and complicated the development of administrative law, vital though it is to the functioning of the modern State—clearly saw the growing importance of statutory legislation as an instrument of legal and social change.

Nearly half a century has passed since the first edition of Dicey's *Law and Opinion in England during the Nineteenth Century*. It has produced changes of staggering magnitude, not only on the battlefields and in the political position of the major States of the Western hemisphere, but also in their social structures. The social welfare State and the technique of planning have developed far beyond the stage which Dicey thought was advanced Socialism. This has meant a profound change in the structure and function of legal institutions, no less fundamental because in England it has come gradually. It is surely time for an attempt to re-assess the function of law and legal institutions in the vastly changed social pattern of contemporary England. Much brilliant work has been done on various aspects of this transformation, such as the judicial function in relation to social problems, the interpretation of statutes, the growth of standard contracts and collective bargaining, or the change in the structure and function of the law of property. But there have been few if any attempts to co-ordinate these various evolutions and to assess the interrelation of law and social change in present-day British society. It is the purpose of this book to discuss at least some aspects of this subject.

The first part analyses the transformation of some fundamental institutions of the common law. Utilising the work of some distinguished scholars, mainly American, it shows that contract is no longer predominantly the instrument of free bargaining between independent individual wills, but an institution with a vastly different function. Standard contracts, collective agreements, statutory terms incorporated into contracts, the growing number and significance of contracts to which a public authority is a party, these and many other factors make the modern law of contract a very different thing from what it was half a century ago and as it is still represented in most text-books on the subject.

Property in English law has never been the object of theoretical definitions similar to Romanistic and Continental jurisprudence. Hence the change in the meaning and function of the law of property has been less conspicuous. It has been none the less fundamental. In the nineteenth century, the owner of land, chattels, patents, leases, the employer of services, was presumed to use and dispose of his property freely, subject only to minor restrictions. In the age of the social welfare State, the powers of property have increasingly become a residue of rights, left after statutory restrictions on its use, compulsory licences, social insurance, statutory terms of employment and many other public law restrictions have transferred much of the substance of property from the private to the public sphere.

The growth of social insurance has made a comparable impact on the law of tort. As the State assumes responsibility for the various vicissitudes of life, for death, sickness, accidents, and old age, the function of tort, which is primarily that of adjusting the incidence of damage to person or property, according to principles of individual responsibility, undergoes a gradual transformation. The relevant chapter shows how the law of tort has been profoundly affected but not yet eliminated by the growth of State-sponsored social insurance.

Criminal law too requires—and has to some extent received, especially by American jurists—a new analysis in the light of the growth of State functions and of the use of criminal law as an administrative sanction. A brief study on this matter, provoked by an Australian decision, deals with the significance of these ' Public Welfare Offences ' and their impact on the principles of criminal liability. The last two chapters in this part are concerned with the impact of changes in industrial and social organisation on legal institutions. The first traces changing judicial interpretations of freedom of trade in contract and tort, resulting from the growth of trade unionism, corporate organisation in business, industry and the professions, and the evolution of public opinion. The second re-examines Maitland's analysis of the social function of trust and shows how the concentration of industry as well as the tax policies of the Welfare State has favoured the use of corporate devices.

The second part of the book is concerned with the increasingly important, though still largely uncharted, role of public law in the contemporary English legal system. Of the three chapters making up that part of the book, the first traces the growth of public law thinking in a number of leading English decisions of recent years and shows how public law problems are increasingly mixed up with problems of contract, tort, statutory interpretation and other matters which are still predominantly the province of the law courts. The second chapter deals with the legal position of the public corporations, a characteristically English attempt at blending the public ownership and management of industries and other public services, with elements of private law and individual enterprise. The third chapter deals with the much neglected, though extremely important, topic of public law remedies. Here again, in the absence of any comprehensive system of administrative procedure and jurisdiction, British and American law courts have adapted old equitable remedies, the declaratory judgment and the injunction, to new purposes.

The third part of the book is perhaps most directly connected with the theme of Dicey's analysis, for it discusses some aspects of statute law in the light of modern social developments. Despite the overwhelming importance of statute law, it is still, on the whole, the Cinderella of legal science and judicial wisdom. The main purpose of the two studies in that part is to suggest an approach to the interpretation of statutes better adapted to the great variety of subject-matters with which modern legislation is concerned, and also to plead for a reconsideration of outdated rules which still give the Crown an immunity from statutes suitable to a past age of royal privileges and State functions, but out of place in our time.

The last part of the book attempts to discuss a problem of great political, as well as juristic significance. How can the vastly increased functions of the modern State be reconciled with the tradition of the common law and, in particular, with the principles of democracy and individual rights inherent in the British tradition, although not incorporated in a written constitution? The analysis comes to the conclusion that such reconciliation is possible, provided there is a far greater readiness to adapt legal thinking to the social realities of the twentieth century.

It is hardly necessary to add that this is a preliminary and incomplete attempt to analyse problems which range over the whole field of jurisprudence. But if this study succeeds in stimulating more thinking and research on the problems which it indicates, it will have fulfilled its main purpose.

PART ONE

THE COMMON LAW
IN A CHANGING SOCIETY

THE FUNCTIONS OF PROPERTY IN MODERN ENGLISH LAW

THE recent English edition of a Continental classic on the social function of property[1] offers a welcome opportunity for the English lawyer to reflect on the meaning and function of property in English law, and the impact of modern legal policies on the law of property.

Renner's main concern is to show how the legal institution of ownership, which was adequate and just in a society where property, work and use in the economic substrate coincided, came to fulfil an entirely different function in the capitalist age. The following is a brief summary of Renner's thesis:

Originally, in medieval society, ownership, which in law means the absolute power of disposing over a thing, symbolises a unit of which the family form is typical. It comprises a complex of things, not only the house, the implements of work, stock, etc., but also the place of work and production, the place of consumption, the market and the family. In that stage, the legal conception of ownership represents, on the whole adequately, its economic substrate. But economic evolution gradually alters the function of ownership. When ownership of a complex of things, now regarded as capital, no longer coincides with the substrate of personal work, it becomes a source of a new power of command. Marx had given the underlying thought:

> The capitalist is not capitalist because he directs (the work), but he becomes an industrial commander, because he is a capitalist. Industrial command becomes an attribute of capital, as under feudalism the power of command was, in war and in the law, an attribute of ownership of land.

By means of this power, the capitalist exercises a quasi-public authority over those who are tied to him by the contract of service. The juristic institution is still the same as at the time when the worker also owned the means of production, but its function has changed. The owner of certain things can use his ownership to control other persons. Legally this is done by the use of ownership as the centre of a number of complementary legal institutions (*Konnexinstitute*), such as sale,

---

[1] Karl Renner, *The Institutions of Private Law and their Social Functions*, 1949, ed. O. Kahn-Freund, LL.M., Dr. Jur.

loan, tenancy, hire and, above all, the contract of service. By means of the latter the worker agrees to hand over the substrate of work to the owner of the capital. Formally this contract, an institution of private law, is concluded between equals. In fact the liberty of those who do not own the means of production is confined to a certain choice between those to whom they are compelled to transfer, by contract, their share in the product. Behind the fiction of equality there stands the reality of the capitalist, exercising a delegated public power of command. The real expression of this power is not to be found in the contract of service, but in the internal rules regulating the conditions of work.

Another change of function takes place. The unity of ownership typical of the former economic conditions, is broken up as specialisation in the various functions of ownership develops.

Property now becomes a source of power (control of factories), profit (owning shares in undertakings), interest (lending capital), rent (letting property) and so forth. At the same time the legal ownership ceases to represent the real control of the thing. The complementary legal institution assumes the real function of ownership. which becomes an empty legal form. Thus the owner of a completely mortgaged property is the legal owner, but the economic function of ownership is in the hands of a mortgagee. The principal shareholder in a company, who controls the undertaking legally, merely owns some documents and certain claims against the company which formally has full ownership. In all these cases the *Konnexinstitut* has taken some of the functions of ownership. Thus it becomes possible to expropriate without formal expropriation. Because of the complementary functions of the contract of service, the workers' share in the product which, according to certain legal theories, gives the title to ownership, can never be actual. By means of the contract of service, the right to appropriate is once and for all conferred on the owner of the material.

To sum up, ownership has ceased to be what it was. While remaining, in legal form, an institution of private law implying the total power of doing with the thing what one likes, it has in fact become an institution of public law (power of command), and its main functions are exercised by complementary legal institutions, developed from the law of obligations.

The law eventually takes account of this change of function by giving property an increasingly public law character. Private ownership in public means of transport, for example, develops into what in Continental jurisprudence is expressed by *Anstalt*, and in English jurisprudence by ' public corporation '. The conditions of work become the object of collective agreements which are subject to public law. Renner asks socialists to abandon their passive attitude towards the law and to create the legal norm which adequately expresses the trend of social development.[1a]

Before examining what truth and value this analysis has for contemporary English society and law, we should first dispose of the question, how far Renner's whole analysis is conditioned by Romanistic and Continental legal institutions. If this were so to any large extent, English jurists and sociologists might regard his work as a matter of theoretical and historical interest rather than of acute concern for themselves. The Continental definition of ownership offers a basis for comparison.

The lawyer who exalts legal definitions, concepts, and systems, without considering the social and economic use to which they are put, might well dismiss the whole of Renner's thesis by pointing out that English law knows nothing like the Continental definitions of property. The definitions of the French, German and Swiss civil codes agree substantially in defining property as a comprehensive right of absolute enjoyment and power of disposal, subject to the restrictions of the law and the rights of third persons.[2]

English law knows nothing of the sort. Property, as the learned editor points out, is a ' bundle of powers '. The development of the English legal system through forms of action, through remedies rather than substantive rights, has left its trace. The rights of ownership are measured by the extent of the power to prosecute trespassers, to obtain injunctions against nuisance, to demand damages for conversion, to follow money into the hands of third parties. Moreover, ownership may be divided between the trustee, who has the power to dispose, and the beneficiary, who has the right to enjoy. Maitland showed

[1a] This summary is taken from Friedmann, *Legal Theory* (2nd ed., 1949), pp. 243-5.

[2] French Civil Code, Art. 544: ' La propriété est le droit de jouir et de disposer des choses de la manière la plus absolue, pourvu qu'on n'en fasse pas un usage prohibé par la loi ou par les règlements '.
German Civil Code, s. 903: ' Der Eigentümer einer Sache kann, soweit nicht das Gesetz oder Rechte dritter entgegenstehen, mit der Sache nach Belieben verfahren und andere von jeder Einwirkung ausschliessen '.
Swiss Civil Code, Art. 641: ' Wer Eigentümer einer Sache ist, kann in den Schranken der Rechtsordnung über sie nach seinem Belieben verfugen '.

many years ago[3] what difficulties German lawyers would have in understanding the meaning and function of trust. On the other hand, the English notion of ' property ' is wider and less technical than the Continental ' ownership '. Property is a complex of things, rights, powers, documents; it comprises not only tangible things but ' choses in action '—patents, copyright, trademarks, shares. ' The English lawyer does not find it incongruous to say that a claim for a repayment for a loan, a mortgage on another man's land, and a share in a limited company belongs to a person's " property " '.[4] Yet these conceptual and juristic differences have not prevented English and Continental law from finding similar solutions for substantially similar social and economic problems. Codification, and the formulation of comprehensive rights, as compared with the casuistic and procedural approach, may produce certain differences of judicial outlook and legal training. But it is relatively insignificant whether Continental legislation restricts the theoretically absolute right of property by police powers, State supervision, expropriation, and taxes, or whether English statutes impose similar restrictions or prohibitions upon the power of an owner to build, or grant a statutory right of inspection of private factories to officials of the Ministry of Health. The extent to which a particular political society wants to restrict or eliminate economic private freedom is far more important than the legal technique by which it does so. The introduction of a Communist, Fascist, Social-democratic or Liberal-Capitalist order of society has not been in any way dependent on, or vitally conditioned by, the differences between Anglo-American and Continental jurisprudence.

Perhaps the only really important difference, for our problem, between the Continental and the English approach, is the greater elasticity of English law, due to its experimental and evolutionary approach to legal problems, which is made possible by the lack of a written constitution and of comprehensive codification. In a roundabout and unsystematic fashion, English law has been better able to give effect to social change than countries dominated

---

[3] Maitland, *Selected Essays*, Chap. 4 (Trust and Corporation).
[4] Kahn-Freund, *loc. cit.*, p. 19.

by written constitutions with fundamental rights, or generally by the habit of theoretical definitions of rights and duties. But here the contrast between English and American law is at least as strong as that between English and Continental jurisprudence. The gradual, often imperceptible evolution of the principles of restraint of trade, conspiracy, property, the recognition of collective bargaining, without any definite theory behind it, the injection of social responsibilities into the common law relationship of employers and employees, have, on the whole, been achieved more painlessly if less systematically, than in countries dominated by the legalistic apex of a written constitution.[5]

It is usually a combination of a formalistic legal outlook with an insular or nationalistic mentality which tends to exaggerate the analytical differences of legal systems and to ignore or belittle the far greater importance of values. All the major legal problems of our generation, such as the reconciliation of growing State responsibilities and functions with the liberties of the citizen, the restriction of private enterprise and the use of ownership in the interests of the community, the imposition of social responsibilities upon the employer, the legal problems of socialised industries, the problem of the judicial interpretation of statutes, have presented themselves to British or French, German or American, Russian or Swiss law. All these countries have witnessed the development of the standard contract in transport, insurance, mortgages; they have experienced the transformation of the joint-stock company, and the passing of control from the individual shareholder to the management, or to a controlling outside interest. These developments have indeed taken many different legal forms, but the decisive divergences are matters of political and ethical values, not of legal technicalities.

We therefore can and must put a further and more important question: 'What have the passage of time, and the impact of

---

[5] This applies in particular to Federal constitutions, where a law court has the ultimate decision on the validity of legislation in the light of the constitution. The judicial history of the American, Canadian and Australian federations amply illustrates the dangers of abstract legal formulations in a rapidly changing society.

nearly half a century of shattering international and social upheavals done to Renner's thesis?' Is private ownership, in particular the private ownership of means of production, still the key to power? Has the law proved either unwilling or incapable of restricting the command power of property in the interests of the community? The answer cannot be in doubt. Contemporary English law, like the law of most other countries, reveals a far-reaching and in many ways fundamental reversal of the position, not because of any inherent differences between Austrian or German and English jurisprudence, but because of a fundamental change in the relation of economic and political power.

A proper assessment of the impact of deliberate State interference with the unrestricted use of property in capitalistic and industrialist society is, however, impossible without first noting a decisive development within capitalism itself, which is ignored by Renner and has gathered momentum since he first wrote. In Renner's contention, the legal owner retains the economic power; he keeps the title to surplus value. He surrenders only the use of his property, ' an item in which he never was interested '. But in the last half-century, corporate enterprise has taken control of all the major fields of industrial production. And with it, ' the economic structure of corporate enterprise has changed almost beyond recognition. Nothing could be further from the truth today than that the legal structure of corporate enterprise does not change the substance of the economic relationship '.[6] Ownership and control have become increasingly divorced. In the words of an American treatise which in many ways takes up the sociological analysis of property in modern society where Renner leaves it,[7] ' ownership continually becomes more dispersed; the power formerly joined to it becomes increasingly concentrated, and the corporate system becomes thereby more firmly established '. Renner saw capitalist owner- ship as an octopus whose numerous tentacles—contracts of service, loan, hire purchase, etc.—enveloped more and more vic- tims. But in the overwhelmingly important field of corporate

[6] Kahn-Freund, *op. cit.*, p. 225.
[7] Berle and Means, *The Modern Corporation and Private Property* (1932), p. 9.

enterprise, the nominal owner, that is, the shareholder, is becoming more and more powerless. He turns into a mere recipient of dividends, often barely distinguishable from the bond or debenture holder. In the analysis of Berle and Means, control has been wrested from the shareholder owner by five different devices; firstly, control through almost complete ownership; secondly, majority control; thirdly, control through a legal device without majority ownership; fourthly, minority control; fifthly, management control. Of these, only the last four are of major sociological importance. Some of the forms of control, especially those achieved through a voting trust, are peculiar to Anglo-American law, although the delegation of votes to banks or other agents can achieve very similar results in Continental company law. But on the whole the devices which vest control either in a minority directed by interests outside the company itself, or in the management, at the expense of scattered and passive shareholders, are the same in Continental or Anglo-American jurisdiction, for the social and economic factors which account for this transformation are similar: the increase in the vastness and complexity of modern industry in most fields, the dispersal of shares among multitudes of small shareholders whose joint influence does not compare with that of a single compact minority interest, and the increasing importance of the managerial as against the financial element, owing to the technical and administrative complexities of modern large scale enterprise.

Among the devices for separation of ownership and control discussed by Berle and Means, two seem particularly significant. A group of entrepreneurs—industrial or financial—may build up a pyramid of corporations. They need the ownership of a majority or near-majority of shares, at most at the top of the pyramid, preferably in a holding company. The holding company acquires a controlling interest in a series of operating or other holding companies, each of which acquires a controlling influence in the company next below in the pyramid. By this device, the original group of entrepreneurs can acquire a decisive or even

monopoly control over an entire industry or utility.[8]
Ownership and control are even more completely divorced where
the management of a vast and complex corporate enterprise
can either govern undisturbed because of the dispersal of share-
holdings among multitudes of small owners, or because it can
if necessary stir up the majority of shareholders in order to
fight the dominant minority.

The steady progress of control through management as
against ownership, is to some extent inherent in Marxist analysis,
although it has taken very little note of it. It accompanies the
increasing concentration and amalgamation of industrial
enterprise, which Marxist analysis predicted. But it also
indicates a new phase in sociological and juristic development,
whose significance far transcends the sphere of economic
corporate enterprise. What Burnham has characterised, with
some oversimplifications, as ' the managerial revolution ' is
becoming the main preoccupation of contemporary sociologists
and political philosophers, of many nations: the emergence of
the new élite, small groups of highly trained and masterful
politicians, industrialists, engineers, scientists, and soldiers,
able to control, through the unprecedented concentration of
power and technical knowledge in a few hands, through the
machinery of modern government, through the skilfully perverted
slogans of democracy, the minds and bodies of the masses. The
progress of control at the expense of ownership has another
significant lesson for the jurist and social reformer: it means that
he must get away from the pre-occupation of early Marxist
thought—which still dominates Renner's analysis—with technical
legal ownership as the key to economic power. The transfer
of ownership from private into public hands may no longer be
the decisive or even the necessary means of shifting control,
large though it still looms in the programmes of socialist parties.
As we shall see, modern government provides many other legal
and administrative methods of control.

Modern public opinion, working through an increasingly

---

[8] Berle and Means give as an example the Brothers van Sweringen. In
1930, an investment of less than $20,000,000 was able to control eight
Class I Railroads, with combined assets of over two billion dollars.

active legislative machinery, has reacted powerfully against the concentration of more and more unchecked economic power in the hands of fewer and fewer people. But there are two different ways of doing so. One is the use of legislative and judicial machinery for the restoration of smallness and balance in economic life, for more freedom with competition, and altogether a closer approximation to the identity of ownership and enterprise, which modern capitalism has increasingly destroyed. Most States have attempted to tackle this problem after a fashion. The German Cartel Law of 1923 provided some half-hearted official supervision over cartels, and the British Monopoly Act of 1948[9] enables the Board of Trade to refer certain monopoly practices to a Commission for investigation and report. But the only serious and sustained effort at countering the increasing concentration of economic power through legal measures aiming at the restoration of competitive conditions has been made in the U.S.A. The Sherman Act of 1890 and the supplementary Clayton Act of 1914 have been analysed and discussed by so many experts that a brief reference to the general conclusions will be sufficient here.[1] American anti-trust legislation has acted as an important brake on the unhindered development of monopoly and of trading conditions which would hamper the independent manufacturer and trader. The Anti-Trust Division of the Department of Justice has been strengthened. It is constantly on the watch for monopolistic trade conditions, such as ' Base Point ' charges.[1a] The Federal Trade Commission has attempted to break up some chain store enterprises. Yet the attempt has failed in its major purpose. The concentration of capital and economic enterprise has continued. At the beginning of 1930, two hundred big companies, covering all the important non-banking economic activities, controlled 49·2 per cent. of all non-banking corporate wealth,

---

[9] Monopolies and Restrictive Practices (Inquiry and Control) Act, 1948.
[1] Cf. among many other analyses, Thurman Arnold, *Bottlenecks of Business* (1945); H. Mannheim (1944) 7 M.L.R. 13. Symposium on the Sherman Antitrust Act and its Enforcement, Law and Contemporary Problems, vol. 7 (1940), pp. 1–160.
[1a] An arrangement by which transport charges are calculated from certain " base points ", so as to eliminate price differences caused by the great variations in distance between producer and consumer.

while the remaining half was owned by more than 300,000 smaller companies.[2] In 1947, 113 firms, each of them with assets of over $100,000,000, controlled 46 per cent. of the total capital assets of American manufacturing corporations.[3] Modern social and economic conditions increasingly favour economic concentration. Only large and wealthy undertakings can afford the frequent replacement of machinery and other equipment necessary for modern mass production; only they can maintain the highly skilled scientific and technical staffs and the huge laboratories which lead to the invention and commercial utilisation of such products as synthetic rubber or nylon. World tension and rearmament which demand standardised mass production, greatly favour large scale enterprise. For collective bargaining, which increasingly governs labour conditions in the U.S.A. as elsewhere, the trade unions often prefer to deal with big combines and enterprises. In view of all these developments, State intervention designed to break up the economy into balanced and self-contained units—quite apart from its problematic value—requires an increasingly complex official apparatus. The American Military Government in Germany maintained a staff of many hundreds for years, for the sole purpose of breaking up the I.G. Farben concern into autonomous units. The British attempted a similiar surgical operation in regard to the vertical coal and steel syndicates of the Ruhr. As Allied control slackens, the dismembered parts are rapidly being joined together again. Paradoxically it is only with the help of a complex and intricate bureaucracy that ' free ' competitive enterprise could be laboriously put on to its feet. Vast spheres remain of course, in which competition and small scale enterprise maintains itself without State intervention; for example, in retailing and many secondary industries. But the basic problem cannot be solved by an endless series of breaking-up operations. One community after another has been driven to the alternative of public control and restriction of private economic power through the deliberate action of the State.

[2] Berle and Means, *op. cit.*, p. 28.
[3] Report by the Federal Trade Commission quoted in (1949) *Economist*, 617.

The following survey will attempt to outline briefly the ways in which English law has taken up the challenge thrown out by Renner many years ago. This reaction may be classed under two guiding principles. The first is the attempt to restore equality of bargaining between employers and employees. The other is the restriction of the economic utilisation of private property in the public interest.

RESTORATION OF EQUALITY OF BARGAINING

In Maine's classical formulation, progressive societies have developed from status to contract. Renner's analysis shows the antithesis: the perversion of theoretical freedom and equality of contract into a state of inequality and dependence, in which the capitalists' power over the worker appropriates the surplus value of his product in return for a subsistence wage, and is able to dictate conditions. But we have moved a long way since then. Freedom of contract, in so far as it survives today, no longer pertains to the individual. One trend of development leads to the totalitarian State in which the employee is deprived of both individual and collective freedom of contract and association. In return, he obtains a quasi-feudal security. Nazi legislation destroyed all vestiges of autonomous trade unionism, but it preserved and in some respects strengthened the existing legal protection of the employee against dismissal. In Communist Russia, trade unions occupy an important and honoured position, but their main function is administration and welfare. Their executives are subject to the same political party and creed as the managements of the State Trusts, their counterparts. Both are executives of a central economic plan. Collective bargaining, let alone a strike, which would impair the execution of the master-plan, is outlawed in fact if not in theory, and subject to the most severe sanctions.

The alternative, which predominates in the non-totalitarian industrial countries of today, is the substitution of collective for individual bargaining. Employers and trade unions, either representing a particular factory or business, or, more and more frequently, bargaining on behalf of the entire industry, make contracts, which bind the individual. Sometimes, collectivism leads to the ' closed shop ' principle, by which employers agree to employ only members of the union with which they have bargained. Even where this is not the case, the predominance of major trade unions is usually sufficient to ensure practical compliance without legal sanction. Sometimes a collective agreement between the major parties of an industry is declared binding for an entire industry by State action.[4] Sometimes State organs themselves authoritatively fix the conditions of labour.[5] Whatever the solution, the helplessness of the worker as against the capitalist owner of property and employer is now largely a matter of the past. How closely this development is connected with the ideology of property is shown by American legal developments. For many years the U.S.A. Supreme Court stubbornly invalidated the legislative regulation of labour conditions as contrary to the Due Process Clauses of the Fifth or Fourteenth Amendment,[6] and thereby regarded any restriction on the freedom of contract of the individual employer and employee, as a violation of the right of property. This trend was reversed only in 1936.[7]

Owing to the absence of a Code of Fundamental Rights, English law has abolished or restricted the command power of capital, and restored equality of bargaining more gradually and on the whole more painlessly. The most important aspects of this process are: firstly, the abolition of the crime of conspiracy, and the gradual recognition of strikes, boycotts, and similar economic collective measures, as a legitimate means of pursuing the interests of workers without liability for criminal or civil conspiracy.[8]

---

[4] Cf., for example, the Cotton Manufacturing Industry (Temporary Provision) Act, 1934.

[5] In Britain, State awards occupy a relatively minor position. Cf. Kahn-Freund, ' Collective Agreements under War Legislation ' (1943) 6 M.L.R. 112 and ' Legislation through Adjudication ' (1946) 9 M.L.R. 269, 429. But in Australia the Commonwealth Arbitration court has power to determine the basic wage and other vital conditions of employment, on the application of a registered trade union or employers' association. While awards are not directly enforceable, de-registration of members and punishment for contempt of court provide sanctions which can be severely felt. See further below, pp. 48–55.

[6] Cf. *The Adkins Case*, 261 U.S. 525 (1923), and the *Lochner Case*, 198 U.S. 45 (1904). *Schechter Case*, 295 U.S. 495 (1935).

[7] *Steward Machine Co.* v. *Davis*, 301 U.S. 548 (1936); *West Coast Hotel Case*, 300 U.S. 379 (1937).

[8] For a discussion of the main judicial developments see below, Ch. 6.

Secondly, the recognition of collective bargaining as a normal form of regulating the conditions of employment. The present state of English law is very complex, and ranges from autonomous collective bargaining to compulsory State awards.[9]

Thirdly, social security legislation culminating in the National Insurance Act and the National Insurance (Industrial Injuries) Act, both of 1946. Social insurance legislation is not primarily aimed at the restoration of equality of bargaining. But indirectly, in a free society, it strengthens the power of bargaining through the elimination of the worst fears arising from unemployment or incapacity to work.

Fourthly, the courts have played an important part in the legal interpretation of the employment contract. They have gradually reduced the discriminatory effect of earlier common law doctrines, such as *volenti non fit iniuria*, or common employment, and they have simultaneously strengthened and developed the statutory common law duties of the employer. This has been done in a multitude of ways, which cannot be analysed in detail here.[1] The more important aspects of this judicial evolution are an interpretation of certain social legislation such as anti-slum statutes in a manner less prejudiced in favour of the owner[2]; the formulation of certain duties of the employer in common law, in regard to the selection of personnel, the safety of plant, and the adequacy of its operation[3]; in the interpretation of ' statutory duties ' such as the fencing of machinery, as duties imposed for the protection of the individual, and thus giving him a right of action. In the field of contract, the most important judicial development has been the elaboration of principles by which the contract restraining the freedom of an employee to use his labour after the termination of the contract is presumed to be void, except in special cases.[4]

---

[9] For detailed analysis, cf. Kahn-Freund (1948) 11 M.L.R. pp. 269, 429.
[1] Cf. Friedmann, ' Social Security and Recent Development in the Common Law ' (1943) 21 Can. Bar Rev. 369, reprinted in *Legal Theory* (1st ed.), chap. 25. For some later developments, see below, p. 84 ff.
[2] *Summers* v. *Salford Corporation* [1943] A.C. 283.
[3] *Wilsons & Clyde Coal Co* v. *English* [1938] A.C. 57.
[4] This dates from the decision of the House of Lords in *Mason* v. *Provident Clothing Co.* [1913] A.C. 724; for the present state of authorities, see Cheshire and Fifoot, *Law of Contract*, pp. 230–7.

Lastly, the relationship between employer and employees is further transformed when industries are socialised. The State now becomes both the representative of the community and an employer. We shall deal with this aspect of the law of property later.

RESTRICTIONS ON THE USE OF PRIVATE PROPERTY

Two aspects of private property have challenged social and political reformers throughout the history of Western civilisation; the advantages which it affords for the enjoyment of the amenities of life, and the power which it conveys. The extreme inequalities of wealth have in pre-capitalist times provided the main incentive to reform and revolution. But the power over men and things conveyed by the ability to use property for the creation of capitalist enterprise now presents by far the more important and complex problem, and it is this aspect of the institution of property which predominates in Renner's analysis.

The following brief survey of the main ways by which contemporary English law is restricting or taking away this unhindered power of utilisation of property will show what distance we have travelled in recent years.

(i) In recent years, comparative lawyers have devoted their attention to the problem of abuse of rights. They have contrasted the attitude of modern Continental civil codes with that of English law, still dominated by a decision of the House of Lords of 1895.[5] Continental legal systems such as the French, German and Swiss, make the abuse of property rights a good defence where the predominant objective of the exercise of a property right has been chicanery, or the intent to do injury to another party.[6] English law still basically adheres to the principle that a person can do with his property what he likes, except for specific statutory restrictions. But the practical significance of the whole doctrine is very much smaller than its theoretical interest. In the practice of French, German, or Swiss courts, it means little more than that the very unusual kind of landowner who creates obstacles out of spite for his neighbour, or who prefers to leave a piece

---

[5] *Bradford Corporation* v. *Pickles* [1895] A.C. 597.
[6] For detailed discussion, cf. Gutteridge, 5 Camb.L.J., pp. 22–45.

of land unused rather than grant a right of passage, may be restrained by the courts. Continental courts have understandably refrained from developing the principle into a more fundamental social doctrine by which the use of property is subject to the needs of the community. The same principle has a much wider meaning in Soviet civil law, which withholds protection from private rights "exercised in contradiction to their social and economic purpose." [6a] It is not even certain that a Continental court would apply the doctrine of abuse of rights in a case like *Bradford* v. *Pickles*, where a landowner dug a hole in his ground in order to abstract water from a neighbouring property, and thus force a local authority interested in that property to buy him out at a high price.[7]

(ii) A far more fundamental aspect of abuse of rights is the problem how far a patentee may, through various devices, withhold the use of a patent from the community. This question touches the very foundations of modern industrial society. The danger that scientific and technological progress may be impeded through the ability of powerful industrial interests, either to patent their own inventions or to buy up other people's inventions for non-use or to attach such conditions to the grant of licences that they become virtually unusable, has recently called for the appointment of a departmental committee, whose main recommendations are embodied in the Patents and Designs Act, 1949. The committee found that, on the whole, there was little evidence of a deliberate suppression of inventions in British industries, and that the power of cartels rested mainly on the economic, financial, and technical predominance of certain firms rather than on the monopolisation of patents. Yet, the committee found a number of dangerous weaknesses in the existing law which the new Act purports to remedy. English law now provides, at least theoretically, an impressive array of legal restrictions on the abuse or non-use of patents, which may be briefly summarised as follows.

[6a] Sec. 1, Civil Code of the R.S.F.S.R. cf. Gsovski, *Soviet Civil Law* (1948) vol. 1, pp. 314–338.
[7] Professor Gutteridge believes that the German law would afford a different solution. For some criticism of this view, cf. (1943) 21 Can. Bar Rev. p. 374.

(*a*) The Comptroller of Patents now has considerable powers to counter the abuse or insufficient use of patent rights by granting compulsory licences.[8] The main grounds are failure to use a commercially workable patented invention to the fullest extent that is reasonably practicable: or the refusal by a patentee to grant licences on reasonable terms.[9]

(*b*) The Comptroller of Patents has somewhat stronger powers to grant licences as of right for the utilisation of patents relating to food or medicine.[1]

(*c*) At any time after the expiration of two years from the date of an order granting a compulsory licence, the Comptroller may, on application, revoke the patent if he is satisfied that the purpose of the compulsory licence has not been achieved.[2]

(*d*) Lastly, the Crown enjoys certain privileges in regard to the use of patented inventions. The power of the government to make use of a patent for the services of the Crown in times of war, or other periods of emergency, is now nearly unlimited.[3] In normal circumstances, these powers are considerably more restricted, although any invention or article required for the defence of the country is automatically deemed to be an invention ' for the services of the Crown '.[4]

The theoretical powers of the law restricting the liberty of the patentee to do with the patent what he likes, are thus considerable. The most important progress made by the recent reform is a restriction of the patentee's power not to use the patent at all. By contrast, American law still holds that ' an owner can, of course, prohibit entirely the manufacture, sale,

---

[8] Patents and Designs Act, 1949, ss. 16–19.
[9] As the Committee pointed out, the former, less far-reaching provisions, coupled with unnecessarily restrictive judicial interpretation, resulted in no more than four orders granting compulsory licences between 1919 and 1946.
[1] Patents and Designs Act, 1949, s. 20.
[2] For details, and the appeal procedure, see Patents and Designs Act, 1949, ss. 21–24.
[3] For details, see Patents and Designs Act, 1949, s. 30.
[4] Patents and Designs Act, 1949, s. 27.

or use of a patented article '.[5] The reform hardly touches the root-problem of the power derived from economic concentration or monopoly. As the committee pointed out, the utilisation of inventions often depends more on the ' know how ' than on the terms of the patent. Quite often important inventions are not patented at all. Such factors as laboratory equipment, a highly qualified scientific staff, ample resources for research and experimental machinery—cannot be changed by patent legislation. Yet legislative development indicates an important evolution of public policy.

(iii) The progress of the welfare state ideology has combined with the economic emergencies of the war and post-war periods to produce a multitude of official restrictions on the use of property. No more than a few illustrations can be given to show the extent of these developments.

(a) Statutory duties affect factory owners, public utilities, retailers, in a multitude of ways. There are provisions for the safety of machinery or mines, for sanitation and drainage, for the purity of foods and water. They enjoy the sanctions of criminal and civil law; statutory penalties for these ' public welfare ' offences[6] do not normally require a *mens rea*. The protection of civil law is often a twofold one: the extension of the obligations of the manufacturer towards the consumer[7] has greatly widened the scope of protection of the public against deficient products. Courts have also increasingly awarded damages to individuals for the breach of statutory duties as such; for example, to a third party injured in a car which, contrary to Statute, had no third party insurance,[8] or to a ratepayer poisoned by impure water supplied by a local authority.[9]

---

[5] Brandeis J. in *Carbide Corporation of America* v. *American Patents Development Corporation*, 283 U.S. 7, 31 (1931). But three dissenting opinions in the recent case of *Special Equipment Co.* v. *Coe*, 324 U.S. 370 (1945) indicate a change in public opinion. Moreover, the suppression of patents may be part of a combined action which offends against Federal Anti-Trust Laws. See *Hartford-Empire C.* v. *U.S.*, 323 U.S. 386, 324 U.S. 570 (1945).

[6] On these, see further below, ch. 5.

[7] Following *Donoghue* v. *Stevenson* [1932] A.C. 562.

[8] *Monk* v. *Warbey* [1935] 1 K.B. 75.

[9] *Read* v. *Croydon Corporation* (1939) 108 L.J.K.B. 72.

(*b*) Official Acts and Regulations increasingly not only forbid but also prescribe. Britain's economic emergency has greatly accentuated this development. The State lays down utility standards for a wide range of consumers' products; or it allocates scarce raw materials or foreign currencies according to priorities. The most powerful and dangerous of State pressures, direction of labour, has not so far been used, except in war, to any considerable extent, but an aggravation of the economic crisis would almost certainly bring it back.

(*c*) One of the most interesting legislative developments is the power of the Minister of Agriculture to dispossess inefficient farmers in certain contingencies, by either compulsory purchase or an order directed to the owner to let the farm to an approved tenant. Coupled with this are statutory standard terms for agricultural tenancies.[1] This is of course a most significant restriction of the rights of private property, in the interest of the community. It expresses the recognition of agricultural land as a national asset, which private owners and tenants must use to the advantage of the community. The power exercised by urban or agricultural landowners through tenancy and the power of the mortgagee to appropriate the substance of the power following from landownership, plays a considerable part in Renner's analysis.[2] This type of legislation shows a new technique: Positive administrative action now displaces private terms of contract, instead of negative administrative measures (clearance orders) as used by the Housing Acts.

(*d*) Taxation is one of the most important weapons by which the State can mitigate the two objectionable aspects of unrestricted private property: firstly, the inequalities of wealth, and secondly, the power to use property for private profit, and without regard to community purposes. In popular consciousness, the first aim still predominates. By graded taxation and surtax on high incomes, gross inequalities of wealth are evened out more easily

---

[1] For details, see Agriculture Act, 1947, Pt. II.
[2] Dr. Kahn-Freund's comparison of the different ways in which ownership in land and agricultural lease can in English law, cover widely different economic situations, is particularly valuable (see *op. cit.* p. 9, n. 1, p. 33 ff.). The forms of tenancy in English law here account for many differences from Continental law, but this does not affect the importance, in either system, of the developments outlined in the text.

than by the equalisation of incomes or the abolition of private property. But the second aspect of taxation policy is becoming increasingly more important. On the one hand, taxation is a cheap means by which the State finances its costly social service schemes. Under the National Health Service Act, 1946, medical services are free for all. The cost of medical services is no longer met by millions of contributions of varying magnitude from private pockets, but out of public revenue. This means that income and property taxes largely pay for the medical services of the poorer classes. To the extent that the State contributes to the cost of national insurance (National Insurance Act, 1946) the same applies.

On the other hand, differential taxes and customs duties form part of national economic planning. The import of non-essential goods is penalised by higher duties. A purchase tax is put on luxury goods, which are earmarked for export instead of home consumption. The law of taxation is gradually revolutionising private as well as public law. The incidence of taxation will be one of the main considerations determining the lawyer's advice on the form of a settlement or a will, or the constitution of a subsidiary company. The rise of the incorporated charitable Foundation[2a] is largely a result of the incidence of taxation on large estates.

(e) Public control of financial credit is another means by which the State curtails privately financed capital. Low interest rates may limit the income from private credit and other banking transactions, but by far the more important aspect of official credit restrictions is the curtailment of the power of private capital to influence the national economy, through the expansion or restriction of credits. Dr. Kahn-Freund has some illuminating comments on the extent to which agricultural banks in Germany and other Continental countries have, through their mortgaging policy, influenced the structure of national economy.[3] In Britain, credit policy is now controlled through the nationalised Bank of England. In Australia, the Banking Act, 1945, gives to the Governor-General, acting with the advice of the Federal

[2] Cf. below, ch. 7.
[3] *Op. cit.*, pp. 185–7.

Executive Council, and to the Commonwealth Bank important supervisory powers over gold and foreign exchange reserves and, above all, over interest rates to be charged by Banks.

PUBLIC OWNERSHIP

Finally, the transfer of property, and of industrial property in particular, from private to public ownership, is the most radical answer to the socialist challenge, and to Renner's analysis. The domain of public property has been vastly extended in most countries. In Germany, posts and railways, for example, have almost from the beginning been State owned enterprises. Similarly, British postal services have been for many years administered by the State under a junior minister of the Crown. However, the most interesting and problematic aspect of the transformation of private into public property is the socialisation of industry. In Soviet Russia, most major industrial enterprises are now operated as semi-autonomous State trusts with separate legal personality, but subject to a central economic plan and strict political supervision.[4] In Germany and France, the acquisition of blocks of shares, and a corresponding degree of control in private enterprises by the State or other public authorities, has become an important feature of public life since the end of the first World War. French public law has also developed the concept of *domaine public*, a type of property distinct from that of private property, through its dedication to public use and a number of other restrictions following from its public character. The doctrine, which is by no means uncontested in France, has not established itself in Germany.

Outside Soviet Russia, Great Britain has now gone further than any other State in the transfer of industrial property from private into public ownership. A separate concept of public property would, of course, be entirely contrary to the tradition of English law, nor would much be gained by its introduction. The chosen legal instrument of English law for the socialisation of property is the public corporation. Basic industries and other public services are constituted as separate legal personalities.

---

[4] Cf. Schlesinger, *Soviet Legal Theory*, pp. 137 ff., 193 ff., 247 ff.; Berman *Justice in Soviet Russia*, pp. 66 ff.; Friedmann, *Legal Theory* (2nd ed.), pp. 249 ff.

They are as often as possible placed on the same legal footing as private corporations, and subject to commercial auditing. They are generally independent in the management of their business but responsible to a Minister—who may give general directions on policy—and through the Minister to Parliament. This is not the place to discuss the complex legal problems of this new type of public enterprise in which public and private law are blended in a novel way.[5] In so far as industrial property, through State ownership or through public corporations, which are independent of private capital and responsible to the nation, has been transferred to public ownership, Renner's challenge has been met. It is, however, already obvious that the correctness of Renner's analysis is, in the public as in the private sphere, affected by the shift from ownership to management control. The relatively short experience of the management of industrial enterprises and social services by public corporations has already shown a similar tendency towards managerial preponderance.

The members of the board are appointed for long terms, and as a debate in the House of Commons in March, 1948, showed, the responsible Minister can mostly protect the public corporation from Parliamentary questions, by shielding behind the principle of managerial independence. The problem of public enterprise is of course infinitely more complex in a mixed economy, operating in a Parliamentary democracy, than it is in the centrally directed, one-party system of Soviet Russia. There, the problem is one of managerial and administrative efficiency; in contemporary Britain, public enterprise must be fitted into a Parliamentary democracy, and it must also observe certain rules of fair competition in relation to the still much larger private enterprise sector.

PRIVATE PROPERTY AND THE JUDICIARY

The evolution and adaptation of English law has not been hampered by the embodiment of ' natural rights ' in a rigid constitution, which perpetuates the political and social ideologies of a past period and confronts the judiciary with an almost

---

[5] For some constitutional aspects, see Wade [1949] *Current Legal Problems*, pp. 172–82; for the general legal structure, see below, ch. 9, pp. 187–216.

insoluble problem.[6] English law has both the advantages and disadvantages of a flexible and empirical approach to new legal problems. This is fully reflected in the judicial attitude to the changing function of property.

(*a*) Under a well established though ill-defined rule, there is a presumption that a statute should not be held to interfere with private property unless it plainly says so. This has been described by Professor Willis[7] as ' a sort of fourteenth amendment '. Although it has sometimes led to restrictive interpretations of social service legislation, the rule is not on the whole of great practical significance.[8]

(*b*) Of far greater importance is the judicial approach to taxation statutes. In this respect English courts, largely under the influence of war and other economic emergencies, have undergone a profound change. Not many years ago, the House of Lords could still pronounce that taxpayers ' incur no legal penalties and, strictly speaking, no moral censure if, having considered the lines drawn by the legislature for the imposition of taxes, they make it their business to walk outside them '.[9] But in several recent cases, the House of Lords and the Court of Appeal have forcefully supported the legislator in his attempt to curb the evasion of taxes, and strongly emphasised the unsocial behaviour of the taxpayer who, by evasion, throws a greater burden on the community.[1]

A similar judicial revolution has occurred in the attitude of the courts towards administrative authorities exercising ' quasi-judicial ' functions. In the period of great extension of various public activities which followed the first World War, the predominant attitude of the law courts was one of distrust. In the leading case of *R.* v. *Electricity Commissioners*,[2] the Court

---

[6] Cf. *Legal Theory* (2nd ed.), chap. 24.

[7] 16 Can. Bar Rev, 23.

[8] There is a hint of a different judicial approach to ' planning statutes ' in Lord Greene's judgment in *Taylor* v. *Brighton Corpn.* [1947] 1 K.B. 740. For a fuller discussion of the problem of statutory interpretation, cf. below, ch. 11. pp. 237–265.

[9] Lord Sumner in *Levene* v. *Inland Revenue* [1928] A.C. 217.

[1] Cf. below, p. 243. But for an even more recent return to the former approach, see *Vestey's (Lord) Executors* v. *Inland Revenue Commissioners* [1949] 1 All E.R. 1108.

[2] *R.* v. *Electricity Commissioners* [1924] 1 K.B. 171.

of Appeal went so far as to describe the compulsory constitution
of joint committees of public and private electricity undertakers
by the Electricity Commissioners as quasi-judicial and thus
subject to prerogative writs, because such a scheme affected
private rights. But in recent decisions the House of Lords and
the Court of Appeal have repeatedly refused to hamper the
administrative discretion conferred upon a minister by
Parliament by construing various ministerial decisions as quasi-
judicial.[2] This change in the judicial approach is not directly
concerned with private property, but by either enlarging or
narrowing the scope of judicial supervision over the decisions of
public authorities which are almost invariably concerned with
the restriction or expropriation of private property for public
purposes, the courts can exercise a considerable influence.

(c) Another aspect—of equal importance to the lawyer,
economist, and sociologist—is the increasing robustness with
which law courts ' pierce the veil of corporate personality '.
Until recently, American courts were far ahead of English courts
in refusing to countenance tax evasion, the circumvention of
statutory prohibitions, or misleading profit and loss accounts,
through the fiction of an impenetrable legal distinction between
the corporation and the people who control it. But recently
not only have English courts more and more frequently
abandoned this fiction, consecrated in the leading case of *Salomon*
v. *Salomon*,[4] but modern British legislation has appended to
important statutes a definition of ' control ' which goes far in
tearing away the cloak of corporate personality, by attaching
legal consequences to the economic realities of control, rather
than legal form.[5] The changing attitude of the courts towards
the relative significance of taxation and private rights has also
encouraged a more robust judicial approach to the problem of
the ' veil of corporate personality '.

(d) On the other hand, the private property approach still
predominates in many fields not yet sufficiently penetrated by
new social problems and an understanding of public law.

[2] *Franklin* v. *Minister of Town and Country Planning* [1947] A.C. 87; and
Johnson v. *Ministry of Health* [1947] All E.R. 395. Cf. below, p. 170.
[4] *Salomon* v. *Salomon* [1897] A.C. 22.
[5] Cf., *e.g.*, Schedule to Transport Act, 1947.

Among these are the limitation of the injunction and the declaratory judgment, as public law remedies, to matters where a ' quasi-proprietary ' interest can be ascertained. English courts have recently gone some way towards enabling the Attorney-General to intervene on behalf of the public, and the need to ascertain the respective spheres of private and public enterprises may greatly increase the necessity for such a procedure. But Australian courts still adhere to the notion of a quasi-proprietary interest.[6] Similarly, the legal status of the host of people who are now empowered to enter private property in the exercise of a public function, whether as police, factory inspectors, or air raid wardens, is still judged by the unsuitable private law categories of invitees or licensees.[7]

While it is therefore difficult to formulate any clear or coherent reaction of the judiciary to the growing impact of public law on private property, the recognition of the growing significance of public law and the corresponding restriction of private property, has found judicial recognition in many fields.

CONCLUSIONS

When Renner published the first edition of his work, he could rightly ask lawyers, and socialist lawyers in particular, to abandon their passivity and shape legal norms more in accordance with social reality. At the time of the second edition, much had already been done to lessen the gap between legal norm and social function. This chapter has attempted to give some indications of the position as it obtains another twenty years later, in a country living under a vastly different legal system. The analysis should show beyond doubt that the law has long shaken off its passivity and become an increasingly active and articulate agent of social change. The law of contemporary Britain goes far to answer the challenge of Renner, and of other critics of the law as a citadel of a conservative and capitalist social order. This is not the place to examine how far, in

---

[6] For a detailed discussion of this highly controversial matter, see below, p. 218.

[7] On this problem, see Wallis-Jones (1949) 65 L.Q.R. 367; Friedmann (1943) 21 Can. Bar Rev. pp. 79–90.   Paton (1941) 19 Can. Bar Rev. 1.

contemporary Britain, private capital can still exert political influence through Parliament, through international affiliations, through frustration of government planning and other means. Certainly British law has changed sufficiently to show what happens if private property is transformed into public ownership, and the power to use private property is drastically restricted. To a large extent Renner's analysis is vindicated. The social substratum of contemporary British law is indeed vitally different from that of half a century ago. Britain today is a social democracy—whose principles are largely accepted by all major political parties—and its law reflects this transformation. But two new dangers have emerged, and it is to them that contemporary jurists and sociologists must devote their critical attention. Firstly, we have to study the limits of law as an agent of social change. Few States today suffer from legislative lethargy. The danger rather is that legislation on price control, production quotas and taxation may be regarded as having a magic power to change economic realities. The laws of supply and demand, the profit incentive, the stimulating effect of competition, are not altogether matters of the past. Modern industrial society must solve the problem how to restore to the individual some of the freedom of movement formerly derived from ownership, without restoring power to private capital.

The second and even more fundamental danger is the new menace of excessive concentration of power, which threatens to transcend the differences between Capitalism and Socialism, Fascism and Communism, and which creates a ' band of brothers ' of generals, politicians and scientists, establishing a new aristocracy of power.

CHAPTER 3

CHANGING FUNCTIONS OF
CONTRACT AND THE COMMON LAW

THE social function of contract in the formative era of modern
industrial and capitalist society may be summed up in four
elements: freedom of movement, insurance against calculated
economic risks; freedom of will; and equality between parties.
These four elements are closely linked, and to some extent, overlapping, but each has a distinct meaning. The problems of legal
adjustment and interpretation, however, which they have posed
in a rapidly changing society, are not of the same order. The
first two of our four elements are essentially formal in character,
the latter two also express political and social ideologies. The
difficulty of bridging the gap between the formal and substantial
aspects of both freedom and equality is evident in the pathetic
contrast between the law of contract as it is taught in most
textbooks, and modern contract as it functions in society.

THE CORNER-STONES OF CONTRACT IN
THE ' CLASSICAL ' ERA

Freedom of Movement.

For a developing industrial society contract supplied the legal
instrument which enabled men and goods to move freely. It
is this aspect of contract above all which is expressed by Maine's
theory that progressive societies have developed from status to
contract. As against a legal status determined by ties and conditions outside personal decisions, contract allows the individual
to change his country or employment. In the American Civil
War, the contest between status and contract stood behind the
ideological struggle between slavery and personal freedom. The
static rural and patriarchal society of the South wanted a
hierarchal immobility. The slave, as part of the estate, was at
the bottom of the social scale, although, as the future showed,
his economic and social lot was often better than under the

34

mobile and free economic society which the industrialised and commercialised North wanted and achieved. Freedom to hire and fire, and the unrestricted mobility of labour, were essential to this society, which regarded economic bargaining value as the main standard by which the demand for labour was regulated.

The evolution from status to contract, from immobility to mobility, gradually pervaded all spheres of life, beyond the fields of commercial and labour contracts. It invaded family relations, and the law of succession. It became the basis of club and union membership. Gradually it penetrated even into the law of land tenure, sale and succession. In the English property legislation of 1925, the right of free disposal over land, including the power to dis-entail, is finally recognised.[1] In some respects, this movement from status to contract still continues, especially in so far as the modern State gradually abandons its ancient legal privileges, as the price to be paid for the vastly increased functions of modern government. The British Crown Proceedings Act of 1947, and corresponding legislation in the Dominions,[2] abolishes petition of right as the form of proceedings between subject and Crown, as well as the immunity of the Crown from liability in tort, based on the feudal and absolute status of the Sovereign. It introduces instead ordinary actions in contract, tort, and property, as between subject and Crown.

But this aspect of contract is increasingly overshadowed by a return to a new kind of immobility resulting from the profound changes produced by the social welfare responsibilities of the modern State, by group organisation and collective bargaining in industry and commerce, and, last, but not least, the state of industrial mobilisation into which international strife has forced Western states since the outbreak of the first World War.

---

[1] By-products of the former immobility and non-commercial characterisation of land ownership remain, *e.g.*, in the rule in *Cavalier* v. *Pope* [1906] A.C. 428, under which the landlord is exempt from liability to his tenant for dangers existing on the premises.

[2] *E.g.*, West Australian Crown Proceedings Act, 1947.

INSURANCE AGAINST CALCULATED ECONOMIC RISKS

The economic correlate of common law contract in its formative phase is a free enterprise society, in which the economic rewards for enterprise or speculation are restricted only within very wide limits, if at all. The functioning of such an economic system depends on the guarantee of the law that enterprise or speculation, in so far as it implies contracts for labour, goods, or shares, will be protected by the award of damages or specific performance. At this stage, we need not discuss the various theories of contract, especially the controversy between those who see the essence of contract in the legitimate expectation of its performance, and those who see it in the guarantee against loss by damages. [3] On either assumption, the sanctions of contract enable the hirer of services, the manufacturer of goods, the speculator in land, or the purchaser of shares, to engage in calculated economic risks. This part of contract has been comparatively free from difficulties of ideology or adaptation to social change. It is a significant application of the Aristotelean principle of distributive justice, which demands the equal treatment of those equal before the law. It assumes that parties entering into a contract are equal before the law, and therefore entitled to the same remedies for breach of contract. It need not enter into the problem of social or economic equality between the rich and poor, capitalists and workers, groups and individuals. The courts have been mainly concerned with working out the comparatively technical or to some extent logical, problems of possession, of remoteness of damage, and of ' positive ' and ' negative ' interest. Occasionally, social and economic problems intrude. The *Liesbosch Case* [4] arose in tort, but might equally have arisen in contract. The owners of a dredger, under contract to a third party to complete special work in a given time, were put to much greater expense in fulfilling this contract because they were too poor to buy a substitute for the dredger sunk by the negligence of the

---

[3] For a survey of the different theories, cf. Paton, *Textbook of Jurisprudence*, s. 80; M. Cohen, *Law and the Social Order*, pp. 69–111; Pound, *Introduction to the Philosophy of Law*, chap. VI.

[4] *Liesbosch Dredger* v. *Edison S.S.* [1933] A.C. 449.

defendants. Was this poverty too remote a consequence to be
taken into consideration? The House of Lords held that it was,
and assumed that, for the purposes of the law of damages, poverty
is a misfortune for which the law cannot take responsibility.
A similar philosophy was adopted by the English courts during
the few years when ' expectation of happiness ' played an
exciting though slightly fantastic role in English law.[5] As Lord
Simon put it, in *Benham's Case*, ' Lawyers and judges may . . .
join hands with moralists and philosophers and declare that the
degree of happiness to be attained by a human being does not
depend on wealth or status '. But on the whole, the problem
of sanctions for breach of contract, while vital to its function
in modern industrial society, has remained relatively technical.

Freedom of Will.

In one sense, freedom of will is only another way of
expressing the essential mobility of contractual obligation. But
freedom of contract has acquired a wider and more problematic
significance, because of its philosophical and political
connotation. Freedom of will goes both to the making and to
the terms of contract. It means that a servant, an agricultural
or an industrial worker, must be free to change his employer
and his job. It means, on the other hand, that an employer can
hire and fire at will, according to economic motives or personal
dislikes, or for other reasons for which he is not generally
accountable to anybody but himself. It means that a landowner
can give notice to quit to a farmer-tenant whether his husbandry
is good or not, and whether the land will go to waste or not.
Freedom to make or unmake a contract also implies that a
person cannot tie himself indefinitely to another. In other words,
contract must not become a disguised form of status. This issue
has not often come before the courts, but in *Horwood* v. *Millar's
Timber and Trading Co.*,[6] the Court of Appeal held a contract

---

[5] Between the decisions of the House of Lords in *Rose* v. *Ford* [1937] A.C.
826, and *Benham* v. *Gambling* [1941] A.C. 157. In the latter case, the
House reduced the amount of damages to be awarded for loss of expectation
of happiness in respect of a child two and half years old, from £1,200 to
£200.

[6] [1917] 1 K.B. 305.

illegal by which a man had, without any limitation of time, assigned his salary to a moneylender, contracted with him never to terminate his employment without the moneylender's consent, never to obtain credit, move from his house, and in several other respects, to restrict his personal movements.

Most of the legal restrictions current in the classical age of contract are concerned with safeguarding this essential freedom. Contract is supposed to be a meeting of free wills. The once-famous controversy between the *Willenstheorie* and the *Erklärungstheorie* is now a matter of purely historical and speculative interest. Whether it is the inner minds or the declared intentions of persons which go to make an agreement, it is essential to the theory of contract that they should not act under the pressure of external forces. This accounts for the rules, jointly worked out by common law and equity, in regard to mistake, duress, undue influence, and misrepresentation.

This freedom also applies to the terms of contract. The parties, it is assumed, are free to bargain out among themselves the conditions and terms of agreement. The classical theory of contract assumes the legal individual also to be a physical individual. The foundations of the theory were shattered when corporations increasingly displaced physical persons as legal individuals, and as parties to commercial and industrial contracts. Because the theory was that two or more individual persons freely bargained with each other, control over the terms of contract was limited to a few categories of illegality. The idea that the State on behalf of the community should intervene to dictate or alter terms of contracts in the public interest, is, on the whole, alien to the classical theory of common law contract. It is true that contracts in restraint of trade are supposed to be void if they are ' unreasonable ', and reasonableness is measured by the interests of the parties as well as the interests of the public. Yet, in the long series of cases in which English courts have dealt with contracts in restraint of trade, there is only one case [7] in which consideration of the public interest produced a decision different from that resulting from a consideration of the interests of the parties. It was used to deny the plaintiff a pension

[7] *Wyatt* v. *Kreglinger* [1933] 1 K.B. 793.

which the defendants had promised him, on condition that he
would not compete against them in the wool trade. Although
the plaintiff did not plead restraint, but was anxious to comply
and take the pension, the contract was held void as against the
public interest.[8]

Equality.

To some extent, the concepts of freedom and equality in
contract are interchangeable. Lack of freedom to make or
unmake a contract, or to bargain on its terms, also implies
lack of equality. As long as we restrict both concepts to the
limited meaning which the orthodox theory of contract gives
them, one usually implies the other. In so far as a person is
free from physical restraint or other direct compulsion to make
and unmake a contract, he is also assumed to be in a position of
equality. Because the law will impartially award damages or
an injunction according to the same principles of distributive
justice, to the employer and to the employee, it is not generally
concerned with the inequality resulting from the fact that one
may be a corporation controlling the entire oil or chemical
industry of the country, and the other a worker on weekly wage
and notice. And formal equality, to vote, to make contracts,
to migrate, to marry, was regarded by early utilitarianism and
democratic theory as automatically conducive to social liberty
and equality.

The increasing gap between this theory and the reality of
developing capitalist society, which led to the gradual reversal
of the earlier Benthamite theory,[9] had its particular effect on the
law of contract, the legal symbol *par excellence* of this society.
It is the main purpose of this chapter to analyse the extent to
which a mixture of legislative developments and judicial
interpretations have bridged the growing gap between the
early philosophy of contract and the reality of contemporary
society. It will become apparent that the evolution of the law of
contract in response to fundamental social changes has

---

[8] For a criticism of this extremely questionable use of the notion of public
interest, see (1933) 49 L.Q.R. 465–7. Cf. further below, pp. 125 ff.
[9] This is brilliantly analysed in Dicey's *Law and Public Opinion in England
during the Nineteenth Century.*

overwhelmingly occurred outside the court room. Unfortunately, cases still form the almost exclusive material for English text-books.[1]

It would not, however, be correct to infer that the courts have been entirely blind to the discrepancy between the formal postulates of freedom and equality in contract and the social reality. There are, of course, well into recent times, judges who continue to uphold the assumptions of the early nineteenth century, either believing that they are still a true reflection of society, or that the law should not attempt to take note of any social evolution.

Perhaps the most telling expression of this view is that of Justice Pitney in *Coppage* v. *Kansas*.[2] But the majority of judges have striven, in however haphazard a way, to mitigate at least some particularly blatant consequences of the earlier theory. If they have not achieved very much, this is to some extent due to judicial conservatism, but to a far greater extent, to the organic weakness of judicial law reform. It is easy enough to detect inarticulate premises or prejudices, or ignorance of economic and social realities, in English and American case law. It is far more difficult to suggest an alternative. Vital developments of modern contract, especially in the sphere of collective bargaining, have largely proceeded outside the law courts. But even in so far as law courts can and wish to take into account the social implications of legal concepts, how far are they to go ? Within the framework of the American Constitution, the Supreme Court has, since 1936, reversed the priority of values. It has,

---

[1] The most recent English textbook, by Cheshire and Fifoot, first published in 1945, does not even refer to the term or meaning of ' standard contract ', or ' contract of adhesion ', or to the impact of public law on contract. This is all the more regrettable, as Eastwood and Wortley drew attention, in 1938, to some of the impacts of administrative law on contract ([1938] S.P.T.L. 23–31).

[2] 236 U.S. 1, 17, (1915): Cf. also Dodd 43 *Columbia Law Review* 667: ' It is impossible to uphold freedom of contract and the right of private property without at the same time recognising as legitimate those inequalities of fortune that are the necessary result of the exercise of those rights. . . . Indeed, a little reflection will show that whenever the right of private property and the right of free contract co-exist, each party when contracting is inevitably more or less influenced by the question whether he has much property or little or none: for the contract is made to the very end that each may gain something he needs or desires more urgently than that which he proposes to give in exchange '.

on the one hand, departed from the long line of decisions by which the court had interpreted the due process clauses, so as to invalidate for example, maximum hour legislation, or the legislative prohibition of " yellow-dog " contracts. In this way the court recognised that the main responsibility for translating the postulates of equality, freedom, and other political values, into legal reality, was normally the job of the legislator in which the court ought not to interfere except in extreme cases. On the other hand, the court has in recent years emphasised the provisions of the constitutions which guarantee political and social equality, regardless of race and religion.[3] What Professor Corwin has described as a ' Constitutional Revolution Limited ', is a judicial revolution made possible as well as limited by the political principles incorporated in a written constitution and accessible to judicial interpretation. Even so, the American courts can only play a minor part in the fundamental changes in the function of contract which are taking place all the time. The judicial function is far more limited in Britain, where the courts have no specific catalogue of political rights to interpret.

Neither in English nor in any other developed system of law has there ever been absolute freedom of contract, or complete passivity in the face of patent inequality between the parties. It is largely as a result of the early constructive influence of equity that the protection of infants and of beneficiaries under trusts has been extended, that remedies against both innocent and fraudulent misrepresentation and undue influence, have been developed, and that generally property rights of persons suffering legal disabilities, such as married women or infants, have been protected against the encroachments of rapacious husbands or parents. But equity shows even more clearly the strict limitations of such judicial interference. Anyone who approaches the study of equity by looking at its twelve maxims must beware of reading too much into such noble phrases as: ' Equality is Equity ', or ' Equity will not suffer a wrong to be

---

[3] Cf. among many others, Pear, ' The United States Supreme Court and Religious Freedom', (1949) 12 M.L.R. 167 : Schwartz, ' The Changing Role of the United States Supreme Court', (1950) 28 Can. Bar Rev. 48.

without remedy '. Their scope does not extend much beyond
the adjustment of property rights, such as the rights between
joint tenants, co-mortgagees, or co-sureties.

The prevailing attitude of the courts has been to protect
freedom and equality of contract against physical coercion,
inequality, or the use of ' unlawful ' means. But what are
unlawful means ? It is obvious that signatures obtained at the
point of a pistol, by unlawful imprisonment, or blackmail,
are not freely obtained and therefore not binding. But as a
line of English decisions, culminating in *Thorne* v. *Motor Trade
Association* [4] shows, even blackmail brings in an element of.
uncertainty, caused by the difficulty of classifying economic
boycott. Is the blacklisting of a trader by a powerful association
an unlawful means to obtain compliance with prices fixed by
the association, or is it a legitimate means of economic pressure?
After a long controversy, [5] the House of Lords decided that
blacklisting was a legitimate means of economic pressure.
There are parallel problems in the law of conspiracy. In the
Mogul Case, [6] the House of Lords had decided that for an
association of tea traders to bring about the ruin of a rival by
exerting strong economic pressure on merchants in China to
boycott him, was a legitimate means of competition. For many
years, English courts tended to decide differently where the
boycotting organisation was a workers' trade union. [7] But in
the *Crofter Case*, [8] the House of Lords finally recognised that
group pressure, applied for economic or social ends, as distinct
from personal malice, and carried out by means not in
themselves unlawful, was a legitimate weapon of modern
economic and social conflict. [9]

English courts have thus gradually come to sanction judicially
the restoration of a rough equality in the economic and social
conflicts, by recognising group pressure as legitimate. They
have gone somewhat further in counteracting social or economic

---

[4]   [1937] A.C. 797.
[5]   Cf. Allen (1938) 54 L.Q.R. 130.
[6]   *Mogul Steamship Co.* v. *MacGregor Gow and Co.* [1892] A.C. 25.
[7]   *Quinn* v. *Leathem* [1901] A.C. 495.
[8]   *Crofter Harris Tweed Co.* v. *Veitch* [1942] A.C. 435.
[9]   For a short account, cf. Salmond *Law of Torts* (10th ed. Stallybrass),
sec. 156. For a fuller discussion, see below, Ch. 6.

inequality in twentieth century decisions on restraint of trade. Going back to the *Nordenfelt Case*,[1] they have held that restrictive covenants are generally valid, if entered in consideration of the sale of a business goodwill.   The parties in such situations are presumed to be generally equal in economic power.   On the other hand, since *Mason's Case*,[2] a covenant by which an employee engages himself not to use his skill and labour, has been held to be void, because the employee is presumed to be in a weaker bargaining position, and the restriction on his main or only capital, that is, labour and skill, is not to be encouraged.[3] Here the courts have touched at least the fringe of that great and dominating problem, the gap between the formal equality of parties free to make contracts as they wish, and the actual inequality and lack of freedom caused by stark differences of economic bargaining power.   Yet it is obvious that the courts can only go a very limited distance along that road.   The sphere of law which is not actually or potentially touched by the legislator, is steadily shrinking.   Over a century ago, English courts invented the doctrine of common employment.   A century later, its abolition though favoured by the judiciary, had to be left to the legislator.[3a]   Judicial temperament, and beliefs, will make some courts go much farther than others in the reform of injustices through the discriminating use of precedent or the manifold other devices of judicial reform.[4]   But it would be idle to expect, even if it were desirable, that the courts could be the main instrument in adjusting law to new economic and social conditions.   They can do this no more than they can develop the principle of abuse of rights or of unjust enrichment, or the maxims of Equity, into general instruments of reforming justice and social change.   In the law of contract the main changes have been the result of extra-judicial developments, and—in so far as it is reflected in deliberate legal change—of legislation.

[1] *Nordenfelt* v. *Maxim Nordenfelt Guns and Ammunition Co.* [1894] A.C. 535.
[2] *Mason* v. *Provident Clothing Co.* [1913] A.C. 724.
[3] Employees' covenants are generally valid if they prohibit the use of trade secrets acquired in the employment: cf. *Morris* v. *Saxelby* [1916] 1 A.C. 688.
[3a] Law Reform (Personal Injuries) Act, 1948.
[4] Cf. Friedmann, *Legal Theory* (2nd ed.) chaps. 23 and 24.

THE MAIN SOCIAL CAUSES OF THE TRANSFORMATION OF CONTRACT

Four major factors may be regarded as being mainly responsible for a transformation in the function and substance of contract, which is creating a widening gap between legal reality and the traditional textbook approach. The first is the widespread process of concentration in industry and business, corresponding to an increasing urbanisation and standardisation of life. Its legal result is the ' standard ' contract, or ' contract of adhesion '.

The second factor is the increasing substitution of collective for individual bargaining in industrial society. Its legal product is the collective contract between management and labour, with a varying degree of State interference.

The third factor is the tremendous expansion of the welfare and social service functions of the State in all common law jurisdictions; its legal product is two-fold: on the one hand, it has led to a multitude of statutory terms of contract, substituted for, or added to the terms agreed between the parties; on the other hand, it has led to a vast increase of contracts where government departments or other public authorities are on one side, and a private party on the other. The effect of this on the law of contract, though as yet little explored, is profound.

All these developments affect the theory and practice of contract, but in different ways. The social security ideology means emphasis on stability and a corresponding lack of mobility, especially in employment contracts. The standardisation of contract greatly restricts the freedom of the weaker party, and is usually accompanied by inequality of bargaining power. Collective bargaining, on the other hand, has substantially restored equality of bargaining power between employers and employees, though increasingly at the cost of individual freedom, as the legal or practical compulsion to join employers' associations and trade unions progresses. The imposition of statutory duties in the interest of social justice largely sacrifices mobility for stability and security. The increasing participation of public authority in contract creates the wider and as yet generally unexplored problem of the dual function of the State, as a superior and as an equal.

Lastly, the economic security aspect of contract, the elaboration of remedies for breach, is increasingly affected by the spread of such political, economic, and social upheavals as war, revolution, or inflation. Its legal result is the doctrine of frustration of contract, with its consequent extension of legal excuses for the non-performance of contract.

STANDARDISATION OF CONTRACT[5]

In extreme cases, a single corporation controlling an entire industry or business can impose its conditions upon an unorganised multitude of individual parties. In the vast majority of cases, the firms operating in a particular industry or business are organised in an association, through which they formulate general conditions, which, by virtue of their membership, they are under an obligation to incorporate in their individual transactions. Most contracts which govern our daily lives are of a standardised character. We travel under standard terms, by rail, ship, aeroplane, or tramway. We make contracts for life or accident assurances under standardised conditions. We rent houses or rooms under similarly controlled terms; authors or broadcasters, whether dealing with public or private institutions, sign standard agreements; government departments regulate the conditions of purchases by standard conditions.[6] In many ways, this standardisation of contract terms simplifies business; indeed, it is an inevitable aspect of the mechanisation of modern life. The working out of thousands of individual contract terms for substantially similar transactions would be as uneconomical as the use of antiquated machinery. It has even been suggested that 'By standardising contracts, a law increases that real security which is a necessary basis of initiatives and tolerable risks'.[7] At the same time, it is certain that the standardisation of contracts affects both freedom and equality of bargaining, except where groups of approximately

[5] Cf. Prausnitz, *Standardisation of Commercial Contracts in English and Continental Law* (1937); Llewellyn; 'What Price Contract?' 40 Yale L.J. 704; Book Review, 52 Harv.L.R. 700: Kessler, 'Contracts of Adhesion', 43 Col.L.R. 629.

[6] Cf. *Standard Conditions of Government Contracts for Store Purchases*.

[7] Morris R. Cohen, *Law and the Social Order*, p. 106.

equal strength confront each other. This is seldom the case
in the type of transaction mentioned earlier. Freedom is affected
in so far as the individual has a purely fictitious alternative to
accepting the terms presented to him. The traveller may have
a choice between different airlines or shipping companies, but
it will hardly ever be a choice between different terms. The same
applies to those who wish to insure themselves, mortgage their
houses, or buy goods on hire-purchase. A shipping company
or a government department will not agree to individual
modifications of terms, where a standard voyage or purchase is
in question. In a recent case which concerned the effect of
conditions printed on the back of a railway pass, Scott, L.J.,
spoke of a " misuse of contract which makes the legislature tend
to substitute status."[7a] The absence of such freedom is, however,
important, mainly because of the ensuing inequality of bargaining
power. Standard terms invariably detract from common law
rights: by limiting or excluding liability[8]: by making the landlord
the judge of whether the tenant has infringed certain terms of the
tenancy agreement[9]: by making a government department as
contractor the sole judge of whether it is justified to terminate
a contract because of altered circumstances.[1] Courts, or even
the legislature, can do very little to alter this situation, which
is inherent in modern conditions of life. It is difficult to see how
it would be practicable for courts to ' enforce only those terms
to which a reasonable offeree would have agreed if he had enjoyed
equal bargaining power with the offeror '.[2] The more likely
approach is that of deconcentration by legislation, as attempted
by the American anti-trust legislation, with inconclusive results.
At least the courts have a certain weapon in so far as they are
called to interpret such legislation in civil or criminal law.[3]
But it is fair to say that, while a certain degree of competition
may be restored or preserved by such legislation and

[7a] *Henson* v. *L.N.E.R.*, [1946] 1 All E.R. 653.
[8] *E.g.*, in the typical Shipping or Air-Transport contract.
[9] Frequent clause Landlord and Tenant agreements.
[1] *Standard Conditions of British Government Contracts for Store Purchases* (1947 ed.)
[2] Editorial comment, 63 Harv.L.R. 504.
[3] Cf. Mannheim, 7 M.L.R. 13, Stone, *Province and Function of Law*, pp. 640–46 ff.

jurisdiction, its effect on the standardisation of terms as between industry and the customer, is small. The legislator and the courts have been somewhat more active in countering another form of inequality, that resulting from the fact that one party draws up terms of contract as a result of experience, long consideration, and expert advice, while the other party has no more than a hasty opportunity to scrutinise the terms. In some cases, the legislator has attempted to counter this inequality, for example, in the English Hire-Purchase Act, 1938, which makes the enforceability of a hire-purchase agreement dependent upon the delivery to the hirer of a note which sets out the essential terms of the agreement, and contains a legible note of the hirer's rights in a form prescribed by the Act. The so-called *Ticket Cases* have also touched this problem, although, as it appears, with inconclusive results, in both English and American law.[4] To some extent at least, the courts have recognised that the customer is not bound by terms of which he cannot reasonably be expected to have taken notice, because they were unusual, inconspicuous, or unreasonable on some other ground. But again, it would go much too far to pretend that this haphazard and occasional legislative and judicial control has substantially altered the position for the great majority of people. A significant exception is, in English law, provided by s. 97, Road Traffic Act, 1930, which, in the case of public service vehicles, invalidates any contractual limitation of the carrier's liability.

As regards the lack of real as distinct from nominal freedom to refuse to enter a contract where the other side holds the monopoly or overwhelming power, a modification of this position would again require a fundamental alteration in the economic and social organisation. Only a return to large numbers of fiercely competing railways, shipping lines or insurance companies, not legal prohibition, would alter the position. Some attempt has, however, been made to counter this lack of freedom

---

[4] Cf. Cheshire and Fifoot, *Law of Contract* (1945) pp. 83–87; Kahn-Freund, *Law of Inland Transport*, 2nd ed. (1949) pp. 331–337; ' Contract Clauses ' 62 Harv.L.R. 594, 2504.

by a corresponding compulsion on the other side to offer a contract to all comers. To some extent, legislation imposes an obligation upon the providers of vital utilities such as water, to provide services under certain conditions laid down in the Act. Moreover, American courts have, to some extent, developed a theory by which a party holding a practical monopoly of service is assumed to have incurred a duty to render public service, and cannot therefore arbitrarily refuse to contract. Yet ' the field of genuine compulsory contract has not on the whole transcended that of public utilities and compulsory insurance '.[5] It is this problem of squaring the *de facto* exercise of public functions with the private law liberty of making or refusing to make a contract, with all its ensuing powers of discrimination and abuse, which has led to the demand for the socialisation of public utilities and insurance.[6]

COLLECTIVE BARGAINING AND THE LAW OF CONTRACT

The increasing substitution, in all the common law jurisdictions, of collective bargaining for individual contract, is steadily supplanting, for the vast majority of employees, the traditional master and servant relationship. In Britain, neither legislature nor courts have had a major part in this development.[7a]

In England the growth of collective bargaining has proceeded almost unnoticed by the law. The term does not appear in the most recent textbook on industrial law.[8] The overwhelming legal significance of collective bargaining in modern English law would be almost unknown except for the work of a German-trained jurist.[9] Collective bargaining is taken for granted in England as a predominant method of regulation of conditions in industry and agriculture, but despite the

[5] Lenhoff, 43 Col.L.R. 595.
[6] In Britain the transport, electricity, gas, coal and iron and steel industries are now the property of the State, administered by autonomous public corporations. The original Labour demand for socialised insurance has been replaced by a proposal to put all insurance on a mutual and co-operative basis.
[7a] In the U.S.A., as well as in the British Dominions, the share of both has been considerably greater.
[8] Cooper, *Outlines of Industrial Law* (1947).
[9] Cf. Kahn-Freund, ' Collective Agreements under War Legislation ' (1943) 6 M.L.R. 112: cf. also the same author in (1948) 11 M.L.R., 269, 429.

tremendous growth of State intervention in recent legal history, governmental interference in the regulation of labour conditions has been extremely cautious and, on the whole, exceptional. Where it has happened, it has been done mainly in the form of minimum wage legislation, that is, through the compulsory determination of minimum terms of remuneration in the relevant contracts.[1] Indirectly, collective bargaining is recognised through ' Fair Wages ' clauses, incorporated in many statutes or directions to enter into collective bargaining. Moreover, the Nationalisation Acts enjoin the boards of the public corporations managing the nationalised industries, ' to enter into consultation with organisations, appearing to them to represent substantial proportions of the persons in the employment of the board ', for the purpose of negotiating terms and conditions of employment. The validity of the ' closed shop ' as a contractual term has never been legally tested in Britain.

The actual strength of trade unionism in most major industries is such that the practical compulsion of union membership is sufficient, and also preferable, to legal compulsion. Occasionally, a single trade union is recognised as exclusively entitled to bargain on behalf of the employees.[2] But on the whole, the collective labour agreement, for all its tremendous importance in the lives of millions of people, has remained outside the sphere of the English law courts, and that means it is still on the bare fringe of interest for the legal profession and writers of textbooks. Strictly, the collective contract is not enforceable before an English law court. Section 4 of the Trade Union Act, 1871, says that ' nothing in this Act shall enable any court to entertain any legal proceedings instituted with the object of directly enforcing or recovering damages for the breach of . . . any agreement made between one Trade Union and another ' (this includes employers' associations). Thus there is no direct

---

[1] As Kahn-Freund points out, this has mainly happened in weakly organised industries, where employees' organisations cannot take care of themselves: cf. Catering Wages Act, 1943; Agricultural Wages Act, 1948; and for the general machinery, Wages Councils' Act, 1945.

[2] *E.g.*, in a recent agreement made between the British Transport Authority and the Transport Workers Union.

enforcement of what, in a Continental terminology now increasingly familiar in the common law jurisdictions, is termed the contractual or obligatory aspect of collective agreement.[3] But the lack of direct legal enforceability compares starkly with its social strength, in a society in which group bargaining has almost entirely displaced individual bargaining. As to the ' normative ' aspect, that is, the question how far an individual contract of employment must conform with the terms laid down in the collective agreement as to wages, holidays, and other important matters, the only English decision on the point[4] decided that no individual member of an association could bring an action on the terms of an agreement made between that association and another. Similarly, two recent English decisions[4a] held that the provision of the Conditions of Employment and National Arbitration Order, 1940, which directed that all employers shall observe " certain " terms of employment settled by negotiation or arbitration, did not create enforceable rights for the workers concerned. Yet, at the present day, it could probably be said that the terms laid down in collective agreements would, by custom or usage, be presumed to be the terms of individual employment contracts between those affected by the collective agreement, unless there is an express stipulation to the contrary. However, to some extent, statutory minimum wage legislation has covered this aspect. In so far as it applies, the terms of collective agreement in certain industries are automatically terms of individual contracts.[5]

The growth of collective bargaining in the U.S.A. is of far more recent origin.[6] The suddenness and the size of its growth, as well as its association with the New Deal legislation, have brought it far more within the purview of legal discussion and adjudication than in Britain. The National Labour Relations

[3] Cf. Kahn-Freund (1943) 6 M.L.R. 112: Thomson, 1 University of West Australia L.R. 80: Lenhoff, *Labour Law Cases and Materials*, vol. 2 (preliminary ed.) compiled by a group of teachers of Labour Law.
[4] *Holland* v. *London Society of Compositors* (1923) 40 T.L.R., 440.
[4a] *Hulland* v. *Sanders* [1945] 1 K.B. 78 (C.A.); *Simpson* v. *Kodak Ltd.* [1948] 2 K.B. 184.
[5] *E.g.*, under the Cotton Manufacturing Industry (Temporary Provisions) Act. 1934.
[6] Cf. Kahn-Freund, *loc. cit.* p. 118.

Act, 1935, made it compulsory upon employers to bargain collectively with the chosen representatives of the employees. The National Labour Relations Board, established under that Act, and the courts deciding on appeal from that board, have given hundreds of decisions trying to elucidate what type of action by the employer complies with the direction of the Act. It is not necessary in our context to pursue that question.[7] The Labour Management Relations Act of 1947, made collective agreements specifically the subject of suits for enforcement in the Federal court. The position therefore now differs from that in English law, where collective agreements are still not directly enforceable. As regards the normative force of collective agreements, on individual contracts of employment the attitude of the courts is not unanimous.

Precedents can be found for almost any conceivable view: that collective agreements impose a mere moral obligation upon the parties [8]; that collective agreements create a usage, the incorporation of which into labour agreements is a question of fact [9]; that collective bargaining agreements are void for want of consideration [1]; that collective agreements give both parties the full armoury of equitable remedies, especially injunctions and specific performance [2]; that the violation of a collective agreement is an unfair labour practice [3]; that individual employees may assert rights under collective agreements, either because the Union has acted as their agent, [4] or as third party beneficiaries. [5] On the whole, there has been a definite development towards full legal status and enforceability of collective agreements. They are increasingly given statutory recognition and protected

---

[7] Cf. Cox and Dunlop, 63 Harv.L.R. 389–432.

[8] Cf. Teller, Labour Disputes and Collective Bargaining, Volume I, Section 157.

[9] Cf. *Moody* v. *Model Window Glass Company*, 145 Ark. 197, 224 S.W. 436 (1920).

[1] *Wilson* v. *Airline Coal Company*, 215 Iowa 855, 246 N.W. 753 (1933).

[2] *Schlesinger* v. *Quinto*, 201 A.D. 487, 194 N.Y.S. 401 (1922).

[3] *J. I. Case Company* v. *N.L.R.B.* (1944) 321 U.S. 332.

[4] The practical difficulties of this theory are shown in *Shelley* v. *Portland Tug and Barge Company*, 76 P. (2d) 477 Oregon (1938).

[5] Cf. authorities quoted in Teller, Section 168, Note 83.

by various private as well as public law sanctions.   But their legal classification remains a problem. [6]

The legal position in Canada is, as in many other fields, a blend between British and American legal developments.   Substantially the same view as in *Holland's* case is taken in a decision of the Judicial Committee, on appeal from a Canadian court. [7] In that case, the plaintiff had sued a railway company for damages for wrongful dismissal, basing himself on a collective agreement between the Canadian Railway Board and a division of the American Federation of Labour.   The Judicial Committee did not exclude that such an agreement might establish directly enforceable rights for an individual but held that in this case the collective agreement appeared " to be intended merely to operate as an agreement between a body of employers and a labour organization. . . . .   If an employer refused to observe these rules, the effect would be, not an action by any employee, not even an action by the Union against the employer for specific performance or damages, but the calling of a strike until the grievance was remedied ".   A number of later Canadian cases have also held that an individual workman cannot derive actionable rights from a collective agreement. [8]   Subsequent Canadian legislation, both Federal and provincial, has put collective agreements on a statutory basis and given them definite legal effect, as between the parties to the agreement. [9]

A third type of collective bargaining is represented by Australia and New Zealand, where the machinery of collective bargaining entirely dominates labour conditions, but with a significant difference in that the terms of collective bargaining can be hardened, and thus be turned from group law into State

---

[6] Cf. Teller, *op. cit.* Volume I, Chapter 10.

[7] *Young* v. *Canadian Northern Railway Company* [1931] A.C. 83.

[8] E.g. *Aris* v. *Toronto, Hamilton and Buffalo Railway Company* [1933] O.R. 142; *Wright* v. *Calgary Herald* [1938] 1 D.L.R. 111.

[9] Cf. the Federal Industrial Relations and Disputes Investigation Act, 1948 and, among others, the Ontario Labour Relations Act, 1950.   Under the 1950 Ontario Act, for example, the sanctions for violation of a collective agreement consist in the right of either party to call for arbitration, in the power of the arbitrator to make awards which are sometimes tantamount to damages, and in the power of criminal prosecution for non-observance of the arbitrator's award.

law, by an award of the Arbitration court.[1] This may be either by a consent decree, or an award adjudicating between contesting points of view.   Here the machinery of group bargaining is the basic factor, but the State machinery, in a capacity half-judicial, half-legislative, is super-imposed upon it.

The vital significance of collective bargaining for the law of contract thus lies in its following aspects: firstly, it resembles a standard contract of business and industry in that standardised terms regulate the conditions of employment of millions of individuals. Secondly, it is a most important instance of a public law function delegated, by the permissive or even imperative authority of the State, from government to social groups. Thirdly, the freedom of the individual to bargain on his terms of employment is inevitably curtailed by the prevalence of collective bargaining. It is even excluded where the ' closed shop ' is recognised either legally or *de facto*. Fourthly, this lack of freedom is compensated by a substantial restoration of equality of bargaining power. It is not the individual employee who has regained equality, but the trade union negotiating on his behalf. Although the trade union is not, strictly speaking, the agent, it has in effect absorbed and consolidated the bargaining power formerly vested in the individual.

It has been suggested[2] that collective agreements should not be viewed as contracts at all but as a new legal category. What this new category is remains the object of speculation. It has been likened to the organism of the constitution as well as to

---

[1] The precise classification of the Australian and New Zealand systems is not easy. Recent developments in the Australian practice tend to reduce the collective bargaining element in industrial relations, and to emphasise increasingly the part of the Arbitration Court in laying down minimum terms for an entire industry or even all industries. The main share of the parties in that procedure lies in setting the machinery in motion (through application of a registered association of employers or employees). Once the conciliation and arbitration machinery has started to operate in a particular dispute, it is doubtful how far any right to collective action (*e.g.*, by strike or lock-out) still remains. On this point, recent decisions are conflicting. For a brief survey of the general position, cf. Thomson, ' Voluntary Collective Agreements in Australia and New Zealand ' 1 University of Western Australia A.L.R., 80–90. Further; Foenander, *Industrial Regulation in Australia* (1947).

[2] Cf. *Rice*, Collective Labour Agreements in American Law, 44 Harv. L. Rev. 572, 606, and cf. also *Duguit* in 29 Col. L. Rev. 441, 459.

group insurance.[3] That the modern collective agreement has a
social and economic significance different from that of the
common law contract is certain. It establishes, in the form of
group agreement, a code of conduct between powerful sections
of the population controlling the vital factors of national production. They not only involve the groups concerned but also
the public. Hence the need for a varying degree of state interference. It has been shown that collective agreements have
gradually absorbed certain elements of contract and equity as
well as of public law. It is probably too early to make a final
assessment of their place in the legal system.

The future of the collective contract in the common law
jurisdictions is ultimately dependent on the degree to which
group autonomy can survive in the planned society. In the
completely planned state, as represented by Soviet Russia, the
collective contract between management and labour survives, but
it is overwhelmingly an instrument of planning and social
solidarity, leaving only limited scope to complementary bargaining by individual plants or industries.[4] There are model
collective contracts with all the emphasis on maximum production and labour discipline. Supplementary plant collective
contracts mainly concentrate on social aspects, such as schools,
nurseries, clinics and houses. In the Soviet state, management
and labour can represent conflicting interests only within very
strict limits, in complete subordination to the state plan. It is
more than doubtful whether these collective contracts create any
legally enforceable obligations.[5] By contrast, the individual
rights of workers, in regard to wages, dismissal, holidays, are
protected by an elaborate administrative and judicial procedure.[6]
This position is not far removed from that of Nazi labour law
which merged all collective workers' organizations in a compulsory state labour front, but preserved the labour courts for
the protection of individual rights. The modern totalitarian

[3] Cf. *Teller, op. cit.*, Section 172.
[4] Cf. Soviet sources quoted in Hazard and Weisberg, Cases and Readings
on Soviet Law, pp. 144 ff.
[5] Cf. *Berman*, Justice in Russia, p. 262.
[6] *Berman, op. cit.*, pp. 263–269; Cases quoted in Hazard and Weisberg,
op. cit., pp. 156–60, 164–74.

" organic " state destroys the autonomy and freedom of its workers but gives them security and protection in return. Anglo-American society is still far removed from such a state, but the ever-growing emphasis on defence and production, and the increasing responsibilities of government for the economic well-being of the people, are steadily increasing the public policy and planning elements and reducing the autonomy of groups.

COMPULSORY TERMS OF CONTRACT AND THE PUBLIC INTEREST

The growing range and volume of activities usually summed up in the term 'social service State' or 'welfare State' affect the law of contract in two different ways. The first, and by far the more familiar way, is legislative or judicial interference with the terms of contract, for reasons of public policy. The second and less explored aspect, is the modification of contract through the growing participation of government departments or incorporated public authorities as parties to contracts.

The variety of impacts of public law on contract is almost infinite, but three broad methods of public control over the terms of contract may be sufficient for our purposes:[1]

(1) Public policy, through statutory or judicial prohibitions, may declare contracts void, either wholly or in particular, in so far as they offend against certain principles of social or economic equality. Reference has already been made to the line of cases which have invalidated restrictive covenants between employers and employees, purporting to restrict the exercise of the employee's skill and labour. This is a relatively rare instance of judicial correction of an inequality of bargaining power. A statutory parallel may be seen in the Truck Acts prohibiting the payment of wages in goods instead of money.[2] These Acts invalidate contracts by which an employer undertakes to pay any part of a workman's wages otherwise than in current coin, or lays down conditions as to the manner or place in which the workman had to spend his wages, (*e.g.*, by having to buy at the

---

[1] Cf. for a slightly different classification Eastwood and Wortley, [1938] J.S.P.T.L. pp. 23–24.
[2] Mansfield, *Outlines of Industrial Law*, p. 213 *et seq.*

employer's store). Subject to certain exceptions laid down in the
Act, the employer cannot make any deduction from wages in
respect of meals or other benefits in kind.[3] The practical
importance of these forms of legislative or judicial protection has
of course been greatly diminished by the far-reaching restoration
of equality of bargaining power through collective bargaining.
They retain importance mainly in regard to unorganised
employees.

(2) Of greater practical importance are the many forms of
compulsory terms incorporated in contracts for the enforcement
of certain social policies. The most frequent way of incorporating
social duties in contracts is by means of statutory duties, which
come into existence as by-products of the master-and-servant
relationship. Technically, the breach of such statutory duties
will usually be sanctioned by either penalties or by actions for
damages akin to tort actions. For example, the breach of a
statutory duty to fence dangerous machinery, or provide
minimum standards of sanitation, may result in an action for
damage by the person injured through neglect of these provisions.
Workmen's compensation legislation—now replaced in Britain
by the comprehensive National Insurance (Industrial Injuries)
Act—provides a statutory obligation, regardless of fault, for
compensation in the case of accidents suffered in the course of
employment. Sometimes legislation of this type imposes
statutory duties of a quasi-contractual type, added to a contract
proper, for example, between landlord and tenant. A familiar
example in English social legislation is the Housing Act of 1936,
by which lessors of houses below a certain rateable value incur a
statutory warranty of ' fitness for human habitation '. The
relation of this statutory provision to the contractual terms has
been the subject of some judicial differences of opinion. The
Court of Appeal subordinated this statutory warranty to the
principles of private contract by holding that where a tenant of a
house coming under the provisions of the statute had been
injured by the breaking of a sash-cord, he could not recover
damages in the absence of notice of the defect given by the tenant
to the land-owner, in accordance with the common law conditions

[3] Cf. *Pratt* v. *Cook* [1940] A.C. 437.

of the landlord and tenant contract.[4] The Housing Act, however, did not provide for any such notice, and some years later,
the House of Lords criticised this approach[5] although its decision
did not rest on that point. All the judgments expressed strong
doubt whether contractual conditions such as notice of defects
should be imported into statutory terms added to the contract
in the public interest.

Another type of compulsory term imposed upon private
contracts is that resulting from minimum wage legislation. Two
kinds of minimum wages legislation have recently gained
importance in English law. The first type makes it compulsory
for contracting parties in a number of industries to incorporate
' fair wages ' standards, that is, to negotiate wages in accordance
with recognised standards. These principles have been embodied
in particular in a large number of Acts which provide assistance
to industries and public authorities, by way of grant, loan,
subsidy, guarantee or licence.[6] This means that contracting
parties are compelled to adopt minimum conditions determined
by reference to standards outside their own volition and control.
The second type of minimum wages regulation directly imposes
statutory minimum standards on a number of industries. Wage
fixing is normally done through boards or councils, known
as ' wage regulating authorities ', which make their orders after
having heard the parties concerned. In substance, this is sometimes much like a process of collective bargaining, but in form
it is a State Act which, by means of a statutory order, imposes
terms on the parties themselves. In Britain this machinery is
used in a few industries where collective organisation is weak,
notably in agriculture, catering[7] and in the retail trade.

(3) Another way of imposing public law upon private
agreements, is the variation of certain terms of contract by public
authority, that is, either automatically by statute, or, more
frequently, by ministerial order. In as far as collective agreements

---

[4] *Morgan* v. *Liverpool Corp.* [1927] 2 K.B. 131.
[5] *Summers* v. *Salford Corporation* [1943] A.C. 283.
[6] Cf. *Industrial Relations Handbook* (1944), pp. 133–138: Kahn-Freund
(1948) 11 M.L.R. 269, 429.
[7] For details, see *Industrial Relations Handbook*, Sec. VIII: Kahn-Freund,
97 Penn. L.R. 778, 784 *et seq.*

are made automatically binding on individual contracts between employers and employees, the terms of the collective agreement are automatically substituted for those of the individual contract, to the extent that it derogates from the collective terms.[8] The Agriculture Act, 1947, provides an interesting example of a ministerial variation of contractual terms in the name of national agricultural policy. Section 36 empowers the Minister, either on the application of the landlord or the tenant, or otherwise, to vary a contract which provides for the maintenance of certain land as permanent pasture, by directing that certain parts of the land shall be treated as arable land. In this way the State ensures that the land is cultivated according to what appear to be paramount national interests, in preference to the agreement of the parties. Another section of the same Act empowers the Minister to make regulations about the maintenance, repair, and insurance of fixed equipment, which shall be deemed to be incorporated in every contract of tenancy concerning an agricultural holding. The Landlord and Tenant (Rent Control) Act, 1949, provides another example of modification of contractual terms in the public interest. Either the landlord or the tenant of a dwelling house, subject to the Act, may apply to a Rent Tribunal for determination of a reasonable rent, and such rent is substituted for that agreed between the parties.

(4) An increasingly important type of official interference with contract is the statutory frustration of certain contracts which occur consequent upon the nationalisation of an industry. Thus, the Coal Industry Act, 1949, section 3, gives the corporation power to terminate certain long-term contracts, for the sale of products as well as for the employment of a person ' if the board is of opinion that they are, or are likely to be, hampered in the efficient performance of their functions by the operation of provisions of a contract '. If the board exercises this power, it is liable to pay compensation, which, in default of agreement, is determined by arbitration. If the contract is effectively

---

[8] Cf. Kahn-Freund, ' Collective Agreements under War Legislation ' (1943) 6 M.L.R. 112, 121. On the position in legal systems outside the common law, cf. Lenhoff, *Labour Law, Cases and Materials*, vol. 2 (Preliminary ed.) pp. 44–62.

terminated, provisions of the Law Reform (Frustrated Contracts) Act, 1943, apply.

The Iron and Steel Act, 1949, like other Nationalisation Acts, gives the Iron and Steel Corporation power to disclaim certain agreements and leases, made before a certain date, by a company subsequently transferred to public ownership, where the corporation are of opinion that

the making or variation of that agreement or lease was not reasonably necessary for the purposes of the activities of the company, or that the agreement or lease was made or varied with an unreasonable lack of prudence on the part of the company.

The party affected by such notice may appeal to an Arbitration Tribunal, which can either revoke or confirm the notice, and determine claims arising under the agreement or lease, by application of the relevant provisions of the Law Reform (Frustrated Contracts) Act, 1943. The application of that Act follows from the statutory provision that where notice is given, and not revoked by the Arbitration Tribunal,

the agreement shall be deemed to be frustrated, or, as the case may be, the lease shall be deemed to be surrendered on the date on which the notice of disclaimer becomes final. [9]

The purpose of such provisions is to enable a public corporation to disclaim certain extravagant agreements (for example, for pensions or supplies), which the companies may have made in the expectation of impending nationalisation.

PUBLIC AUTHORITIES AND THE LAW OF CONTRACT

The modifications of the traditional principles of contract discussed so far are familiar to all common law countries. Moreover, it is their frequency and importance, rather than their existence, which is a fairly recent development. By far the most important modification of the law of contract, however, results from the increasing role played by the government, by local authorities, and the growing number of incorporated public authorities, as owners and managers of industry, as providers of public utilities, administrators of social services, or in some other capacity, which requires the making of contracts. It is

[9] Sect. 13 (3).

perhaps not surprising that this problem has as yet been so little explored in the common law systems. It is a familiar problem in Continental systems, where the relations between public authority and the citizen have, for many decades, been the concern of the science of public law. The legal classification of conflicts between public authorities and the citizen is also indispensable for the allocation of a particular dispute, either to a Civil Court or an Administrative Tribunal. In the common law systems, on the other hand, public law has crept in gradually and by stealth. As all common law countries now have highly developed government machineries, social services, public utilities, and publicly owned industries, the significance of public law in these countries is steadily growing. But public law has to be developed mainly out of the categories of common law. Legal discussion has been overwhelmingly concentrated on the problem of administrative justice and procedure. The impact of public law on common law concepts, however, is of at least equal significance. It presents itself in two forms. Firstly, government departments or other public authorities are employers, buy and sell goods, manage factories, grant loans, repair dykes, or regulate watercourses, and exercise a multitude of other activities which bring them into legal contact with the citizen. On the other hand, public authorities contract with each other. The British Transport Commission must buy coal from the National Coal Board, and the National Coal Board uses nationalised railways.

CONTRACTS BETWEEN PUBLIC AUTHORITIES AND PRIVATE PERSONS

Continental Law.

Continental legal literature and decisions have worked for many years on tests by which to distinguish a private law contract between a public authority and a private person from transactions of an administrative and public law character. The basic distinction in French law is between *gestions publiques* (jurisdiction of administrative courts), and *gestions privées* (jurisdiction of civil courts). Generally speaking, the nature of the service and the activity in question is the decisive test. As the public activities and functions of public authorities are now manifold and diverse, this is not an easy test, unless one were to adhere to the now discredited theory that commercial and industrial activities are not proper functions of the State. In effect therefore, the main criterion is the nature of the particular transaction. If it is of a predominantly financial or commercial character, if it is in the form of an ordinary contract, or if it can be surmised from other circumstances that the State or a public authority adopted the form of a private transaction, it will be adjudged to be a *gestion privée*. Recent decisions have, for example, held a contract between the Minister of Posts and Telegraphs with the Society of Authors and Composers, concerning broadcasting rights, to be a private contract. They have similarly interpreted a guarantee given by a local authority for a loan contracted by a building society, or a promise of indemnity given by the State to a railway company for any obligations incurred as a consequence of fires caused through the operation of a powder factory. On the other hand, contracts let for the execution of public works or transport services are usually held to be administrative, not civil, contracts. Contracts arising in connection with an industrial or commercial activity of the State or any public authority, are usually deemed to be private contracts. Contracts arising in connection with the organisation of defence, police, or other traditional public services, would presumably be held to be administrative contracts, unless there were special circumstances to indicate the contrary.[1]

In German administrative law, the general approach is similar. The basic distinction is between the State as authority and fiscus. Although it is indivisible, the State thus has two legal aspects. It has a Janus head. In its capacity as fiscus, the State descends on the plane of private law and behaves like a private law person. The problems of distinguishing between the one and the other capacity become more intricate as the functions of public authority extend. Generally, however, the presumption will be, as in French law, that the State operates as a private law subject, and in the forms of private law, when

[1] Cf. Waline, *Manuel de Droit Administratif* (4th ed., 1946), pp. 52–63, 475–487.

it buys land, operates an industrial or commercial service, or lets property. The difficulty is that a public authority may sometimes undertake the same activity in a public or private law capacity. It may, for example, undertake the supply of water in the form of a public law concession of a private law contract.[2] This is connected with the notion of *Anstalt*, that is, a corporation of public law devoted to public purposes. These functions include public utilities such as electricity, gas, water, telephones; but it has increasingly come to be recognised that such services may be run on a private law basis as well as on a public law basis.

If a certain activity undertaken by a public authority is defined as a transaction of administrative law, this does not normally deprive the other party of its rights. It allocates the matter to administrative law and jurisdiction, under which the private party may obtain injunctions or damages and is, on the whole, not much worse off than under a private law contract.[3] The main difference is that the element of discretion in public policy, including for example, the right to terminate a contract in certain circumstances, gives to the public authority a greater latitude than in a private law transaction.

This kind of approach will still sound unfamiliar to the vast majority of common lawyers. Yet the similarity of the social problems which have faced the common law jurisdictions has brought them up against problems very close to those of Continental systems, although the similarity is veiled by differences of legal terminology and thinking. In recent years, a number of English decisions have groped for tests by which to distinguish transactions in which the public law element prevails, from those in which the State or public authority is held by the

---

[2] Cf. Jellinek, *Verwaltungsrecht*, (3rd ed., 1931), pp. 20–28.

[3] It is in regard to administrative contracts that the famous doctrine of ' imprévision ' was first developed. Since 1905, French administrative tribunals have adjusted terms of administrative contracts in favour of the private contractor where a change of circumstances, such as a substantial rise in costs, would make it inequitable to hold him to the terms of the agreement. This has inspired most of the recent developments of the doctrine of frustration. Cf. below, p. 67 ff. On the French law, cf. Waline, pp. 340, 414, 483.

ordinary rules of private contract. The category of 'Administrative Contracts' is of course unknown to the common law tradition. If a bilateral transaction to which the State or a public authority is a party is not held to be a contract, the alternative is that the authority is not bound at all. Many of the problems of the Continental law have, however, been solved by the device of the public corporation, which combines features of the *Anstalt* with those of a private company. Predominantly industrial, commercial, and managerial operations, such as the provision of transport, electricity, or gas, or the management of health services, are now normally carried out by incorporated public authorities, which are subject to the rules of private law, although responsible to Ministers and Parliaments for the general conduct of the operation. The T.V.A. in the United States, or the National Coal Board, the British Electricity Authority, the Regional Hospital Boards in Britain, are liable in contract and tort as they are liable to pay rates and taxes in the same manner as private legal persons.[4] But the problem of defining the public policy area from the private law area remains important, especially where government departments, local authorities, or other public authorities of a non-commercial character, enter into legal relations with the public. This problem is best illustrated by some recent English decisions. In *Kent* v. *East Suffolk River Catchment Board*,[5] the majority held that the execution of dyke repairs by a public authority was not in the nature of a contract. But in a later judgment,[6] the Court of Appeal held a catchment board liable for breach of contract, where it had negligently executed drainage work, with the result that the plaintiff's land was flooded.

A most interesting illustration of the conflict between public policy and private interest, is the decision of the Court of Appeal in *Ransom and Luck* v. *Surbiton B.C.*[7] where the Court of Appeal held that a public authority could not be presumed to have restricted its planning powers, for which it was responsible to Parliament, by means of a private contract.

---

[4] Cf. further below, p. 206.
[5] [1941] A.C. 74. For facts and detailed discussion, see below, p. 175.
[6] *Smith* v. *River Douglas Catchment Board* [1949] 2 K.B. 500, see below, p. 176.
[7] [1949] Ch. 180, see below, p. 162.

These decisions clearly illustrate a problem familiar to Continental jurisprudence. The relative prevalence of public policy or private interests must decide whether a transaction involving a public authority is a private law contract, in which both parties are in a position of equality, or a public law transaction where the public authority enjoys unilateral privileges.

In the common law, the main problem is therefore the establishment of the borderline between administrative discretion and public policy on the one hand, and the binding force of undertakings on the other. On the whole, this question will have to be solved according to considerations similar to those of Continental law, except that the incorporation of commercial and industrial activities would create a strong and possibly irrebuttable presumption that transactions classifiable under private law were, in fact, subject to private law. This is one more instance of how the alleged discrepancy between Continental and common law thinking has been greatly reduced by the pressure of common social factors.

It is of course possible for the government to safeguard the public interest, even where it enters into a definite private law contract. It can do so by means of standard conditions, and to that extent exercise the same power that insurance or transport companies exercise in regard to the individual customer, by virtue of their superior bargaining power. Thus, the Standard Conditions of Government Contracts for Store Purchases provide that: ' the authority shall have power to determine the contract at any time, by giving to the contractor written notice '. In the event of such notice, the authority must take over from the contractor at a fair and reasonable price unused and undamaged materials, and indemnify him against unreasonable or improperly incurred liabilities or expenditure.

The common law systems are thus gradually coming to grips with the problem of infiltration of public law into contract, within the confines of the common law itself, but it can hardly be denied that the absence of a clear-cut system of administrative law and tribunals greatly impedes and retards the clarification of this increasingly important branch of the law.

CONTRACTS BETWEEN PUBLIC AUTHORITIES

To an increasing extent, government departments or incorporated authorities now deal with each other. The greater the sector of socialised industry, the more important is this type of transaction. Against a different legal background, it has become the predominant form of contract in the Soviet system, where all industry is nationalised. Through the establishment of the different industries as quasi-autonomous legal corporations, Soviet law has treated them as separate legal managerial and accounting units, which are able to make contracts. But contracts between State owned corporations working under an overall economic and political plan, are obviously different in substance, if not in form, from the private law contract of both common law and the civil law systems, which are based on the principle of individual ownership and free economic enterprise.

In modern Soviet jurisprudence, contract has been restored as the chief legal instrument in the relations between state enterprises. Earlier Soviet jurists, who, under the leadership of Pashukanis, relegated all law, and contract in particular, to the scrap-heap, as an instrument of bourgeois society, have been purged and castigated as " wreckers ". But the restitution of contract to a place of honour serves mainly the purpose of administrative decentralization, and of the accountancy of state enterprises to the political planners. " The two—contracts and plans—bear a polar relation to each other ".[8]

In general the Soviet Civil Code of 1922, which is in many ways modelled upon the modern civil codes of Continental Europe, applies to the transactions between state enterprises. Liability for breach of contract depends upon fault; the familiar rules of civil law regarding mistake, impossibility, unjust enrichment, illegality, are applied.[9] Special commercial courts, the *Gosarbitrazh*, adjudicate on disputes between state enterprises. Though separate from the ordinary courts and closely linked with the administrative branch of government, these courts have been increasingly directed to apply law rather than general equity

[8] Berman, in (1947) 35 Cal. L.R., p. 225.
[9] For details cf. Berman, *loc. cit.*, pp. 191–234.

or policy principles.[1] Yet the interpretation and enforcement of contracts between Soviet enterprises—which are above all instruments of national planning—accounts for at least two distinctive features: firstly, in the decisions of the *Gosarbitrazh*, administrative and penal sanctions are coupled with civil sanctions. Where the court regards a particular breach of contract as injurious to the national economy, it will report to the superior authorities.[2] Secondly, the ability to fulfil a contract is often influenced by policy and planning decisions outside of the control of the parties. This is perhaps only a difference of degree as compared with the present position in Britain or the United States, where the official allocation of raw materials, the prohibition of certain transactions, the imposition of price controls and other aspects of a semi-planned economy are becoming increasingly frequent. The Soviet commercial contract is of necessity part of an over-all plan laid down by the superior authority. The latter enter annually into general contracts on the basis of which the subordinate enterprises conclude local contracts.[3] An unjustified delay in the conclusion of a local contract will expose the defaulter to penalties.[4] But where a cartographical factory had ordered 17 million pieces of tin stamp from the plaintiff trust and then refused to accept the goods because its planned task only called for 8 million pieces, the *Gosarbitrazh* held the defendant liable.[5]

In non-Socialist society, the penalty of miscalculation is a financial one, although the increasing intervention of government considerably cushions such effects of a *laissez-faire* economy, by

[1] Cf. the Soviet authorities quoted by Berman, *Justice in Russia*, p. 65.
[2] Thus, in a case reported by Berman, 35 Cal. L.R., 230, a factory, operating under the paper machine construction trust, which was insufficiently equipped for the manufacture of pergament machines, had contracted to manufacture such a machine. It was rejected as faulty by the plaintiff, a Siberian paper factory of the People's Commissariat of Timber. Not only were the defendant factory and its superior administration held liable for the breach of contract, but the court also notified the People's Commissariat of General Machine Construction that no steps had been taken by the defendant administration to remedy the position.
[3] Cf. Decree of the Council of Ministers of April 21, 1949; Berman, *Justice in Russia*, p. 72.
[4] Cf. the case reported in 35 Cal. L.R. at p. 234, where the defendant was ordered to pay 13,915 roubles penalty for delaying the conclusion of a local contract by one month.
[5] Berman, *Justice in Russia*, p. 74.

guarantees, compensation clauses, and other means. In Soviet law the sanctions of contract are used as a whip. Damages will show up in the accounts of the enterprises concerned; penalties will bring it into bad odour; court reports to the superior authorities will expose the management to disciplinary measures. Even though the form and sanctions of contract are largely similar to those of non-Soviet law, its social function is different.

Similar situations will increasingly occur, in contracts between the different public corporations operating the nationalised industries in Britain. Their autonomy of management goes far, but the general direction of policy is in the hands of the competent minister. Most of the problems which may arise through a change in national planning policy will be adjusted by negotiations behind closed doors, between the managers and the ministers concerned. Moreover, the British public corporation still represents less than 20% of the national industry, and therefore operates far more within the existing common law than the Soviet industries, which represent practically the entire industrial life of the nation. What develops in a fully socialised economy is not public law, in the way in which the French and other Continental systems have elaborated it during the nineteenth and early twentieth centuries. The limitation of the powers of public authority in relation to individuals, requires an elaborate system of legal rules. Where the predominant type of legal transaction is between public authorities, law becomes far more closely linked with and dependent upon State policy and planning.

STABILITY OF CONTRACT AND ECONOMIC UPHEAVALS

Before the first World War, physical or legal impossibility was the only means by which contract could be discharged, apart from breach of contract. The first World War produced the problem of frustration of contract, as a result of political, social, or economic upheavals. A great further impetus was given to the doctrine by the post-war inflation in Germany, which led to important judicial developments, especially to the doctrine of 'foundation of contract'. The French doctrine of *imprévision* in administrative contracts also had considerable influence. What emerged was a doctrine which, in civil,

commercial, and industrial relations, supplemented the strict
categories of impossibility by ' frustration ' of contract, where
war, devaluation, major social unrest, or similar factors beyond
the control of the parties had vitally affected the ability of one
or both parties to perform. By now the doctrine of frustration
is an established part of most civil and common law jurisdictions.[1]
This is mainly a reflection of the vicissitudes and uncertainties
of a period of wars, international tensions, social revolution,
and economic upheavals. The law recognises that these factors,
due to national or international policies, go beyond reasonable
calculation of economic risk, to safeguard which is the function
of the law of contract. This is not the place to discuss in detail
the extent to which the doctrine of frustration has now been
incorporated in the law of contract of the Western systems, both
in the common law and the civil law[2] systems. Frustration of
contract is still predominantly a judicial doctrine, although it
has been incorporated in a recent civil code.[3] A vital change of
circumstances may lead sometimes to the complete discharge,
and sometimes to the judicial modification of the terms of
contract.[4] The doctrine of frustration has recently gained
increased importance in English law. This is a natural
consequence of the upheavals of war, inflation, and any such
social and legal changes as are produced by the nationalisation
of industries. Reference has already been made to the instances
of statutory frustration, where the boards of nationalised
industries are empowered to disclaim certain contracts and
leases. In English law the doctrine owed its main expansion to
the first and second World Wars. But the courts stopped short

---

[1] Cf. the comparative survey in *Journal of Comparative Legislation*, vol.
28, pp. 1–25 (Scots law, French law, and German law): Vol. 29, pp. 1–18
(American law and Soviet law): Vol. 30, p. 55 (Swiss law). Also, Zepos,
*Frustration of Contract in Comparative Law and the new Greek Civil Code
of 1946* (1948) 11 M.L.R. 36–46.
[2] For details, see the articles quoted in the J.C.L., see above, n. 1.
[3] Greek Civil Code, article 388, cf. Zepos, *loc. cit.*, pp. 36, 42.
[4] The latter is the normal effect of *imprévision* in French law; German
courts have applied similar principles under sec. 242 German Civil
Code ; sec. 388 of the Greek Civil Code of 1946, specifically empowers
the court to reduce the promisor's obligation, or decree the discharge
of the contract, where because of a change due to extraordinary and
unforeseen events, the obligation has become excessively onerous.

of varying the terms of contracts, until in a recent decision,[5] the Court of Appeal followed some Continental models and boldly revised the terms of contract. A contract between the commissioner of works and a private firm had stipulated that the sum to be paid to the contractor ' should not be greater than the actual cost plus a net profit remuneration of £300,000 '. The parties had contracted for about £5,000,000, but extra work ordered brought the total cost up to £6,683,000. The court awarded the contractors extra remuneration in proportion to the excess cost. In another recent case,[6] a contract for the supply of newsfilms made during the war was to continue until a Cinematograph Film Order, made in 1943, under the Defence Act, 1939, was cancelled. When the Defence Act expired after the war, the order was continued under the Supplies and Services Act, 1945. The Court of Appeal considered the circumstances which had led to the agreement and came to the conclusion that the order had been continued for reasons different from those leading to the original Cinematograph Film Order, and it discharged the defendants from further performance of the contract, despite its clear wording.

If the ensuing turn of events was so completely outside the contemplation of the parties that the court is satisfied that the parties as reasonable people cannot have intended that the contract should apply to a new situation, then the court will read the words of a contract in a qualified sense.[7]

Such developments clearly show the increasing impact of social and economic changes upon the law of contract. The major effect of this doctrine—which is itself a reflection of the political and social instability of our time—is the substantial limitation of the sphere of breach of contract, and, with it, the diminution of the value of contract as a measure of security against economic risks. This is a development for which none

---

[5] *Sir Lindsay Parkinson & Co. Ltd.* v. *Commissioner of Works & Public Buildings* [1949] 2 K.B. 632.
[6] *British Movietonews* v. *London & District Cinemas Ltd.* [1950] 2 All E.R. 390.
[7] The House of Lords has now reversed the decision and repudiated the wider significance attached to the doctrine by the Court of Appeal, especially in the judgment of Denning L.J. [1951] 2 All E.R. 617.

of the current theories of contract can adequately account.[8]
The general trend of opinion has been critical of Holmes' view
that ' the only universal consequence of a legally binding promise
is that of the law making the promisor pay damages if the
promised event does not come to pass '.[9] This criticism has been
mainly based on the ground that the law does not leave a promisor
freedom to choose between performance and the payment of
damages where he is able to perform.[1] But Holmes' theory
comes far nearer than any of the others to the position of contract
under contemporary conditions. Modern developments strongly
underline the view put by M. Cohen,[2] that contract is ' a number
of rules, according to which courts distribute gains and losses,
according to the equities of such cases ', and that ' the
interpretation of a contract is really a method of supplementing
the original agreement by such conditions as are necessary to
determine the point at issue '. This aspect of contract, in which
the judicial adjustment of rights and obligations plays a vital
part, makes it ' a way of enforcing some kind of distributive
justice within the legal system '. To the extent that strikes,
shortages of materials, national or international policies, affect
the ability to perform—and they do so to an increasing extent—
contract is no longer primarily directed towards performance.
It is essentially the foundation on the basis of which the court
determines how the risk of non-performance shall be distributed.

CONCLUSIONS

It has not been possible, in this attempt at synthesising the
various changes in the structure and function of contract, to
give more than a general picture of developments which require
the most detailed study. It should, however, suffice to justify
some general conclusions. First, it is clear that contract is
becoming increasingly institutionalised. From being the

---

[8] For a lucid discussion of the current theories described as ' sanctity of
promises theory, will theory, injurious reliance theory, equivalence theory,
formalistic theory, and distribution of risks theory ', see M. Cohen,
Law and the Social Order, pp. 88–102.
[9] *The Common Law*, p. 301.
[1] Cf. Buckland, 8 Camb.L.J. 247: Cohen, *loc. cit.*, p. 100: Paton, *Text
Book of Jurisprudence*, p. 297.
[2] *Loc. cit.*, p. 101.

instrument by which millions of individual parties bargain with each other, it has to a large extent become the way by which social and economic policies are expressed in legal form. This is another way of saying that public law now vitally affects and modifies the law of contract.

In as far as the basic industries and economic commodities are now subject to standardised regulation by private insurance, transport, or public utility undertakings, these exercise functions of public law. Because of the inability of the other party to bargain effectively on terms, such private enterprises exercise, by permission of the State, a quasi-legislative power. Where ' the sense of injustice ' [3] is strongly aroused, public law intervenes further, either by the imposition of statutory conditions, by the compulsory restoration of competition, or, in the last resort, by the transfer of the industry or utility concerned into public ownership.

The exercise of public law functions through nominally private law groups is even more marked in the position of collective bargaining. By permitting or even directing the regulation of industrial conditions through collective contract, the State transfers a vital law-making function to the recognised organisations of employers and employees. Sometimes it formally strengthens this position by making the terms of representative collective agreements compulsory, sometimes it modifies them by State award.

In another way, collective bargaining narrows the gap between the mobility of contract and the stability of status. The paramount purpose of collective bargaining on an industry-wide or nation-wide scale, is the stabilisation of industrial conditions. The more successful the collective bargaining, the greater the approximation of the status of the employee to that of an official. Recently American collective agreements in industry have been pre-occupied with the right to pensions. The most important of a series of collective agreements, that between General Motors and the Automobile Workers Union, guarantees conditions for five years, grants pensions, and goes

[3] Cf. Cahn, *The Sense of Injustice* (1949).

further than any previous agreement towards giving all employees a quasi-' official ' status.

In the relations between government and the community at large, the parallel development is the increasing imposition of statutory terms or other public law controls upon private contract, for the sake of equalising justice.

Lastly, the increasing use of contract as an instrument of economic State policy, through the extension of government functions and the socialisation of industries, makes contract largely the legal expression of economic and social policies. This weakens the degree to which contract can any longer fulfil the function of security against calculated economic risks. This is further emphasised by the development of the doctrine of frustration, which allows for the statutory or judicial consideration of circumstances beyond the control of the parties. To that extent, contract becomes increasingly the foundation for a broad adjustment of risks in which private agreement and public policy are mingled.

CHAPTER 4

SOCIAL INSURANCE AND THE PRINCIPLES
OF TORT LIABILITY

THE impact of social insurance upon the common law liability in tort is a problem which, although it has so far received little attention from theorists, is of outstanding importance to the further development of the common law. The problem was outlined by Oliver Wendell Holmes in 1881, in the following words:

> The state might conceivably make itself a mutual insurance company against accidents, and distribute the burden of its citizens' mishaps among all its members. There might be a pension for paralytics, and state aid for those who suffered in person or estate from tempest or wild beasts. As between individuals it might adopt the mutual insurance principle *pro tanto*, and divide damages when both were in fault, as in the *rusticum judicium* of the admiralty, or it might throw all loss upon the actor irrespective of fault. The state does none of these things, however, and the prevailing view is that its cumbrous and expensive machinery ought not to be set in motion unless some clear benefit is to be derived from disturbing the *status quo*. State interference is an evil, where it cannot be shown to be a good. Universal insurance, if desired, can be better and more cheaply accomplished by private enterprise.[1]

Today we must regard the advance of social security measures—ranging from pensions or unemployment assistance to public health services and universal State insurance against ill-health, accidents, unemployment, or old age—as a development common to all modern industrial countries.

Within the common law system it is in Britain that the trend has gone furthest. The National Insurance Act of 1946, has extended and co-ordinated the many different branches of social insurance into one comprehensive system. It covers benefits for sickness, unemployment, maternity, and widowhood; retirement

[1] Holmes, *The Common Law* 96 (1881).

73

pensions; guardians' allowances; and death grants. It covers everybody, employed persons as well as self-employers, housewives, and other non-employed persons. It is supplemented by the National Insurance (Industrial Injuries) Act, 1946, which replaces the former system of workmen's compensation by a corresponding system of insurance against industrial accidents arising in the course of employment, and the National Health Service Act, 1946, which provides free medical and dental treatment for everybody. Between them these acts provide a comprehensive system of minimum grants, insuring everybody, regardless of personal and financial status, against the major vicissitudes of modern life, and providing a bare minimum subsistence, but no more. It is easy to see that such a universal social insurance system must influence and cause a readjustment of principles of civil liability developed over the centuries, under social conditions which made an individual the only or at least the main source of compensation for injuries inflicted wrongfully by him on somebody else, whether an employee or a member of the general public.

This problem, still relatively remote in most common law countries, has now become acute in contemporary Britain. The infusion of social security principles into the common law has, however, been a process of many years; and a study of the interaction between changes in judicial ideology and common law principles on the one hand and the growth of statutory rules on the other makes a fascinating contribution to the study of legal theory. It will be the general thesis of this chapter that English developments during the last quarter of a century have shown a give-and-take between the judicial absorption of new social ideas and public policies, and the systematic and comprehensive adoption of such ideas by Parliament. It will further show that, after a period of initiative and leadership in the adaptation of the law of tort to the new principles of public policy, the English judiciary is now reverting to a more cautious and conservative attitude as an ever-swelling number of statutes give articulate expression to new social policies.

RECENT TRENDS IN THE LAW OF TORTS

It is not intended here to give more than the most general survey of some of the developments, mainly between the middle twenties and the early forties of this century, which have profoundly modified the English law of tort.[2] The background against which these developments must be seen is the traditional teaching of the law of torts, according to which fault is the basic principle of delictual liability, while for a number of specific torts, like nuisance, damage by fire, damage by escaped animals, or the situation of *Rylands* v. *Fletcher*,[3] a stricter though certainly not an ' absolute ' liability is imposed. Meanwhile a relatively new tort, negligence, is extended steadily and increasingly overlaps with some of the older torts.

Duties of Controllers of Property towards the Public

(1) In the field of manufacturers' negligence, *Donoghue* v. *Stevenson*[4] disposes of the rule that contractual liability of A to B excludes tort liability of A to C.[5] Simultaneously it introduces the positive principle that for manufacturers of dangerous substances any potential consumer is a ' neighbour ', to whom a duty of care is owed by the manufacturer, with corresponding liability for negligence in the manufacture of the product.[6]

The range of this legal responsibility has been greatly widened by subsequent cases, mainly in four directions: first, the term

---

[2] For a fuller analysis, see C. A. Wright, ' The Law of Torts': 1923–1947, (1948) 26 Can. Bar Rev. 46; Friedmann, ' Modern Trends in the Law of Torts ' (1937) 1 M.L.R. 39; Friedmann, ' Social Security and Some Recent Developments in the Common Law ' (1943) 21 Can. Bar Rev. 369. Cf. Isaacs, ' Fault and Liability ' (1918) 31 Harv.L.R. 954.

[3] [1868] L.R. 3 H.L. 330.

[4] [1932] A.C. 562.

[5] Noted in (1933) 46 Harv.L.R. 530. Cf. *MacPherson* v. *Buick Motor Co.*, 217 N.Y. 382; 111 N.E. 1050 (1916) discussed in Seavey, ' Mr. Justice Cardozo and the Law of Torts ' (1939) 52 Harv.L.R. 372, 376–79.

[6] The growing American tendency to hold suppliers of certain commodities liable on warranty, without regard to negligence, is noted in (1938) 52 Harv. L.R. 328.

' manufacturers ' has come to include repairers, makers of tombstones, local authorities responsible for water supply.[7]

Second, the concept of ' dangerous ' in this and other torts has been so widened as practically to lose any distinctive meaning. Any chemical, a hair-dye, electricity, a motor car, ginger beer, rusty wire, a rock, a flagpole, may be dangerous in certain circumstances.[8] In other words, no article or substance is in itself either dangerous or non-dangerous: the conduct, circumstances, and relations of the parties concerned determine whether it has become dangerous in a particular instance. At most the presumption is stronger in the case of some articles than of others, but this is only a variant of the question of duty of care.[9] A recent decision of the Court of Appeal [1]—which has been rightly criticised [2]—has, however, revived a moribund concept, by holding that a boiler without a safety-valve is not a noxious and dangerous thing and no duty of care is therefore owed by the landlords who gratuitously installed it, to a tenant injured by the explosion of the boiler.

Third, the liability of the manufacturer has been extended through the use of *res ipsa loquitur*.[3] Thus in *Grant* v. *Australian Knitting Mills*,[4] where a buyer of woollen underwear was injured by an excess of sulphur, the manufacturer of the finished product was held liable although the plaintiff could not positively prove

[7] See the cases cited in Salmond, *Torts* (10th ed., Stallybrass, 1945) 434 n. In the United States, manufacturer's liability is imposed also on those who purport to have manufactured: see, *e.g.*, *Slavin* v. *Francis H. Leggett & Co.*, 114 N.J.L. 421, 177 Atl. 120 (Sup. Ct. 1935). Liability of building contractors for injury to strangers as a result of defective construction has not kept pace in the United States with the extension of manufacturer's liability, but is growing; see *Moran* v. *Pittsburgh-Des Moines Steel Co.*, 166 F.2d 908 (3d Cir.), *cert. denied*, 334 U.S. 846 (1948).

[8] See Stallybrass, ' Dangerous Things and the Non-Natural User of Land ' (1929) 3 Camb.L.J. 376.
Compare the list in Prosser, *Torts* (1941) 678–79: ' automobiles, electric appliances, furnaces and boilers, coffee urns, a sanitary napkin, a ladder, a chain, an oxygen tank, a gasoline tank, and a cigarette '.

[9] As Paton has pointed out in ' Chattels Dangerous Per Se ' (1941) 2 Res Judicatae 197, the notion of chattels ' dangerous per se ' is still used in negligence and entails a duty of full and adequate warning. There is, however, no reason why this should not be treated as an ordinary instance of negligence.

[1] *Ball* v. *L.C.C.* [1949] 2 K.B. 159.
[2] Cf. Goodhart, 65 L.Q.R. 518.
  MacPherson v. *Buick Motor Co.*, 217 N.Y. 382, 111 N.E. 1050 (1916).
  [1936] A.C. 85.

negligence, while the defendants could show that they had sold over four million similar garments without any complaint. By the application of the maxim *res ipsa loquitur*, the onus of proof was in effect shifted to the defendant: it was for the manufacturer to show that a cause outside his sphere of responsibility had intervened.[5] " The appellant is not required to lay his finger on the exact person in all the chain who was responsible " (*per* Lord Wright).

Finally, while the manufacturer's liability was originally thought to be terminated by the intervention of a third party who had ' opportunity of inspection ', after some judicial vacillations this opportunity was interpreted to mean a commercial ' probability ', in other words a situation which created a reasonable necessity, not a mere physical opportunity, of inspection.[6] For example, a retailer of underwear is under no obligation to examine the chemical components of his ware, and the fact that he could physically do so is not sufficient to exclude the manufacturer's liability.

One historical and completely antiquated principle has resisted the impact of *Donoghue* v. *Stevenson*: the rule in *Cavalier* v. *Pope*,[7] which exempts the seller or lessor[8] of a dilapidated house from any liability in tort for fitness of the premises.

The scope of the rule in *Donoghue* v. *Stevenson* is at present quite uncertain, for two judicial tendencies conflict. One is to restrict the rule to the narrowest possible scope, *i.e.*, liability of the manufacturer to the consumer in certain special circumstances; the other is to widen the rule into a general duty of care.[9] If the latter tendency prevails, the rule will absorb the

---

[5] *Contra*: the much criticised decision in *Daniels* v. *R. White and Sons, Ltd.* [1938] 4 All E.R. 258 where a ' foolproof ' process for filling lemonade bottles was held to rebut evidence of negligence resulting from the poisoning of a consumer through carbolic acid contained in a bottle which had been subjected to this process.

[6] Cf. *Haseldine* v. *C.A. Daw and Son, Ltd.* [1941] 2 K.B. 343; see *Paine* v. *Colne Valley Electricity Co.* (1938) 160 L.T. 124, 126.
See *Flies* v. *Fox Brothers Buick Co.*, 196 Wis. 196, 218 N.W. 855 (1928); Prosser, *Torts* (1941) 682–83.

[7] [1906] A.C. 428; see also *Otto* v. *Bolton* [1936] 2 K.B. 46.

[8] For a survey of the American cases on a lessor's tort liability to persons injured on the premises, see Note (1949) 62 Harv.L.R. 668.

[9] Cf. Morison, ' A Re-examination of the Duty of Care ', 11 M.L.R. 9, 33–34 (1948).

many limited and special categories of tort which now confuse the picture. Denning, L.J., in a recent case, made a valiant though unsuccessful attempt to apply the principle of *Donoghue* v. *Stevenson* to the negligent preparation of accounts by a firm of accountants who knew that the plaintiff was relying on their statement to decide whether to invest in a company or not.[1] The majority of the Court of Appeal dissented. On the other hand, in *Horton* v. *London Graving Dock Co.*[1a], two of the three judges based the wider interpretation of the duties of an occupier towards an invitee on the principle of *Donoghue* v. *Stevenson.*[2] Such a view would merge the duties of occupiers of premises in the wider principle.[2a] In a Canadian case[3] the Nova Scotia Supreme Court considered the possible liability of an Air Line for the damage to breeding caused by the noise of aeroplanes flying over a mink ranch, with specific reference to *Donoghue* v. *Stevenson.* All this shows that the decision in *Donoghue's* case itself was only a partial and incomplete generalization, a provisional attempt to adapt legal responsibilities to new social conditions which cannot remain confined to the manufacturer-consumer relationship. No generalization can, of course, determine when a duty of care exists. But it can provide the framework for a more rational application of legal categories to changing social conditions.

(2) The extension of liability of a principal for the torts of an independent contractor has gone far. The traditional principle of non-liability has been so riddled with exceptions that in modern decisions the cases where the exemption applies are far outnumbered by those in which, under one exception or another, the principal is held liable.[7] Negligent employment of contractors, duties where the principal cannot be allowed

---

[1] *Candler* v. *Crane, Christmas & Co.* [1951] 1 All E.R. 426.
[1a] [1950] 1 K.B. 421.
[2] Similarly, O'Halloran J.A. in the Canadian case of *Kennedy* v. *Union Estates Ltd.* [1940] 1 D.L.R. 662.
[2a] It was, however, repudiated by a majority decision of the House of Lords, which reversed the Court of Appeal. *London Graving Dock Co.* v. *Horton* [1951] 2 All E.R. 1. Cf. below, p. 96.
[3] *Nova Mink Ltd.* v. *T.C.A.*, [1951] 2 D.L.R. 241.
[7] See *Pacific Fire Ins. Co.* v. *Kenny Boiler & Mfg. Co.*, 201 Minn. 500, 503, 277 N.W. 226 (1937): ' Indeed it would be proper to say that the rule is primarily important as a preamble to the catalogue of exceptions '.

to transfer the risk to any contractor, cases of absolute liability, the creation of dangers in a highway, acts done under statutory authority, and so-called extra-hazardous acts, are the main instances of exceptions. There appears to be only one recent major decision,[8] where a visitor was injured in a lift due to the negligence of the engineers in charge of repairs, in which the negligence of the independent contractors was held to exclude the principal's liability. Whether or not it is correct to say that the principle is now in fact one of liability rather than non-liability[9] does not matter for the purpose of this study. The undoubted great extension of liability certainly indicates an advance of the idea that the injured shall not suffer from the acceptance of internal manufacturing or business arrangements but shall be able to hold liable the person who has general control of the enterprise involved.

(3) A parallel evolution of the action of nuisance has subjected the occupier of houses or other installations apt to injure a member of the public to obligations similar to those of the manufacturer. Although the development of the law of nuisance is plagued with technicalities, the broad principle emerges, applied again and again in recent cases, that the occupier of property is liable in tort for any damage the possibility of which he foresaw or ought to have foreseen.[1]

---

[8] See *Haseldine* v. *C.A. Daw and Son, Ltd.* [1941] 2 K.B. 343.

[9] See Salmond, *Torts* (10th ed., Stallybrass, 1945) 113–20; Chapman, ' Liability for the Negligence of Independent Contractors ' (1934) 50 L.Q.R. 71; Friedmann, ' Modern Trends in the Law of Torts ' (1937) 1 M.L.R. 39, 54.

[1] For an analysis of this position see Paton, ' Liability for Nuisance ' (1942) 37 Ill.L.R. 1; Friedmann, ' Incidence of Liability in Nuisance ' (1943) 59 L.Q.R. 63. For a recent judicial affirmation see the dictum of Lord Goddard in *Caminer* v. *Northern & London Investment Trust, Ltd.* [1948] 2 All E.R. 1101, 1103 (K.B.). The decision of the Court of Appeal in *Wringe* v. *Cohen* [1940] 1 K.B. 229 (C.A. 1939), goes further by stating that ' [i]f premises become dangerous as the result of something done by an occupier and they cause damage, the occupier is liable although he did not know of the danger and was not negligent in not knowing '. *Id.* at 248. This is qualified by the statement that the act of a third party or a latent defect exempts the occupier from liability unless he has knowledge or means of knowledge. This brings the decision in substance into line with others, for the occupier in *Wringe* v. *Cohen* was held liable for the defect of a gable which had last been inspected two years before the accident and had been in defective repair for three years. See now *Mint* v. *Good* [1950] 2 All E.R. 1159, where a landlord, who had no covenant to repair

(4) Simultaneously with the extension of negligence and the broadening of liability in nuisance, there occurred a widening of the liability under the rule in *Rylands* v. *Fletcher*. I have analysed that extension elsewhere [2] and shall restate only the main points here. Reference has already been made to the widening of the notion of things dangerous in themselves. This applies equally to the ' things likely to do mischief ' under the rule in *Rylands* v. *Fletcher*. The most important development, however, has come in making more precise the concept of ' natural user of land '. In the original interpretation of the courts this was, as Professor Bohlen in particular has shown, [3] understood as uses of land appropriate to an agricultural society. It included farming, residential occupation, and mining operations, but not industrial undertakings. In course of time the concept was transformed into ' ordinary user '. The decision of the House of Lords in *Rickards* v. *Lothian* [4] marks the transition. In Lord Moulton's formulation, liability under *Rylands* v. *Fletcher* was excluded where the activity in question was ' merely . . . the ordinary use of the land or such a use as is proper for the general benefit of the community '. [5] As developed in further decisions, liability does not arise from ordinary domestic activities and installations, but it does arise from special industrial activities such as the escape of water from the washing of films for industrial purposes, [6] although the manufacture of explosives in wartime under government directions may be an ' ordinary user '. [7]

No less significant has been the gradual abandonment of the condition of *ownership* of the land. In later decisions, *occupation* both by the plaintiff and by the defendant has been held sufficient to bring the rule into operation. In a case decided in 1914,

---

with the tenant, was held liable for the collapse of a well on a highway. Compare the American cases considered in Bohlen, ' Fifty Years of Torts ' (1937) Harv.L.R. 725, 740–47.

[2] Friedmann, ' Modern Trends in the Law of Torts ' (1937) 1 M.L.R. 39, 49–53.
  The American cases are analysed in a Note, ' Absolute Liability for Dangerous Things ' (1948) 61 Harv.L.R. 515.

[3] Bohlen, ' The Rule in *Rylands* v. *Fletcher*' (1911) 59 U. of Pa.L.R. 298, 320–25, reprinted in Bohlen, *Studies in the Law of Torts* (1926) 371–77.

[4] [1913] A.C. 263.

[5] *Id.* at 280.

[6] *Western Engraving Co.* v. *Film Laboratories, Ltd.* [1936] 1 All E.R. 106.

[7] See *Read* v. *J. Lyons & Co.* [1945] K.B. 216, 240, *per* Scott L.J.

the rule was applied as between two companies using a highway as licensees under statutory authority, one for the conduct of water, the other for the transmission of electricity by underground cables.[8] The concept of 'escape', however, has been applied strictly. The attempt to extend the rule in *Rylands* v. *Fletcher* to explosions occurring within the defendant's premises has been rejected repeatedly, last and most authoritatively by the House of Lords in *Read* v. *J. Lyons & Co.*[9]

The rule in *Rylands* v. *Fletcher* has, of course, never imposed *absolute* liability. Intervention by a third party, the so-called act of God, normal or ordinary user of land, and, according to the terms of the authority conferred, statutory power, are all good defences. As liability in nuisance and negligence was extended, it became increasingly difficult to draw a clear distinguishing line between these bases for liability and that in *Rylands* v. *Fletcher*. In one case decided by the Privy Council[1] negligence proved stricter than the rule in *Rylands* v. *Fletcher*: The plaintiff's hotel was destroyed by fire caused through the escape and ignition of gas from a defective joint belonging to the defendants, a gas company operating under statutory authority. The leak was caused by work undertaken by the city. This interposition of an act of a stranger excluded liability under *Rylands* v. *Fletcher*, but the Privy Council held the defendants liable in negligence because they ought to have foreseen the danger of leaks from the operations of the city, and their failure to act constituted negligence.

To sum up these complex, unsystematic, and somewhat erratic developments: A series of torts, led by negligence and concerned principally with the liability of manufacturers, occupiers of land, and other property owners, are slowly converging into a general broad principle of legal responsibility towards the public flowing from the control of property. The fault principle is not eliminated, but the gap between strict and non-strict liability is steadily narrowing. Owing to the many developments that have been described, it is becoming

---

[8] *Charing Cross Electricity Supply Co.* v. *Hydraulic Power Co.* [1914] 3 K.B. 772.
[9] [1947] A.C. 156.
[1] *Northwestern Util., Ltd.* v. *London Guarantee & Acc. Co.* [1936] A.C. 108.

more and more difficult for the defendant to disprove negligence; in practice, if not in theory, the burden of proof is lightened for the plaintiff.[2]

(5) A similar though much less definite tendency can be detected in the judicial development of the rules concerning occupiers of dangerous premises or structures. This part of the law is still very confused. I have suggested elsewhere that instead of the five categories, of persons entering as of right, contractees, invitees, licensees, and trespassers, with children forming a possible sixth category, three categories would be perfectly sufficient: apart from persons entering by contract, and those entering in pursuance of a public duty, the general duty of care and the principles of negligence would cover all others.[3] Be that as it may, the duties of occupiers have been extended, first by the judicial inclination to impose stricter standards where children are on the premises,[4] and more particularly by the tendency so to construe *actual knowledge*, required as a condition of liability towards bare licensees, as to include *means of knowledge*. This is best illustrated by the case of *Ellis* v. *Fulham B.C.*,[5] where a borough council was held liable for the injury suffered by a child from broken glass at the bottom of a pool

---

[2] This view, put forward by the present writer in 1937, ' Modern Trends in the Law of Torts ' (1937) 1 M.L.R. 39, is substantially shared in C. A. Wright's masterly survey of twenty-five years' development in tort law: C. A. Wright, ' The Law of Torts: 1923–1947 ' (1948) 26 Can. Bar Rev. 46, 79.

[3] Friedmann, ' Liability to Visitors of Premises ' (1943) 21 Can. Bar Rev. 79. On part of the same problem, see Wallis-Jones, ' Liability of Public Authorities as Occupiers of Dangerous Premises to Persons Entering as of Right ' (1949) 65 L.Q.R. 367. Paton, in 21 Can. Bar Rev. 440, 444, suggests a reclassification into four categories, ranging from the duty to use reasonable care to make the premises reasonably safe, owed by contractors, public utilities and invitors, to the duty not intentionally to injure owed to trespassers. Prosser, 20 Can. Bar Rev. 357, sees the unifying principle in the assumption of responsibility by the occupier for the safe condition of premises thrown open to the public, as distinct from situations where an individual enters the premises, for the performance of contracts or other economic purposes from which an assurance of safety can be implied.

[4] *E.g., Glasgow Corp.* v. *Taylor* [1922] 1 A.C. 44 (1921). The American doctrine of ' attractive nuisance ' appears to distinguish cases involving infant trespassers by tests for liability more specific than are found in the English cases. See Restatement, *Torts* (1934) § 339; Bohlen, ' Fifty Years of Torts ' (1937) 50 Harv.L.R. 725, 737–39.

[5] [1938] 1 K.B. 212 (C.A.).

in a public park. The court held that the defendant council was aware of the possibility of there being broken glass in the pool, as shown by the fact that an attendant raked the pool periodically. This seems an indirect way of saying that the defendants ought to have been aware of the presence of glass.[6] In this branch of the law of tort it is particularly difficult to detect any consistent principles; but, as most cases are covered by the categories of contractee, invitee, or licensee, the general trend of the decisions adumbrates a general duty of care towards visitors other than trespassers.[6a] There is no reason, other than history and the haphazard generalizations of the precedent system, why the duties of occupiers towards persons on the premises should be kept distinct from the duty of care towards any member of the public. The border line is thin enough where a private wall collapses and injures a passer-by on the highway.[6b]

(6) Certain historical anomalies remain. The rule in *Cavalier* v. *Pope* has already been mentioned. Another island resisting the general tide is liability for animals. The rules governing this branch of the law, many of them ancient, have resisted both co-ordination and logic longer than almost any other branch of the law of tort. One of its many peculiarities consists in the contrast between strict liability of the landowner for a trespass of cattle on his neighbour's land, and his immunity from liability for injury to the public done by animals that escape from his land to the adjoining highway.[7] This immunity was reaffirmed in *Heath's Garage, Ltd.* v. *Hodges*,[8] where escaping sheep collided with a motor car. The later case of *Deen* v. *Davies*[9] seemed to point to a softening of this attitude, for in that case a farmer was held liable for the injury done by a pony which he had tied up on a public highway. The old rule was reluctantly confirmed by the

---

[6] In this sense, see Goodhart, Note (1938) 54 L.Q.R. 160, 161. Friedmann, ' Liability to Visitors of Premises ' (1943) 21 Can. Bar. Rev. 79, 84–85. But see Salmond, *Torts* (10th ed., Stallybrass, 1945) 484.

[6a] But see now, for an unconvincing revival of old distinctions by the House of Lords, *London Graving Dock Co.* v. *Horton* [1951] 2 All E.R. 1.

[6b] *E.g.*, in *Mint* v. *Good* [1950] 2 All E.R. 1159.

[7] Most of the American cases in point deny this immunity and put liability on the ground of negligence. *E.g.*, *Galeppi Bros., Inc.* v. *Bartlett*, 120 F.2d 208 (1941); see Note (1949) 34 Iowa L.R. 318, 323.

[8] [1916] 2 K.B. 370 (C.A.).   [9] [1935] 2 K.B. 282 (C.A.).

[1] [1943] 1 K.B. 574 (C.A.).

Court of Appeal in *Hughes* v. *Williams*,[1] where horses in darkness collided with the plaintiff's stationary motor car. It was severely criticised by Lord Greene M.R.:

> The rule appears to be ill adapted to modern conditions. A farmer who allows his cow to stray through a gap in his hedge on to his neighbour's land, where it consumes a few cauliflowers, is liable in damages to his neighbour, but if, through a similar gap in the hedge, it strays on to the road and causes the overturning of a motor omnibus, with death or injury to 30 or 40 people, he is under no liability at all.[2]

But the House of Lords reaffirmed the rule categorically in *Searle* v. *Wallbank*,[3] which will be discussed later.[4] Subject to these anomalies, however, there was an unmistakable tendency to develop broader principles of responsibility towards the public.

Legal Duties of Employers to Employees.

At least as remarkable as the extension of liability of manufacturers and controllers of property towards members of the public has been the gradual extension of the liability of employers towards employees. The courts have been concerned with this in two capacities, *viz.*, through the development of common law liabilities and through the interpretation of modern statutes. Through both media they have greatly extended the social security of employees.

(1) The decision of the House of Lords in *Wilsons & Clyde Coal Co., Ltd.* v. *English*[5] laid down a threefold common law duty of the employer towards his employees: the provision of a competent staff of men; the provision of proper and safe appliances for the work; and a proper system of operation and efficient supervision.[6] This comprehensive statement of duties replaced a series of vacillating and often contradictory decisions, and it left relatively few cases of accidents arising in the course of industrial employment where the employer was not liable. Negligence of a foreman, a defect in machinery, or a breakdown in the safety system not attributable to the negligence of the employee himself—all these became, in the relation between

---

[2] *Id.* at 576.
[4] See p. 95 *infra.*
[3] [1947] A.C. 341.
[5] [1938] A.C. 57.
[6] These rules are substantially equivalent to the employer's duty, apart from statute, in the United States. See Prosser, *Torts* (1941) 505–11.

employer and employee, the responsibility of the former, although the employer might of course indemnify himself against those directly responsible for the damage. A subsequent decision of the Court of Appeal [7] applied the rule of the *Wilsons Case* to the injury suffered by stevedores from a broken rail on a ship whose cargo they were unloading; delegation of the duty could not transfer responsibility to the foreman, whose negligence therefore was no defence for his employers.

The limiting factor is, of course, negligence. The employer will not be liable even under *Wilsons' Case* for an accident which he could not reasonably have foreseen, such as the intervention of a stranger not under his general control. Whether under this rule an employer is liable for a defect in machinery which he could not be expected to detect remains doubtful.

(2) The significance of this extension of common law duties was enhanced by the restrictive interpretation which English law courts have in recent years applied to some legal rules obnoxious to modern social conscience and public policy. Thus, the defence of *volenti non fit injuria* has been steadily narrowed down, since the House of Lords in *Smith* v. *Baker* [8] held that knowledge of a danger did not imply consent, especially in the case of a workman. The rule of common employment, [9] now abolished by the Law Reform (Personal Injuries) Act, 1948, was for a number of years steadily whittled down by the courts under the leadership of the House of Lords, through a series of ingenious distinctions dominated by the motive of doing everything short of open overruling of precedent to restrict its scope. [1] Contributory negligence, on the other hand, is still a good defence against actions for breach of statutory duties, though it does not succeed easily. [2]

[7] *Speed* v. *Swift* [1943] K.B. 557.
[8] [1891] A.C. 325.
[9] Equivalent to the ' fellow servant ' rule in the United States; see Prosser, *Torts* (1941) 514–18, indicating a similar erosion of the doctrine.
[1] See Winfield, *Textbook of the Law of Tort* (4th ed. 1948) § 32.
See also Radin, ' The Trail of the Calf ' (1946) 32 Cor.L.Q. 137, 143.
[2] Cf. *Caswell* v. *Powell Duffryn Collieries* [1940] A.C. 152 (defence of contributory negligence failed; *Barcock* v. *Brighton Corp.* [1949] 1 All E.R. 251 (plaintiff workman failed to recover on breach of statutory duty because it was he who had broken it after it had been delegated to him but recovered at common law despite plea of contributory negligence.

(3) An increasing number of employers' duties are regulated by statute. This fact, as well as the limitations attaching even to the wide sweep of modern common law duties, gives particular significance to the modern judicial interpretation of statutory duties. A leading English decision in this direction is that of the House of Lords in the *Lochgelly Case*,[3] which laid down that, where a statutory duty is framed in absolute terms, negligence, apart from breach of the statutory duty, need not be proved against the employer responsible for its fulfillment, nor is evidence of absence of such negligence relevant. Moreover, there is a tendency to construe statutory duties in this field very strictly against the employer.[4]

Problems of construction similar to those under statutes imposing duties on employers are created by the many modern statutes that are concerned with specific social improvements; but in interpreting statutes of this latter class, the courts on occasion have obstinately frustrated their clear objective, causing much resentment. Thus, in *Morgan* v. *Liverpool Corporation*[5] it was held that a statutory warranty under the Housing Act, 1925, to keep houses under a certain rateable value ' in all respects reasonably fit for human habitation '[6] did not include the breaking of a defective sash cord which crushed the plaintiff's hand while she was cleaning the window. The same view had been taken by a divisional court in regard to a house overrun from time to time with rats.[7] But the House of Lords decisively repudiated that view in *Summers* v. *Salford Corporation*,[8] where the facts (except on a matter of notice to the landlord) were identical with those in the *Morgan Case*. In the words of Lord Wright:

> The sub-section must I think be construed with due regard to its apparent object, and to the character of the legislation to which it belongs. The provision was to reduce the evils of bad housing accommodation and to protect working people by a compulsory

---

[3] *Lochgelly Iron & Coal Co.* v. *M'Mullan* [1934] A.C. 1.
[4] See *Riddell* v. *Reid* [1943] A.C. 1, 24. See p. 92 *infra*, comparing the Coal Mines Act, 1911, with the Factories Act, 1937.
[5] [1927] 2 K.B. 131.
[6] Sec. 1 (1).
[7] *Stanton* v. *Southwick* [1920] 2 K.B. 642.
[8] [1943] A.C. 283.

provision, out of which they cannot contract, against accepting improper conditions. . . . It is a measure aimed at social amelioration. . . . It must be construed so as to give proper effect to that object.[9]

This change in the judicial approach to specific social legislation marks a most important break with long tradition.[1]

THE IMPACT OF THE
NEW SOCIAL INSURANCE LEGISLATION

Until recently, modern social insurance legislation, such as Housing, Health Service, Workmen's Compensation, and Factory Acts, represented a partial and unsystematic expression of a spirit of social reform, a growing tendency to mitigate the evils of economic insecurity for the underdog. This ideology increasingly influenced the direction in which English courts have in recent years developed the common law within the limits set to them by precedent and the haphazard character of judicial law-making. The problem how far social insurance would altogether undermine common law liability had only arisen occasionally: for example, on the question of election by a workman between his common law remedy and his statutory remedy under the Workmen's Compensation Act.

An altogether new situation arose when the Beveridge Report[2] outlined, and subsequent legislation implemented, a comprehensive system of social insurance. Instead of mitigating certain specific evils, the legislature now aimed at an over-all insurance for the citizen. This has been implemented by a series of Acts, of which the most important are the National Insurance Act, 1946; the National Insurance (Industrial Injuries) Act, 1946; and the National Health Service Act, 1946. The relation between social insurance and tort liability was outlined in the Beveridge Report and discussed at length by a special departmental committee,[3] whose final report was published in July, 1946, and was partly implemented by the Law Reform

---

[9] *Id.* at 293 ff.
[1] Cf. below, p. 239 ff.
[2] Social Insurance and Allied Services, Report by Sir William Beveridge [1942] Cmd. No. 6404.
[3] Final Report of the Departmental Committee on Alternative Remedies [1946] Cmd. 6860.

(Personal Injuries) Act, 1948. Only a few major points in that report can be considered here.

In the first place, the committee pointed out that, for employed as well as for non-employed persons, the scale of benefits under the new social insurance legislation would remain very substantially below the amount of damages recoverable in a common law action. A non-employed married man with one child, for example, would obtain in benefits less than £130 for an incapacity lasting one year[4]; an employed person in the same position would receive just under £200 in benefits,[5] whereas in damages he would receive about £350 if earning £3 a week and £700 if earning £10 a week. In either case the difference is so substantial as to make a common law action still very much worthwhile.

The next and more important question was whether it was justifiable to permit an injured person to recover both his social insurance benefit and common law damages, beyond the maximum which he could recover from either source alone.[6] The Beveridge Report had said that ' an injured person should not have the same need met twice over '.[7] On this point a sharp division arose in the committee. The majority thought that to give an injured person full compensation from both sources would certainly mean more than fair compensation, but a minority, representing employees' organisations, took an entirely different line. It regarded social insurance as but another and more comprehensive form of insurance comparable to private insurance.[8] Without question private insurance, having been paid for in premiums, need not be set off against damages. Why then should the position be different where payments were made under the national insurance scheme? The majority replied, first, by distinguishing private insurance as the reward of thrift, from national insurance, which is compulsory and to

---

[4]   *Id.* at ¶ 27.
[5]   *Id.* at ¶ 16 (computed).
[6]   For a detailed analysis of this problem from the American standpoint, see Note, ' Mitigation of Damages because of Availability of Social Benefits through Public Programs ' (1949) 63 Harv.L.R. 330.
[7]   [1942] Cmd. No. 6404 at ¶ 260.
[8]   [1946] Cmd. No. 6860 at Annex A.

which everybody contributes, directly or by taxation.[9] Second, it said that full compensation from both sources would lead to an increase in litigation because the risk of common law action was lessened by the certainty of insurance benefit.[1] Lastly, the argument that even double compensation was far from compensating for such irreparable injury as the loss of a limb applied to any pecuniary compensation in law; it could never completely redress such a loss.[2]

Nor did the majority accept a modified proposal made on behalf of the Trades Union Congress that damages exceeding five twelfths of the amount of the insurance benefit should be retained, as the proportion of the insurance met by contributions from the employees. The majority thought that such a scheme would compel the corresponding taking into account of employers' contributions. Moreover, it would entail different proportions for different classes of cases, whereas the object of national insurance legislation was a uniform standard.[3] Finally, the majority did not accept the opinion of one member, a King's Counsel, who thought that benefits should be assessed by the National Insurance Fund after the injured person had been compensated by the payment of damages so that the difficult valuation of future benefits could be eliminated.[4] The majority report recommended that in the case of both non-employed and employed persons the injured person or his dependants should not be permitted to recover by way of damages and pecuniary benefits more than the maximum which he could recover from either source alone,[5] and that the court when assessing damages should take into account either benefits already paid or the value of future benefits.[6]

The Act itself[7] adopted a compromise which some may regard as a model of Solomonic justice and others as a model of expediency. It contains the following clause:

[9] *Id.* at ¶ 32.
[1] *Id.* at ¶ 33.
[2] *Id.* at ¶ 32.
[3] *Id.* at ¶ 35.
[4] *Id.* at Annex B.
[5] *Id.* at ¶ 113 (2).
[6] *Id.* at ¶ 113 (4).
[7] Law Reform (Personal Injuries) Act, 1948.

In an action for damages for personal injuries (including any such action arising out of a contract), there shall in assessing those damages be taken into account, against any loss of earning or profits which has accrued or probably will accrue to the injured person from the injuries, one half of the value of any rights which have accrued or probably will accrue to him therefrom in respect of industrial injury benefit, industrial disablement benefit or sickness benefit for the five years beginning with the time when the cause of action accrued. . . . This subsection shall not be taken as requiring both the gross amount of the damages before taking into account the said rights and the net amount after taking them into account to be found separately.[8]

It also stipulated that, despite the comprehensive National Health Service which had since come into operation, it would still be legitimate to claim private medical expenses, though it is for the court to determine whether they are reasonable.

This compromise aroused remarkably little discussion either in the Commons or in the Lords. It was admitted that logically there was no more to be said in favour of allowing half the benefits to be set off than for any other proportion. As Lord Porter put it during the debate in the House of Lords, the compromise was effected ' rather by the rule of the thumb, which after all is the way in which juries arrive at their results '.[9] In a sense, the clause is a compromise between Left views and Right views. It saves for the time being the law of tort and makes common law actions still worth while. On the other hand it concedes to the insured, among whom employees are the most powerful group, that the new national insurance is an additional benefit for which the insured pays, partly in the form of an insurance contribution, and partly as a citizen of a nation which has decided through its Parliament that the wealthier sections should by taxation help to mitigate the inequalities of the social system. That for the time being leaves both sides reasonably satisfied.

The general underlying problem cannot be solved purely by arithmetic, but only by a sociological valuation. The trade union suggestion that benefits should be deducted in proportion to the contribution of the insured is not convincing, for the benefit received under national insurance is a standardised one and not

[8] *Id.,* s. 2 (1).
[9] (1947) 152 H.L. Deb. 1202.

dependent upon the rate of contribution. Having regard to the history of the Act and to its general scheme, there can be no doubt that it is dominated first by the objective of a general public insurance against the worst vicissitudes of life, and second by a desire to finance this insurance by a levelling procedure, that is to say, by throwing a relatively greater burden on the wealthier part of the population. In a system of graded taxation this follows from the fact that one sixth of the contributions comes from the State, that is, from the taxpayer, but it also follows from the fact that the benefit is uniform, whereas contributions differ; for example, as between employed, non-employed, and self-employed persons. The logical conclusion from this argument would be that insurance benefits should not be taken into account at all, and this was in fact the argument of a minority not only of the committee but in Parliament. The concession to the other view that benefits should be taken into account is due to a balancing argument of expediency, not of logic. By allowing a partial offsetting of benefits against damages, the insured is reminded that part of the social insurance benefits is provided for him by a benevolent State, and the danger of the odd case in which a relatively light injury would be compensated out of proportion to the damages suffered is reduced. The Act steers a middle line between two conflicting philosophies.

Another aspect of the report is of outstanding interest for the relation between social insurance and tort liability. Having recommended that civil liability in tort should continue to lead a legal existence independent of statutory social security, the committee was worried by the problem of how to differentiate the criteria of liability in tort from those of social security obligations. The report made short shrift of the proposal that the common law liability of the employer for a failure to take reasonable care for the safety of his workmen should be limited to cases of serious and wilful misconduct or gross negligence of himself or of persons exercising superintending functions on his behalf. An acceptance of this proposal would have meant the adoption of the concept of ' gross negligence ', alien to the English though familiar to Continental law and not unknown in the United States.[1] A far more serious problem was the existence of certain absolute statutory duties. Both the Coal Mines Act, 1911, and the Factories Act, 1937, impose upon employers statutory duties to observe safety provisions laid down in the Acts. Both Acts also provide penalties for offences, but qualify them by the requirement of ' due diligence to enforce the execution of this Act and of any relevant order or regulation made thereunder '. In regard to civil liability, only the earlier Coal Mines Act contains a provision that ' the owner of a mine shall not be liable to an action for damages as for breach of statutory duty . . . if it is shown that it was not reasonably practicable to avoid or prevent the breach '. The Factories Act, inexplicably, contains no similar provision, thus making the employer's civil liability more extensive than his criminal liability. The malice of a servant acting outside the scope of his employment, or the interference of a stranger, is no defence.

Apart from the inconsistency between different statutes, the committee obviously felt that the extension of social security benefits should go parallel with the reaffirmation of the fault principle in tort. It therefore recommended that

wherever any Act or Regulation imposes a duty on the defendant designed for the protection of workmen, and there is a failure to comply with that duty, the defendant shall be excused from liability in civil proceedings by the injured workman founded on that breach of statutory duty if he proves that it was not reasonably practicable for him or for his servants or agents, other than (i) the injured person, or (ii) another servant or agent who committed the breach while acting outside the scope of his employment, to avoid or prevent the breach.[2]

The government at first accepted this recommendation but dropped it from the Bill in the second reading.[3] Government spokesmen did not attempt to provide juristic justification for this change of mind. It seems that the government had been influenced by trade union representatives objecting to any whittling down of industrial safety provisions.

[1] See Prosser, *Torts* (1941) 258, 260.
[2] [1946] Cmd. No. 6860 at ¶ 82.
[3] (1948) 449 H.C. Deb. 2161–66.

THE RETURN TO JUDICIAL CONSERVATISM

The Alternative Remedies Committee did not attempt to tackle the wider problem of the fundamental relation between social insurance and tort. The judicial reaction to the sweeping advance of social security in contemporary British legislation may not be deliberate; but there is an undoubted judicial tendency to answer the extension of social security obligations with a more cautious interpretation of tort obligations and a return to a more conservative, historical, and casuistic approach to precedent. In *Adams* v. *Naylor*[4] the House of Lords refused to countenance judicially the practice by which, in tort actions in which a government department as defendant was protected by the immunity of the Crown, the department concerned would nominate an officer as defendant and honour any judgment against him. The British Crown Proceedings Act,[5] which abolished the immunity, did in fact follow shortly afterwards; and the line taken by the House of Lords may well have lent greater urgency to the need for legislative reform. There have, however, been some other recent decisions displaying a similar judicial approach in situations where statutory reform is not in sight. This may be to some extent due to judicial changes—of the two outstanding modern judicial reformers of the law of tort in the House of Lords, Lord Atkin has died and Lord Wright has retired—but the desire to protect the law of tort from complete merger with the law of social insurance is probably a more important factor.

The most important decisions in this regard are those of the Court of Appeal and the House of Lords in *Read* v. *J. Lyons & Co.*[6] In that case a factory had in wartime manufactured high-explosive shells on behalf of the government. The plaintiff, who had been directed by the Minister of Labour and National Service to work in the factory as an inspector, was injured by the explosion of a shell through no negligence on the part of the defendants. The plaintiff brought an action for damages, alleging applicability of the rule in *Rylands* v. *Fletcher* and liability for

---

[4] [1946] A.C. 543.
[5] Crown Proceedings Act, 1947.
[6] [1945] K.B. 216, *affd.*, [1947] A.C. 156.

things dangerous in themselves. In the Court of Appeal Lord Justice Scott delivered a learned judgment for the defendant in which he discussed at great length sections 519–521 of the American Law Institute's *Restatement of the Law of Torts*. This imposes strict liability for ' ultrahazardous activities ', that is, activities which ' necessarily involve a risk of serious harm to the person, land or chattels of others which cannot be eliminated by the exercise of utmost care ', and which are ' not a matter of common usage '.[7] The learned judge pointed out that the existence of such statutes as the Coal Mines or Factories Acts in English law confirms the absence of a general principle of strict liability for ultrahazardous activities;[8] that the rule in *Rylands* v. *Fletcher* did not apply to accidents occurring inside the defendant's land or premises,[9] and that the extension of the rule was a matter for the legislature, not for judges. The other Lord Justices did not go as deeply into principles, but they confirmed unanimously that the rule in *Rylands* v. *Fletcher* was not to be extended so as to eliminate the condition of ' escape ' from land occupied by the defendant.

Relying on Holdsworth's *History of English Law*,[2] Lord Macmillan in the House of Lords set forth the proposition that

the process of evolution has been from the principle that every man acts at his peril and is liable for all the consequences of his acts to the principle that a man's freedom of action is subject only to the obligation not to infringe any duty of care which he owes to others. The emphasis formerly was on the injury sustained and the question was whether the case fell within one of the accepted classes of common law actions; the emphasis now is on the conduct of the person whose act has occasioned the injury and the question is whether it can be characterised as negligent.[3]

No less significant is the statement that

your Lordships' task in this House is to decide particular cases between litigants and your Lordships are not called upon to rationalise the law of England. . . . Arguments based on legal consistency are apt to mislead for the common law is a practical code adapted to deal with the manifold diversities of human life and as a great American judge

---

[7] Restatement Sect. 520 (1938).
[8] [1945] K.B. 216, 231–32.
[9] *Id.* at 238.
[2] See Holdsworth, *History of English Law*, vol. 8, p. 446 *et seq.*
[3] [1947] A.C. 156, 171.

has reminded us ' the life of the law has not been logic; it has been experience '.[4]

The other Lords were content to emphasise that rules of strict liability like that of *Rylands* v. *Fletcher* were an exception to the general principles of fault liability and were to be interpreted strictly.

Reference has been made earlier to the immunity of the owner of land from liability for the harm done by escaping animals to users of the highway, and to the severe strictures placed upon this rule by Lord Greene in *Hughes* v. *Williams*. Such criticism, and the general tendency in the modern law of tort to extend the responsibility of controllers of property towards the public, probably encouraged the plaintiff in *Searle* v. *Wallbank* to bring an action for damages against the owner of a horse which had strayed from an adjoining field onto the highway during a wartime blackout and injured the plaintiff cycling along the highway. The immunity of the keeper of non-mischievous animals from any duty towards the public to fence the land or provide other safeguards against escape is of course qualified by the general liability in negligence. But as Lord du Parcq pointed out in his judgment,[5] this general liability is subject to the twofold qualification that in the absence of special circumstances, where a tame animal does a dangerous act contrary to its ordinary nature, then, first, mere failure to provide against that possibility does not constitute negligence; and, second, even if a defendant's omission to control or secure the animal was negligent, such negligence may not be regarded as the direct cause of such an act. In the absence of negligence, the House firmly refused to construe anything like a general duty of an occupier of land adjoining a highway to prevent animals from escaping onto it. The approach of the House to the problem was largely historical. There had always been the contrast between the strict liability of the owner of animals for trespass to his neighbour, and the liability of the highway public to take the land as they found it, that is to say unfenced. As several of the opinions pointed out, the problem has become acute only since the advent of motor cars and other fast-moving vehicles. But whereas the law of tort has been generally adjusted to the

[4] *Id.* at 175. [5] [1947] A.C. 341, 360.

advent of industry and modern technical inventions, and the actions in negligence, nuisance, and trespass in particular have been so developed as to impose upon the occupier of land a general responsibility for damage to the public which he could have avoided by reasonable control, the House of Lords has refused to impose similar duties on the landowner and farmer as keeper of animals. From the general angle of a reasonable distribution of burdens in modern economic society there is no reason for this differentiation between industry and agriculture, in the age of farm subsidies, guaranteed prices, production quotas, and import tariffs. Farmers invoke State insurance against risks no less than industry.

The House of Lords again struck a conservative note when, in *Jacobs* v. *L.C.C.*[6] it refused to hold a landlord liable for the injury caused to a tenant's visitor who suffered injury from a protruding stop-cock on the forecourt. The House relied on *Fairman's Case*,[7] which regarded such a visitor as the landlord's licensee, and the latter liable for actual knowledge only. Scott, L.J., had cast some doubt on the *ratio decidendi* of this case,[8] and *Ellis' Case*[9] makes the distinction between knowledge and means of knowledge questionable.

Finally, in *London Graving Dock Co.* v. *Horton* [1951] 2 All E.R. 1, the House of Lords dismissed the action of a welder injured while working on a trawler under unsafe conditions against which he had vainly protested. The majority repudiated any general duty of care on the part of an invitor. As Lords MacDermott and Reid (dissenting) pointed out, the result is unreasonable and based on a questionable interpretation of an ambiguous phrase used by Willes J. in 1866. This branch of the law is now more beset than ever by distinctions unrelated to principle or common sense.[1]

[6] [1950] 1 All E.R. 737.   [7] [1923] A.C. 74.
[8] In *Haseldine* v. *Daw* [1941] 3 All E.R. 156.
[9] [1938] 1 K.B. 212. Cf. above, p. 82.
[1] The Court of Appeal favours a less orthodox approach. Cf. its recent decisions in *Horton* v. *London Graving Dock* [1950] 1 All E.R., which treated liability to an invitee as an aspect of the general duty of care, and *Cassidy* v. *Min. of Health*, [1951] 1 All E.R. 574, where, for the first time, a hospital authority was held liable for the professional negligence of a surgeon in its employment. On the other hand, the deplorable decision in *Ball* v. *L.C.C.* (above, p. 76) unconvincingly revives the moribund concept of things ' dangerous per se '.

CONCLUSIONS

The first and most general principle is that the main function of the law of tort is the reasonable adjustment of economic risks in a capitalist—though not necessarily in a capitalist—society and not the expression of certain absolute moral principles. It may be sufficient to compare the classical formulation in Holmes' *Common Law*, first published in 1881, with the restatement of the problem by a modern American jurist in 1947. This is what Holmes says on the subject:

> Be the exceptions more or less numerous, the general purpose of the law of torts is to secure a man indemnity against certain forms of harm to person, reputation, or estate, at the hands of his neighbours, not because they are wrong, but because they are harms. The true explanation of the reference of liability to a moral standard, in the sense which has been explained, is not that it is for the purpose of improving men's hearts, but that it is to give a man a fair chance to avoid doing the harm before he is held responsible for it. It is intended to reconcile the policy of letting accidents lie where they fall, and the reasonable freedom of others with the protection of the individual from injury. . . . As the law, on the one hand, allows certain harms to be inflicted irrespective of the moral condition of him who inflicts them, so, at the other extreme, it may on grounds of policy throw the absolute risk of certain transactions on the person engaging in them, irrespective of blame-worthiness in any sense.[2]

Jerome Hall states that ' torts deal with individual damage which need not have been effected by morally culpable conduct '.[3] The view that liability in tort is essentially a matter of balance between various social and economic policies is also brought out in the following passage:

If attention is centred on the injured plaintiff, it is thought that he certainly ought to have reparation. . . . On the other hand, countervailing moral principles induce equal insistence that actual fault is the only proper ground for shifting the loss. These various objectives and policies run at cross-purposes. To many the escape from the dilemma is offered by insurance—the injured person is compensated but the loss is distributed over a wide field—hence both the monetary judgment against a particular person and his want of culpability are of minor consequence.[4]

[2] Holmes, *The Common Law* (1881) 144–45.
[3] J. Hall. *General Principles of Criminal Law* (1947) 213.
[4] *Id.* at 242.

It follows from this recognition of the law of tort as a set of rules designed to distribute economic harm according to changing principles of public policy that the law of tort should be clearly dissociated conceptually from the law of crime despite the parallelism of their recent developments. It is true that a large section of the modern law of crime has moved away from the older principles of mens rea, in a way comparable to the manner in which civil social insurance liability has moved away from the fault principle in tort; both trends are aspects of the growing complexity of modern industrial society and the consequent need to promote the observance of certain standards of conduct by penalties on the one hand, and strict or near-strict civil liability on the other. Because of the basic difference between punishment for murder or embezzlement, and fines imposed on a business undertaking for offences against certain safety provisions, health regulations, or food standards, many modern writers have recommended the complete separation of ' administrative penal law ' or ' public welfare offences ' from the main body of criminal law.[5] Once this operation is performed, it is easier to subscribe to Hall's suggestion that, while ' moral culpability is of secondary importance in tort law—immoral conduct is simply one of various ways by which individuals suffer economic damage ', in penal law ' the immorality of the actor's conduct is essential '.[1] If we follow the mere procedural test, distinguishing criminal from civil offences according to whether they are initiated by prosecution or civil action, there is much overlapping. No useful purpose is served, nor can consistency be obtained, by linking liability in tort to criminal liability, notwithstanding their once close historical association. It may be desirable to make the standard of conduct in public welfare offences conform to that of civil liability for statutory duties, but our general problem of the relation between social insurance and tort liability must be considered on its own merits.[2]

---

[5] See, *e.g.*, Sayre, ' Public Welfare Offences ' (1933) 33 Col.L.R. 55; J. Hall, *op. cit. supra.* See further below, p. 107.

[1] J. Hall, *op. cit. supra* note 85, at 203.

[2] The relatively few wrongs in which malice or intention is essential are of no importance for our purposes; they are not wrongs which concern primarily the adjustment of economic harms.

Finally, it seems clear that the part of the law of tort with which we are dealing here is itself concerned not with states of mind but with standards of conduct, whatever the merits of the theoretical controversy may be in general. Objective evidentiary tests determine whether a statutory safety obligation has been broken, whether a car has been driven at excessive speed, or whether an excess of sulphur in woollen underwear is due to the maker's negligence.

Having cleared the ground, we can attempt a summary of the principles governing our problem. First, that part of the law of tort which concerns us here has steadily moved closer towards a social insurance principle, although the two have not yet merged. The standards of care imposed upon the manufacturer of goods, the occupier of land, the driver or keeper of fast-moving vehicles, have been tightened, and the range of defences has steadily decreased. Certain defences, like common employment, have disappeared, and others are becoming steadily more difficult, *e.g.*, non-liability for an independent contractor, lack of knowledge of a defect in a building, unawareness of the operations of a third party, or the selection of adequate supervisors. Even if there is still some substance theoretically in the difference between ' strict ' and ' negligence ' liability in common law, from the broader angle of the adjustment of social harm the difference in a given modern situation is of subordinate significance.[3]

There remain certain islands amidst the stream of extending common law liability, such as the relative immunity of the keeper of animals in regard to users of the highway. They hardly affect the general trend and are significant rather as an expression of the determination of courts to maintain the common law in its historic structure and growth.

It would be tempting to eliminate, for the sake of simplicity, what appears to be a relatively small difference between tort liability dependent on negligence in the broad modern sense, and strict social insurance liability. It has in fact been suggested that the maintenance of the fault principle in tort liability is futile,

---

[3] For a summary of the remaining differences, see Paton, ' Evolution of Negligence ' (1949) 23 Aust.L.J. 158. For enterprise liabilities of the type analysed in the text, Ehrenzweig suggests the paradoxical term ' Negligence without Fault '. (U. of Cal. Press, 1951.)

because the modern manufacturer and employer, or the motor-car owner, must invariably insure himself, and that insurance against harms done to employees or third persons should simply be considered as everyday expenses: a small burden attendant upon the profits of enterprise in a capitalistic society.[4] There are, however, three conclusive answers to this. In the first place, the law of torts even today affects large numbers of people who are neither employers nor manufacturers, but ordinary members of the public not covered by insurance. For them the difference between strict and non-strict liability is still important.[5]

Secondly, the coupling of tort liability with standards of conduct, and with negligence in particular, is not without practical significance. Under modern business conditions the interest in the observance of these standards often passes from the defendant enterprise to the defendant's insurance company, which, where liability is not strict, has a definite pecuniary interest in careful conduct of the insured. It is therefore clearly in the public interest, and in particular in the interest of workmen operating machines, to have liability dependent on the maintenance of certain standards of conduct. This adds to any civil or penal sanction against the employer or manufacturer the financial interest of the insurance company in the maintenance of standards.[5a]

[4] See, for example, the remarks of Mr. Silverman, M.P., in the debate on the Law Reform (Personal Injuries) Bill (1948) 449 H.C. Deb. 2187.

[5] Even the radical Automobile Accident legislation of Saskatchewan which compulsorily insures both motor car owners and the public against accidents caused by motor vehicles, though a special fund administered by a Crown Corporation on a non-profit basis, preserves the right to bring a tort action for negligence and to retain the excess of damages over compensation. For details, see Green, Automobile Accident Insurance Legislation in the Province of Saskatchewan, 31 J.C.L. 39-53, reprinted in Lawson, *Negligence in the Civil Law,* pp. 315 ff. It should also be remembered that a number of important torts—defamation, injurious falsehood, malicious prosecution, and others not causing a physical disability that can be covered by social insurance—remain outside the problem considered here.

[5a] It should, however, be pointed out that for many years Canadian legislation has substituted Workmen's Compensation, administered by Boards, for tort actions by workmen, injured by accidents arising out of and in the course of employment, against their employers. No right of election or waiver is permitted. Cf. Ontario Workmen's Compensation Act, 1950 (Ch. 430).

Third, as the Attorney-General said in the debate on the Bill,[6] an increasing number of industries in Britain have become or are becoming the property of the nation, and any profits made by a nationalised enterprise are made on behalf of the nation. In these cases, where both damages and benefits however computed will be at the expense of the government, the extent of civil liability as affecting the apportionment of recovery becomes purely a matter of proper business management and accounting principles, which are as important for public as for private enterprise.[7] Certainly it is no less realistic to reflect damage payments due to negligence in the liabilities of the negligent enterprise than it is to charge them to an insurance fund. Indeed, this would serve as a check on efficiency and proper management, for, while the negligent individual will not feel a financial burden directly, his carelessness may lead to his dismissal or to curtailment of the budget of his organisation. Thus, although the day may come when the compensatory functions of the law of tort are assumed entirely by State insurance—as Holmes envisaged—the enforcement of standards of conduct need not become entirely a matter of penal law; the ' accountancy ' principle of socialised enterprise[8] may demand not the abandonment, but the strengthening of the principle of fault.[9]

---

[6] (1948) 449 H.C. Deb. 2164.
[7] Cf. below pp. 187, 191–93.
[8] For its significance in Soviet law, see Schlesinger, *Soviet Legal Theory* (1946) 193, 247; Friedmann, *Legal Theory* (2nd ed. 1949) 249–50. Gsovski, *Soviet Civil Law*, Vol. 1, chap. 11.
[9] Soviet jurisprudence has completely abandoned earlier theories which repudiated fault liability, as the expression of an un-Marxian free-will philosophy. It has now reverted to a fault theory close to modern West European doctrine. Cf. Gsovski, *op. cit.*, chap. 14. In cases of injury to the earning power of a person, the amount of damages must not, however, exceed the rates payable in similar cases as social insurance. (Sec. 415, Civil Code of the R.S.F.S.R.)

CHAPTER 5

PUBLIC WELFARE OFFENCES, AND THE PRINCIPLES OF CRIMINAL LIABILITY

A RECENT decision of the High Court of Australia[1] has—for the first time as it seems—raised a problem of considerable theoretical and practical importance, part of the wider question of how to adjust old legal concepts and theories to twentieth-century conditions of government and society.

Under the Australian Commonwealth Re-establishment and Employment Act, 1945, employers are under a duty to reinstate persons who have completed a certain period of war service, in their former employment. A further section provides that they shall not without reasonable cause terminate or vary such employment. Offenders are liable to a penalty of £100, to be imposed by a court of summary jurisdiction. Other sections of the Act provide, for certain other offences, imprisonment not exceeding six months, alternatively or in addition to a penalty. The whole Act is specifically declared binding upon the Crown.

The defendant, who was a manager of a Commonwealth munition factory, was prosecuted before a court of petty sessions in Victoria for unlawful termination of the plaintiff's employment. Conviction was possible only under section 5 of the Commonwealth Crimes Act, which provides that ' any person who procures or by any act of commission is in any way directly or indirectly knowingly concerned in or party to any offence against any law of the Commonwealth, shall be deemed to have committed that offence, and shall be punishable accordingly '. Although there is increasing support for the view that the person who can act directly on behalf of a corporate body is its organ or alter ego,[2] the defendant in this case was only in the position of a servant.

---

[1] *Cain* v. *Doyle* 72 C.L.R. 409 (1946).
[2] *Lennard's Carrying Co., Ltd.* v. *Asiatic Petroleum Co., Ltd.* [1915] A.C. 705 ; cf. Winn, ' Criminal Responsibility of Corporations ' (1929) 3 Camb.L.J. 398, and Welsh, ' Criminal Liability of Corporations ' (1946) 62 L.Q.R. 345.

His conviction was therefore dependent upon his being an accessory to an offence committed by the Crown. Although the High Court decided by a bare majority to confirm the order of the magistrate dismissing the information, the majority of the judges did not reject the possibility of the Crown being convicted for a criminal offence. A short analysis of the different judgments well illustrates the strains to which the steady expansion of commercial and managerial government activities in the ' mixed economy ' of Britain and the Dominions exposes traditional legal thinking.

Only the Chief Justice (Latham C.J.) dismissed the idea that the Crown might commit a criminal offence as unacceptable in principle. His objections were, first, that the fundamental idea of the criminal law is a prosecution of offences against the King's peace; secondly, that the Crown itself would have to be a prosecutor in the case of serious offences; thirdly, that the Commonwealth would have to pay a fine to itself; and fourthly, that where imprisonment was at least an alternative penalty, the Crown could not be included as it could not be imprisoned.

Dixon J., with whose judgment Rich J. concurred, took a less rigid view. He did not regard the imposition of a criminal liability upon the Crown as a theoretical impossibility. But he thought that there was the strongest presumption against such an interpretation of any statute: ' It is opposed to all our conceptions, constitutional, legal and historical. Conceptions of this nature are, of course, not immutable, and we should beware of giving effect to the strong presumption in their favour in the face of some clear expression of a valid intention to infringe upon them. But we should at least look for quite certain indications that the legislature had adverted to the matter and had advisedly resolved upon so important and serious a course '. The following reasons persuaded Dixon J. that the present Act did not displace the presumption: first, there was no court with summary jurisdiction over the Crown; secondly, any fine would go to the Federal Treasury, which would thus have to pay fines to itself; thirdly, the Crown had power to remit fines; fourthly, if the answer were different, two or more ministers or other Crown servants could be held guilty of conspiracy. All these technical considerations were, however, in the opinion of Dixon J., only illustrations of the wider principle 'that the King is not under the coercive power of the law'. Like Latham C.J. he drew a distinction between the penal and the merely directive aspects of the statute. Even without penal sanctions, an Act might still impose certain duties on officers of the Crown and their neglect might be remedied by injunction or mandamus or civil remedies.

The dissenting judgments of Starke and Williams JJ. took an entirely different line. Starke J. emphasised that 'Sovereign bodies may create rights and obligations against themselves and submit the determination of those rights and obligations to the jurisdiction of the courts and provide means for enforcing them', and that 'A penal sanction does not seem an impossibility, especially when, as in this case, the judicial authority may order that portion of the penalty be paid to the employee'. He thought that if the duties imposed on governments could not be enforced against them, the effectiveness of the Act would be seriously impaired. Similarly, Williams J. saw no constitutional difficulty in the way of the Sovereign binding himself in Parliament. Both judges pointed out that the Commonwealth had been subject to liability in contract and tort since the Judiciary Act of 1903. Williams J. did not regard difficulties of enforcement as decisive, as the Crown might be presumed to meet its legal obligations out of the money's provided by Parliament.

Thus, four out of five judges of a court which is not noted for either radicalism or disrespect for the principles and traditions of the common law, did regard the criminal conviction of the Crown as at least theoretically possible. It is submitted that this conclusion is not only theoretically correct, but that it represents one of the necessary adaptations of legal thinking, if the inevitable extension of governmental responsibilities and functions is to be balanced by an extension of the rule of law. This means a removal of the lingering remnants of the historical identification of the Crown with the person of the King, and of both with the modern State.

All the specific reasons produced in the High Court against criminal liability of the Crown seem unconvincing. First, the subjection of the Crown to summary procedure is a mere technical matter, not an objection of principle. A comparable technical obstacle was overcome when the (English) Criminal Justice Act, 1925, s. 33, provided for the trial of corporations by indictment. Nor is there any reason why submission of the Crown to summary procedures should not follow from an Act which is specifically declared applicable to the Crown. Secondly, the possibility that the Treasury might both pay and receive fines presupposes the unity and indivisibility of the Crown, which should now be discarded. The purpose of a fine, especially in penalties for administrative or social welfare offences, is not always primarily to hurt the defendant financially. It is to attach a stigma—pronounced by independent law courts—on the breach of legal obligations which have been imposed in the interest of the community. If a modern giant industrial concern is fined for a statutory offence, this does not normally hurt an individual. But an accumulation of such convictions will deservedly impair the standing and reputation of such a concern. Nor is there any doubt that public corporations such as the National Coal Board or the Transport Commission could be fined for statutory offences. Yet they are in substance part of the government machinery, and their finances are, in a more or less direct way, linked with government finance.[3] But there is no reason why the often merely technical difference between a government department separately incorporated as a statutory authority, and a government department which remains technically part of the Crown, should be elevated into a matter of principle. The apparent absurdity of the Crown paying a fine to itself is part of nineteenth century legal thinking applied to twentieth century conditions.

The same applies to the further argument that the Crown could not be imprisoned. In *R. v. I. C. R. Haulage, Ltd.*,[4] the Court of Criminal Appeal held that an indictment for a common law conspiracy to defraud lies against a limited company. It also disagreed with the earlier decision of *R. v. Cory Bros.*,[5] where the

[3] Cf. below, Ch. 9, p. 191, also 22 Australian L.J. 11 *et seq.*
[4] [1944] K.B. 551.
[5] [1927] 1 K.B. 810.

court refused to indict a company whose directors had caused the
death of an unemployed coalminer by charging a fence with
electric current. It held that it is sufficient if a fine is at least an
alternative punishment. This is strongly supported by both Winn
and Welsh.[6] On the other hand, ' Where the only punishment
which the court can impose is death, penal servitude,
imprisonment or whipping, or a punishment which is otherwise
inappropriate to a body corporate, such as a declaration that the
offender is a rogue and a vagabond, the court will not stultify
itself by embarking on a trial in which, if a verdict of guilty is
returned, no effective order by way of sentence can be made '.[7]
There is no reason why these considerations should not apply
to the Crown. If an Act is declared specifically applicable to
the Crown, this applicability should go as far as is technically
possible whether the literal or the mischief rule of statutory
interpretation is applied to the construction of the statute.

All these points are, however, aspects of a wider problem.
The absurd fiction that because modern government is still
nominally carried out in the name of the King, the government
is above the law, has at last been discarded for the sphere of civil
law.[8] But, ironically enough, it is conservative legal thinking
on this subject that still impedes the implementation of Dicey's
principle of equality before the law. The only reason for
differentiating between civil and criminal liability would be
that an imposition of criminal liability upon the Crown would
offend against elementary principles of constitutional law and
public policy. This leads us to a distinction of two types of
criminal law which is becoming more and more important.
The common law type of criminal offences, from murder to
larceny, which demands a *mens rea*, still dominates the textbooks,
but a type of criminal offence which is mainly administrative
in character and does not involve a moral stigma is steadily
gaining in importance. This kind of statutory offence is essentially
an instrument of government, a formalised protection of social
welfare provisions. Safety or health provisions in factories,

[6] See note 2, above.
[7] Welsh, *loc. cit.*, p. 363.
[8] Crown Proceedings Act, 1947.

purity of foodstuffs or beverages for sale, compliance with directions on price control, standards of production, or building restrictions, are some of the innumerable illustrations of this growing branch of administrative penal law, which the last war in particular has made familiar to thousands. On the Continent this has long been known as *Verwaltungsstrafrecht*. American authors have recently introduced a corresponding category called ' public welfare offences '.[9] Liability for such offences is normally strict. It is designed to ensure a standard of conduct in the social interest rather than to punish a state of mind of the individual. As long ago as 1846, an English court held a retail dealer guilty of having adulterated tobacco, although he neither knew nor had any reason to suspect it was adulterated.[1] Since then, the range of strict statutory offences has widened immensely. It includes the sale of food, liquor and narcotics, traffic offences, building regulations, safety devices in mines, factories, docks, and a multitude of other activities closely connected with public order and social welfare. As Hall points out, these public welfare statutes represent ' relatively recent adaptations to an intricate economy ', and ' their occurrence does not arouse the resentment that characterises the affective attitudes directed at the perpetrators of traditional crimes '. There is nothing shocking in the suggestion that the Crown—whether it acts through a government department or through a separate corporation—should be subject to this type of penal liability. The public policy which has led to the constitution of an increasing number of government activities in the form of public corporations, fully liable in public and private law, and as nearly as possible on the same footing as a private individual, applies with equal force to liability for statutory offences, which are one way of ensuring public order and the minimum of social standards in services. And just as separate budgeting, accounting, and auditing of public corporations—whether or not they are entirely financed by the government—is regarded as an essential means of ensuring efficient management and honest accountancy, so

---

[9] Sayre (1933) 33 Col.L.R. 71; Hall, *Principles of Criminal Law* (1947) 281. Cf. above, p. 98.
[1] *R.* v. *Woodrow* (1846) 153 Eng. Rep. 907.

the liability of the Crown and other public authorities to fines must be seen, not as a means of making them suffer financially, but as a means of ensuring a standard of public conduct at least equal to that which the Crown demands of its subjects.[2]

[2] There is no need to go into the further question whether the Crown, like other corporations, might also be liable for criminal offences which demand a *mens rea*. Welsh has recently analysed the criminal liability of corporations in general, in the light of three English decisions of 1944, which have held corporate bodies liable for crimes in which a guilty state of mind was an essential element. The actions of other ' primary representatives ', *i.e.*, representatives who are organs rather than mere servants or agents of the corporations, were imputed to the bodies corporate. Both Welsh and Winn (*loc. cit.* note 2) advance powerful arguments for the general extension of criminal liability of corporations, except for a limited number of crimes such as bigamy, incest, and rape, which could not be committed by a corporation, and certain crimes which are not punishable by the infliction of a fine, at least as an alternative to a heavier penalty. The main difficulty in extending this wider criminal liability of corporate bodies to the Crown lies probably in constitutional law, as Dixon J. pointed out in *Cain* v. *Doyle* (72 C.L.R. at p. 425).

CHAPTER 6

FREEDOM OF TRADE, PUBLIC POLICY
AND THE COURTS

IT is not often that an English decision openly reveals the political and social ideals which support the law. American law, in this respect, is very different. The constitution, as the supreme source of law, enforceable by the courts, necessitates a legal interpretation of the political, economic and social principles, such as freedom of person or property, which it formulates in broad terms. But in English law, principles such as freedom of property or trade, form merely the basic theme. There is, in the absence of a specific law, no basis for an action founded on freedom of property, person or trade. These and other principles appear at random in judgments when a judge wishes to give emphasis to a decision; but their chief importance lies not in any specific legal protection for the citizen; it lies in a mental background and in principles of interpretation which they supply to those administering the law. Consequently they remain vague and indistinct. That has the advantage of adaptability and elasticity, but the disadvantage of all inarticulate and vague ideology.

The *Harris Tweed Case*[1] not only demonstrates more clearly than any previous decision the elusiveness of the ideal of freedom of trade, it also shows the evolution which economic individualism has undergone in the last fifty years—the development from an almost pure Benthamism to a position where well organised economic groups struggle with each other, with authority looking on as an umpire who attempts to interfere little and to be impartial.

The *Harris Tweed Case* is a conspiracy case. For the analytical jurist it adds one more to the massive number of decisions which have attempted to grapple with that mysterious tort in great

---

[1] *Crofter Hand Woven Harris Tweed Co., Ltd* v. *Veitch and Another* [1942] A.C. 435.

length but with scant success. The chief stages are marked by the
' trilogy ' consisting of the *Mogul Case*,[2] *Allen* v. *Flood*[3] and
Quinn v. *Leathem*,[4] by *Sorrell* v. *Smith*,[5] *Thorne* v. *Motor Trade
Association*[6] and now the *Harris Tweed Case*. No attempt will be
made, here, to add to the numerous efforts to reconcile these
and lesser cases on analytical grounds. After many hesitations
and discussions, it is now generally accepted [7] that conspiracy,
to be actionable, requires (*a*) joint action by at least two persons,
(*b*) malice, to be understood as action devoid of a reasonable
purpose. Both these propositions are affirmed by the House of
Lords in the *Harris Tweed Case*,[8] and both demonstrate the
complete impasse in which this purely analytical approach has
landed the law. The origin of conspiracy in criminal law may do
as an historical explanation, but the result, as often pointed out,
is that the joint action of two unemployed can be conspiracy,
while the action of a limited company, controlling, perhaps,
the entire steel or oil output of a country and ten thousands of
people in its employment, cannot. As for the test of malice, it is
enough to refer to the brilliant analysis of Evatt J. in *McKernan*
v. *Fraser* [9] which disclosed no fewer than twenty-four definitions
of malice and eventually came to the conclusion that only
' disinterested malevolence '[1] that is pure spite unconnected with
any economic purpose could be actionable malice. It is significant
that, of all the leading English decisions, only *Quinn* v. *Leathem*[2]
was based on malice. The jury found that the defendants had
maliciously conspired to induce the plaintiff's customers or
servants not to deal with the plaintiff or not to continue in his
employment, and a House which was not too friendly towards
collective labour action, awarded damages. The comment of

[2] [1892] A.C. 25.
[3] [1898] A.C. 1.
[4] [1901] A.C. 495.
[5] [1925] A.C. 700.
[6] [1937] A.C. 797.
[7] Cf. Salmond, *Torts*, s. 156; Winfield, *Tort*, s. 13.
[8] Cf. in particular, the judgments of Lord Simon, L.C. and Lord Wright in
the *Harris Tweed Case*.
[9] (1931) 46 C.L.R. 343.
[1] A formula used by Cardozo J. in *Nanay* v. *Raimist* 255 N.Y. 319 (1931).
[2] [1901] A.C. 495.

Lord Wright, in the *Harris Tweed Case*,[3] shows that the decision is difficult to support; in every subsequent case, some economic object was found to exist on the part of the defendants. Indeed, it is difficult to imagine the costly and risky apparatus of collective action being started to satisfy personal spite, in the absence of economic objects, for the purpose of securing some direct or indirect advantage for the group involved. This test, coupled with that of ' joint action ' has served to divorce the law of conspiracy from social reality. This chapter will attempt a brief survey of the matter in terms of the type of social conflict involved, and though conspiracy provides most of the material, it will include certain aspects of the law of contract (restraint of trade) and of the law of associations (discipline over members).[4]

Our central theme will be the principle of freedom of trade. What is its precise meaning in the English law today, and what evolution has it undergone since it was stated in its classical and, on the face of it, still authoritative form? The following appear to be the principal types of social conflict by which the meaning, scope and limitations of freedom of trade can be assessed—

1. Competition between business rivals (single firm *versus* single firm or combine).

2. Conflict between groups of trade interests.

3. Conflict between labour and employers (single or combine).

4. Conflict between rival labour groups.

5. Conflict between rival business groups, with employers and labour within each group collaborating.

The necessary complement to the legal limits of collective action against another party is provided by the extent to which the law protects internal group discipline. There are three main types of cases—

1. Contractual action arising out of cartel agreements (controlling prices or production).

---

[3] [1942] A.C. 435, 472.
[4] The problem of freedom of labour, which was originally regarded as one aspect of freedom of trade has, of course, been profoundly transformed by the development of collective bargaining and must be treated separately. Cf. above, pp. 48–55.

2. Actions by and against trade associations (black lists and fines).

3. Disciplinary actions arising out of reglementation or boycott by trade or professional organisations (trade unions, British Medical Association, etc.).

FREEDOM OF BUSINESS COMPETITION

1. The *Mogul Case* [5] provides not only a striking illustration of unfettered and ruthless competition between business rivals; it is also the best starting point for our analysis, as the classical embodiment of Benthamite economic liberalism in the law. Like a number of other House of Lords decisions from the last decade of the nineteenth century, the *Mogul Case* reflects the outlook of a judiciary brought up in conceptions and under conditions which had already largely lost their validity at the time of the judgment. The defendants, a group of shipping companies, had ousted the plaintiff, a rival trader, by threatening his agents with boycott if they continued to act for him, and by deliberately undercutting the plaintiff, at a temporary loss to themselves. The House found that there was no malice as required for a conspiracy action, but it is the economic creed of the law lords, which gives the clue to the decision. Lord Watson said—

I cannot for a moment suppose that it is the proper function of English courts of law to fix the lowest price at which traders can sell or hire, for the purpose of protecting or extending their business without committing a legal wrong which will subject them to damages. [6]

If this statement rather avoids the question whether the means employed did not overstep the limits of law, it certainly reflects the emphatic distrust of any controlling function of public authority which would interfere with the free play of economic forces. Even more sweeping are Lord Halsbury's categorical words—

' All are free to trade upon what terms they like '. [7]

---

[5] *Mogul Steamship Co.* v. *McGregor Gow & Co.* [1892] A.C. 25.
[6] *Loc. cit.* p. 40.
[7] *Loc. cit.* p. 38.

Only a few years later Dicey, in his *Law and Opinion in England during the Nineteenth Century,* clearly saw the writing on the wall. He brilliantly analysed the dialectic antithesis to which Benthamite individualism coupled with its legislative zeal to ensure individual freedom had led, and foreshadowed state socialism; but such thoughts were far from the minds of the judiciary for a long time to come.

2. A comparison between the decision in the *Mogul Case* and those given by the Court of Appeal in the next year, in *Temperton* v. *Russell,*[8] and by the House of Lords, some years later, in *Quinn* v. *Leathem,*[9] shows how difficult it was for the judiciary to apply the principles of freedom of trade so eloquently and categorically formulated for business competition to similar action taken by organised labour against employers. In *Temperton* v. *Russell,* the defendants, as members of a joint committee of trade unions in Hull, prevented the supply of building materials to a firm of builders who refused to comply with a rule agreed upon by the unions and designed to make the master builders of Hull observe certain rules regarding building operations thought to be for the benefit of the union members. In the words of Lord Esher, M.R., the defendants were not

actuated . . . by spite or malice against the plaintiff personally in the sense that their motive was the desire to injure him, but they desired to injure him in his business in order to force him not to do what he had a perfect right to do.

Nevertheless, the action succeeded, the chief authority being *Lumley* v. *Gye.*[1] Inducing persons not to enter into a contract was held to be on a par with inducement to break a contract.

The effect of this decision, remarkable when contrasted with the *Mogul Case,* was somewhat tempered by the decision of the House of Lords in *Allen* v. *Flood.*[2]

Here a liberally minded House dismissed an action for damages by two shipwrights against the delegate of an ironworkers' trade union, who had told their employer that all ironworkers would be called out by the union, unless he dismissed

[8] [1893] 1 Q.B. 715.
[9] [1901] A.C. 495.
[1] 2 E. & B. 216.
[2] [1901] A.C. 495.

the plaintiffs. This decision, given a few years after the *Mogul Case*, seemed to assimilate the legal position of labour pressure to that of business pressure against rivals. But in *Quinn* v. *Leathem*, a differently composed House took great pains to explain *Allen* v. *Flood*, somewhat artificially, as being concerned with the unauthorised and self-styled action of a single union official, and therefore not being concerned with conspiracy at all. In *Quinn* v. *Leathem*[3] the defendants, as officials of a trade union, wished to compel the plaintiff, a butcher, to dismiss non-union men by threatening his chief customer with the calling out of his employees. The plaintiff, after the first warning, had declared his willingness to let his men join the union and pay their fines and entrance money, but the defendants had refused the offer, apparently in order to show the men that it was unwise to remain outside the union. This was ruthless action, but no more ruthless, and no less directly connected with the attainment of a legitimate economic object than the action of the defendants in the *Mogul Case*. Yet few of the Lords in *Quinn's Case* even referred to the *Mogul Case*, so remote seemed the idea that what was legitimate coercion in the business world was also legitimate in conflicts between labour and employers. The union action in *Quinn* v. *Leathem* was harsh, but there was no evidence of any personal motive in the action against the plaintiff or his employees. There was probably no conscious discrimination, but simply the difficulty in the minds of judges versed in the ways of business and trade to grasp fully the implications of organised Labour action.[4] Theoretically, Lord Lindley's statement is impeccable.

According to our law, competition, with all its drawbacks, not only between individuals, but between associations, and between them and individuals, is permissible, provided nobody's rights are infringed. The law is the same for all persons, whatever their calling; it applies to masters as well as to men; the proviso however is all-important, and it also applies to both, and limits the rights of those who combine to lock out as well as the rights of those who strike. But coercion by threats, open or disguised, not only of bodily harm,

[3] [1901] A.C. 495.
[4] Cf. among others, the pungent comments of Holmes J. in *Vegelahn* v. *Guntner* (1896) 167 Mass. 168, and of Evatt J. in *McKernan* v. *Fraser*, 46 C.L.R. 382.

but of serious annoyance and damage, is, *prima facie*, at all events, a wrong inflicted on the persons concerned; and in considering whether coercion has been applied or not, numbers cannot be disregarded.[5]

But the real crux of the matter lies in the limits of the ' rights ' which must not be infringed. In attempting to distinguish the case before him from the *Glasgow Fleshers' Case*[6]—where a butchers' union was held not liable in damages for threatening salesmen that they would not buy from them, if they continued to sell meat to the plaintiff, with the object of limiting competition—Lord Lindley held that in the latter case no one's rights had been infringed, whilst, in *Quinn's Case*, the coercion of the plaintiff's customers and servants had infringed their liberty as well as his. As Scrutton L.J. pointed out in *Ware and De Frevill* v. *Motor Trade Association*,[7] this distinction is quite unintelligible.

While *Temperton's* and *Quinn's Cases* thus left organised labour in a position much more unfavourable than that of business competitors, the balance was more than redressed by the Trade Unions Act of 1906, which gave trade unions an immunity for actions which would otherwise be actionable conspiracy. The Act of 1927 narrowed the field of application of this immunity by the much more restricted definition of trade disputes, but left it untouched in principle.

Thus, after the removal of the disabilities which, at first, had outlawed collective labour action, the law no longer presented essential obstacles to the important social and economic development, which made individual freedom of trade and individual rivalry more and more a matter of the past, and substituted for it the disciplined organisation and collective action of groups within the State.

Employers' federations and labour unions, production and price cartels, trade associations and professional organisations, all tended to close their ranks against growing pressure from conflicting interests and organisations. Capitalists attempt to

---

[5] [1901] A.C., at p. 539.
[6] *Scottish Co-operative Wholesale Society* v. *Glasgow Fleshers' Trade Defence Association*, (1898), 35 S.L.R. 645.
[7] [1921] 3 K.B. at p. 68.

organise a particular industry by complete regimentation and standardisation of production, prices, marketing, conditions of labour, etc. Trade unions aim at a monopoly of collective bargaining, the fullest expression of which is the ' closed shop ' principle, so hotly contested in the United States. Professional organisations discipline members' conduct and activities, jealous of outsiders and competitors.

Individual freedom of movement is more and more curtailed. Meanwhile the law, reflecting State policy, attempts to remain a neutral umpire, content to check certain excesses, but otherwise leaving the contending groups to fight it out and maintaining all the time uneasily the myth of individual freedom of trade.

3. The Trade Union Act of 1906, is probably responsible for the absence of any House of Lords decisions on conspiracy and other problems of combined action until well after the first World War. For *Conway* v. *Wade* [8] only deals with a side issue, and reflects the desire of the House to counteract the effects of the Act by a restrictive interpretation of the scope of legitimate trade union activity, a tendency continued (by a severe restriction of the scope of legitimate strikes) by the Act of 1927.

Meanwhile, group organisation and action had become more and more predominant, and the next great case after the ' trilogy ', *Sorrell* v. *Smith*, [9] deals with a conflict between two powerful trade groups, a trade union of newspaper retailers on one side, and a committee of newspaper proprietors on the other. The dispute arose from a conflict of economic policy. The retailers wished to prevent competition by new retailers, the proprietors wished to encourage sales by an increase in retailers. Both exerted pressure upon the middle-men, wholesalers; the plaintiff, at the order of his union, by transferring his custom from a wholesaler who also supplied newcomers, to another wholesaler; the defendants, by threatening the latter wholesaler to stop supplies, unless he ceased to deal with the plaintiff. The plaintiff's suit for an injunction to restrain the defendants was unsuccessful, and the decision seems obviously right. Not only from a formal legal point of view, the attitude of judicial neutrality towards

[8] [1909] A.C. 510.
[9] [1925] A.C. 700.

economic groups struggling for enforcement of their economic aims, in a State which has itself no active economic policy, here happened to correspond to a rough balance of strength, between the contending groups, proprietors and retailers. But the case illustrates how far social reality was already removed from the state of affairs idealised by the *Mogul Case*, where every individual had full economic freedom and, so Bentham thought, all would come out well for the community.

4. Such conflicts are not confined to rival business groups or to a struggle between capital and labour. At least two important decisions deal with conflicts between rival labour associations. *Reynolds* v. *Shipping Federation* [1] reveals, in the first place, a struggle between the powerful National Union of Seamen and Firemen, attempting to create a single source of supply of seamen and firemen for British shipping, and a rebel union which wanted to break this monopoly. In the second place it shows, as later the *Harris Tweed Case*, co-operation between employers and labour against outsiders, and it shows that the unity of the working class is often a myth. In this case, the Shipping Federation, comprising nearly all the shipowners of the country, and the National Union, had agreed to recognise the decisions of the National Maritime Board, a kind of successor to the war-time official board established by the Ministry of Shipping. The labour supply was controlled by the issue of a card to members of the National Union, without which it was impossible to obtain employment on any ship belonging to the Federation. It was against this method that the plaintiff, a member of the rebel union, unsuccessfully brought a conspiracy action.

The Australian case of *McKernan* v. *Fraser* [2] also concerned a conflict between rival unions of seamen. The members of the established union refused to sail with those of a rebel union. The case gave the occasion for the masterly judgment of Evatt J. which exposes the fallacy of the malice test when applied to class and group action of the type dealt with in all the judgments hitherto analysed.

[1] [1924] 1 Ch. 28.
[2] (1931) 46 C.L.R. 343.

The two decisions give us a glimpse of the social trends that are gradually taking shape: labour is getting organised—at least in some parts of the world and in some branches of the industry—in such strength that the main trade union movement can aim at not only controlling individual workmen, but at establishing a monopoly of labour supply and conditions. Any new labour organisation must fight not so much against employers who sometimes support or welcome it—as against the existing labour organisation. This development towards guild monopoly is reinforced by the tendency of State authority to reduce labour strife by leaning upon the predominant trade union movement, and a corresponding tendency on the part of employers' federations which, for different reasons, have come to prefer negotiation to strife no less than the officially recognised labour movement. They may want protection from foreign competition, or from an internal rival, or they may live on State orders, as in times of rearmament or war. Where employers and labour co-operate within a particular industry, without official intervention, we get different types of syndicalism; where the State deals with and protects the respective organisations of employers and workmen, we get, after a time of transition, an active social and industrial policy dependent upon the political philosophy of the government.

5. The *Harris Tweed Case* [3] arose shortly before the outbreak of the second World War from a situation which war developments have greatly modified. The conflict was one between the original Harris tweed industry of the Outer Hebrides, which has the yarn spun by hand in the islands and woven there in the crofters' cottages, and some competing island mills, which had their yarn spun on the mainland by cheaper commercial methods, but the cloth woven by island crofters. This latter method also qualified for the trade mark ' Harris Tweed '. By far the greater part of the Harris tweed industry on the island of Lewis was apparently in the hands of millowners, organised in an association and employing members of the Transport and General Workers Union; to the same union belonged all the dockers at the port

[3] [1942] A.C. 435.

where imported yarns were unloaded. The union wanted to protect its members and fight non-union mills, by depriving them of their means of competition; the Millowners' Association wanted to rid itself of the competition of mainland spun yarn. The Transport and General Workers Union and the Millowners' Association thus had parallel interests and co-operated in every way. The action taken was a refusal by the dockers, who, though not in the Harris tweed industry, were members of the same union, to unload any more yarn imported from the mainland and consigned to the plaintiffs, seven small producers. On the part of the trade union, this was part of a wider policy designed to secure a minimum selling price for island cloth and a collective bargaining agreement with the Millowners Association. These latter negotiations did not lead to any result, and there was some difference of opinion among the judges whether the secretary of the association was a party to the alleged conspiracy of the two defendants sued as officials of the union. The result was not affected since the combined action was held not to be an actionable conspiracy. What is certain is that the employers' association and the workers' union co-operated against a number of outsiders who were owner-producers.

The action was, apparently by agreement, not brought against the officials as agents of the trade union, but as individuals, so that the Trade Union Act of 1906 could not apply and the problem was one of common law conspiracy. The lords were unanimous in dismissing the action, and their judgments show how greatly the understanding of modern British judges for collective action in industrial strife has increased. There was no shadow of disagreement on the decisive point: that the action taken by the union was not ' malicious ', but for the protection of legitimate interests. Such legitimate interests are the prevention of undercutting and unregulated competition, or the creation of a better basis for collective bargaining. In the judgment of Lord Simon L.C. it is sufficient that such objects should form the predominant purpose, even if it should be accompanied by feelings of personal satisfaction at teaching the opponent a lesson. Lord Simon felt strongly critical of the use of ' motive ' and ' intention ' in this connection and replaced these by ' object '

or ' purpose '. This shows a significant realisation of the impasse
to which the investigation of subjective feelings and motives has
led in the field of the social struggle between groups and classes.
Lord Wright strongly reinforced this view, which is the only
sensible approach to economic problems, as well as a necessary
brake on jury prejudice. To quote Lord Wright—

> To leave to a jury to decide on the basis of an internal mental
> state, rather than on the facts from which intent is to be inferred,
> may be to leave the issue in the hands of the jury as clay to mould at
> their will. . . . Mere malevolence does not damage anyone. I cannot
> see how the pursuit of a legitimate practical object can be vitiated
> by glee at the adversary's expected discomfiture. Such glee, however
> deplorable, cannot affect the practical result.[4]

The chief interest of Lord Wright's judgment lies in the way
in which it faces some of the economic and social implications of
the dispute instead of being content with the occasional quotation
of such stock phrases as ' freedom of trade '. It deals both with
the limits of such alleged ' freedom ' and with the respective
position of employers' and workmen's interests in an issue like
the present one.

> It cannot be merely that the appellants' right to freedom in conduct-
> ing their trade has been interfered with. That right is not absolute or
> unconditional. It is only a particular aspect of the citizen's right to
> personal freedom, and, like other aspects of that right, is qualified
> by various legal limitations, either by statute or by common law.
> Such limitations are inevitable in organised societies, where the
> rights of individuals may clash. In commercial affairs, each trader's
> rights are qualified by the right of others to compete. Where the rights
> of labour are concerned, the rights of the employer are conditioned
> by the rights of men to give or withhold their services. The right
> of workmen to strike is an essential element in the principle of
> collective bargaining . . . [5]

That one of the paramount problems of law is the
reconciliation of the freedom of one individual with that of every
other in the society, has indeed been the pre-occupation of most
legal philosophers. Starting from widely different premises, Kant,
Spencer, Bentham, Stammler, among others, agree in seeing the
aim of law in the securing of the maximum freedom for every

---

[4] *Loc. cit.* p. 471.
[5] *Loc. cit.* p. 463.

individual which is compatible with an equal measure of freedom for everyone else. The problem of a legal order lies not in the recognition of this elementary truth, but in the way to realise it, in the light of changing social and economic conditions. In regard to personal freedom, the law of every civilised State has long recognised the need to limit the freedom of each individual by criminal law, police supervision and a host of other restrictive measures. But the glittering ideology of freedom of trade, particularly appealing to a legal profession whose social background was the same as that of the commercial and industrial *entrepreneur* who, for the greater part of the nineteenth century, derived benefit from an unrestricted interpretation of freedom of trade, has obscured the inherent contradiction of such an ideal. Many years before the *Mogul Case* Marx pointed out how the economic freedom of capitalist enterprise would lead to its own extermination, by the formation of groups and monopolies which would suppress the small *entrepreneur*. But even to lawyers unversed in Marxist dialectics, the *Mogul Case* might have shown the fallacy of unchecked freedom of trade. In that case, the stronger association could, in the name of that freedom, squeeze the weaker out of business. As pointed out, in the absence of an active economic State policy, the various economic interests within the State resorted to an increasingly rigid corporate policy, in order to counterbalance pressure from other organised interests. But it is obvious that this policy must also lead to a deadlock; either one group proves decidedly stronger and crushes opponents, or various groups, such as employers and workmen's unions, producers and retailers, or competing undertakings within the same industry, keep each other in check, with an effect which is bound to be paralysing at times of economic stress or national emergency. On this aspect of the matter, neither Lord Wright nor any of the other law lords had any comment to make. But Lord Wright did remark on the question of the struggle between capital and labour—

It is true that employers and workmen are often at variance because the special interest of each side conflicts in the material respect, as, for instance, in questions of wages, conditions of hours of work, exclusion of non-union labour, but, apart from these differences in interest, both employers and workmen have a common interest in the prosperity of their industry, though the interest of one side may be in profits and of the other in wages. Hence a wider and truer view is that there is a community of interest.[6]

The *Harris Tweed Case* demonstrates that the theory of the necessary conflict between capital and labour is an over-simplification, or, at any rate, to some extent overtaken by developments not existent in the earlier stages of industrial revolution. The alternative theory of the community of interest between employers and workmen is no less subject to qualifications, unless one accepts unreservedly either the syndicalist theory of enterprise or the Fascist theory of labour. The analysis of the eclipse of freedom of trade must be supplemented by a survey of the internal legal structure of the group entities which have largely replaced the individual in the economic struggle.

THE ENFORCEMENT OF CORPORATE DISCIPLINE IN TRADE MATTERS

The growth of group action in the pursuit of economic interests could be effective only if the group organisation concerned could exercise adequate control over its members and those within its sphere of action.

Enforcement of Cartel Agreements.

A number of actions has arisen out of agreements within a particular trade or industry, by which the parties, in the common interest, agreed to observe a certain price or a production quota, to form a pool or to employ another of the many methods adopted in modern economic life. These actions are purely contractual, and the small number of court decisions reported seems to show a definite movement from the protection of individual economic freedom to the recognition of the legitimate purposes of group control. But it is difficult to follow a clear line, because the decisions, like those on conspiracy, avoid any conscious appreciation of the social and economic issues involved and contain, instead, haphazard and improvised excursions into economic theory.

---

[6] *Loc. cit.* p. 479.

In *Hilton* v. *Eckersley*[7] eighteen millowners agreed to conform with the resolutions of a majority present at any meeting, in regard to wages, working hours, engagement of workmen, and general management. The Court of Exchequer held that ' a contract by which the obligors agree to carry on their trade not freely as they ought to do, but in conformity to the will of others . . . is contrary to public policy '.

In *Joseph Evans* v. *Heathcote*[8] a number of cased tube manufacturers had, by agreement, regulated prices and output. Any manufacturer who exceeded his quota of production, had to pay a certain proportionate amount into a pool, from which those who had not reached their quota were to be compensated. The association was not compelled to buy from the individual manufacturers, but they were under an obligation to sell to the association. The plaintiff claimed his share, in accordance with the agreement, not having reached his quota, and, strangely enough, it was the association which successfully pleaded invalidity of the agreement, on the ground of the plaintiff's restriction of economic freedom. The defence succeeded (though the plaintiff recovered on another ground) because, in the judgment of Scrutton L.J., (1) the plaintiff was bound not to sell except to five named firms, which were under no obligation to buy from him; and (2) the plaintiff had no power to withdraw from the agreement.

A similarly strong attachment to individual freedom of competition and economic initiative was shown by the House of Lords, in the *Irish Dairy Case*.[9] An Irish co-operative society for the manufacture of cheese and butter took all the milk output of its members at current prices. The members were not to sell, without consent, to any other creamery within a certain area. They had no right to withdraw from this obligation except by transfer of their shares. The majority judgments, especially that of Lord Birkenhead, thought that the consent to a transfer of shares, which was necessary, would not be given ' unless in the most exceptional cases ', and a member was thus practically tied

[7] (1855), 6 El. & Bl. 47.
[8] [1918] 1 K.B. 418.
[9] *McEllistrim* v. *Ballymacelligott Co-operative Agricultural and Dairy Soc.* [1919] A.C. 548.

for ever to this restriction of his economic liberty, whereas Lord Parmoor, in his dissenting judgment, said that ' there is positive evidence that whenever a person has applied for a transfer it has been granted . . .'. There was, thus, a conflict of opinion as to the degree to which the economic freedom of members had, in fact, been restricted.[1] But the main difference was on the principle. Lord Finlay expressed the majority view by the following words—

> Public policy requires that every man shall be at liberty to work for himself and shall not be at liberty to deprive himself or the State of his labour or talent, by any contract that he enters into. This is equally applicable to the right to sell his goods.[2]

Lord Parmoor's dissenting judgment struck a very different note. It emphasised two aspects ignored by the majority: (1) that a co-operative society was a voluntary association for the common benefit of all its members who share in the shaping of its policy; and (2) that the obligations and restrictions were not unilateral, but the consideration for the obligation of the plaintiff not to sell milk to other persons or societies was to be found in the society's obligation to purchase all his milk.

> The basic idea is co-operation . . . . No member of the society is subjected to the risk of selling his produce at a price dictated by an outside purchasing body, for the purposes of profit, and I can see no reason for the suggestion that the appellant, and other members of the respondent society, are subjected to unreasonable conditions by an obligation to sell milk at a price to be fixed by a committee of their own choice in the interest of the members of the society, and which it should be assumed, in the absence of evidence to the contrary, will be fairly fixed in the common interest of all parties concerned.[3]

The distinction between contractual and corporate relationship is familiar to Continental, but unfamiliar to English

---

[1] There is nothing in the reported judgments of either the House or of the lower courts [1918] 1 I.R. 313, to contradict Lord Parmoor's statement of the facts. Barton J. only said that ' it would be difficult for a man with ten or twenty cows, and still more difficult for a man with forty or fifty cows to find, within the area of the Society's operations, a transferee . . ., if this rule is a good and binding one '. He went on to point out that company law refused to interfere with the decision of the directors, unless they had acted improperly, which it was for the complainant to prove. It was not disputed that the defendants would not encourage a proposed transfer which would strengthen a rival creamery.

[2] [1919] A.C. at p. 571.

[3] *Loc. cit* at p. 598.

legal thinking. Maitland has brilliantly analysed[4] the way in which contract and trust are made to explain and represent all the relations arising from membership of an unincorporated association. This difference of approach is itself a symbol of the individualistic tradition of English law, and Lord Parmoor had probably a keen appreciation of the shape of things to come when he thought that the discipline enforced by an association upon its members could not be brushed aside by an invocation of an imaginary freedom of economic movement, which economic developments might long have made illusory. There is no doubt that the categories of contract and trust are no longer adequate to explain the legal character of group action, whether by corporate or unincorporated groups. Subsequent decisions which present, of course, an incomplete and somewhat haphazard selection from the different types of economic action show an increasing judicial recognition of the power of the group to enforce the restrictions of economic freedom on the individuals whose economic interests it represents. But before we attempt an analysis of these decisions, and of the trend which they reveal, it should be observed that, even at the time of *Evans'* and *McEllistrim's Cases*, the House of Lords and other high tribunals had repeatedly recognised combined action which restricted the economic freedom of the members for a common purpose. In *Att.-Gen. of Australia* v. *Adelaide S.S. Co.*,[5] agreements between various coal-mine and ship owners designed to cut out competition were held not to infringe the Australian Industries Preservation Act, 1906, since they were not concluded with intent to restrain trade or commerce to the detriment of the ' public ' nor an attempt to monopolise.

Lord Parker, who delivered the judgment of the Judicial Committee, said that, though, speaking generally, it was the interest of every individual member of the community that he should be free to earn his livelihood in any lawful manner, and the interest of the community that every individual should have this freedom, yet, in certain circumstances it was in the interest

---

[4] *Selected Essays*; cf., in particular, ' Trust and Corporation ', and ' Moral Personality and Legal Personality '.
[5] [1913] A.C. 781.

of the individual to contract in restraint of such freedom, and the community, if interested in maintaining freedom of trade, was equally interested in maintaining freedom of contract within reasonable limits. The decision of the House of Lords in the famous *Salt Case*[6] was no less emphatic in stressing the benefits of restrictive agreements to control supply and prices. The plaintiff company was a combination of salt manufacturers established in order to regulate supply and keep up prices. It had practical control of the inland salt market. The members of the combination were entitled to be appointed as distributors. The defendants, themselves not members of the company, undertook to supply to it, for four years, 18,000 tons of salt per annum at a price of 8s. per ton and not to make other salt for sale. They had an option of buying back the whole or part of the supply at the current selling price, which was no less than 18s. per ton, and to act as distributors. This agreement was held to be valid. The most objectionable aspect of the decision is its omission to consider whether an agreement is in accordance with public interest that quite obviously enables a combine to maintain a monopoly over a vital commodity, and to enforce prices the reasonableness of which in regard to the public can be judged by the difference between the purchasing price of 8s. and the selling price of 18s. per ton. Although the law is quite clear that not only the interest of the parties but that of the public is to be considered in testing the validity of an agreement in restraint of trade, the latter is invariably brushed aside with the observation, that only in exceptional cases what is reasonable between the parties is not also reasonable towards the public.[7] This is indeed a remarkable judicial contribution to the social and economic problems of monopoly control of commodities, but we cannot pursue this aspect of the matter any further here. The House certainly had no doubt that the restriction of economic freedom imposed upon the plaintiff was not unreasonable. Lord

[6] *North Western Salt Co.* v. *Electrolytic Alkali Co.* [1914] A.C. 467.
[7] The only decision in the field of restraint of trade, which may be said to rest on the notion of public interest in *Wyatt* v. *Kreglinger* [1933] 1 K. B. 793, where a grant of a pension in return for a restrictive covenant on the part of an employee was invalidated against the wishes of the employee, who was anxious to take up the pension. This decision is a remarkable perversion of the notion of public interest.

Haldane observed that an illregulated supply and unremunerative prices may be a disadvantage to the public. It is difficult to see why similar considerations should not have applied in the *Irish Dairy Case*. This confused and erratic and sometimes prejudiced attitude of law courts towards economic problems goes together with the widespread judicial illusion—expressed by Lord Finlay in *Crown Milling Co.* v. *The King* [8]—that it is not for any tribunal to adjudicate between conflicting ' theories of political economy ', but every decision commented on in this chapter shows how often judges have taken sides in economic issues, though often unconsciously and mostly in the form of improvised and unscientific theories.

A decade after *Evans* v. *Heathcote*, the Court of Appeal had no hesitation in declaring valid an agreement by which the defendant had joined a society formed to organise the marketing of home-grown hops through the society, and the defendant undertook to deliver to the plaintiffs all hops grown on certain land. He attempted to get out of his obligation by leasing his land, with hops almost ready to pick, to a company which he himself controlled. Scrutton L.J. emphasised that courts now viewed with favour restraints of trade imposed between equal contracting parties for the purpose of avoiding undue competition and carrying on trade without excessive fluctuations and uncertainties. [9]

The steady increase of collective action for the protection of certain economic interests has more and more led, from a comparatively loose contractual form, to a tighter structural organisation, mostly in the form of trade and other, usually unincorporated, associations. The principal object of these associations is the maintenance of minimum prices by a rigid control of wholesalers and retailers. Obviously such control can be effectively attempted only where competition between producers has been decisively curtailed or excluded. Price control within any industry is the direct result of a combination which makes substantial control of the market possible. The most rigid and universal price control scheme in Britain is that of the

---

[8] [1927] A.C. 394.
[9] *English Hopgrowers, Ltd.* v. *Dering* [1928] 2 K.B. 174.

tobacco trade, and it is the tobacco industry where manufacture is almost completely monopolised. But effective schemes have been evolved by many other trades, among them the proprietary articles trade, the book trade and the motor trade. Though there is variety in details, the basic principles are the same. An association is formed which comprises sometimes manufacturers only, but often wholesalers and retailers as well. The association, whose main object is usually the fixing of wholesalers' and retailers' prices (manufacturers' prices are not fixed) concludes a number of agreements with the different sections of the trade, by which both wholesalers and retailers undertake not to supply to or buy from price cutters. The principal means of enforcement is the black list system, which has come before the courts on several occasions. The contractual side is revealed, for example, in *Imperial Tobacco, Ltd.* v. *Parslay*,[1] where the plaintiffs had fixed liquidated damages of £15 for every breach of the clause in the agreement with the retailer forbidding undercutting. The legality of the black list scheme was finally recognised by the House of Lords in *Thorne* v. *Motor Trade Association*,[2] which settled the protracted controversy between the Court of Appeal and the Court of Criminal Appeal. Both the placing of a member on the stop list and the alternative of a fine to prevent black-listing were declared legal, provided the action is a reasonable pursuit of legitimate business interests. In that case it is neither criminal blackmail nor civil conspiracy. From the judgments in *Thorne's Case* it can be surmised that only action dictated by personal or vindictive motives, Justice Cardozo's ' disinterested malevolence ' or the demand of an extortionate fine would make the action illegal. Thus a further important step was taken in legitimating collective action for the protection of economic group interests. The law authorised corporate action which eliminated freedom of trade for the individual, and it refused to interfere, except in very rare cases. The attitude was still neutrality, with silent abandonment of the liberal economic ideals of previous generations.

[1] 52 T.L.R. 585.
[2] [1937] A.C. 797.

The autonomy of group organisation and the power of discipline of the corporate institution which represents a particular interest, is further strengthened by the refusal of law courts to interfere with disciplinary measures, save in exceptional circumstances. An interesting illustration is *MacLean* v. *Workers' Union*,[3] where Maugham J. refused to interfere with the expulsion of a member of a trade union as a disciplinary measure unless certain elementary principles were ignored.

There is no legal right of redress if he be expelled according to the rules, however unfair and unjust the rules or action of the expelling tribunal may be, provided that it acts in good faith.

The same principles have been applied to all sorts of professional organisations which have thus been enabled to exercise a guild-like control over the particular field in which they operate. Thus, in *Weinberger* v. *Inglis*[4] the House of Lords refused to examine the merits of the expulsion of a naturalised German member by the Stock Exchange (then unincorporated) during the war. In *Thomson* v. *British Medical Association*[5] the Judicial Committee refused to follow the attempt made by McCardie J. in *Pratt* v. *British Medical Association*,[6] to control and make actionable the boycotting and professional ostracism of a medical practitioner by the organised medical profession, and similar principles apply, of course, to other professions, such as the Inns of Court, the Law Society, and the Accountants' organisations. In *General Medical Council* v. *Spackman*[7] the House of Lords invalidated, however, the disciplinary proceedings of the General Medical Council, where it had refused to hear fresh evidence from a practitioner who had been found guilty of adultery in divorce proceedings. This decision indicates that the courts will exercise a somewhat stricter supervision over tribunals equipped with compulsory statutory jurisdiction than over voluntary associations. Socially, this is a somewhat artificial distinction. Under modern economic and social conditions, the power of a manufacturers' or trade association, of a trade

---

[3] [1929] 1 Ch. 602.
[4] [1919] A.C. 606.
[5] [1924] A.C. 764.
[6] [1919] 1 K.B. 244.
[7] [1943] A.C. 337.

union and of many voluntary professional associations, is such that expulsion may make it impossible for the expelled member to earn a livelihood in his trade or profession. It has recently been pointed out[8] that the whole law on this subject needs reconsideration in the light of modern conditions.[9]

CONCLUSIONS

Two factors, above all, make it difficult to draw full and satisfactory conclusions from the decisions analysed in this article. One is the relative paucity of cases dealing with freedom of trade and cartels which come before the courts, as compared with arbitration or settlement by corporate discipline. The other is the almost universal refusal of the British judiciary to enter into the economic implications of law, even where it is most closely related to economics. Nevertheless, it is possible to trace a fairly clear pattern of development. It may be thus summarised—

1. Attachment to the ideal of individual freedom of trade and economic movement has dominated the British judiciary in the past few generations. It has been shaped mainly against the background of free competition in business and trade.

2. Individual freedom of economic movement, in all spheres, has increasingly been displaced by the self-organisation of the different economic interests. It has led both to a predominance

---

[8] Cf. Lloyd, 'The Disciplinary Powers of Professional Bodies' (1950) 13 M.L.R. 287. Further, on this problem, below, p. 142 ff.

[9] The first report published by the Monopolies and Restrictive Practices Commission in December, 1950, on the supply of dental goods in the United Kingdom well illustrates the economic power exercised by 'non-compulsory' associations. An association covering nine-tenths of both manufacturers and dealers of the dental trade enjoys such powers that, in the words of the report, 'If they break any of the A.D.M.T.'s rules, manufacturer or dealer members can be boycotted by an overwhelming majority of the trade', and 'A manufacturer or dealer cannot leave the A.D.M.T. through disagreement with its rules or method of government without losing most of his business and so risking his livelihood'. Control is exercised mainly through the usual clauses which bind manufacturer and dealer members only to deal with each other, and through the unrestricted power of the council to refuse admission, and to apply drastic sanctions including expulsion, when it considers the conduct of a member 'detrimental to the interests of the association or the trade'. Even the mighty Imperial Chemical Industries were compelled to join the association in order to find a market for a new denture-base material.

of collective action against opposing interests, and to a rigid policy of disciplinary control and, if necessary, ostracising of outsiders or rebels within a particular group by the predominant organisation.

3. The courts have gradually come to recognise as legitimate, within very wide limits, the power of group organisation to replace the individual in the economic struggle. The recognition, at first halting in the case of collective labour action, is now extended to all types of labour, trade and professional organisations, and the checks imposed by the test of reasonableness (in regard to conspiracy, restrictive convenants and blackmail) would operate only in very exceptional cases.

4. The public at large, representing the bulk of consumers and users, in the absence of group organisation, remains no more than a spectator and, often, a victim in the struggle of organised interests. In dealing with restraint of trade, conspiracy and similar problems, the courts have conspicuously failed to develop the notion of ' public interest ' to any real significance. The first major attempt to give expression to the interest of the unorganised public may be found in the statutes nationalising a number of basic industries and creating consumer councils.[1]

5. The courts, in conformity with the general policy of English law, have striven—though not always successfully—to maintain neutrality in the struggle of economic and social interests. In practice, this attitude leads to the attainment of a largely monopolistic control by the most powerful group.

6. While, to this extent, Marxist analysis has been vindicated, by social and legal development, this is not the case in regard to the unity of working-class action. A number of recent cases shows working-class organisations in co-operation with employers' organisations, sometimes against a rival working-class organisation.

In this, as in other fields, the common law is gradually being overshadowed by extra-judicial and statutory developments. The tort of Conspiracy has probably been buried by the decision in the *Harris Tweed Case*. The questions which the common law

[1] Cf. further below, p. 195.

once tried to solve by this tort are now overwhelmingly dealt with by collective agreements, anti-strike legislation, arbitration acts and other new instruments of social policy. Perhaps one problem in this sphere may sometime come before the courts. The ' closed shop ' agreement has never occupied the attention of courts and legislators in England to anything like the same extent as in the United States. The probable reason is that public opinion in England, including the trade unions themselves, still overwhelmingly opposes compulsion to join a union. This was recently confirmed when the Durham County Council attempted to force its employees, including teachers, doctors and other professionals, into union membership as a condition of employment. It was ordered by a Labour Minister of Education to desist. The tendency towards union membership as a condition of employment is, however, growing and strikes against the employment of non-union members are not infrequent. It is possible that sometime a court may have to decide whether an agreement incorporating the closed shop principle is compatible with public policy.

CHAPTER 7

TRUSTS, CORPORATE BODIES AND
THE WELFARE STATE

IN several striking passages Maitland has characterised the social function of the English trust as that of supplying a personalised substitute for the far more comprehensive use of corporate devices in German law.

'But there are two achievements of the trust which in social importance and juristic interest seem to eclipse all the rest. The trust has given us a liberal substitute for a law about personified institutions. The trust has given us a liberal supplement for a necessarily meagre law of corporations. The social importance of these movements will appear by and by. The juristic interest might perhaps escape us if we could not look abroad.'[1]

'. . . Many reformers of our "charities" have deliberately preferred that "charitable trusts" should be confided, not to corporations, but to "natural persons". It is said—and appeal is made to long experience —that men are more conscientious when they are doing acts in their own names than when they are using the name of a corporation.'[2]

'Our *Anstalt*, or our *Genossenschaft*, or whatever it may be, has to live in a wicked world: a world full of thieves and rogues and other bad people. And apart from wickedness, there will be unfounded claims to be resisted: claims made by neighbours, claims made by the State. This sensitive being must have a hard, exterior shell. Now our Trust provides this hard, exterior shell for whatever lies within.'[3]

'But apparently there is a widespread, though not very definite belief, that by placing itself under an incorporating *Gesetz*, however liberal and elastic that *Gesetz* may be, a *Verein* would forfeit some of its liberty, some of its autonomy, and would not be so completely the mistress of its own destiny as it is when it has asked nothing and obtained nothing from the State.'[4]

Maitland's main theme is the contrast between the personalised English concept of trust and the impersonal,

---

[1] Maitland, *Selected Essays*, pp. 135-136.
[2] *Ibid.*, pp. 182-183.
[3] *Ibid.*, p. 188.
[4] *Ibid.*, p. 207.

' collectivised ', German concept of an association (*Verein*), an incorporated public institution (*Anstalt*), or a private charity (*Stiftung*). The trust, he points out, is hardly intelligible to the clear conceptual thinking of Roman or German lawyers, but though being neither a clear ' jus in personam ' nor a clear ' jus in rem ', has served to facilitate all sorts of legal developments without State interference; above all, it has enabled hundreds of important corporate institutions to remain unincorporated because ' the hedge of the trust ' made possible a continuity of legal relationships and a stability of property rights which Continental law cannot provide without a corporate form. In times of religious intolerance the trust has permitted the fulfilment of many worthy purposes without recourse to State protection. On the other hand, the combination of trust and contract relations has enabled institutions, of the immense social and economic significance of the Stock Exchange or the Inns of Court, to remain unincorporated.

Looking at Maitland's thesis, and its implications half a century later, we find, in the first place, that the contrast between Continental and Anglo-American legal devices in the field of unincorporated associations and endowments seems to have narrowed down considerably; in the second place, that unincorporated associations have acquired so many attributes of legal personality that the difference between incorporated and unincorporated bodies, while still important, is no longer fundamental; in the third place, that the reluctance of charities and other institutions to become incorporated has greatly lessened. The advantages of incorporation steadily gain against the snobbism of aloofness, while in the United States and Canada, the heavy taxation demands of the modern welfare State have led to a veritable flood of incorporated charities, genuine and otherwise.

But perhaps the greatest problem suggested by Maitland's thesis is the social and political danger of the assumption that an association, corporate or unincorporated, merely by being in form private rather than public, should still enjoy the far-reaching immunity from judicial or other official control which the courts have accorded it. In this field above all, economic and social developments of the last half century make a re-examination necessary.

DISADVANTAGES OF UNINCORPORATED STATUS

In the first place, it is true that the trust is legally unique. It vests full power in the trustees to deal with property like owners. The rules regarding appointment and replacement of trustees enable property to be held without transfer of title despite fluctuation of membership. On the other hand, the rights of beneficiaries are far more powerful than the rights of parties to a contract. Corporate life can flow behind the hedge of the trust. Moreover, as Maitland points out, the whole moral and legal conception of trust has flowed over from the private into the public sphere. As he foresaw, the trust concept inspired the institution of mandates under the League of Nations and of trusteeship under the United Nations Charter.[5] Under German law, it is not possible to vest club property in a body of trustees in the same easy manner as in English or American law, yet German unincorporated associations—of which there are thousands—have used a similar though more clumsy device by giving the management fiduciary ownership of the property of the association. The only difference with English law is that any change of management makes a transfer of title necessary.[6] Moreover, German courts have increasingly applied by analogy the provisions of the Civil Code dealing with incorporated associations to unincorporated bodies. This is true, for example, of the methods of appointing and dismissing management, of the rights of members and the rules regarding expulsion or other disciplinary measures. The courts have done that in order to reduce the legal clumsiness of unincorporated associations. They cannot, for example, sue as such, although they can be sued; they cannot sign bills or be registered owners of property. If an unincorporated association succeeds to an estate or receives a legacy under a will, this is interpreted as a gift to the members subject to the obligation of donating their shares to the association. Above all, liability for contracts made by the

---

[5] See *Selected Essays*, p. 221.
[6] Cf. Palandt, *Burgerliches Gesetzbuch*, 7th ed., (1949) p. 34.

management on behalf of the association is governed by the rules of agency, nor is there vicarious liability of the association for torts committed by the management on its behalf.[7] As regards contractual obligations, the German, like the English courts, often imply a presumption that the liability of members is, by the membership rules, limited to the extent of their contributions.

In English law, the trust device makes things easier. The membership nexus, while in theory contractual, can, by standard rules, be brought close to the rules governing corporate membership of commercial companies and other incorporated associations. The vesting of property into a management committee as trustees is more elegant than anything that Continental jurisprudence can offer. Yet, in English as in German law, a number of difficulties remain which to some extent account for the increasing tendency towards incorporation. A representative action is possible actively and passively, but it is not easy to achieve in practice.[8] The courts have interpreted narrowly ' the common interest ' which must be proved to enable such action to be brought or defended in a representative capacity on behalf of the members of an unincorporated association.[9] While the standard rules of membership can, as in German law, bring the contractual rules close to those of corporate membership, members can never be liable in tort for the actions of management except where they have authorised the tort. Gifts to an unincorporated association will often fail for uncertainty, and in this respect the English trust rules appear to be stricter than the German rules.[1]

On the other hand, the position of unincorporated associations has in many ways been assimilated to that of corporate bodies. In the *Taff Vale Case*[2] the quasi-corporate ' trade union ' was declared liable for the torts of its servants. Such associations can also sue and be sued in defamation, while a libel directed against the members of an ordinary unincorporated society may in

[7] Cf. ss. 54, 278, 831 of the German Civil Code.
[8] Lloyd (1949) 12 M.L.R. 419-423.
[9] Cf. in particular *Ideal Films* v. *Richards* [1927] 1 K.B. 374; *Barker* v. *Allanson* [1937] 1 K.B. 463; *Walker* v. *Sur* [1914] 2 K.B. 930.
[1] Cf. authorities quoted in Lloyd, *Law of Unincorporated Associations*, pp. 169-170.
[2] [1901] A.C. 426.

certain circumstances give ground for action to its members.[3] In some cases an unincorporated association may be indicted for certain offences.[4]

INCORPORATION OF CHARITIES IN MODERN ENGLISH PRACTICE

There is thus considerable truth in Maitland's dictum that ' it would not . . . be easy to find anything that a corporation could do and that is not being done by this *nicht rechtsfähiger Verein* '.[5] But in an age in which limitation of liability and smoothness of commercial transactions have become increasingly important features of economic life, the disadvantages of lack of incorporation are sufficient to drive more and more institutions into corporate status. As a modern writer has put it, ' the persistence of the unincorporated form of society in the case of most social clubs and of many other non-commercial institutions, notwithstanding the facilities for corporation provided by the Companies Acts, is perhaps to be explained merely as an example of legal conservatism '.[6] But modern English Company Law provides an alternative which is increasingly used for charitable purposes and by other non-profit-making societies wishing to avail themselves of the advantages of the Companies Act. The Companies Act, 1948,[7] provides for companies limited by guarantee, with or without a share capital. The liability of the members is limited and every member undertakes to contribute to the assets of the company in certain contingencies up to a limit of £10. Moreover, companies limited by guarantee and pursuing such objectives as the running of schools for blind people or a non-profit-making magazine, usually avail themselves of the permission to dispense with the word ' limited ' after their name. A licence to do so may be granted where an association is about to be formed for promoting science, religion, charity or any other useful object and the founders are willing to form it on the footing that its profits or income shall be applied in

---

[3] Cf. Lloyd, *op. cit.*, p. 155.
[4] Cf. Road Traffic Act, 1934, s. 26.
[5] *Selected Essays*, p. 194.
[6] Lloyd, *op. cit.*, p. 23.
[7] Ss. 11, 454; Tables C and D. Sched., 1.

promoting its objects only, and that no dividend shall be paid to its members. A leading authority on company law has described the advantages of incorporation for such associations in the following words:

' The association gains in stability, public estimation, and credit. It becomes a body corporate with perpetual succession, just as if it were incorporated by Royal Charter or special Act of Parliament. It can adopt in lieu of " company " a more suitable name, such as chamber, club, college, guild, association. It can have a common seal; it can hold property in its own name without the intervention of trustees; it can contract and take and defend legal proceedings in its own name; its affairs can be conducted much more efficiently, and— finally—its officers and members are freed from personal liability '.[8]

As the same authority points out, at first the applications came almost exclusively from law societies, chambers of commerce and trade protection societies, but the advantages offered by the section are now better appreciated, and associations of all kinds apply.

THE AMERICAN FOUNDATION

Perhaps the most important modern development in this field—and it contrasts dramatically with Maitland's picture of clubs, religious associations and charities preferring the hedge of the trust and the anonymity of unincorporated status—is provided by the ' foundation ' flourishing in contemporary America. It is an indirect result of the modern welfare State, for it is the effect of the heavy taxation on large estates which accounts above all for this significant juristic development.

The foundation is largely an American creation. No doubt the accumulation of vast wealth was one reason for its rise; another—at least in the days when Carnegie, Rockefeller and others perpetuated their names through their now world-famous bequests—was unquestionably a desire of wealthy and successful men to purge their consciences before God and man by leaving a vast proportion of their wealth for the benefit of mankind. But without question, in recent years these original objectives of earlier foundations have receded, and the incorporated foundation or trust has become predominantly a business device,

---

[8] Palmer, *Company Law*, 19th ed. (1949), p. 240.

a paramount instrument in the struggle between the demands of the modern welfare State and the wish of the individual *entrepreneur* to perpetuate his fortune and his name. The desire to give, and to perpetuate the name of the donor, are undoubtedly still important motivations, but the immense increase of foundations in recent years [9] suggests that material advantages play an increasing role. By either bequeathing or giving during lifetime a proportion of his estate to a permanent institution established for officially recognised charitable purposes, the donor, usually the controller of an industrial or business empire,[1] achieves a number of purposes.[2] In the United States, gifts to such organisations are exempt from the gift taxes, and bequests to them are deductible for estate tax purposes. The organisations themselves are normally exempt from income tax, excess profits tax, property tax and other taxes. A charitable gift *inter vivos* is an allowable deduction from the taxable income of the donor. The arithmetics of these benefits vary from year to year and are, of course, subject to legislative changes. Unless, however, there were to be a fundamental change in legislation in regard to charitable gifts,[3] the advantages of transferring both capital and the annual income from a personal estate of a taxpayer in the high income brackets or from the income of a corporation are very considerable.[4] But in the age of the managerial revolution

[9] According to an article in *Fortune* (1947) p. 109, the Treasury Department estimated that there were then in the United States more than 10,000 foundations.

[1] There are, however, also numerous examples of smaller family foundations whose main purpose is to secure an income for dependents from a less highly taxed capital fund.

[2] Cf. the article in *Fortune* quoted above; also an excellent note in (1948) 34 Virg.L.R., pp. 182-201.

[3] Political rivalries have led to such legislation in the Province of Ontario, Canada. (13 Geo. 6, (1949), chap. 10). The owner of a successful Liberal newspaper established a charitable foundation in which he vested the bulk of the shares. The founder members and controllers were the management and editors of the newspaper. Political opposition was largely responsible for an Act providing that, except for religious organisations:
    ' Wherever any interest in any business that is carried on for gain or profit is given to or vested in any person in any capacity for any religious, charitable, educational or public purpose, such person shall dispose of such portion thereof that represents more than a ten per centum interest in such business '.
    Such disposal must be carried out within seven years after the interest was vested, unless the Supreme Court extends the period.

[4] For detailed calculations cf. *Fortune, loc. cit.*, p. 108.

and the welfare State, a motive at least equal to that of providing a suitable mechanism for philanthropy and a tax-free reservoir for an otherwise highly taxable income is the power which the foundation gives to the controller of a business or industry to perpetuate his control.

' It is this peculiar circumstance—*retention of control*—which largely explains the emergence of family foundations as the dominant feature on the foundation scene today. Men who have built successful enterprises and seen the value of their equity swell have sought, naturally, to keep control within the family. They have accordingly established charitable family foundations, minimised their tax, enjoyed the satisfaction of promoting good works, and retained practically all but the dividend benefits of ownership. Such persons, it has been said, actually do not give away their property at all, but only the income thereon—though this is perhaps an overstatement '.[5]

The recently established Ford Foundation, for example, with assets estimated at $625,000,000, will undoubtedly increase substantially the scope of educational and other charitable activities to which foundations have contributed so much in the United States, but it also preserves the bulk of the Ford fortunes in the hands of the family; all its stock is non-voting stock, whereas the small voting stock of the Ford Company remains within the Ford family. The Ford family thus continues to control the Ford Company through holding the voting stock, and it controls the foundation through the terms of the will establishing it.

A detailed analysis of the many methods and purposes for which the modern American foundation is used, would greatly exceed the scope of this chapter. It clearly represents a development strikingly different from the state of affairs which Maitland pictured. As many modern sociologists have pointed out,[6] the modern industrial enterprise has become a corporate empire within the State in which control of management is more important than nominal ownership of shares. Modern government attempts to counter the accumulation of private wealth and power partly by supervisory regulation and partly by heavy

[5] (1948) 34 Virg.L.R., pp. 188-189.
[6] Cf. in particular Berle and Means, *The Modern Corporation and Private Property* (1932); Renner, *Institutions of Private Law* (ed. Kahn-Freund) (1949); and such more general analyses as Arnold, *Folklore of Capitalism*, and Burnham, *The Managerial Revolution*.

taxation. The controllers of enterprises counter—and that is a novel and fascinating feature of this recent development—by divesting themselves of assets and at the same time sanctifying their name through the establishment of charitable institutions. Examples are known of large business concerns vesting their entire real property assets in a charitable foundation controlled by them and renting them back from the foundation.[7] As long as charities retain the legal benefits and advantages which they have traditionally enjoyed—and it would be difficult for any Legislature to take them away[7a]—the modern business corporation gains by diminishing its assets and its income. By this device persons and corporations not only reduce their liabilities without losing control but can also make their name a household word in philanthropy. And the very complexity and size of the enterprises involved makes it necessary to establish these foundations as permanent and, almost invariably, incorporated institutions. They are mostly incorporated as membership or non-profit-making charitable corporations.[8] While they hold no capital stock and may not distribute dividends or profits, and while they must hold their funds in trust for the charitable objects defined in the charter, their organisation is very much like that of the usual business corporation. The charter is the empowering instrument; a board of directors, managers or trustees administers it; and the larger foundations have vast staffs of executive officers, many of them highly paid. Provided its income is destined for charitable purposes, a corporation does not lose its charitable character by conducting a business enterprise.[9] The reasons why English associations increasingly choose the form of the company limited by guarantee have been pointed out earlier.[1] Similarly, the advantages for incorporation for the American type of foundation have been formulated as follows:

---

[7] Cf. the examples given in *Fortune*, *loc. cit.*
[7a] For a discussion of tax reform proposals, cf. Latcham (1950) Penn. L. R. 617–653.
[8] (1948) 34 Virg.L.R., pp. 193–194. Latcham, *loc. cit.*
[9] In a recent case, a testator devised to a foundation established by his will a ceramics manufacture business. The income of the foundation was to go to the promotion of the ceramic arts, but a sum actually exceeding its average income was for five years to be paid to the testator's wife. The foundation was held charitable. (Reported in 34 Virg.L.R. 225).
[1] Cf. p. 137 above.

'The advantages of the corporate form are many. In several States exemption of the property of charitable institutions from taxation is limited to incorporated organisations. Also, corporations may generally be created for perpetual duration, thus eliminating questions as to reversion or the difficulties occasioned by death of an individual trustee. Furthermore, where there are restrictions upon the investment of trust funds, they may be found inapplicable to corporations or subject to removal by charter or bye-laws. The principal advantage, however, is undoubtedly the insulation of the "trustees" from personal liability '.[2]

To revert to Maitland's theme, trust and corporation are no longer alternatives, nor is a committee of trustees any longer the favourite hedge behind which corporate life can flow without formal incorporation. On the contrary, the purposes of the charitable trust are carried out through incorporation, and in the depersonalised manner which distinguishes the modern large-scale corporation from the old-fashioned trustee.[3]

PRIVATE ASSOCIATIONS, PUBLIC POLICY AND JUDICIAL CONTROL

In his essays, Maitland deals only incidentally with the wider problem of the relation between the private association, incorporated or otherwise, and State authority. Although, in other writings[4] Maitland was clearly aware of the inevitable increase of State functions, the implication in these essays is that the social development of associations protected by the hedge of the trust has benefited from not being dependent on the State. There is, of course, much to be said for this view, although the mere device of incorporation and registration, by authority of the law, counts for little as compared with the political philosophy of the government in power, and its attitude towards freedom of association.

---

[2] (1948) 34 Virg.L.R., p. 195.

[3] A similar development can be traced in the increasing prevalence of the Public trustee or trust corporations as the professional executor of wills. Although these institutions act as trustees for remuneration and often constitute large-scale business concerns, they still operate to a large extent under the old rules of trust law designed for the individual trustee acting without remuneration against a background of personal fiduciary relationships. Professor Keeton has recently analysed the social causes and significance of this change in the position of the trustee ((1950) 3 *Current Legal Problems*, pp. 14–29).

[4] Cf. *Constitutional History of England* (1908).

But a problem which Maitland touches only incidentally is now assuming overwhelming importance. It is whether the theoretically private character of an association, incorporated or otherwise, still justifies the far-reaching degree of immunity from judicial or other official control which it has traditionally enjoyed. Commercial companies are, of course, subject to a measure of court supervision mainly from the angle of commercial probity, honesty of accounting and fairness of dealings as between creditors and shareholders, or between different groups of shareholders. But it is the non-commercial associations, pursuing social, political, religious or charitable purposes, whose legal position is now becoming a major social and political problem. Associations of this type include professional organisations such as the British Medical Association or the Law Society. They include churches, labour unions and trade protection societies. Between them these associations have always exercised an immense influence on the body politic, an influence which inspired the pluralistic theory of the State. Recent developments have increased their significance further, and once again it seems as if the law badly lags behind social realities. British courts still stubbornly adhere to the view that the activities of what are often called ' domestic tribunals ' are, with rare exceptions, beyond the control of the courts. A certain amount of supervision is exercised over those bodies which by law exercise a statutory jurisdiction over a profession. By controlling the admission, conduct and expulsion of doctors, lawyers, pharmacists, nurses and others, the relevant bodies enjoy a judicial power directly delegated to them by act of State. Consequently, in such cases a prerogative writ will lie to a court, and as the recent case of *General Medical Council* v. *Spackman* [5] shows, such writ will occasionally be granted. In this case the House of Lords granted *certiorari* against the General Medical Council, which had removed a doctor from the medical register on the ground of adultery committed with a patient. The Council had accepted the evidence of a previous divorce suit without allowing the appellant's request for fresh evidence, purporting to refute the correctness of the conclusions of the Divorce Court. The House of Lords

[5] [1943] A.C. 627.

considered that the Council had violated its obligation ' of due inquiry ' and emphasised the gravity of the responsibilities conferred upon it by the Medical Act. However, even with statutory bodies of this kind, judicial interference is very rare, as the courts are most reluctant to interfere with a strong British tradition of autonomy in matters of professional discipline. A graver problem is presented by such bodies which, like churches, employers' organisations, trade associations or labour unions, exercise a *de facto* compulsory control over vast sections of the population while still enjoying the legal privileges of private organisations. Maitland himself drew attention to the celebrated case which showed the limitations of the trust concept as a controlling device for a living religious organisation. In the *Free Church Case* [6] a majority of the House of Lords held that the minority of the Free Church of Scotland was to retain control of the trust property although a majority had decided to unite with the United Presbyterians. The majority might alter the dogma or practices of the church, but it could not affect the property the use of which was unalterably determined by the trust. In Maitland's classical phrase, ' the dead hand fell with a resounding slap upon the living body '. [7] The effect of the decision was overcome by Act of Parliament, but the wider problem raised by it remains with us. The control of courts over private associations is still limited by two principles : on the one hand such associations enjoy complete autonomy in their internal dealings, including the admission, expulsion of members and other disciplinary measures. This is limited only by the so-called principles of natural justice which, in practice, are reduced to the two modest propositions that a fair hearing must be granted and that nobody must be judge in his own cause. Yet in practice even these modest principles are hardly applied to private associations. In *Weinberger* v. *Inglis* [8] the House of Lords refused to review the action of the Stock Exchange which during the first world war had expelled a naturalised British subject of German birth. The deed of settlement constituting the Stock

[6] [1904] A.C. 515.
[7] *Selected Essays*, p. 237.
[8] [1919] A.C. 606.

Exchange provided that the committee should admit members
' as they think proper '. The House unanimously thought that
there had been no improper exercise of the discretion though
there were some rather timid expressions of view to the effect
that the discretion would have to be exercised ' honestly '. In
MacLean v. *Workers' Union*[9] Maugham J. similarly refused to
scrutinise the resolution of a union which had expelled the
plaintiff. Although the learned Judge mentioned the rules of
natural justice, he specifically stated that even an unfair or an
unjust decision made by a domestic tribunal of this type could not
be reviewed, provided it was given ' honestly and in good faith '.
On the other hand, the ability even to start proceedings is severely
limited by the dead hand of equitable jurisdiction whose basis
is property right. It is consistently held by British courts that no
civil remedies will be available against a ' voluntary association '
unless the rules were either intended to create contractual relationships between the members so as to sustain an action for damages
or a declaratory judgment, or the members enjoyed under the
rules a civil right of a proprietory nature so as to sustain a suit
for an injunction. In the instructive Australian case of *Cameron*
v. *Hogan*[1] the Australian High Court therefore dismissed an
action brought by an expelled member of the Australian Labour
Party against its executive. The court held that even if it were
procedurally possible to construe an action by one member of a
large body of persons for damages for breach of contract against
all the others,[2] a political association of this kind was not normally
meant to create enforceable or contractual proprietory rights.
The contingent interest of a member of a vast organisation in a
share of such funds as there might be in the case of the dissolution
of the organisation was regarded as too vague and remote to
give rise to legal claims. In many other cases courts have consistently stressed the social and club character of associations of
this kind, thus underlining corporate discretion and autonomy

[9] [1929] 1 Ch. 602.
[1] (1934) 51 C.L.R. 358.
[2] The difficulty being that either all members must be joined or a representative action must be brought. In the latter case, the plaintiff could recover
damages only from the common fund which represents him as well as the
other members.

and minimising the scope of enforceable rights of an injured member.

Such an attitude can be attacked on two grounds. It can either be contended that the contractual element in membership relations of this kind should be strengthened, in view of the growing economic consequences which expulsion or other disciplinary action might have. This view has recently been put forward by a learned writer.[3] But a widening of the scope of contract in this sphere would imply an all but complete reversal of judicial practice.[4] The other ground of attack is public policy, and there is at least the glimpse of such an approach in the recent decision of *Russell* v. *Duke of Norfolk*.[5] It is not without irony, that it was the withdrawal of a trainer's licence by the all-powerful English Jockey Club which gave rise to some judicial observations on the power of monopoly, and the possible application of public policy.[6] The action failed on the ground that there had been no actual departure from the rule of natural justice, as the plaintiff had been given a fair hearing. But there was some divergence of judicial opinion on the possible limits of absolute discretion of an association which held a position of power and monopoly. As Denning L.J. put it, ' The Jockey Club has a monopoly in an important field of human activity. It has great powers with corresponding liabilities'. The learned Lord Justice thought that where no mere question of discretionary administration but a penalty for misconduct was involved, the rules of natural justice had to be applied more strictly, and he further suggested that a specific provision permitting the expulsion of members unheard might be contrary to public policy. This is, of course, an *obiter dictum*. It indicates an approach distinctly different from a consistent judicial tradition. Even more important to the general public than the activities of the Jockey Club are those of trade

---

[3]   Lloyd in (1950) 13 M.L.R., pp. 281, 301.

[4]   The only judicial support for this view appears to be a decision by Farwell J. who, in *Donaldson* v. *Institute of Botano-Therapy* (1937) 184 L.T.J.O. 384, granted a declaration of restoration to an expelled member of the Institute partly on the ground that benefits might accrue from the subscription.

[5]   [1949] 1 All E.R. 109.

[6]   In the many cases dealing with Conspiracy, Restraint of Trade, Blackmail and other situations of economic pressure the courts had conspicuously failed to do so. Cf. above, pp. 125–128.

associations or labour unions. [6a] In recent years, English courts have increasingly recognised the legitimacy of collective action by organised economic interests. In *Sorrell* v. *Smith* [7] the House of Lords refused to hold that action and counteraction in a war between the associations of newspaper proprietors and newspaper vendors constituted a tort of conspiracy. In *Thorne* v. *Motor Trade Association* [8] the House of Lords settled a controversy of long standing by holding that blacklisting of a motor trader by the Association for an offence against its rules did not constitute blackmail. In the *Harris Tweed Case* [9] the House of Lords applied the same principle to the action of a labour union against a rival union. A boycott organised by the union did not constitute a conspiracy if the predominant purpose was that of pursuing certain lawful economic objectives rather than personal malice. Taken together, these and other decisions recognise the legitimacy of collective action without considering the wider aspects of public policy. This is one of the most important and unsolved legal problems of our time. The corporate and collective organisation of industry, both on the employers' and the workers' side, has now proceeded to a point where in the more highly industrialised democratic countries it stops little short of *de facto* compulsion. The lone dissenter, or a rebel who criticises the management, will not only be expelled but he will normally be unable to find work in his trade. Where business men must comply with price rules, production quotas and other conditions of business, the workman must comply with the policy of his union. Freedom to organise is rapidly becoming compulsion to organise. This is not the place in which to discuss the various ways in which the legislature has attempted to emphasise the element of public policy. Apart from wartime conditions, when the power of government is vastly greater in the

---

[6a] The Privy Council in *White* v. *Kuzych* [1951] 2 All E.R. 435 avoided the general issue of public policy, raised by O'Halloran J. A. in the British Columbia Court of Appeal where a welder had been expelled by his union for opposing the ' closed shop ' policy. It dismissed the plaintiff's action because he had failed to use his right of appeal to the Shipyard Workers' Federation, as provided in his contract with the Union.

[7] [1925] A.C. 700.

[8] [1937] A.C. 797.

[9] *Crofter Hand Woven Harris Tweed Co.* v. *Veitch* [1942] A.C. 435. Cf. above, pp. 116–122.

name of national emergency, the democratic State is still loath
to interfere with collective bargaining, having come to recognise
it as a predominant and legitimate means of regulating industrial
conditions.[1] As regards the related problem of public control
over corporate action, there will be little general enthusiasm for a
vastly extended use of the supervisory jurisdiction of the courts,
whether by means of injunctions or the prerogative writs which at
present are not applicable to private associations. There are too
many examples of the abuse of the prerogative jurisdiction. For
many years the English courts, following the decision of the Court
of Appeal in *Rex* v. *Electricity Commissioners*[2] extended the
notion of ' quasi-judicial ' administrative action beyond all
reason. And there is much evidence of similar attitudes taken
by American courts.[3] In recent years English courts have
exercised far greater restraint. Both the House of Lords and the
Court of Appeal have repeatedly stressed that government is a
function of the Executive supervised by Parliament, and that it
would be improper for the courts to enforce their views on the
desirable extent of administrative powers by unduly widening
the notion of quasi-judicial or by stretching the concepts of
natural justice.[4] The opposite danger exists in relation to private
associations whose all but complete immunity from judicial
control is out of step with their present economic and social
significance. Perhaps the best solution is that attempted by some
recent English legislation. Under the Solicitors' Act, 1932, an
appeal lies to the King's Bench Division, and further to the
Court of Appeal, where a solicitor has been struck off the roll
for professional misconduct. Under the Legal Aid and Advice
Act, 1949, any solicitor or barrister who has been removed from
the panels of those willing to act for assisted litigants has a right
of appeal to the High Court. Under the Medical Act, 1950,

---

[1] Among the common law countries Australia and New Zealand probably
go furthest in giving an arbitration court power to lay down the basic
conditions of working hours and wages with compulsory effect.

[2] [1924] 1 K.B. 171. For a general survey of the use of the remedy in English
law, see Wade & Phillips, *Constitutional Law*, 4th ed., (1950) pp. 247-304;
Friedmann, *Principles of Australian Administrative Law* (1950) pp. 80–85.

[3] Cf. Davis in 44 Ill.L.R., pp. 613 ff.

[4] Cf. *Franklin* v. *Minister of Town and Country Planning* [1948] A.C. 87;
Johnson v. *Minister of Health* [1947] 2 All E.R. 395.

an appeal from the Medical Disciplinary Committee lies to the Privy Council.

The development of the corporate power of economic and industrial associations is a social fact which cannot be easily controlled by legal rules, but a careful combination of statutory appeals in the case of professional bodies exercising disciplinary jurisdiction, with a judicious application of public policy in cases where private associations have abused their monopoly power and interfered with fundamental principles of personal freedom, would impose some check on social situations which bear less and less resemblance to the picture as Maitland painted it.

Maitland's world, as it emerges from his essays, is that of private donors using their accumulated wealth for the pursuit of philanthropic or other social purposes, in an age when a liberal government did little to interfere with the private accumulation of wealth as well as its disposal. The corporate counterpart is the club, the informal association of gentlemen who pursue their social, professional or economic objectives as loosely organised as possible, held together by common traditions, and their position in society, to which the law of trust is admirably adapted. But our world is that of giant industrial concerns, battling for economic power with governments which, in the name of social justice or defence, make increasingly heavy demands. It is also a world in which the values of the Victorian era, dominated by middle class power and ideology, has given way to a restless and toughly organised society. It is no longer the club which matters most—not even the Jockey Club—but the closely organised employers' or manufacturers' association and the labour union. And between these powerful and intolerant groups stand millions of unorganised citizens, whose interests modern government cannot ignore. Such social transformations demand new legal solutions; they demand among others a re-assessment of the extent of public control over corporate organisations, and of the scope of public policy.

PART TWO

THE PLACE OF PUBLIC LAW IN CONTEMPORARY ENGLISH JURISPRUDENCE

PUBLIC LAW PROBLEMS IN RECENT ENGLISH DECISIONS

THE PLACE OF PUBLIC LAW IN THE ENGLISH LEGAL SYSTEM

IT is no longer necessary to argue whether public law has a place in the English legal system. Public law confronts us with increasing frequency and urgency. But what is still obscure is the precise scope and function of public law, and its relation to the common law tradition. Dicey's famous heresy has probably retarded an appreciation of the problem. Under his influence, the systematic and theoretical study of public law was neglected until the flood of new social services, ministerial powers, administrative tribunals, and public corporations injected public law problems into English law far in advance of its theoretical study. It is apparent that all these new institutions and relations cannot simply be treated within the legal categories and relations of private law, that they demand a new analysis of the different types of legal relations between public authority and the citizen. But how far these developments take place inside or outside the common law, is still rather obscure.

PUBLIC LAW IN CONTINENTAL JURISPRUDENCE

A brief glance at the place of public law in Continental jurisprudence might help to get the problem clear. Dicey rejected public law because he alleged it to be incompatible with the rule of equality of all, governors and governed alike, before the law. In Continental legal systems, the dichotomy of private and public law is well established, but not uncontested. Duguit, rejected the distinction on grounds somewhat reminiscent of Dicey's thesis. He thought that it contradicted the principle of social solidarity, which was the basic fact of society, and should compel obedience from governors and governed alike. Kelsen, on the other hand, rejects the dichotomy because it interferes with

153

the hierarchical structure of pure legal norms. As all norms are deduced from an ultimate *Grundnorm*, a division between public and private law is arbitrary. All norms derive their authority from the supreme norm, public authorities making decrees and regulations, as much as individuals making contracts. The division of law into public and private law is, to Kelsen, not only scientifically wrong, but also politically objectionable. He regards it as an attempt for absolutist and autocratic tendencies to legitimise the arbitrariness of autocratic State power. This analysis is more fully developed by Marxist jurists, in particular by Renner,[1] who regards the institutes of private law in capitalist society as a means by which the owners of capital exercise a delegated power of command. In effect, the private law of capitalist society enables the owners of factories, banks, and other economic institutions, to wield authority under the guise of formal legal equality.[2]

Early Soviet jurisprudence took up this challenge, and one of its best known spokesmen, Pashukanis, developed Renner's thesis by saying that all real law was private law.[3] Private law enabled those in control of the means of production to exercise power over the others. Public law therefore was only an unsuccessful attempt of capitalist legal science to transfer the notions of law to a sphere where it had no place. As, in a socialist community, there was no scope for autonomous private legal relations, but only for regulation in the interest of the community, all law was converted into administration; all fixed rules into discretion and utility. Pashukanis's theory has long been regarded as utterly heretical by Soviet jurisprudence, which now accepts the division of public and private law, although there is much controversy as to the borderlines between the two.[4]

In Soviet law the emphasis has, of course, decisively shifted, from economic relations between private individuals or corporations to relations between State enterprises. Most of the private law sphere has been absorbed by the socialisation of industry and farming, and this has imported certain private law

[1] *The Institutions of Private Law* (Eng. ed., Kahn-Freund 1949).
[2] For a full analysis, see above, p. 9 *et seq.*
[3] *Allgemeine Rechts-und Staatslehre*, (German ed., 1927).
[4] Cf. Schlesinger, *Soviet Legal Theory*, pp. 252 *et seq.*

notions into the public law sphere. As the history of both the Nazi and the Soviet regimes shows, the differences between public and private law are more formal than real in a totalitarian society. As the entire life of the community is directed by the government, as the law courts are expected and commanded to interpret law in accordance with the philosophy of the government, as the doctrine of separation of powers is rejected and political justice absorbs a vast part of both criminal and civil law, the distinction between public and private law is not really important. It is maintained for reasons of convenience and respectability. But it is not surprising that the criticisms of Duguit or Kelsen have had little if any influence on the systems against which they were directed. Democratic societies need the dichotomy of public and private law. They have a rapidly increasing number of public bodies, law-making authorities, and social services, of all kinds, which cannot be treated on a par with contract or property relations between private parties yet must be brought within ascertainable legal rules. Public law as first developed in France during the nineteenth century, means an attempt to restrict the unfettered discretion of public authorities by legal rules enforceable before courts, which recognise the needs and characteristics of administration, but impose certain clearly defined limits upon administrative discretion.

Here, as in so many other fields, the much-vaunted differences between Continental and Anglo-American legal thinking are less important than the legal problems posed, in both systems, by different types of society. In a Communist or Fascist Britain, Germany, France, or Russia, the distinction between public and private law becomes relatively unimportant. But a democratic France and a democratic Britain are confronted with basically similar problems of how to blend the expanding administrative tasks of the social welfare State with the protection of individual rights and the legal prevention of abuse of power. This does not mean that the technical ways in which the different democratic legal systems attempt to solve this problem are identical. Rather too much attention has been paid in recent years to the problem of administrative tribunals. English jurists have found that the multitude of *ad hoc* administrative tribunals set up during the last few decades prevents a systematic development of public law, and facilitates the abuse of public power. There has been much argument on the way in which a kind of administrative justice could be developed within the English legal system.

But the main advantage of a comprehensive administrative jurisdiction in Continental legal systems has been the stimulus which this has given to constant thinking on public law problems, and in particular on the borderline between public and private law. The first problem which every administrative tribunal faces, is that of jurisdiction. Whether a particular dispute is to be decided by a civil or an administrative court, depends mainly though not entirely on the allocation of the subject-matter to public law or private law. This has meant, for example, the juridical development of the dual capacity of the State as sovereign and fiscus, as a subject of public and private law relations. It has also compelled the analysis of legal transactions for the purpose of allocating them to the one or the other sphere. As has been shown above,[5] the solutions are far from being unanimous or definite. But the problem can be dealt with more clearly and systematically than in English law.

In English law it would be inadequate to look for the main problems of public law in the largely unpublished decisions of administrative tribunals, or even in the prerogative jurisdiction exercised by the King's Bench Division, through the orders of mandamus, certiorari, and prohibition. Many of the most important public law problems appear in ordinary common law actions: in actions for damages against a local authority; for nuisance against a public hospital; for a declaratory judgment against a public corporation; for breach of contract against a government department; in such defences as immunity from statutes pleaded by Crown departments or public corporations. The more fundamental public law problems appear more often in a King's Bench or Chancery judgment than in the award of a compensation or pensions tribunal, but they are so scattered, and often so disguised, that their true significance in the changing pattern of British society has hardly been seen.

---

[5] Pp., 60–62; see also below, p. 178.

SURVEY OF PUBLIC LAW PROBLEMS IN RECENT ENGLISH DECISIONS

It is difficult to systematise the public law problems which have occupied both legislature and courts in recent years. It may be convenient to consider them according to three broad though closely interconnected problems:

(1) The conflict of public interest and private rights.
(2) The borderlines between administrative discretion and legal duties.
(3) The problems of sovereignty and equality in the legal relations between the State and other public authorities on the one side, and the individual citizen on the other.

These problems are interconnected, because the prevalence of public interest as against private rights usually goes hand in hand with the scope of administrative discretion, and the allocation of a particular State activity to its sovereign rather than to its non-sovereign sphere. Yet emphasis on the one or the other of these three aspects will help to clarify the problems.

THE CONFLICT OF PUBLIC INTEREST AND PRIVATE RIGHTS

The adjustment between public interest and private rights can be most clearly followed in the judicial interpretation of statutes.

There are no constitutional guarantees of personal liberty in British law. Its main protection lies in the strength of public opinion, and in the determination of an independent judiciary to protect the basic liberties, unless they are directly and clearly restricted by legislation. Yet the courts are sometimes prepared to sacrifice the protection of personal liberty for *raison d'etat*. They will do this only in times of war or exceptional political emergency. The decision of the House of Lords in *Liversidge* v. *Anderson*[6] showed the House of Lords, during the last war, clearly prepared to depart from ordinary canons of statutory construction, in order to give precedence to the national interest. Regulation 18B, Defence Regulations, 1939, gave the Home Secretary certain powers of detention where he ' has reasonable cause

[6] [1942] A.C. 206

to believe any person of hostile origin or associations . . . '.   In
an action for false imprisonment against the Home Secretary,
the majority of the House decided that it could make no order for
particulars to compel the Secretary of State to prove the facts
justifying the order for detention. The majority based their
judgments mainly on general policy considerations. They held
that a regulation of this kind had to be interpreted with a view
to the emergency of which it was a consequence; that compulsion
to disclose facts before the court would gravely interfere with
public policy and national safety, and that these considerations
prevailed over the grammatical formulation and normal rules
of interpretation.   Lord Atkin, in his dissenting judgment, had
little difficulty in showing that ' has reasonable cause to believe '
is different from ' thinks that he has reasonable cause to believe '.
He produced overwhelming evidence from other statutes and
regulations, illustrating the difference between objective and
subjective formulation. In the absence of any specific direction
to the contrary, Lord Atkin held that the question whether the
Home Secretary has reasonable cause was clearly the subject
of judicial evidence and decisions. Logically, it is submitted,
Lord Atkin's argument is unassailable. The difference between
him and the majority was not a matter of logic but of policy.
The majority were prepared to ignore ordinary rules of
interpretation, because they regarded the public interest of
national safety in times of war as superior to the normal
safeguards for the liberty of an individual.

Similar considerations moved the House of Lords in the
Thetis Case[7] to confirm the privilege of the Crown in regard to
discovery of documents, in an action by next of kin of the
victims of a submarine disaster, against the shipbuilders. The
House urged that the Crown ought to claim privilege only where
national security required it. This rule was later confirmed in
the Crown Proceedings Act, 1947.

The paramountcy of State interests in matters concerning the
defence of the realm has a long history, and the courts are less
reluctant to sacrifice the interests of the individual to those of
the State in such situations. Present day social and international

Duncan v. *Cammell Laird and Co.* [1942] A.C. 64.

developments may make the distinctions between war and peace, between emergency situations and normal situations, more and more precarious. The recent Australian Act outlawing the Communist party and affiliated organisations, and subjecting persons declared to be Communists to serious disabilities, was based on the defence power of the Commonwealth.[7a] The very term ' cold war ' indicates the twilight atmosphere between war and peace, which will make it more difficult for the judiciary to have one approach in times of war, and another in times of peace. But it is still broadly correct to say that English law courts will interpret State powers restricting individual rights far more strictly in times of peace than in times of war. In *Nakkuda Ali* v. *M.F.De S. Jayaratne*,[8] the Privy Council was concerned with a motion for a certiorari, to quash an order to the Ceylon Controller of Textiles, who had withdrawn a dealer's textile licence. The relevant regulation provided that ' Where the controller has reasonable grounds to believe that any dealer is unfit to be allowed to continue as a dealer, the controller may cancel the textile licence or textile licences issued to that dealer '.[9] Except in the substitution of the word ' ground ' for ' cause ', this was identical with Defence Regulation 18B. The Privy Council expressed its disagreement with *Liversidge* v. *Anderson* in unmistakable terms:

It would be a very unfortunate thing if the decision of *Liversidge's Case* (*supra*) came to be regarded as laying down any general rule as to the construction of such phrases when they appear in statutory enactments. It is an authority for the proposition that the words ' if A.B. has reasonable cause to believe ' are capable of meaning ' If A.B. honestly thinks that he has reasonable cause to believe ' and that in the context and surrounding circumstances of Defence Regulation 18B they did in fact mean just that. But the elaborate consideration which the majority of the House gave to the context and circumstances before adopting that construction itself shows that there is no general principle that such words are to be so understood; and the dissenting speech of Lord Atkin at least serves as a reminder of the many occasions when they have been treated as meaning ' if there is in fact reasonable cause for A.B. so to believe '.

[7a] The Act was declared unconstitutional by the High Court of Australia, in March, 1951.
[8] (1950) 66 T.L.R. 214.
[9] (1950) 66 T.L.R., p. 216.

After all, words such as these are commonly found when a legislature or law-making authority confers powers on a Minister or official. However read, they must be intended to serve in some sense as a condition limiting the exercise of an otherwise arbitrary power. But if the question whether the condition has been satisfied is to be conclusively decided by the man who wields the power the value of the intended restraint is in effect nothing. No doubt he must not exercise the power in bad faith: but the field in which this kind of question arises is such that the reservation for the case of bad faith is hardly more than a formality. Their Lordships therefore treat the words in regulation 62 ' where the controller has reasonable grounds to believe that any dealer is unfit to be allowed to continue as a dealer ' as imposing a condition that there must in fact exist such reasonable grounds, known to the controller, before he can validly exercise the power of cancellation.[1]

Most of the decisions concerned with the adjustment of public interest and private rights have arisen from the extension of social services and public duties, and their corresponding limitation of private rights.

Housing legislation provides an illustration of this conflict of interests. Such legislation has deliberately sought to restrict freedom of property and, to some extent, of contract, in order to achieve certain minimum standards of social welfare.

The Housing Act, 1925, in a clause later re-enacted in the Housing Act, 1936, imposed on the lessor of houses below a certain rateable value a statutory obligation to keep the house ' in all respects reasonably fit for human habitation '. An identical situation was treated first by the Court of Appeals in 1927,[2] and fifteen years later by the House of Lords.[3] The defective sashcord in a working class house had caused the window to fall and crush the plaintiff's hand while she was cleaning the window. The Court of Appeal in the earlier decision adopted the approach of Salter J. in a case decided some years earlier that ' the standard of repair required by those Acts is naturally . . . a humble standard '.[4] The Court of Appeal by a majority held that the breaking of the sashcord did not prevent the house from being in all respects reasonably fit for human

---

[1] (1950) 66 T.L.R., p. 219.
[2] *Morgan* v. *Liverpool Corp.* [1927] 2 K.B. 131.
[3] *Summers* v. *Salford Corp.* [1943] A.C. 283.
[4] *Jones* v. *Green* [1925] 1 K.B. 659, 668.

habitation, and Lawrence L.J. went so far as to describe a different attitude as ' somewhat fantastic '.[5]

It was indicative of the same ' private rights ' approach to a public law statute that the court regarded the statutory warranty as contractual, so that damages could not be recovered unless notice as required by common law was given by the tenant to the land-owner (although the Housing Act did not stipulate any notice and the defect might be hidden). The decision of the House of Lords—given in the middle of the last war when the people of Britain had transferred to the government almost unlimited powers over their persons and properties, and when the hope for a better social order inspired the vast majority of Britons to suffer danger and privation—struck a note very different from that of the Court of Appeal fifteen years earlier. The House rejected both the contractual approach and the somewhat cynical interpretation of what sort of house is fit for the underdog to live in; as Lord Wright put it:

> The provision was to reduce the evils of bad housing accommodation and to protect working people by a compulsory provision, out of which they cannot contract, from accepting improper conditions. Its scheme is analogous to that of the Factory Acts. It is a measure aimed at social amelioration, no doubt in a small and limited way. It must be construed so as to give proper effect to that object. . . . ' In all respects ' must mean in all respects material to the enjoyment of the tenement, and the unfitness of one room may be a most material detraction from that enjoyment. ' Human habitation ' is in contrast with habitation by pigs, horses or other animals, or with use as warehouses, and the like, but I think it also imports some reference to what we call humanity or humaneness.[6]

In other words, the statutory obligation is to be interpreted in the spirit of the statute which contains it, as a deliberate measure of restraint on the use of property and the freedom of contract; it is not to be thwarted by conceptions of freedom of contract and property which the statute deliberately sets out to restrain.

A similar problem is shown in another pair of recent decisions. The Paddington Borough Council, following some individual

---

[5] [1927] 2 K.B. at p. 152.
[6] [1943] A.C. at 293.

complaints by tenants, had applied to the rent tribunal set up under the Furnished Houses (Rent Control) Act, 1946, for the review of rents for an entire block of 555 flats. The tribunal made orders reducing the rents of eight of these flats. The landlords then moved for an order of certiorari, which was granted. Lord Goddard C.J., delivering the judgment of the court,[7] considered that such block reference to the tribunal was not a bona fide exercise of the powers conferred by Parliament on the local authority. The tribunal was there to deal with individual cases. There was no doubt that under the statute the local authority had power to refer the tenancy contracts to the tribunal, nor had any other section of the Act been infringed. The court, therefore, had to fall back on the mala fides test by giving its own interpretation of the objects of this Act. Its underlying attitude was the minimisation of statutory interference with freedom of contract. It is once again a matter of balancing conflicting policies and interests. As the Act was expressed, it was no less legitimate to consider the rent tribunal as an institution generally supervising the fairness of rents, on application by one of the interested parties, than it was to make its jurisdiction dependent on a specific complaint by a specific party to the local authority which referred the case to it. The decision depends on the respective value attributed to the right of the landlord to use his property on his own terms, and the rights of the State to ensure some fairness between the parties, at a time of a general housing shortage.

The public interest prevailed in a recent decision of the Court of Appeal.[8] Under a now superseded Town and Country Planning Act, the owners of certain land had been given permission for interim development, subject to certain conditions laid down in two agreements between themselves and the local authority. Under these agreements, the parties apportioned the responsibilities and cost of development of the estate and the plaintiffs undertook to dedicate certain land to public use (which they did). The war halted further development. After the war, the so-called Greater London Plan had included the area in

[7] *R.* v. *Paddington and St. Marylebone Rent Tribunal* [1949] 1 K.B. 666.
[8] *Ransom & Luck Ltd.* v. *Surbiton Borough Council* [1949] 1 Ch. 180.

question among those which were not to be developed. Consequently, the Minister, exercising powers conferred by a new Act, withheld permission for further development, although the plaintiffs had already laid out some money in the construction of sewers. They claimed that the defendants had assumed a contractual obligation by which they had bound themselves not to exercise any existing or future statutory powers in such a way as to restrict the development of the land in accordance with the agreement. Lord Greene, with whom the other two judges agreed, pointed out that the planning authority could not bargain away its statutory powers of planning conferred on it by an Act in the public interest.

Is it likely that Parliament, . . . without express words to that effect would do anything so unusual, so explosive, as to enable a planning authority to do that which all the principles laid down and observed by the courts and the legislature in regard to statutory duties of this kind forbid, namely, to tie its hands and contract itself out of them ? [9]

He went on to point out that the agreements into which the authority had entered were not contractual, but mainly a manner, permitted by the act, of carrying out certain statutory duties, and they were subject to the overriding purpose of the statute as a whole.

ADMINISTRATIVE DISCRETION AND LEGAL DUTIES

How to limit administrative discretion so as to maintain a reasonable balance between the needs of administration and the legal security of the individual, may well be described as the cardinal problem of administrative law. The absolute State knows no such limitations, except by the grace and concession of the sovereign. The completely liberal State, on the other hand—reflected in Dicey's theory of the rule of law—regards the rules of private law as paramount and binding upon governors and governed alike. But the philosophy and practice of modern democracies, concerned with the balance between the social welfare and individual freedom, must attempt to solve the problem of administrative discretion. It is at the very heart of

[9] [1949] 1 Ch. at p. 195.

the Continental doctrine of administrative law. Slowly, the Continental administrative courts have developed principles by which the State and other public authorities are made accountable for the excess and abuse of administrative powers.

In English law, the problem is no less important. But owing to the lack of canalisation of public law problems in a hierarchy of administrative tribunals, it appears in the most diverse places: sometimes in King's Bench decisions granting or refusing a prerogative order, and sometimes in actions for damages or injunctions against public authorities.

One aspect of the problem is illustrated by the decisions which have laid down the limits of judicial supervision over the exercise of discretion by a local authority. English courts have given themselves the power to invalidate the by-laws of local authorities and other statutory bodies not only for excess of powers in the strict sense but also for abuse of power, that is, for an exercise of their powers which is ' manifestly unjust, shows bad faith, is oppressive, or a gratuitous interference with the rights of those subject to them, as could find no justification in the minds of reasonable men '.[1] In the highly controversial decision of *Roberts* v. *Hopwood*,[2] the House of Lords, at a time when the English courts often took an unsympathetic attitude towards new social legislation, interpolated the word ' reasonable ' in a statute which had given local authorities power to fix wages for their employees ' as they think fit '. The House confirmed the surcharge of the district auditor against the members of a London borough council which had fixed a uniform minimum wage of £4 a week for all its male and female employees. It rejected the very conception of a basic minimum wage for all employees as not being a reward for labour.[3] It also considered the amount fixed as grossly extravagant, an outburst which in its betrayal of political prejudice is very exceptional in English courts. Lord Atkinson said that the council ' allowed themselves to be guided in preference by some eccentric principles of socialist philanthropy, or by a feminist

[1] *Kruse* v. *Johnson* [1898] 2 Q.B. 91.
[2] [1925] A.C. 578.
[3] The House was apparently unaware that at that time, as now, the basic wage had already become the cornerstone of Australian industrial law.

ambition to secure the equality of the sexes in the matter of wages in the world of labour '.[4] The question is not, of course, whether the borough council were wise or cautious in fixing the wage as they did. It is whether the House of Lords, by reading the words ' as they think fit ' as ' as they think reasonably fit ', and regarding themselves as the arbiters of reasonableness, did not transgress from the judicial into the policy sphere.

By contrast, in 1944, the Court of Appeal unanimously refused to uphold the district auditor's surcharge against the councillors of the Birmingham Corporation, which had decided to pay a fixed weekly war bonus, with the addition of a children's allowance in the case of married men, widowers or widows.[5] The court was obviously right in holding that this was a perfectly reasonable decision, in accordance with public policy and the practice of good employers, but it had some difficulty in overcoming the obstacle of *Roberts* v. *Hopwood*. There were, of course, differences between the two cases which the court pointed out. Yet the later decision shows clearly a different approach to the problem of judicial interference in administrative policy. The Court of Appeal, unlike the House of Lords in the earlier case, was unwilling to set itself up as judge of how— short of abuse or bad faith—a local authority, responsible to its ratepayers on the one hand and to the Minister of Health on the other hand, ought to exercise its statutory powers.

Differences of judicial outlook on the scope of public powers are again illustrated by some very recent cases. In *Middlesex County Council* v. *Miller*,[6] a licensing authority, under the Nurses Act, 1943, had power to grant a license to a person desiring to carry on an agency for nurses, subject

to such conditions as they may think fit for securing the proper conduct of the agency, including conditions as to the fees to be charged by the person carrying on the agency, whether to the nurses or other persons supplied, or to the persons to whom they are supplied.

In the exercise of this power, the county council imposed on the granting of a licence the condition that the licensee was not to

---

[4] [1925] A.C. at 594.
[5] *Re Decision of Walker* [1944] 1 K.B. 644.
[6] [1948] 1 K.B. 438.

demand in respect of the services supplied any sum in excess of the amount appropriate to the service ' calculated in accordance with a scale of charges approved by the council and furnished to the licensee '. In short, the council had coupled the fees which the agency might claim with a maximum scale of charges for the nurses, presumably in order to prevent the shortage of nurses resulting in extravagant offers from those able to make them. The court held that this condition had nothing to do with the proper conduct of the agency, but meant an indirect limitation of the fees or wages for which nurses were willing to work. But it is difficult to see why this should not have been an aspect of the ' proper conduct of the agency ', within the terms of the statute. The supporting judgment of Singleton J. said that the condition imposed here was not in any sense ' necessary ' for securing the proper conduct of the agency. The Act, however, does not use the word ' necessary ', but the phrase ' such conditions as they may think fit '. The approach of the court here resembles that of the House of Lords in *Roberts* v. *Hopwood*, and it contrasts with the decision of the Court of Appeal in the recent case of *Associated Provincial Picture Houses, Ltd.* v. *Wednesbury Corporation.*[7] The licencing authority here, in granting licences for cinemas to be opened on Sundays, had power to impose ' such conditions as the authority thinks fit to impose '. The defendant authority in this case had allowed Sunday cinema performances in its area, provided that children under the age of fifteen were excluded. Lord Greene, with whom the rest of the court agreed, once again emphasised that it is not the function of a court to impose its own views of public policy on those of the local authority:

> Some courts might think that no children ought to be admitted on Sundays at all, some courts might think the reverse, and all over the country I have no doubt on a thing of that sort honest and sincere people hold different views. The effect of the legislation is not to set up the court as an arbiter of the correctness of one view over another. It is the local authority that are set in that position, and, provided they act, as they have acted, within the four corners of their jurisdiction, the court, in my opinion, cannot interfere.[8]

[7] [1948] 1 K.B. 223.
[8] [1948] 1 K.B. at p. 230.

These conflicting approaches to the problem of how far the law courts should go in controlling administrative authorities which are constitutionally responsible to higher administrative or political authorities, are closely parallel to the uncertainties surrounding the notion of ' quasi-judicial ', which is the key to the scope of prerogative jurisdiction affecting ministerial authorities. [9] In a somewhat different setting, the same problem arose recently in the important decision of the Court of Appeal in *Blackpool Corporation* v. *Locker*. [1] The problem here was, how far a Minister, exercising statutory powers, could treat the requisition of a private dwelling-house as an internal administrative matter, rather than as delegated legislation. If the former interpretation was correct, the householder affected by the requisition had no right to be informed and heard. If the latter view was correct, certain duties of publication, analogous to those incumbent on delegated legislation proper, had to be observed by the Minister. The Minister of Health had power under the Defence Regulations, 1939:

to such extent and subject to such restrictions as he thinks proper, to delegate all or any of his functions . . . to any specified persons or class of persons.

The Minister had delegated his power to take possession of vacant dwellings to local authorities. He had done so by means of circulars, in which he laid down certain conditions, which were not published to any but the administrative authorities concerned. A local authority requisitioned the defendant's house, in breach of the conditions laid down by the Minister, but the Minister subsequently purported to ratify the action of the local authority. The Court of Appeal held that the Minister, by delegating his powers, had for the time being divested himself of these powers. He ' retained only those powers which, in his sub-delegated legislation, he had expressedly or impliedly reserved for himself '. The circulars, although not disclosed to the public, were held to contain, in a manner binding upon the Minister, the terms of sub-delegation. By refusing to the local authority any privilege of non-disclosure for the

[9] See below. p. 169 ff.
[1] [1948] 1 K.B. 349.

circulars, the Court of Appeal emphasised its strongly held view that the terms of Ministerial sub-delegation of powers should be made available to the public affected by it.

The decision apparently had a wholesome effect upon administrative practice. Requisitioning powers are now delegated, not summarily but for each individual case, and a copy of the instrument is made available to the owner or his agent.[2]

The wider problem remains, however. It stems from the increasing difficulty of neatly defining the three branches of government, in accordance with the doctrine of separation of powers. In modern administration, not only are administrative and judicial functions closely mingled—this is illustrated by the extreme difficulty of finding a satisfactory definition of ‘ quasi-judicial ’ functions—but legislative and administrative functions are equally mixed. Between the issue of a general norm, applicable to an indefinite number of persons, and the issue of a particular order, affecting a specific individual group of persons or corporations, there is a difference of degree rather than of principle.[3] A circular by the Ministry of Education which lays down rules on the lighting and sanitation of schools, or the principles which are to govern the appointment of teachers, has legislative as well as administrative elements. Similarly, the order of the Australian Vegetable Seeds Committee, addressed to vegetable seeds merchants, to destroy particular stocks of seeds,[4] or a requisition order applicable to certain types of houses, contained both legislative and administrative elements. In the *Blackpool Corporation Case*, Scott L.J. described the problem as being one of ‘ sub-delegated legislation ’; where the powers conferred upon a public authority are of the quasi-legislative character, the principles of publication and the rights of objection developed in regard to primary delegated legislation should, in the opinion of Scott L.J., apply. But as the distinction between legislative and administrative actions cannot

[2] de Smith (1949) 12 M.L.R., p. 43.

[3] This incidentally provides an interesting confirmation of the so-called Stufentheorie of the Vienna school. Cf. *Legal Theory* (2nd ed.) p. 111 *et seq.*

[4] *Yates* v. *Vegetable Seeds Committee* 72 C.L.R. 37 (1946)

be drawn absolutely, the classification of a particular official act will still largely depend on a careful weighing of the needs of public administration, against the legitimate interests of the individual.

The difficulty of drawing a clear borderline between administrative functions on the one hand and judicial or ' quasi-judicial ' functions on the other hand, has particular significance for the problem of administrative discretion. It is the main touchstone for the applicability of the prerogative orders of certiorari and of prohibition. If a particular activity of an administrative authority, Ministerial or otherwise, is classified as ' quasi-judicial ' the courts will quash or review proceedings if they do not conform with ' natural justice '. Despite the many decisions on the subject, an accurate test has not yet been found. Probably it cannot be found—because almost any decision of an administrative character affects the rights of somebody. The problem therefore becomes what is a right in this particular context, and whether, on a general appreciation of the situation, the judicial or the administrative aspects prevail. This is less a matter of logic than of common sense, and the decisions on this subject reflect to a particular degree the conflicting opinions of courts on the respective value of public power and private rights. In the decade following the end of the first World War, the law courts were inclined to take a sceptical and even hostile attitude towards the extension of administration. One result of this was the dangerous extension of the notion of ' quasi-judicial '. The decision of the Court of Appeal in *R.* v. *Electricity Commissioners* [5] is a high water mark. The Electricity Commissioners were a public authority with strictly defined statutory powers to formulate schemes for the improvement of the electricity supply and to make orders subject to confirmation by the Minister of Transport. The commissioners made an order by which they constituted a joint authority, in terms which in the opinion of the Court of Appeal were ultra vires. But the court had further to prove that the scheme constituted the exercise of a quasi-judicial function, although it was subject to confirmation. Atkin L.J., who delivered the leading judgment,

---

[5] [1924] 1 K.B. 171.

saw in the ' withdrawal from existing bodies of undertakers of
some of their existing rights, and the imposing upon them of
new duties, including their subjection to the control of the new
body, and new financial obligations '[6] a quasi-judicial decision.
He also gave the following definition of a ' quasi-judicial '
function: ' Wherever any body of persons having legal
authority to determine questions affecting the rights of
subjects, and having the duty to act judicially, act in excess of
their legal authority, they are subject to the controlling
jurisdiction of the King's Bench Division exercised in these
writs '.[7] This of course circumscribes rather than defines the
two main questions, what is a right, and when an authority has
a duty to act ' judicially '. If a scheme of the Electricity
Commissioner reorganising the electricity undertakings in a
district, and subject to approval by the Minister and Parliament
was a ' quasi-judicial ' decision, this should apply *a fortiori*
to a decision of a textile controller cancelling, without appeal,
a licence of a textile dealer.[8] Yet the Privy Council decided
that this was an administrative, not a ' quasi-judicial ' action.
The decision of the controller affected an individual right, namely
the right to trade, far more directly than the decision of the
Electricity Commissioners. Nor was it subject to appeal. The
Privy Council considered that his action was administrative,
because it was not regulated by any special procedure. But apart
from the duty to hold a local inquiry, this is also true of the
Electricity Commissioners' powers. Both the House of Lords and
the Court of Appeal have, in recent decisions,[9] denounced the
idea that a ' quasi-judicial ' function could be derived from an
obligation to hold an inquiry for the purposes of hearing
objections. All these recent decisions indicate a reversal of the
earlier judicial tendency to extend the scope of judicial supervision
by construing as many administrative actions as possible as
' quasi-judicial '. The English courts have realised the
undesirability of piecemeal judicial intervention in a complex

[6] *Id.* at p. 207.
[7] *Per* Atkin L.J. [1924] 1 K.B. 171 at p. 205.
[8] *Nakkuda Ali* v. *M. F. De S. Jayaratne* (1950) 66 T.L.R. 214.
[9] *Franklin* v. *Minister of Town and Country Planning* [1948] A.C. 86: *B. Johnson & Co.* v. *Minister of Health* [1947] 2 All E.R. 395.

administrative process. Consequently, they have restricted the notions both of ' right ' and of the ' duty to act judicially '.[1] But over administrative tribunals proper, the courts have vigorously asserted, and even widened, their prerogative jurisdiction.[2]

STATUTORY IMMUNITIES AND LEGAL DUTIES

It is probably due to the absence of a systematic consideration of public law problems, to their scattered and somewhat haphazard appearance in common law actions, that there has been so much judicial confusion over the effect of statutory immunities and powers conferred upon public authorities. The accidents which occurred during the last war as a result of the general blackout, and of bombing raids, brought the problem to a head. But it was only after years of confusing decisions that the Court of Appeal, in *Fisher* v. *Ruislip U.D.C.*[3] brought some clarity into the matter. Under the Defence of the Realm Act, local authorities were absolved from their normal duty to light streets. They also obtained powers to build both surface and underground air raid shelters. A number of accidents happened, to pedestrians, cyclists, and motorists, who in the general blackout ran into surface shelters, tumbled into fresh bomb-craters, or slipped on the steps of an underground shelter. One would have thought the legal problem to be simple enough; the statutory immunity absolved the local authority concerned from liability for failure to light, but did not affect its duty to exercise this immunity in accordance with the ordinary standards of care. This meant that the local authorities had to take such measures for the protection of the safety of the public as were compatible with the observance of the blackout, and other war-time regulations. Such precautions consisted in the placing of dimmed

---

[1] This self-limitation, evident in *Nakkuda Ali's* case (above, pp. 159, 170) is criticised by H. L. R. Wade, in 67 L.Q.R. 103.
[2] Cf. in particular, the Divisional Court in *R.* v. *Paddington Rent Tribunal* (above, p. 162); *R.* v. *Northumberland Compensation Appeal Tribunal* [1951] 1 K.B. 711; *R.* v. *Fulham Rent Tribunal* [1951] 2 K.B. 1. Lord Goddard C.J., presiding, has repeatedly ' advised these tribunals on the merits of the cases and thus brought the Court close to the function of an Administrative Appeal Court.'
[1945] K.B. 584.

red lights around fresh bomb-craters, the painting of white
lines round surface shelters, and the use of a trained corps of
full-time or part-time air raid wardens, fire-fighters, and other
civilian defence services. Obviously, the standard of care had
to be determined with full regard to war-time circumstances.
It would have been unreasonable to expect a full array of warning
lights in a freshly bombed district. Shortages in manpower and
material must be taken into account. In general, the public
living and moving in an English city during war-time could be
expected to behave with far greater caution than in normal
times. All these are matters of fact, to be weighed in determining
the question of negligence. But there should have been no doubt
on the principle that a local government or any other public
authority was subject to the ordinary principles of common law
liability, in so far as these did not prejudice its duties as a public
authority. Yet the decisions, up to *Fisher's Case*, are
contradictory and confused.[2] The Court of Appeal in *Fisher's
Case*, made a valiant attempt to reconcile the authorities, an
impossible task. It is not necessary now to analyse the many
spurious and contradictory solutions attempted before *Fisher's
Case*. Lord Greene's formulation of the problem provides a
fairly clear guide for the future.

If the right which is being exercised is not a common law right
but a statutory right, a duty to use care in its exercise arises, unless,
on the true construction of the statute, it is possible to say that the
duty is excluded. If, for instance, the statute expressly authorises
the doing of a specific act in a defined manner, no liability arises if
the act is done in the manner defined, even if by taking some
additional precaution a greater degree of safety could be attained.
The question, therefore, in any given case appears to resolve itself
into this—does the statute, on its true construction, in authorising
the act in question, exclude the duty of taking care in its
performance ?[3]

The true view, in my opinion, is that the date of the erection of
an obstruction and the purposes for which it is intended to be used are
(apart from some special circumstances or some special language in
the statute) both immaterial; that the duty to take reasonable care

---

[2] A survey and synopsis up to the beginning of 1945—*i.e.*, shortly before
Fisher's Case—is given in Friedmann, ' Statutory Powers and Legal
Duties of Local Authorities ' (1945) 8 M.L.R. 31, 48.
[3] [1945] K.B. 584.

to prevent danger to the public is present throughout: that so long as the streets are properly lit the duty is *ipso facto* performed: but that when the street lighting is suspended, either as the result of lighting restrictions or (in cases where street lighting is optional) as the result of the local authority's decision to extinguish the street lamps or as the result of a break-down in the lighting system it becomes the duty of the local authority to take such steps to safeguard the public by special danger lights or otherwise, as in the circumstances of the case are reasonably possible.[4]

A closely related though not identical problem is the degree of immunity from legal liability conferred upon a public authority through a statutory power to do certain things which, without such power, would be an infringement of other people's rights. Such statutory authority is currently divided into ' absolute ' and ' conditional ' or ' imperative ' and ' permissive '.[5] ' Absolute authority is authority to do the act, notwithstanding the fact that it necessarily causes a nuisance or other injurious consequences. Conditional authority is authority to do the act, providing it can be done without causing injurious consequence . . . where the authority is imperative and not merely permissive, it is necessarily absolute—that is to say, that the statute not merely authorizes but also directs a thing to be done, then it must be done regardless of any nuisance that necessarily flows from it.' [6] The leading authority for this provision is *Metropolitan Asylum District* v. *Hill*.[7] In that case, a local authority, equipped with statutory power to erect a smallpox hospital, was restrained from building it in a place in which it would cause a nuisance to the residents of the neighbourhood. The statutory power was construed as conferring only a conditional permission to build the hospital, if it could be done without causing a nuisance to anybody.

Technically the decision rests upon the permissive wording in the authorising statute, and on the jury verdict that the defendants did not erect and carry on the hospital ' with all proper and reasonable care and skill with reference to the plaintiff's right '. This obscures the question under what

---

[4] [1945] K.B. 595, 613.
[5] Cf. Salmond, *Torts* (10th ed. Stallybrass), p. 42, para. 9.
[6] Salmond, *Torts*, pp. 42, 43.
(1881) 6 A.C. 193.

circumstances a statutory power must be construed as imposing a public duty which takes precedence over private rights.

The practical importance of the decision is probably far smaller than its theoretical fame. Most statutory powers conferred upon local authorities, public corporations, and other statutory bodies, specifically state the liabilities to which they are subject. Where this is not done, modern decisions seem to take a less destructive view of the meaning of statutory powers than in *Hill's Case*.[8] But *Hill's Case* is still quoted as the highest authority on the subject, and it serves to obscure the genuine public law problems as they present themselves today. Statutory powers are normally conferred in the permissive form. For example, the Civil Defence Act, 1939, conferred upon local authorities the power to erect air raid shelters. This power was in form permissive. As the degree of danger from air raids varied greatly from area to area, it would have been most inadvisable to confer the power in an imperative form. Yet such legislative language permits no conclusions about the character of the power, and the relative importance of public interest and private right. It is difficult to imagine an English court granting an injunction or even damages in lieu of an injunction, to a Poplar or Finsbury resident complaining that the building of an air raid shelter at night, and the use of hydraulic presses, disturbed his sleep. In *Oakes* v. *Minister of War Transport*,[9] Singleton J. refused damages to a plaintiff injured by a projecting tank trap, constructed under a war-time power. In the absence of negligence, the obstruction which caused the injury had been constructed in the interests of public safety. In short, the rule of *Hill's Case* needs re-stating. The construction of a statutory power must be determined neither by the form of the power nor by any general presumption that private rights should not be interfered with, but by a balance of the interests involved. A power clearly conferred in the public interest, such as the authority to build air raid shelters or tank traps, must take precedence over private rights. But a power

[8] Cf. *Edginton* v. *Swindon Corporation* [1939] 1 K.B. 86: *Oakes* v. *Minister of War Transport* (1944) 60 T.L.R. 319.
[9] (1944) 60 T.L.R. 319.

conferred on a ' local authority ' to run a bus service, should *prima facie* be construed differently. It is not necessary to enter into dubious economic theory or political philosophy by saying that the running of transport services is a matter of private enterprise. The borderlines between public and private enterprise are now extremely fluid, and the sphere of generally accepted State functions has vastly expanded, as compared with the period when *Hill's Case* was decided. But the now frequent constitution of nationalised industries and social services in the form of public corporations, shows that the prevalent principle of public policy is to organise public services of all types, inside and not outside the common law. Public corporations are fully liable in contract, tort, and quasi-contract, and also for taxes, rates, and charges. Similarly, a statutory power enabling a public authority to run a commercial enterprise should normally be construed as being subject to the ordinary liabilities. Only a test of this character can bring this problem into line with the rules governing public corporations, statutory immunities, and other rules which are gradually building the foundations of English public law.

Yet another aspect of this basic problem is illustrated by the recent *Catchment Board Cases*. Under the Land Drainage Act, 1930, these Boards ' shall exercise general supervision over all matters relating to the drainage of land within its district, and shall have such other powers and perform such other duties, as are conferred on Drainage Boards by this Act '. These powers include that of repairing walls, dykes, or banks. In *Kent v. East Suffolk Catchment Board*,[1] the Catchment Board had exercised this power in order to repair a breach which had flooded the plaintiff's farm land with salt water. Owing to negligent execution, the work took 164 days instead of 14 days, which would have been a reasonable period, given proper skill and care. The plaintiff sued for damages, but failed. In the judgments of the majority, three different reasons can be distinguished. The main ground for the majority decision was that the Board's negligence had not caused additional damage since it need not have acted at all. A second point was that a public authority,

[1941] A.C. 74.

operating with limited resources and on a limited budget, had to be judged by a more elastic and milder standard than a private contractor. Lastly, Lord Simon in particular emphasised the public law aspect. A public authority exercising an administrative function and subject to public supervision would be hampered in the proper exercise of its public duties if held to the ordinary standards of negligence. Lord Atkin's powerful dissenting judgment took an entirely different line. He argued that, once having undertaken the work, the Board was in exactly the same position as a private contractor, and liable in damages for failure to carry out the work with the skill reasonably to be expected. The argument of the majority, that the Board did not cause any additional damage, because it need not have acted at all, seems to beg the question. Having once undertaken the work, any discrepancy between a reasonable period of repair and that actually taken, was surely damage in the sense of the law. Such strength as the arguments of the majority possess, derives from public law considerations. It is arguable that a Catchment Board, operating in the interests of a whole area on a limited budget and with limited resources, cannot be taken to be liable according to the standards imposed upon a private contractor, working for profit and on business principles. In other words, a consideration of the administrative position might justify an interpretation of the statutory power conferred upon the Catchment Board in the sense imputed to it by the majority. Unfortunately, the majority judgments emphasise the weaker argument, namely that no new damage was caused. This made it easy for the case to be distinguished in a subsequent decision of the Court of Appeal, which was obviously unsympathetic to the principle of *Kent's Case.* In *Smith* v. *River Douglas Catchment Board*,[2] the Catchment Board had agreed with a number of landowners, including the plaintiff, to build flood banks. The landowners had agreed to make a contribution to the cost of the work. Neither the amount of the contribution, nor the relation it had to the cost of material, labour, and a possible service fee, was mentioned in the agreement; the point was obviously not regarded as relevant

[2] [1949] 2 K.B. 456.

by the Court of Appeal, for no evidence was taken. The court unanimously regarded this transaction as a contract, and the Catchment Board as liable for the damage caused by the bursting of the bank and the consequent flooding of the plaintiff's land. If *Kent's Case* seems to err in the direction of excessive administrative discretion, *Smith's Case* errs in the opposite direction. It gave no consideration at all to the public law problem involved, and simply assumed that some contribution to the cost of the work justified the implication of a contract. Yet in an almost simultaneous decision,[3] the Court of Appeal held another Catchment Board not liable for the nuisance suffered by the owner of a bridge which had been swept away as a consequence of legitimate operations of the Board. The court held that the plaintiff was limited to the statutory compensation provided for in the Land Drainage Act. It was essential that the public authority should not, in the absence of negligence, be impeded in the exercise of its statutory powers by the threat of private remedies.

The facts of these three decisions are sufficiently different to justify different results, but the problems involved are sufficiently alike to emphasise the need for a clearer appreciation of the public law aspects. As pointed out earlier, a public authority, such as a Catchment Board, should clearly be liable, in so far as its legal position can fairly be compared to that of a private contractor. Where, for example, the Catchment Board has prevented the farmer from having repair work done privately, it should be held liable in negligence, or possibly in contract. Where it has entered into an agreement which can fairly be interpreted as a contract, it should be held liable accordingly. But where it can be shown that such liability would impede the carrying out of paramount public functions, the statutory power should be construed as excluding common law remedies.

SOVEREIGNTY AND EQUALITY IN THE RELATIONS BETWEEN PUBLIC AUTHORITY AND THE INDIVIDUAL

English law has no theory of the State. Gradually, a concept of the State as a juristic personality, and a theory of State

---

[3] *Marriage* v. *East Norfolk Catchment Board* [1949] 2 K.B. 456.

functions, is developing out of the maze of historical fictions
which treat the person of the King and the Crown as one and
the same person. Another cause of retardation in the development
of a legal theory of State functions has been the Dicey legacy,
the refusal to recognise the duality of the State, or to admit any
distinction between sovereign and non-sovereign aspects, and
the very existence or necessity of public law. Yet the necessity
to distinguish between the different aspects and functions of the
State is no less urgent in English than in other legal systems.
In Continental jurisprudence, it is of course a problem of primary
importance. Whether the State or another public authority has
acted in its public or private function, is the most important
though not the only factor determining whether the civil or the
administrative courts are competent. A special Conflict Tribunal
decides if necessary conflicts of jurisdiction. The Janus head of
the State—as a fountain of authority (sovereign), and as a
subject of private rights (*fiscus*)—is a familiar feature of
Continental jurisprudence. Recent German and French
jurisprudence has elaborated a parallel distinction between
gestion publique and *gestion privée*, in order to determine
the public or private law character of a transaction.[4] Generally
speaking, public authorities have greater discretion in the
exercise of their public functions than in their private transactions.
But definite rules of liability have been worked out. Both
German and French law know the ' administrative contract '.
Damages and injunctions can be granted before administrative
courts.

The English plaintiff on the other hand must either succeed
in convincing the court of the existence of a common law contract
or tort or an enforceable statutory duty, or he fails entirely.
The government department or the borough council will either
have to answer according to common law, or it can withdraw
behind the protective shield of administrative discretion. Hence,
some recent decisions on the problem of contractual liability
of government and other public authorities acquire particular
significance. They serve to illustrate, from yet another angle,

---

[4] Cf. Waline, *Droit Administratif* (4th ed., 1946), pp. 56–58, see above,
pp. 60–62. Also below, pp. 270–273.

the cardinal problem of the relation of administrative discretion and legal duty.

The first case illustrating the problem without throwing much light upon it, is *Rederiaktiebolaget Amphitrite* v. *The King*.[5] During the first World War, a Swedish ship had, before sailing to England, obtained a promise from the British Legation at Stockholm that the ship would ' earn her own release ', if she carried a cargo of at least 60% approved goods. On the second voyage, made after an express renewal of the promise, the British Government refused clearance, unless it was arranged through the officially recognised Swedish Shipping Committee. The owners were not entitled to apply to that committee because the ship had formerly traded with Germany. The British Government refused its release, and the owners were compelled to sell the ship. They sued for breach of contract. War-time cases often make bad precedents, but Rowlatt J. supported his refusal to award damages by the theory that there was no contract but merely an expression of intention to act in a particular way. ' My main reason for so thinking is that it is not competent for the government to fetter its future executive action.'

Although this decision has ever since figured in textbooks and case books on Constitutional Law, its authority, such as it is, has been greatly weakened by some recent decisions. It would, however, be wrong to assume that these decisions indicate more than a small fraction of the cases in which there are genuine contracts between public authority and the citizen. Contracts between government departments and private firms are normally made under standard conditions, which provide for arbitration.[6] In many other cases, the fact that a government department can bind itself by an ordinary commercial contract, is taken for granted. Thus, in a leading Australian constitutional case,[7] the government department controlling the New South Wales Tourist Bureau had contracted with a newspaper for a series of advertisements. Payment was to be made out of a general fund at the disposal of the Prime Minister. A subsequent government

---

[5] [1921] 3 K.B. 500.
[6] *E.g., Standard Conditions for Government Contracts for Stores Purchases* (1947 ed.), sec. 23.
[7] *N.S.W.* v. *Bardolph* (1935) 52 C.L.R. 455.

attempted to repudiate it. The High Court decision was mainly concerned with the problem, whether such a contract could be enforced without specific appropriation of funds (a question which it answered in the positive). But it did not doubt that a contract of this type, between a government agency and a private business firm, was normal and legitimate.

Lastly, a vast sphere of transactions to which public authority is a party has been removed from the public law sphere by legislation. The public corporations, which operate Britain's nationalised industries, and a considerable number of social services, are clearly liable in contract and tort, like every private law subject. [8]

There remain some important cases illuminating the borderland between administrative discretion and binding promise. In *Robertson* v. *Minister of Pensions*,[9] an officer who claimed that his disability was due to military service had obtained a written reply from the War Office, which contained the following passage: ' I now write to let you know that your case has been duly considered, and your disability has been accepted as attributable to military service '. In reliance on that letter, the claimant obtained no further medical opinion, and took no other steps regarding his disability. The Minister of Pensions later disclaimed liability. Denning J. held that the War Office had acted as an agent for the Crown. It had thus bound the Crown as a whole, including other government departments.[1] Denning J. rejected the doctrine of executive necessity, and dismissed the *Amphitrite Case* on the somewhat dubious ground that it was not based on the doctrine of executive necessity, but on the now doubtful right of the Crown to dismiss its servants at pleasure.[2] The learned judge was obviously

---

[8] A similar conclusion was reached in France by the administrative courts some years ago. Cf. Waline, *op. cit.*, p. 57.

[9] [1949] 1 K.B. 227.

[1] This application of estoppel to government actions, restated by Denning L.J. in the *Falmouth Boat Construction Ltd.* v. *Howell* [1950] 1 All E.R. 538, is criticised by Mitchell (1950) 13 M.L.R. 376.

[2] The current view of the relations between the Crown and its servants has recently been subjected to considerable criticism. (Cf. Logan (1945) 61 L.Q.R. 240; Mitchell (1950) 13 M.L.R., 318–339).

The prevalent opinion is still that the Crown can dismiss both military and civil servants at pleasure (Wade and Phillips, *Constitutional Law,*

anxious to bring this case as close as possible to the ordinary rules of legal liability.

If this was a question between subjects, a person who gave such an assurance as that contained in the War Office letter would be held bound by it unless he could show that it was made under the influence of a mistake or induced by a misrepresentation or the like, none of which appears here. There are many cases in the books which establish that an unequivocal acceptance of liability will be enforced, if it is intended to be binding, intended to be acted on, and is, in fact, acted on.[3]

' In my opinion, if a government department in its dealings with a subject takes it on itself to assume authority on a matter with which he is concerned, he is entitled to rely on it having the authority which it assumes. He does not know, and cannot be expected to know, the limits of its authority. The department itself is clearly bound, and as it is but an agent for the Crown, it binds the Crown also, and as the Crown is bound, so are the other departments, for they also are but agents of the Crown.'[4]

The decision of the Court of Appeal in *Turberville* v. *West Ham Corporation*[5] shows a similar approach. A local education authority, by a resolution made in 1939, had decided to give leave of absence to its employees who joined the Forces with their approval, and to make up their pay to the amount of their salary ' received by them at the date of their being called up for training or service, with such increments, if any, of their grades, which they would have received but for such leave of absence '. Another part of the same resolution said that a cost of living bonus was ' not to be considered as salary or wages, and was not to be payable to employees so granted leave of absence '. The plaintiffs, two teachers employed by the council, were called up in 1940, and until March 31, 1945, received from the council the sums to which they were entitled under the resolution. An order from the Minister of Education of 1945, directed local

---

4th ed., p. 311). But the Crown may bind itself for a fixed term (*Reilly* v. *The King* [1934] A.C. 176), and there is increasing support for the view that the Crown is legally liable to pay its servants for services rendered. This obligation may be grounded in statute, contract, or quasi-contract. (Cf. Logan, *loc. cit.*, and the careful decision of the Supreme Court of Victoria, in *Bertrand* v. *The King* [1949] V.L.R. 49).

[3] [1949] 1 K.B. 227.
[4] [1949] 1 K.B. at pp. 230, 232.
[5] [1950] 2 K.B. 203.

educational authorities to pay to teachers new, improved
scales of pay, as from April 1, 1945. The council wrote to one of
the plaintiffs, to the effect that they would make the necessary
adjustments in their payments, as soon as they had reached a
decision on the applicability of the new scales. Later, however,
the council informed the plaintiffs that they could not augment
their services pay to bring it up to the new rates. The plaintiffs
sued for the difference between the pay received, and that to
which they claimed to be entitled under the new scales. The
council pleaded, *inter alia*, the Limitation Act, 1939, under
which

' no action shall be brought against any person for any act done . . .
in execution, or intended execution . . . of any public duty or authority,
. . . unless it is commenced before the expiration of one year from the
date on which the cause of action accrued '.

The Court of Appeal rejected the defence, and held the
council liable. Having decided that the new scales of pay
came within the resolution of 1939, which affected the plaintiffs,
the court considered that the resolution was in the nature of a
contractual promise, and not therefore within the above-quoted
clause of the Limitation Act. As Singleton L.J. put it:

' they entered into a contract voluntarily, and, when they made
payments under such a contract, they did so in pursuance of the
contract and not in the execution of any public duty '.

The language of the Limitation Act compelled the court to
make the unfortunate choice between ' public duty ' and
' voluntary contract '. From a political and administrative point
of view, there is no such contrast. The local education
authority exercised a public duty in making any promises to
its teachers on war service. The purpose of the decision was,
of course, to widen the sphere of contractual liability
against that of administrative discretion, and to strengthen
the position of the individual in the manifold legal contacts
which he now has with public authorities of all kinds.

Another decision of the Court of Appeal, which has already
been quoted in a different context,[4] shows, however, that

---

[4] *Ransom and Luck* v. *Surbiton Borough Council* [1949] Ch. 180, see above,
p. 162.

contractual liability will not be allowed to hamper the execution of political and administrative responsibilities. Lord Greene, who delivered the judgment of the court, strongly emphasised that a planning authority could not be presumed or permitted to bargain away the exercise of its planning powers by private contract. To this, it might possibly be objected that the exercise of planning powers in the national interest would not necessarily be affected by an obligation to pay damages for promises previously given. It would conclusively dispose only of a suit for specific performance. Presumably, the court's answer to this lay in the brief reference to the statutory compensation provided in the Act for expenses incurred in interim development.

This decision illustrates vividly, if somewhat haphazardly, the cardinal problem of public law: how to preserve the legal security of the individual, in a society in which more and more legal relations pass from the private to the public sphere, without hampering the needs of administration in the social welfare State.

CONCLUSIONS

It is a rather chequered picture which emerges from the discussion of public law problems, as they are illustrated by recent British legislation, and the decisions of the courts. As yet, public law problems are seldom recognised or appreciated in their full importance, in the common law setting in which they usually appear. Nevertheless, it is far easier now than even a few years ago, to extract a number of tentative principles from legislation and decided cases.

1. Not only the legislature but the courts are gradually coming to abandon the former presumption—sanctioned by textbook rules of statutory construction—of interpreting a given provision or legal dispute in favour of the integrity of private rights. War-time decisions, such as *Liversidge* v. *Anderson*, the *Thetis Case*, or the *Amphitrite Case*, tend to go to the other extreme, and place the public interest first, even at the expense of well-established rules of construction. Generally, however, the predominant judicial attitude is now one of balancing the interests concerned without any predisposition

in favour of either public interest or private rights. This is clearly apparent, for example, in recent decisions on tax evasion,[5] and planning powers.[6] Both are now seen as legitimate instruments of public policy, and no longer merely as objectionable interferences with private rights which the courts ought, by their interpretation, to restrict to the minimum. The attempt of an individual to evade a tax is now increasingly regarded as an attempt to attain private benefits at the expense of the rest of the community.

2. The principles limiting administrative discretion are beginning to emerge more clearly. Tentatively, the position might be formulated as follows:

(a) where the imposition of legal liability (in tort or contract, through the imposition of statutory duties, or through the construction of ministerial actions as quasi-judicial) would interfere with the execution of public duties, such legal liabilities will not be imposed on a public authority.

This approach emerges from such decisions as: the *East Suffolk Catchment Board Case*[7]; the *Town Planning Cases*[8]; or *Ransom and Luck* v. *Surbiton Borough Council.*[9]

An application of these principles should lead to a much-needed clarification of the legal effects of statutory powers. Whether all specific statutory powers, conferred upon a public authority, should be construed as overriding private rights or not should be made dependent not on the form of the power nor governed by a presumption in favour of private rights, but by the purpose and nature of the power. Where the urgency of the public interest demands it, but not otherwise, it should be construed as overriding private rights. The principle of *Metropolitan Asylum District* v. *Hill*[1] needs reformulation.

(b) Subject to these reservations, however, public authorities

---

[5] Cf. below, p. 242 ff.
[6] Cf. above, pp. 162, 170.
[7] Cf. above, p. 175.
[8] Cf. above, p. 170.
[9] Cf. above, p. 162.
[1] Cf. above, p. 173.

are now increasingly subjected to the same legal duties as everybody else.

(i) In the field of tort, *Fisher* v. *Ruislip Urban District Council*[1] makes it clear at last that statutory immunities or powers do not convey a general immunity from duties of care towards the public. The rule which limits the liability of highway authorities to acts of misfeasance is an anomaly ripe for removal. The rule has, however, been eroded by recent English decisions.[1a]

(ii) In the field of contract, there is an increasing tendency to treat promises given by public authorities, including the Crown, as contractual, rather than administrative. This is indicated by such recent decisions as: *Smith* v. *River Douglas Catchment Board*[2]; *Robertson* v. *Minister of Pensions*[3]; and *Turberville* v. *West Ham Corporation*.[4] But the *East Suffolk Catchment Board Case*, and *Ransom and Luck* v. *Surbiton Borough Council*, are reminders that considerations of public policy may exclude contractual liability. The borderline will to some extent be determined by the courts' opinion on the respective importance of social welfare and planning powers on the one hand, and the rights of the individual on the other.

The emergence of these public law principles confirms once again that the pressure of social problems is a more powerful factor in legal evolution than technical conditions. The public law problems which legislature and courts now face in common law countries are substantially the same as in Continental systems of similar political and social structure. It may be that common law systems will eventually develop a hierarchy of administrative courts, and thus help to systematise administrative law.

---

[1] [1945] 1 K.B. 584.
[1a] Cf. Wade and Phillips, *Constitutional Law*, 4th ed. p. 286.
[2] See above, p. 176.
[3] See above, p. 180.
[4] See above, p. 181.

Meanwhile, however, public law problems have to be solved within the framework of the common law tradition. Recent developments, both legislative and judicial, show that the adaptability of the common law, which is the pride of English lawyers, can meet this new challenge as it has met many others. It is the jurist's duty to assist both legislature and judges in this task of adaptation.

CHAPTER 9

THE LEGAL STATUS AND ORGANISATION
OF THE PUBLIC CORPORATION

THE public corporation has, since the end of the first world war, become a familiar device for the organisation of public enterprises and services, in many different countries and legal systems.

Both its value and its elasticity can be gauged from the fact that it has been adopted in the Socialist and entirely State-controlled economic system of Soviet Russia as well as in the non-Socialist system of the United States.

The Soviet Union proceeded, only a few years after the Revolution, to develop the institution of the State trusts[1] for the running of major industrial State enterprises. These trusts are constituted as autonomous legal units; they receive their charter from the Supreme Council of National Economy, which also appoints the members of the board; they have two types of capital assets which roughly correspond to the distinction between fixed and floating assets of British company law. The fixed assets belong to the State, the floating assets belong to the trusts. That is to say, they are State property at one remove and can be freely disposed of. The trusts enter into contractual and other legal transactions, and legal disputes between them are settled by special courts which appear to have developed principles of mixed contract and administrative law.[2]

In Germany the public corporation appears in two forms. One makes the State or other public authorities a shareholder in a company. The undertaking is organised in the form of a joint stock company and governed by company law, with the State or other public authorities holding a controlling or substantial interest as shareholder.[3] A more genuine form of

---

[1] The first decree was of April 10, 1923.
[2] Cf. above, p. 65.
[3] This is known as ' Mixed Public Enterprises ' (Gemischt-Wirtschaftliche Unternehmung).

public corporation was devised when the Dawes Plan constituted the German State railways as an independent commercial company, under a control board with allied participation, charged with reparation obligations and separated from the State budget.

An instructive type of public corporation, of great comparative interest for the British lawyer is the Tennessee Valley Authority (T.V.A.), an outstanding example of public enterprise in a non-Socialist economy.

However, it is in Britain and the British Dominions that the public corporation has achieved particular significance. A multitude of enterprises of all kinds are organised in this form: from the British Broadcasting Corporation to the National Coal Board, and the other recently nationalised basic industries; from the Regional Hospital Boards and Management Committees administering the National Health Service, to the Australian Forest and Housing Commissions; from the Trans-Australian Airlines, operating in competition with private air services, to the Canadian Hydro-Power Commissions and the Canadian National Railways; from the British Development Corporations set up under the New Towns Act, to the Australian Repatriation Commission, in charge of the civilian rehabilitation of ex-servicemen. In Britain and the British Dominions, which, despite many differences and changes of government, broadly concur in the blending of an extensive social service State with the preservation of a large degree of private enterprise, the public corporation is regarded as the best way in which to combine the principles of public service and ownership with those of managerial responsibility and financial accountability.

Lastly, the legal form of the public corporation has been adopted by the constitutions of the many functional international agencies created in conjunction with the United Nations Organisation. Such institutions as the Food and Agriculture Organisation, the World Health Organisation, UNESCO, the International Monetary Fund, and others may conveniently be termed international public corporations.[4] Their constitutions

---

[4] Friedmann, ' International Public Corporations ' (1942) 6 M.L.R., 185.
Schmitthoff, ' International Corporations ', Grotius Soc. (1946).

and functions naturally differ somewhat from those of the national corporations, as they are institutions of international law. They share with the national public corporations, however, the essential characteristics of a separate legal personality, and relative autonomy of management, (represented by the Director-General and his permanent staff), coupled with responsibility to a political body (the delegates of the member nations), and financial accountability.

DEFINITION AND GENERAL CHARACTERISTICS OF PUBLIC CORPORATIONS

While the idea of an autonomous corporation, responsible not to private shareholders but to public authority, has thus commended itself to the most diverse legal and social systems, the structure and characteristics of the public corporation are inevitably determined by the difference in the legal and constitutional systems in which they are established. The objective is given in President Roosevelt's classic summary (in his message to Congress in 1933 recommending the formation of the T.V.A.): ' Clothed with the power of governments but possessed of the flexibility and initiative of a private enterprise '; but there are vast differences between the Soviet State Trust, which is under the all-pervading economic and political control of the Soviet Government in a completely socialised system, the T.V.A., whose responsibility towards Congress and President respectively reflects the American system of division of powers, and the British public corporation which, after some experimenting, now reflects the British system of indirect responsibility to Parliament, through the government.

Even within the British legal system, the public corporation stands for a variety of functions and purposes.[5] The first task is as clear a definition of its nature and characteristics as is possible.

[5] The following major statutes establishing public corporations are repeatedly referred to in the text: Agriculture Act, 1947; Air Corporations Act, 1949; Coal Industry Nationalisation Act, 1946; Coal Industry Act, 1949; Electricity Act, 1947; Gas Act, 1948; Iron and Steel Act, 1949; National Health Service Act, 1946; New Towns Act, 1946; Overseas Resources Development Act, 1948; Town and Country Planning Act, 1947; Transport Act, 1947.

From other public authorities such as Borough Councils or other Local Government authorities, or from the Crown itself, the public corporation is distinguished by its functional character. However widely defined its objectives (and such public corporations as the National Coal Board or the British Transport Commission do exercise vast functions and many powers), it is not a multi-purpose authority but a functional organisation, created for a specific purpose: the provision of transport or broadcasting services, the management of hospital and health services, the development of Colonial resources, the administration of compensation for the nationalisation of development rights in land, the provision of houses for certain sections of the population, or the import and sale of raw cotton. The nature of these services thus varies widely, from commercial and trading to cultural and supervisory administrative activities, as well as the provision of social services. As will be shown later, the nature of the services performed is not without importance for the legal status of the corporation. It is, however, possible to outline certain universal legal characteristics of the public corporation, applicable to all types.

(i) The public corporation has no shares and no shareholders, either private or public. Its shareholder, in a symbolic sense, is the nation represented through government and Parliament.

(ii) The responsibility of the public corporation is to the government, represented by the competent minister, and through the minister to Parliament.

(iii) The administration of the public corporation is entirely in the hands of a board which is appointed by the competent minister, sometimes after and mostly without consultation with any special group or industry but invariably not on a basis of representation of specific interests.[6]

---

[6] The board of the Port of London Authority consists of representatives of the directly interested industries. The board of the former London Passenger Transport Board was appointed by trustees. While the former method can be justified for the particular case of a port authority, the latter method has been criticised by both Gordon (*Public Corporations*, 1937) and Robson (*Public Enterprise*, 1937) as removing the board from proper public control. This method of 'appointing trustees' has now been abandoned.

(iv)   Where a public corporation needs capital—those of an essentially administrative character do not—it is provided, in the case of public corporations administering nationalised industries, through assets taken over from private ownership and capitalised through the issue of interest-bearing stock.

Such stock is either government stock or, in most cases, stock issued by the public corporation with a Treasury guarantee. The financial assets of public corporations which have not acquired the assets of formerly private industries (such as the Airways Corporations) consist of corporation stock with a Treasury guarantee, supplemented by the power of the minister to give certain Exchequer grants during the formative period. The industrial public corporations have furthermore the power to borrow money, with the consent of their supervising minister and the Treasury, within limits fixed by the Acts.

(v)   The public corporation has the legal status of a corporate body with independent legal personality.

(vi)   All public corporations are supervised by commercial accounting and auditing as well as some form of public control. But the type of accounting and public control varies according to the type of public corporation.

(vii)   All public corporations have a dual nature; they are instruments of national policy but they are autonomous units, with legal independence and certain aspects of commercial undertakings. The degree of independence varies, however, according to the type and purpose of the public corporation.

THREE TYPES OF PUBLIC CORPORATION

The nationalisation of British industries has brought into prominence the industrial or commercial type of public enterprise. It now looms large, with such giant enterprises as the National Coal Board, the Transport Commission, the British Electricity Authority, the Iron and Steel Board, the Gas Council, the Airways Corporations, the Colonial Development Corporation and the

Overseas Food Corporation. This type of public corporation, which may be described as the ' commercial corporation ', is designed to run an industry or public utility, according to economic and commercial principles but subject to public responsibility to the appropriate constitutional authorities. There is, secondly, what we may term the social service corporation.[7] This type of corporation is designed to carry out a particular social service on behalf of the government. It is represented by such enterprises as the new Town Development Corporation, Regional Hospital Boards and Management Committees, the Central Land Board and the Agricultural Land Commission. These and similar public corporations also have to undertake numerous commercial and managerial functions. They have to employ staff, buy equipment, manage large institutions. But their essential purpose is that of undertaking a social service on behalf of a government department. They enjoy therefore a smaller degree of independence from managerial supervision than commercial corporations. For example, the Agricultural Land Commission manages and farms land vested in the minister and placed by him under the control of the Commission. It also carries out such other functions as may be entrusted to the Commission by the Act. The Central Land Board, it is specifically provided, exercises it functions ' on behalf of the Crown '.[8] Because the Regional Hospital Boards are described as carrying out their functions ' on behalf of the minister ', it is provided that this shall not affect their legal liability.[9]

The differences between these two types of corporations are legally important in various respects.[1] The distinction is also reflected in the provisions regarding accountability. After some considerable discussion, it was decided that the commercial corporations would have their accounts

---

[7] This terminology, suggested in ' The New Public Corporations and the Law ' (1947) 10 M.L.R. 236–37, has been accepted by Professor Glanville Williams: *Crown Proceedings*, p. 28. The term ' commercial public corporation ' is also used by the Court of Appeal in *Tamlin* v. *Hannaford* [1950] K.B. 18 (Denning L.J.).
[8] Town and Country Planning Act, 1947, s. 3 (3).
[9] National Health Service Act, 1946, s. 13.
[1] Cf. the discussion below, p. 207.

audited according to commercial standards and by commercial auditors, but not by the Auditor-General. Such social service corporations as the Town Development Corporation and the Regional Hospital Boards, on the other hand, must submit their accounts to the minister, who has them audited by the Comptroller and Auditor-General. This indicates a difference in the legal status and constitutional position of the two types of corporation.

It is, however, useful to add a third though less frequent type of public corporation. This may be termed the supervisory public corporation. It has essentially administrative and supervisory functions, and it does not engage in commercial transactions, either to fulfil its main objective, or incidentally to the performance of a social service. A good example of this type of corporation within the British legal orbit[2] is the Australian Broadcasting Control Board, created by a Statute of 1948. It is established as a corporate body on the usual lines. Its main function is the supervision of both technical and cultural standards of broadcasting services, (broadcasting in Australia is shared between a Commonwealth-owned public corporation and a number of commercial stations). This board has certain powers of direction, including the power to grant loans for certain purposes, with the consent of the Treasury, but it does not itself undertake any commercial operations. The main reason for giving such institutions separate legal status rather than that of a government department, is the greater degree of managerial autonomy and independence from civil service regulations.

CONSTITUTION OF BOARDS

In all cases the boards are appointed by the competent minister, who is not tied by any consideration of representative interests in his choice. Appointments have in fact been made throughout on an independent, non-party and non-political basis, though the different members naturally represent various

[2] There are also a number of American public agencies of this type, such as the Federal Communications Commission, the National Labour Relations Board, and the Federal Trade Commission.

walks of life and experience.[3] The relevant clause in the Coal
Industry Nationalisation Act is typical: ' The board shall consist
of a chairman and not less than eight, nor more than eleven
other members. The chairman and other members of the board
shall be appointed by the Minister of Fuel and Power . . . from
amongst persons appearing to him to be qualified as having had
experience of, and having shown capacity in, industrial,
commercial or financial matters, applied science, administration,
or the organisation of workers '.[4]

While in some cases the qualifications of the persons whom
the minister should appoint are specified he is left complete
discretion in others.[5] Some Acts specify groups or authorities
which the minister has to consult before appointment.[6]

The minister is usually given power to make regulations
with respect to the tenure of office of the board. A standard
practice is undoubtedly developing in this field.[7] Neither the
members of the board nor the staff of the public corporation are
civil servants. The appointment is for a definite term and upon
conditions as determined by the minister with the approval
of the Treasury. Members of the boards may resign or be
dismissed by the minister, in cases specified in the regulations.
Apart from membership of Parliament, which is incompatible,
the main grounds upon which the minister may ' declare the
office to be vacant ' are the member's engagement in any trade
or business including a directorship of a company, or a position

---

[3] In the National Coal Board, for example, the various members have
   been chosen with regard to their technical knowledge of the coal industry,
   administrative experience, trade union and labour management experience,
   etc.

[4] Sec. 2 Coal Industry Nationalisation Act, 1946, in conjunction with
   sec. 1, Coal Industry Act, 1949. Similar clauses are found in: New Towns
   Act, s. 2; National Health Service Act, Sched. III; Electricity Act, s. 3;
   Transport Act, s. 1; Town and Country Planning Act, s. 2; Agriculture
   Act, s. 65; Gas Act, s. 1; Iron and Steel Act, s. 1.

[5] *E.g.*, in the appointment of the National Assistance Board (National
   Assistance Act, 1948, First Sched.) its members are appointed by His
   Majesty by warrant under the sign ' Manual '.

[6] *E.g.*, the university, the medical professional organisation, and the local
   health authorities, are to be consulted in the appointment of members
   to the Regional Hospital Boards. Cf. Third Sched. to National Health
   Service Act.

[7] Cf., for example, S.R. & O., 1946, No. 1094, regulating appointments to
   the National Coal Board, in pursuance of s. 2. Coal Industry
   Nationalisation Act.

as officer or servant in an organisation of workpeople. But there is also a general power of dismissal in the case of continued neglect of duty (such as absence from meetings of the board for more than six months consecutively and unfitness to continue in office or incapability of performing duties). In all these respects the discretion lies with the minister, who is given power to approve exceptions, for example in regard to membership of a company or of a workmen's organisation. A necessary and wholesome provision in the regulations is the obligation laid upon every member of the board to disclose to the minister full particulars of any interest held either directly or indirectly in any business similar to that carried on by the board. This includes interests in board contracts and membership of any firm interested in such contracts. It has been customary to provide for ' staggered ' appointments so that terms of office of the different members of the board shall not expire simultaneously, to the detriment of the continuity of its administration.

Decentralisation of management and legal responsibilities is a general problem of all the public corporations which administer the basic national industries. But whereas in most cases, for example that of the National Coal Board, it has been left to the board to organise its own decentralisation, the Gas and Electricity Acts provide for Area Boards. The Area Gas Boards, for example, are responsible for the gas supply in specified areas, and for that purpose have a number of ancillary powers, including the manufacture and distribution of gas and certain ancillary products. On a more limited scale, the powers of the Area Boards are parallel to those of the wider National corporation. They are, however, generally responsible to the latter, in a way roughly comparable to the responsibility of the national corporations to their respective ministers. [8]

ADVISORY COUNCILS

The public corporation is not under the control of a shareholders' meeting. Theoretical though the control of shareholders is today in the case of most companies, the link

[8] Cf., for example, Gas Act, s. 2 (iv), s. 4 (ii).

established between the public corporations and Parliament, through the competent minister does not establish sufficient contact between the public corporation and the public. A series of advisory councils or committees has been constituted for the specific purpose of giving independent advice to the minister on behalf of the public in general, or of such groups of the public as are particularly interested in the enterprise concerned. Although the type and composition of these advisory councils varies according to the nature of the industry or enterprise concerned, a general pattern can be discerned. The advisory councils are appointed by the minister ' as the minister may think fit ', or ' as the minister may from time to time determine '. [9] But the minister is directed in the Acts to consult with certain organisations before he makes the appointments. [1] Thus, in the case of the coal industry, an Industrial Coal Consumers' Council and a Domestic Coal Consumers' Council have been established. The minister is to consult on the appointments ' with such bodies representative of the interests concerned as the minister thinks fit ', and he ' shall have particular regard to nominations made to him by the said bodies representative of the interests concerned of persons recommended by them as having both adequate knowledge of the requirements of those interests and also qualifications for exercising their wide and impartial judgment on the matters to be dealt with by the council generally '. The Iron and Steel Act provides for a single Iron and Steel Consumers' Council, consisting of an independent chairman and from fifteen to thirty other members appointed by the minister, after consultation with representative bodies. The Gas and Electricity Acts, in conformity with the policy of decentralisation, establish a number of Consultative Committees, one for each Area Board.

It is the function of these advisory councils to advise and report to the minister on the matters on which they are competent. They are to make annual reports to the minister, who shall lay them before Parliament. The members of the councils are not full-time officials or employees. But provision is made for

[9] This seems an example of needless diversity in terminology.
[1] See Coal Industry Nationalisation Act, s. 4; Transport Act, s. 6; Iron and Steel Act, s. 6.

full-time staffs, whose remunerations are determined by the minister with the approval of the Treasury. There are some strange and apparently unnecessary inconsistencies in the constitution of the different committees.

Thus, the Coal Act lays down that the two consumers' councils shall consist of persons appointed by the minister ' to represent the board '. A similar provision does not exist in the case of the three Transport Users' Consultative Committees. The function of these committees, which is to represent the section of the consuming public concerned (including industry) in a position of independence of the board, and with full power to criticise it, seems incompatible with its representing the board. On the other hand, the Transport Act lays down that the full-time officers and servants of the consultative committees are to be provided by the Transport Commission itself (section 7 (7)). The Coal Industry Nationalisation Act, by contrast, provides that clerks, officers and staff are to be furnished by the minister, with the concurrence of the Treasury. This is both more logical and more sensible if the consumers' councils are to be in a position of independence towards the boards.

How far the advisory councils are in practice fulfilling the function of independent consumers' representatives, is a matter of some doubt. A recent report in *The Economist* [2] asserts that the Coal Consumers' Councils—which have so far issued three annual reports—tend too much to regard themselves as part of the organisation, and to whitewash the boards which it should be their duty to criticise if necessary. The danger of subservience, or at least lack of sufficient independence, is obviously greater where the officers and staff of the councils are supplied by the corporation. This is so with the Coal Consumers' Councils, but not with the proposed Iron and Steel Consumers' Council, or the consultative council set up in the Electricity Act, for each Area Board. The latter are far closer to local opinion; but the chairman of the Area Council is also an ex-officio member of the Area Board. Suggestions have recently been made in Parliament that the Advisory and Consultative Councils should

[2] August 5, 1950.

be made more independent of the boards, by a complete separation of both finance and personnel.

An altogether different institution is the Air Transport Advisory Council,[3] which is constituted in the form of a tribunal with a legally qualified chairman and whose function it is to consider representations from any person ' with respect to the adequacy of the facilities provided by any of the three corporations, or with respect to the charges for any such facilities '. The council has a wide discretion in rejecting representations which they consider as frivolous, vexatious or inexpedient.

Despite its semi-judicial composition, the council has only the power to make recommendations to the minister, and it must make an annual report which the minister shall lay before Parliament, together with a statement of any recommendations submitted by him in consequence, or any recommendations submitted to him by the council. It is difficult to see the reason for this fundamental difference between the Air Transport Advisory Council and the other advisory councils. Both are advisory, but both may have to deal with such matters as charges for goods and services. Nor is it apparent why the Air Transport Advisory Council should be constituted in the form of an administrative tribunal.

LEGAL POWERS OF THE PUBLIC CORPORATION

A comparison of the powers clauses in all the relevant Acts shows that the legislator has chosen wide and elastic formulas giving the corporations almost unlimited scope and discretion.[4]

The formulations are, however, far from identical. The general pattern is that of setting out the specific tasks of the public corporation in question. This is followed by provisions specifying a number of particular activities which the public corporation shall be empowered to carry out, but without prejudice to the generality of the powers granted in the section as a whole. To this is added a general powers clause of varying formulation. Thus, the Coal Industry Nationalisation Act provides:

[3] Civil Aviation Act, 1949, s. 12.
[4] Coal Industry Nationalisation Act, s. 3; Electricity Act, s. 2 (5); Transport Act, s. 2; Air Corporations Act, s. 3; New Towns Act, s. 2 (2); Iron and Steel Act, s. 2.

' The Board shall have power to do anything and to enter into any transaction . . . which in their opinion is calculated to facilitate the proper discharge of their duties under subsection (i)

(which defines the duty of producing and supplying coal)

of this section or the carrying on by them of any such activities as aforesaid or is incidental or conducive thereto '.

The Electricity Act chooses a slightly different formulation:

' . . . which in their opinion is calculated to facilitate the proper performance of their duties, under the foregoing section or the exercise or performance of any of their functions under the foregoing provisions of this section, or is incidental or conducive thereto '.

This is followed by a specific restriction on the powers of an Area Board in regard to the manufacture of electrical plant and electrical fittings, which is reserved to the central authority.

The Air Corporations Act has a different and more complex powers clause. It first defines the duty of the Airways Corporations: ' to provide air transport service and to carry out all other forms of aerial work . . .'. It secondly contains a general powers clause in the following form:

' Each of the three corporations shall have power, such as hereinafter provided to do anything which is calculated to facilitate the discharge of their functions under the preceding subsection or of any other functions conferred or imposed on the corporation by or under this Act, or is incidental or conducive to the discharge of any such functions '.

The Act, thirdly, gives the minister the right to define the previously conferred powers for the purpose of keeping the public properly informed as to the nature and scope of the activities of the public corporation; but it is added that ' Nothing in any such order shall prejudice the generality of the powers conferred by the preceding provisions of this section '. The Act, fourthly, withholds from all three corporations the power to manufacture air frames or aero engines or air screws. It fifthly enumerates certain additional powers, again without prejudice to the generality of the powers previously conferred, to acquire auxiliary undertakings. The Act lastly authorises the minister to issue an order which limits the powers of any of the three corporations, to such extent as he thinks desirable in the public interest, by making their exercise dependent on a general or special authority given by him. Such order must be laid before Parliament, which may annul it within forty days.

The powers clause of the Development Corporations under the New Towns Act is again different. It firstly defines their objects, and enumerates a number of specific powers to which is added a general clause in the following form:

' To carry on any business or undertaking in or for the purposes of the new town, and generally to do anything necessary or expedient for the purposes of the new town or for purposes incidental thereto '.

The Act then specifically excludes the power to borrow money (other than ministerial advances under the Act) and authorises the minister to give directions restricting the exercise of any of the powers of the corporation or to give instructions as to the manner of their exercise. But it is further provided:

' Any transaction between any person and any such corporation acting in purported exercise of their powers under this Act shall not be void by reason only that it was carried out in contravention of such direction unless that person had actual notice of direction '.[5]

The Transport Act, alone of the laws setting up commercial public corporations, defines the powers of the Transport Commission by way of enumeration, without adding a general and elastic clause of the type mentioned before.

The clauses defining the powers of the non-commercial public corporations are markedly different. Their position is more that of auxiliary organs of the minister in the performance of a social service. Thus, section 11 of the National Health Service Act provides that Regional Hospital Boards shall be constituted ' . . . for the purpose of exercising functions with respect to the administration of hospital and special health services in those areas '. Section 65, Agriculture Act, defines the function of the Agricultural Land Commission as:

' (*a*) managing and farming land vested in the Minister and placed by him under the control of the commission; (*b*) advising and assisting the Minister in matters relating to the management of agricultural land and with such other functions as may be entrusted to the commission by the Act '.

[5] New Towns Act, s. 2 (3).

Certain functions, such as the acquisition or the disposal of land except where specifically placed under its control, are excluded from the capacity of the commission, but a general clause similar to those in the Acts regulating the nationalised industries gives the commission 'power to enter into such transactions and do all such things (whether or not involving the expenditure of money) as in their opinion are expedient for the proper discharge of their functions'. These functions are, however, much more limited and specific than those of the commercial corporation.

The degree of elasticity of the powers conferred upon the corporations, and in particular, the choice between an objective and a subjective formulation of those powers, has a direct bearing upon the question of *ultra vires* control. The greater the discretion placed in the hands of the governing body of the corporation, the smaller the scope of judicial control.

As corporate bodies, the public corporations are subject to the ultra vires limitation on contractual capacity[6] and on tortious liability.[7] As public authorities, forming part of public administration, they are subject to the supervisory powers which the courts as guardians of the law of the land exercise over administrative authorities.[8]

The ' powers ' clauses in the Acts constituting the public corporations are therefore likely to be read by the courts in the light of this double limitation. Their width and elasticity, which is analogous to the technique of most modern memoranda of association, may not serve as a protection against the tests which the courts apply to the exercise of administrative powers.

What are these tests? Despite the extreme difficulty of extracting clear principles from the welter of decisions, it is submitted that the two main causes of invalidity for ultra vires are Excess of Power (*excès de pouvoir*) and Abuse of Power

---

[6] *Ashbury Carriage Co.* v. *Riche*, L.R. 7 H.L. 653.

[7] The view, first developed by Salmond (Torts, cf. 10 ed., s. 13), that the ultra vires rule ought not to apply to torts committed by those representing the corporate body (as distinct from servants) now rightly finds increasing support (*e.g.*, by Winfield, Tort, s. 26; Welsh (1946) 62 L.Q.R. 345, at pp. 351, *et seq.*).

[8] Kahn-Freund (1946) 9 M.L.R. 237, appears to suggest that only in the latter capacity, the public corporations are subject to ultra vires control.

(*détournement de pouvoir*).   The first means checking legal acts by the terms of the enabling statute, the second means a check on administrative discretion where motives alien to the administrative purpose have prevailed.

The position is much confused, however, through the nebulous test of ' reasonableness ' which the courts apply to administrative actions.

Few questions are more obscure in English law than the meaning of reasonableness for the purpose of judicial control over the powers of public authorities.   In *Kruse* v. *Johnson*[9] the court limited reasonableness to scrutiny of motives and abuse of powers.   The examples given by Lord Russell were partiality and inequality of bye-laws, manifest unjustness, bad faith, oppressive or gratuitous interference with the rights of those subject to them as could find no justification in the minds of reasonable men.   In *Westminster Corporation* v. *L.N.E.R.*[1] Lord Macnaghten stated three separate requirements: " It must keep within the limits of the authority committed to it.   It must act in good faith and it must act reasonably ".

This seemed to mean that the courts were limited to an examination of excess of power and of improper motives.   But this interpretation was gravely upset by the House of Lords in *Roberts* v. *Hopwood*,[2] a decision somewhat discredited by some more recent cases discussed earlier in this book.[3]   Of the present tendency of English Courts not to use the ultra vires test as an instrument of interference with administrative responsibilities, the following observations of Lord Greene M.R. are representative:

' In making his decision, he may obviously be guided by his own views as to what is " expedient " for the purpose of dealing " satisfactorily " with extensive war damage . . .   How can the Minister, who is entrusted by Parliament with the power to make or not to make an executive order according to his judgment and acts *bona fide* (as he must be assumed to do in the absence of evidence to the contrary) be called on to justify his decision by proving that he had before him materials sufficient to support it?   Such justification, if it is to be

[9]   [1898] 2 Q.B. 91.
[1]   [1905] A.C. 426.
[2]   [1925] A.C. 578.
[3]   Cf. above, p. 164 ff.

called for, must be called for by Parliament and not by the courts, and I can see no ground in the language of the Act, in principle or in authority, for thinking otherwise '.[4]

It is submitted that grave legal uncertainty as well as political danger would follow from any attempt of the courts to interfere in the administrative policy and discretion of public corporations and to examine reasonableness as distinct from (*a*) excess of statutory powers and (*b*) objectionable motives. Not only would such an attitude be an almost open defiance of clear parliamentary language, it would precipitate a dangerous conflict between the judiciary on the one hand and those responsible for policy on the other hand. Where is the limit to be drawn? If the courts examine reasonableness in the wider sense, could they declare invalid as ultra vires a contract by the National Coal Board for the purchase of a rest home for miners' families? Could they invalidate the purchase of administrative headquarters as being extravagant and therefore not ' calculated ' or ' required ' for the proper discharge of their functions? The proper machinery for control is a strict system of auditing and accounting and effective supervision by Parliament, not the haphazard control of law courts.

The different aspects of the ultra vires problem are best illustrated in the Air Corporations Act.[5] The general powers clause should make the corporation immune from judicial interference, except only in case of a *détournement de pouvoir*. For example, the purchase of land at a grossly exorbitant price, when shown to be due to personal interests of a member of the board, would be a clear case of abuse of powers.

The Minister is further empowered to ' define the powers conferred upon the corporation . . . so far as he thinks it desirable so to do for the purpose of securing that the public are properly informed as to the general nature and scope of the activities in which the corporation may engage '. But, as it is specifically provided that such an order is not to prejudice the generality of the powers conferred upon the corporations, it operates as a limitation of authority, not of capacity. The

[4] *Robinson* v. *Minister of Town and Country Planning* [1947] 1 All E.R. 851.
[5] Cf. above, p. 199.

board can be held to account for breach of duty, but a contract which it concludes in violation of the order is not invalidated.

There are, thirdly, statutory limitations upon the powers. If an airways corporation enters into a contract relating to the business of making air frames, or if it exceeds its borrowing authority, these are cases of *excès de pouvoir* and subject to the ultra vires rule.

It remains to ask how the ultra vires question could arise in practice.

Ultra vires proceedings may be started either by the corporation itself, or by third parties.

The former is the normal procedure in the case of companies, the latter in the case of local authorities or other public authorities equipped with statutory powers.

Under the rules in *Foss* v. *Harbottle* [6] and in *Burland* v. *Earle*,[7] the company itself must sue to redress a wrong done to the company or to recover moneys or damages. But where the majority of the shares is controlled by those against whom relief is sought, the complaining shareholders may sue in their own name. A public corporation has no private shareholders. Its shareholder is the nation represented through Parliament which acts through the responsible Minister. Suppose that the purchase, by the National Coal Board or the Electricity Authority, of extensive properties, either for investment or for the development of holiday homes, is criticised in Parliament. It may be that the Minister himself is anxious to stop extravagance, or that a change of Government leads to a change of policy. Again, a particular member of the board may have been extravagant or fraudulent in transactions entered into on behalf of the board. Does the analogy of company law apply? For the reasons given above, it is submitted that it does not. Public corporations are special public authorities, not commercial companies, and the remedy of Parliament and Government must be political, administrative and disciplinary. The Minister cannot be compared to a minority shareholder.

[6] (1843), 2 Hare 461.
[7] [1902] A.C. 83.

But if public corporations are in the position of special public authorities, the remedies normally available against these should apply.

In the first place, there may be an action for damages or specific performance by a third party, arising out of an act purporting to be on behalf of the corporation. It may be in contract or in tort. In either case, it would be the right and the duty of the corporation to plead ultra vires. According to settled principle, the doctrine of estoppel does not apply to ultra vires cases.[8] Such situations will not arise frequently, but they are by no means impossible, especially if the new corporations should develop the desired spirit of healthy enterprise. For example, an Area Board has power to repair and maintain but not to manufacture electrical fittings. The borderline may not always be easy to determine.

In the mixed economy of contemporary Britain, there may be applications for injunctions, or motions for prerogative orders, by private business interests contesting what they consider an undue extension of public enterprise. It is possible, for example, that an airways corporation may wish to start a local shipping service for its passengers, as an activity, ' calculated to facilitate the discharge of its functions', and that either a local shipping line, or shipping lines in general would apply for an injunction to stop the airways corporation. Conflicts of competence may also arise between different nationalised services. An injunction lies against a public authority, at the suit of an individual who claims special damage as the result of an ultra vires action. The Attorney-General may ask for an injunction where the public interest is concerned.[9] The delimitation of the respective competences of several public corporations, or of public and private enterprise, may well be such a public interest.

Again, mandamus lies where no other adequate remedy can be obtained and the claimant can show a clear right to the performance of a duty by the public authority. This is potentially the most important of the legal remedies available

---

[8] Street, *Ultra Vires*, p. 400, and authorities there cited.
[9] See below, Ch. 10, p. 221-232.

to the public, but its scope is far from clear.   It has been refused to a sanitary authority wishing to enforce, by means of mandamus, the carrying out of vaccination by another authority[1]; on the other hand a ratepayer obtained a mandamus to compel the production of the accounts of a local authority for inspection by his agent.[2]   Nice questions may arise as to the extent to which the public duties imposed upon a corporation engender private rights, but the majority of public duties imposed upon the public corporations, such as the mining and distribution of coal, or the creation of a co-ordinated and efficient transport system, must be construed as public duties, not enforceable at the wish of an individual.

The vast majority of potential conflicts are removed from the judicial forum by the width and elasticity of the powers of the corporations.   This increases the importance of adequate public control, by means of ministerial supervision, parliamentary debate, public auditing and periodical check through parliamentary sub-committees.

THE LEGAL STATUS OF PUBLIC CORPORATIONS

Corporate Character.

Substantially similar provisions in all the Acts provide for the establishment of the public corporation as ' a body corporate . . . with perpetual succession and a common seal and power to hold land without licence in mortmain '.[3]

The Acts do not state specifically that the public corporation is to be on the same footing as any private legal person in respect to legal duties, liabilities, charges, etc. That they are to be in such a position can, however, be inferred from two typical sets of provisions.[4]   One says that:

' Nothing in this Act shall be deemed to exempt the corporation from liability for any tax, duty, rate, levy or other charge whatsoever, whether general or local '.

---

[1] *R.* v. *Lewisham Union,* [1897] 1 Q.B. 498.
[2] *R.* v *Bedwelty U.D.C.. ex p. Price* [1934] 1 K.B. 333
[3] *E.g.,* Coal Industry Nationalisation Act, s. 2; New Towns Act, s. 2; Transport Act, 1st. sched.; National Health Service Act, 3rd. sched.
[4] See, for example, the Iron and Steel Act, 1949, ss. 9 and 10.

This clause makes it clear that the public corporations do not participate in any privileges or immunities of the Crown. Another typical provision is as follows:

(1) The Public Authorities Protection Act, 1893, and section twenty-one of the Limitation Act, 1939, shall not apply to any action, prosecution or proceeding against the corporation, or for or in respect of any act, neglect or default done or committed by a servant or agent of this corporation in his capacity as a servant or agent of theirs.

(2) In their application to any action against the corporation sections two and three of the Limitation Act, 1939

(which relate to the limitation of actions of contract and tort, and certain other matters)

shall have effect with the substitution for references therein to six years of references to three years '.

This provision implies that the public corporations are fully liable in law in actions for breach of contract, tort, recovery of property, etc. Their special position, and their duties as public authorities responsible to a minister are reflected only in the privilege of a shortened limitation period.

The normal commercial public corporation, such as the National Coal Board or the Transport Commission, is politically responsible to the minister and through him to Parliament. But legally, it is in no sense an agent or servant of the minister or the Crown. This is brought out clearly by certain differences in the drafting of the relevant statutes. Some of the social services corporations are specifically assigned their functions ' on behalf of ' the executive. Thus, the Town and Country Planning Act, 1947, stipulates that ' the functions under this Act of the Central Land Board, and of their officers and servants, shall be exercised on behalf of the Crown '. The National Assistance Board, which administers assistance to ' persons . . . without resources to meet their requirements', in supplementation of the National Insurance Act, also exercises its functions ' on behalf of the Crown '.[5] The National Health Service Act, 1946, lays down that: (section 13, (1)):

(1) A Regional Hospital Board and the Board of Governors of a teaching hospital shall, notwithstanding that they are exercising functions on behalf of the Minister, and a Hospital Management

[5] National Assistance Act, 1948, 1st sched. s. 9.

Committee shall, notwithstanding that they may be exercising functions on behalf of the Regional Hospital Board, be entitled to enforce any rights acquired, and shall be liable in respect of any liabilities incurred (including liabilities in tort), in the exercise of those functions, in all respects as if the Board or Committee were acting as a principal, and all proceedings for the enforcement of such rights or liabilities, shall be brought by or against the Board or Committee in their own name.

(2) A Regional Hospital Board, Board of Governors or Hospital Management Committee shall not be entitled to claim in any proceedings any privilege of the Crown in respect of the discovery or production of documents, but this subsection shall be without prejudice to any right of the Crown to withhold or procure the withholding from production of any document on the ground that its disclosure would be contrary to the public interest.

The precise legal effect of such provisions is not easy to ascertain. It is possible that the Central Land Board is meant to participate in the privileges and immunities of the Crown, in regard to statutes, taxes, and other rights and liabilities. The Regional Hospital Boards and Management Committees might be in the same position, except for the specific provision of the National Health Service Act. The Australian courts, which are still greatly preoccupied with the problem of the ' shield of the Crown ',[1] would probably so hold. The English Court of Appeal, in *Tamlin* v. *Hannaford*,[2] leaves it at least open whether it would have come to a different decision in the case of the Central Land Board. But it is equally possible that it would separate the question of legal liabilities from that of constitutional responsibilities. The public corporations exercising their functions ' on behalf of ' the Crown are on the ministerial budget, and subject to a far closer degree of ministerial supervision and responsibility. This also means greater latitude for questions in Parliament.

No corresponding provisions exist in regard to any of the commercial corporations. In the only English decision so far on this matter,[3] the Court of Appeal rightly deduced from this difference in drafting, that the British Transport Commission —and this applies to all the nationalised industries—was not a

---

[1] Cf. below, p. 209.
[2] [1950] K.B. 18, below, p. 210.
[3] See note 2.

servant or agent of the Crown, and could not therefore be held
to participate in the Crown privilege of immunity from the Rent
Restriction Acts. The court reinforced its argument by a
consideration of the general structure of the public corporations,
whose characteristic feature is legal autonomy coupled with
political responsibility.

THE SHIELD OF THE CROWN

In short, the Court of Appeal gave the only interpretation
consistent with the true purpose and function of public
corporations in the modern legal and economic system of Great
Britain. It specifically acknowledged that public corporations
are public authorities, but separated this question from that of
their legal relation to Crown and Parliament. It acknowledged
the dual character of this new form of public authority:

' In the eye of the law the corporation is its own master and is
answerable as fully as any other person or corporation. It is not the
Crown and has none of the immunities or privileges of the Crown.
Its servants are not civil servants, and its property is not Crown
property. It is as much bound by Acts of Parliament as any other
subject of the King. It is, of course, a public authority and its purposes,
no doubt, are public purposes, but it is not a government department
nor do its powers fall within the province of government '.[4]

The problem of the so-called ' shield of the Crown ' is no
longer of much significance in English law. Its importance,
has been greatly reduced by the Crown Proceedings Act, 1947,
which makes the Crown itself fully liable in civil proceedings.
There remain, however, a number of important Crown privileges
of which the most considerable are immunity from taxes and rates,
and in particular, immunity from the binding effect of statutes,
unless they are by specific or necessary application applied to
the Crown.[5] It is now clear, partly from express statutory
provisions, and partly from the interpretation of their status and
character as given in *Tamlin* v. *Hannaford*, that the commercial
corporations at least will not participate in any remaining Crown
privileges.

[4] [1950] K.B. 18 *per* Denning L.J.
[5] For a fuller discussion, see below, Ch. 12.

Unfortunately, however, this problem is still a matter of great importance in Australia, which has a multitude of public corporations but none of the unifying legislation which has clarified the status of the modern British public corporations. It is precisely because the dual status of the modern public corporation, its Janus head as a public authority and a legal person of private law, has not been sufficiently appreciated in the Australian courts that the judicial authorities on this subject are in a state of great confusion.

The whole problem can be traced back to some English decisions of the late nineteenth century. In *Mersey Docks Trustees* v. *Gibbs*,[6] one of the earliest public authorities (a Public Harbour authority) was held liable for negligence. Mr. Justice Blackburn observed as follows:

' It is well observed . . . of corporations like the present, formed for trading and other profitable purposes, that, though such corporations may act without reward to themselves, yet in their very nature they are substitutions, on a large scale, for individual enterprise. And we think that, in the absence of anything in the statutes (which create such corporations) showing a contrary intention in the legislature, the true rule of construction is that the legislature intended that the liability of corporations thus substituted for individuals should, to the extent of their corporate funds, be co-extensive with that imposed by the general law on the owners of similar works '.

Some years later, a House of Lords decision held, on the other hand, that land owned by the Justices of the County of Berkshire, used for the building of a Court of Assizes, was exempt from rates and taxes, because the administration of justice was ' a proper and inalienable ' government function.[7] From these cases, a rule gradually emerged, that the status of a particular public authority depended on its purpose and function. If it exercised a proper government function, it was within the shield of the Crown, and shared its privileges; if not, it was outside the shield.

The basic fallacy and impracticability of such a test should be apparent. Without the adoption of a radical *laisser faire*

---

[6]   (1866) L.R., 1 H.L., 93.
[7]   *Coomber* v. *Justices of the County of Berks* (1883) 9 A.C. 61.

philosophy, and the definition of State functions, as they were current in the days of Adam Smith or Herbert Spencer, it is utterly impossible to sort out proper from improper government functions. A moment's thought on the implications of modern defence, government control over industrial research, education or broadcasting, quite apart from direct industrial enterprise, should show the futility of this distinction. At a time when every common law country, the United States as well as Great Britain and the British Dominions, own and operate a multitude of public enterprises, from the Tennessee Valley Authority to the Trans-Australian Airways, or the National Coal Board, it is obviously impossible for the lawyer to lay down an entirely different definition of State functions. The work of such men as Gény, Heck, and others on the Continent, of Dicey in England, of Holmes, Cardozo, Pound, and others in the United States, has shown that the courts must follow the main evolutions of public opinion in their interpretation of general legal problems. As Mr. Justice Holmes observed, the constitution does not enact Herbert Spencer's *Social Statics*. This applies equally to the definition of State functions for legal purposes. Such an approach has now been accepted by the American Supreme Court in the *Saratoga Springs Case*.[8]

In this case the issue was whether the State of New York was liable to the Federal tax on mineral waters on the sale of mineral waters from its State-owned and operated Saratoga springs. Majority and minority judgments, in particular those of Frankfurter J. and of Douglas J., agree on the uselessness of the former test, as laid down by Sutherland J. in *Ohio* v. *Helvering*,[9] that liability to taxation depended on the distinction between the State as government and the State as trader. In the words of Douglas J.[1]:

' A State's project is as much a legitimate governmental activity whether it is traditional, or akin to private enterprise, or conducted for profit. . . . What might have been viewed in an earlier day as an improvident or even dangerous extension of State activities may today be deemed indispensable '.

[8] *New York* v. *U.S.*, 326 U.S. 572 (1945).
[9] 292 U.S. 360 at p. 366 (1934).
[1] 326 U.S. 572 at p. 591 (1945).

At present many functions are exercised by public authority which are not a substitute for private enterprise but the outcome of new conceptions of social responsibility. If Railway Commissioners or the National Coal Board may be regarded as a substitute for privately owned railways, the Forest Commissioners cannot. Their functions are not confined to the purchase or sale of timber but they comprise what Roscoe Pound has described as one of the vital social interests protected by modern law: the conservation of social resources. A Housing Commission exercises many of the functions of a private builder, but it also discharges a social responsibility of the State and is bound to give priority to social policy considerations. Again, the Development Corporations established in the British New Towns Act of 1946 exercise many commercial functions. They acquire and dispose of land, they control building and personnel, they enter into a multitude of contracts. But their essential function is one which cannot be regarded as a substitution for private enterprise: the co-ordinated development of planned townships under a general national plan of redistribution and redevelopment. Commercial and non-commercial aspects are as inextricably mixed as public and private law.

Australian courts have been well aware of the difficulties in defining the proper functions of government. In order to determine the status of a public corporation, they have therefore increasingly relied on a number of subsidiary technical tests.

Latham C.J., in his survey of the problem in the *Grain Elevators Board Case*,[2] enumerates the essential factors: firstly, incorporation; secondly, financial autonomy; thirdly, the amount of independent discretion given to the public authority as towards the government and the public; fourthly, the right of appointment of the members of the authority by the Crown; lastly, the question whether the authority fulfils a governmental or a non-governmental function.

There is also fairly universal agreement that none of these tests singly gives a conclusive answer. It all depends on the words and the implied intention of the statute, on the respective

---

[2]   *Grain Elevators Board (Vic.)* v. *Shire of Dunmunkle* (1946) 73 C.L.R. 70.

weight of any one or several of the above-mentioned tests, and last but not least on the somewhat chancey ideas of the court on the nature of government functions.

The extreme difficulty of deriving any satisfactory and consistent practical conclusions from these tests may be illustrated by a few examples: the New South Wales Forest Commission is liable in tort,[3] but the Victorian Forest Commission is not.[4] The Victorian Railways Commissioners were given the priorities of the Crown for claims arising out of the sale of coal from a coal mine vested in them.[5]

More recently, the Victorian Supreme Court held the Victorian Railways Commissioners not bound by the sectional regulations regarding landlord and tenant,[6] but this decision was subsequently overruled by the Full Supreme Court,[7] which held that the commissioners might be an instrumentality of the Crown for some purposes, but not in their capacity as landlords. On the other hand, the New South Wales Housing Commission was held not to be bound by the building regulations of a Local Government Act.[8] The Commonwealth Repatriation Commission, which among other activities makes business loans to ex-servicemen, was held entitled to the Crown priorities in seizing assets for the satisfaction of its debts.[9] In an earlier decision, however, the Sydney Harbour Trust Commissioners were held bound by the Employers Liability Act.[1] More recently the High Court of Australia—the highest court of the country— held that land vested in the Grain Elevators Board of Victoria (which stores and sells grain) was not ' land the property of His Majesty'. The reasoning of the court, and in particular the judgment of Dixon J., was close to that later adopted by the English Court of Appeal in *Tamlin* v. *Hannaford*[2]; the public

---

[3] *Ex parte Graham*: *Re Forestry Commission* (1945) 45 S.R. (N.S.W.) 379.
[4] *Marks* v. *Forest Commission* (1936) V.L.R. 344.
[5] *Re Oriental Holdings Pty., Ltd.* (1931) V.L.R. 279.
[6] *Victorian Railways Commissioners* v. *Greelish* (1947) V.L.R. 425.
[7] *Victorian Railways Commissioners* v. *Herbert* (1949) A.L.R. 440.
[8] *Sydney Municipal Council* v. *Housing Commission of N.S.W.* (1948) 48 S.R. (N.S.W.) 282.
[9] *Repatriation Commission* v. *Kirkland* (1923) 32 C.L.R. 1.
[1] *Sydney Harbour Trust Commissioners* v. *Ryan* (1911) 13 C.L.R. 358.
[2] See above, p. 208.

functions of the Board were separated from its legal liabilities. In the *Grain Elevators Case*,[3] Dixon J. said:

' It is probably correct to say, that it conducts what is just as much a governmental undertaking as the State railways and that it falls within the department of the Minister for Agriculture of the State of Victoria. But that appears insufficient to overcome the plain intention of the legislation that, like the Victorian Railways Commissioners, the State Savings Bank Commissioners, the State Electricity Commission, and many other statutory governmental bodies, the Grain Elevators Board should be an independent corporation owning its own property legally and beneficially and acquiring its own rights and incurring its own obligations '.

The most recent decision on this subject, however,[4] though of less authority than that of the High Court, held the Electricity Trust of South Australia to be immune from the South Australian Rent Restriction legislation, partly on general grounds, and partly because of the statutory provision under which the trust ' shall hold all its assets for and on account of the Crown '.

This truly disturbing confusion of authorities is a matter of considerable practical as well as theoretical importance. As the scope of the public enterprise grows, such matters as immunity from local rates, or immunity from rent restriction legislation, affect a growing proportion of public life. The finance of local authorities, which depends on rates, is upset: the citizen who can be evicted because his house is owned by Railway Commissioners or a public Electricity Trust, cannot but have a strong feeling of injustice and resentment. The absence of any consistency in the judicature is due mainly to two factors: first, failure to recognise the dual character of public corporations, which is incompatible with the tests usually applied; second, the absence of a clear and simple principle of legal policy.

As regards the first, the test of financial autonomy, the position of the public corporations varies considerably, but none is entirely autonomous. Most have their own capital, some issue government stock, but all carry a Treasury guarantee, and in many cases the Exchequer may make grants or advances for

---

[3] (1946) 73 C.L.R. 70.
[4] *Electricity Trust of South Australia* v. *Lintern's, Ltd.* (1950) Argus L.R. 551.

specific purposes.[5] The commercial public corporations have their separate budgets, and profit and loss accounts. They are expected to make good their own deficits, and apply their profits to the enterprise, but to the extent that they have received grants from public funds, they must of course make repayments into the Consolidated Fund. All the accounts of public corporations must be laid before Parliament, and can be criticised. Some of the social service corporations, such as the Regional Hospital Boards, are carried on the departmental budget, but, as we have seen, this does not affect their legal liability in private actions as well as for public charges.[6]

The same duality of position is apparent in the method of appointment and the degree of autonomy of management. As stated earlier, the normal method of appointment is by the Minister, or, in the Dominions, by the Governor-General-in-Council, or the Governor-in-Council. This provides an obvious and deliberate link with the Executive which is reinforced by the general power to give directions to the boards in matters affecting the national interest. But, in the general conduct of business, there is far-reaching autonomy of management.[6a] Reluctance to restrict it has been the main justification for the British Government's refusal to have the accounts of the commercial public corporations audited by the Comptroller and Auditor-General, as well as by commercial auditors, and for the refusal of ministers to answer questions on details of management in Parliament.[7] There is no contradiction between the principle of the widest possible autonomy of management, and the right of the nation, represented by Cabinet and Parliament, to call the corporations to account on matters of general public policy, or the misuse of public money. Equally, security of tenure goes far, but is not absolute.

The problem just discussed demonstrates the necessity for a

---

[5] *E.g.*, Air Corporations Act, 1949, ss. 13–16; Victorian Railways Act, 1928, s. 103; Electricity Trust of South Australia Act, s. 19.
[6] National Health Service Act, 1946, s. 13.
[6a] The National Coal Board, for example, has hitherto shown considerable independence, *e.g.*, by raising export prices for commercial reasons when the government would have preferred them low for political reasons.
[7] Cf. the debate in the House of Commons, March 3, 1948, 448 H.C. Deb. 391–455, 5th series, 1948.

clearer appreciation of the many new public law problems which confront the court as well as others concerned with the application and development of the law. Precedents are either so scarce or so conflicting that the courts have a relatively free hand, in helping in the evolution of the law. Nor is there, in this case, a conflict of legal policies between which the court might find it difficult to choose. Advocates and opponents of public enterprise are agreed on the necessity to subject it to legal liability and commercial accountability. The public corporation is an institution deliberately designed to integrate public enterprise with the existing common law system. The courts can help this purpose, by a full appreciation and application of the principles governing the public corporation. They can hinder it by applying nineteenth-century ideas to twentieth-century problems.

CHAPTER 10

DECLARATORY JUDGMENT AND INJUNCTION AS PUBLIC LAW REMEDIES

PRESENT day administrative law, in Britain as in other common law countries, suffers greatly from a fundamental weakness; a system of public law which is growing to ever increasing significance still has mainly to use the categories and remedies of a private law system. In the absence of administrative tribunals and a general system of actions for breaches of public law, the protection of public law depends on the more or less haphazard extension of remedies designed for different purposes. At present public law sanctions can be broadly grouped as follows:—

1. Statutes normally contain penalties, of varying adequacy, mostly fines, as a sanction against, *e.g.*, the breach of building regulations, the non-observance of sanitary or safety standards and other regulations for the protection of the public.

2. This sanction may be reinforced by actions for damages or injunctions at the suit of private persons. This is, from the point of view of public law, a haphazard remedy depending upon the construction of each particular statute by the court and the willingness of an individual to take action.

3. In addition, jurisdiction in equity has been developed to a certain extent to provide remedies for the protection of public interest. This operates through two types of action in both of which the Attorney-General is a party. One is an action for a declaratory judgment or an injunction against the Crown represented by the Attorney-General; the other is a suit for an injunction in which the Attorney-General, as guardian of the public interest, is the plaintiff.

Suits Against the Attorney-General for a Declaratory Judgment.

As between subject and subject, the power to make a declaratory judgment, even without giving any consequential

relief (*e.g.* damages or injunction) is familiar in all jurisdictions.[1]
The use of this remedy as a means of defining the rights and
obligations of public authorities, including the Crown itself,
is one of the most remarkable developments of modern British
administrative law. The importance of a declaratory judgment
against the Crown is of course particularly great where ordinary
actions may not be brought against the Crown. In that respect
the remedy is therefore, since the adoption of the Crown
Proceedings Act, 1947, of less significance in Britain than in
Australia where some States still preserve the Crown immunities.[2]
As will be shown later, the importance of the declaratory
judgment is, however, by no means confined to actions against
the Crown. It may well develop into one of the most important
means of ascertaining the legal powers of public authorities in
the intricate mixture of public and private enterprise which is
becoming a distinctive feature of both British and Australian
life. As Jennings pointed out some years ago, the growth of
public law and public authorities is bound to be accompanied
by the increasing importance of declaratory judgments
authoritatively interpreting the law, at the expense of enforceable
judgments which are often neither desired nor possible (for
example because there is no actionable damage). The declaratory
judgment is the symbol of the twentieth century conception of
the law.[3]

The modern use of the declaratory action against public
authorities is generally dated back to *Dyson* v. *Attorney-General*[4]
where an action was brought against the Attorney-General to test
the validity of notices issued by the Commissioners of Inland
Revenue under the Finance Act of 1910. The plaintiffs contended
that the Commissioners had exceeded their powers in the way

---

[1] See Supreme Court Rules, Order XXV, r. 5; High Court Rules, Order IV,
r. 1. For the position in New South Wales, where the Judicature system
is not in force, see *Tooth & Co. Ltd.* v. *Coombes* (1925) 42 W.N. (N.S.W.)
93; *David Jones Ltd.* v. *Leventhal* (1927) 40 C.L.R. 357 and *Hume* v.
Monro (*No.* 2) (1943) 67 C.L.R. 461 at p. 472.

[2] For a survey of the scope of the remedy under the Crown Proceedings
Act, see Glanville Williams, *Crown Proceedings*, pp. 84–97. For an earlier
discussion of the use of the remedy against public authorities see Jennings
(1932) 41 Yale L.J. 407

[3] Jennings, 41 Yale L.J. 416.

[4] [1911] 1 K.B. 410.

in which they had issued the notices. The Court of Appeal went back to the early case of *Powlett* v. *Attorney-General*[5] as authority for a well-established jurisdiction of the Court of Chancery to bring the Attorney-General, as representative of the Crown, before the court ' in some cases '. The remedy is clearly founded in Equity, and more particularly in the protection of property rights by equitable jurisdiction. In *Dyson's Case* the Court of Appeal did not define more closely the nature of property rights for the protection of which the remedy could be granted. It was more concerned with the question whether a declaratory judgment would interfere with the immunity of the Crown or would indirectly compel it to convey a legal estate. It answered both questions in the negative, and thus laid the foundation for a type of remedy against a public authority whose potentialities are still far from exhausted. Subsequent cases have not thrown very much light on the scope of the remedy. The following decisions indicate the use to which it has been put so far, and the limits within which it is confined:

(a) A mere threat to the interests of an individual will not justify the action. Thus in *Anderson* v. *Commonwealth of Australia*[6] the plaintiff was held not entitled to maintain an action for a declaration that an agreement between the Commonwealth and the Government of Queensland restricting the importation of sugar into the Commonwealth was illegal. As a mere member of the public the plaintiff had not a sufficiently defined interest. There is little direct authority on the question what type of interest would enable a private citizen to sue for a declaratory judgment. But as the use of the declaratory judgment and the injunction both spring from the same origin, namely, equitable jurisdiction, the limitations laid down in the case of *Boyce* v. *Paddington Borough Council*[7] apply to the declaratory action as well. In other words, a special private interest or injury must be proved. The Australian High Court has quite recently regarded the interest of a motor car dealer in the sale of new cars as sufficient for a declaration on the validity of a

[5] Hardres' Reports 465.
[6] (1932) 47 C.L.R. 50.
[7] [1903] 1 Ch. 109, cf. below, p. 221.

Commonwealth New Motor Cars Order.[8]   On the other hand, the House of Lords in *Moscrop's Case*[9] held that the plaintiff, in the absence of a private right or special damage, was not entitled to sue for a declaration, without joining the Attorney-General.   The judgment also implied that the Attorney-General could sue for a declaration where a public interest was involved.[1] In another case a private landowner was held not to have a sufficient private interest for a declaration that a local authority had to maintain a drainage system.[2]

(b) Where there are other remedies available the court will exercise its discretion. Where a statute provides for proceedings in a court of summary jurisdiction, the claimant cannot instead ask for a declaration as to his rights.[3]   Where there is a proper appeal procedure against tax assessments the remedy will not be granted.[4] But a police sergeant who claimed that a dismissal order by a Watch Committee was ultra vires obtained a declaration, although he could have appealed to the Secretary of State or obtained a writ of certiorari.[5]

(c) Differences of constitutional structure account for certain divergences as between Britain and Australia. In Britain, the law-making power of Parliament is not restricted. The courts have therefore recently refused to use an injunction—and the same principles would apply to a declaratory judgment—in order to prevent a private bill from being passed by Parliament. The court in such cases ought not to interfere since the questions of public policy involved were more suitable for determination by Parliament than the court.[6]

(d) On the other hand the declaratory judgment which is otherwise used very sparingly by Australian courts, has assumed outstanding importance for questions of constitutional interpretation and the High Court has not hesitated to grant a declaratory judgment at the suit of a State Attorney-General

[8] *Crouch* v. *Commonwealth* (1948) 77 C.L.R. 339.
[9] [1942] A.C. 332, cf. below, p. 228.
[1] On this question, see further below, p. 226 ff.
[2] *Clark* v. *Epsom R.D.C.* [1929] 1 Ch. 287, 298.
[3] *Barraclough* v. *Brown* [1897] A.C. 615.
[4] *Smeeton* v. *Attorney-General* [1920] 1 Ch. 85.
[5] *Cooper* v. *Wilson* [1937] 2 K.B. 309.
[6] *Bilston Corporation* v. *Wolverhampton Corporation* [1942] Ch. 391.

against the Commonwealth to restrain it from giving effect to an unconstitutional Act before it was proclaimed.[7]

Injunctions.

A parallel extension of an ancient equitable remedy for new purposes is the use of the injunction against public authority, and generally as a sanction against breaches of public law. The foundations for this use of the injunction are the same as for a declaratory action. It is the extension of equitable jurisdiction in protection of property rights for new purposes. Two types of cases must be distinguished, although both affect public law liabilities. On the one hand a private citizen may in certain cases sue for an injunction to restrain breaches of public law whether committed by public authorities or private citizens. The conditions limiting this use of the remedy have been laid down in *Boyce* v. *Paddington Borough Council.*[8] An individual citizen cannot sue for an injunction without joining the Attorney-General except:

(1) Where an interference with a public right involves an interference with some private right of his own;

(2) Where, in respect of a public right, he suffers special damage peculiar to himself from an interference.

In *Boyce* v. *Paddington Borough Council*[9] it was held that, as the plaintiff was suing either in respect of an alleged private right to the access of light, or in respect of an alleged interference with a public right from which he personally sustained special damage, he could sue without joining the Attorney-General as a plaintiff.

On the other hand, interesting potentialities of the remedy are shown by a number of cases in which the Attorney-General has obtained an injunction, either at the relation of a private plaintiff or on his own, in order to enforce a duty owed to the public or to prevent a breach of such a duty. A survey of the relevant cases might precede a discussion of the exceedingly difficult question

---

[7] *Attorney-General for Victoria* v. *Commonwealth* (*Pharmaceutical Benefits Case*) (1945) 71 C.L.R. 237; and see *Toowoomba Foundry Pty. Ltd.* v. *Commonwealth* (1945) 71 C.L.R. 545, *per* Latham C.J. at p. 570.
[8] [1903] 1 Ch. 109.
[9] [1903] 1 Ch. 109.

how far the function of the Attorney-General extends in this field.

In *Attorney-General* v. *Ashborne Recreation Ground*,[1] the Attorney-General sued successfully at the relation of a local authority for the enforcement of the bye-laws of the local authority. In *London County Council* v. *Attorney-General*[2] the Attorney-General obtained an injunction against a local authority, at the relation of a group of private bus operators, restraining the authority from running a public bus service in the purported exercise of statutory powers to run a tramway service. In *Attorney-General* v. *Sharp*,[3] the Court of Appeal granted an injunction to the Attorney-General at the relation of the Manchester Corporation to restrain the defendant from continuing to ply for hire in the city without a licence. In this case the defendants had previously been fined on 60 occasions for offences under the Act. In another case, decided shortly afterwards,[4] the Attorney-General obtained an injunction at the relation of licensed motor coach owners to restrain the defendants from operating a coach service without licences. In this case too the Act provided penalties for the breach of the licensing provisions. On the other hand, in *Devonport Corporation* v. *Tozer*,[5] the plaintiffs unsuccessfully asked for an injunction as well as a declaration that they were entitled to remove or pull down work done by the defendants in contravention of regulations by the local authority. The judgment, confirming the decision in *Ashborne's Case*, held that in the absence of a special private interest the action was maintainable only by the Attorney-General.

All these are English decisions. The only Australian decision in which an injunction was granted in similar circumstances, namely, to a Shire Council suing in place and in the position of the Attorney-General, is a New South Wales decision (*Council of the Shire of Hornsby* v. *Danglade*[6]). A few English decisions and practically all Australian decisions on the other

[1] [1903] 1 Ch. 101.   [2] [1902] A.C. 165.
[3] [1931] 1 Ch. 121.
[4] *Attorney-General* v. *Premier Lines* [1932] 1 Ch. 303.
[5] [1902] 2 Ch. 182; affirmed [1903] 1 Ch. 759.
[6] (1929) 29 S.R. (N.S.W.) 118.

hand, while accepting the principle that the Attorney-General can sue for an injunction as representative of the public interest, have refused such an injunction on a variety of grounds. A series of Australian decisions, including an important High Court decision, have refused injunctions in circumstances similar to those where English Courts have granted them. Two cases in particular reveal an Australian interpretation of the remedy which is far more restrictive than that of the English courts. In *Attorney-General* v. *Gill*[7] the Supreme Court of Victoria decided that the Attorney-General of Victoria could not maintain a suit for a prohibitive injunction restraining a landowner from proceeding with the erection of a building, in contravention of a municipal bye-law prescribing a residential area. The judgment of the court was delivered by Dixon A.J., as he then was. It rests mainly on the following grounds:

(a) It is not the function of a Court of Equity to prevent the commission of threatened crimes. Hence, in accordance with the decision of the House of Lords in *Institute of Patent Agents* v. *Lockwood*[8] a court should be reluctant to grant an injunction where the statute prescribed penal sanctions.

(b) The root of the equitable jurisdiction to grant an injunction is the protection of property. Where therefore the infringement of a local statute interferes with a private right and other legal remedies are insufficient, the court can grant an injunction on general equitable principles.

(c) Proprietary rights in this sense need not be exclusively vested in the individual. Rights enjoyed in common, such as the free and unrestricted passage of a highway or navigable river, constitute legally protected interests of the subject within equitable cognisance. The main conditions of intervention by a court of equity are therefore, firstly, the character of the interest, secondly, the sufficiency of the legal remedy, and thirdly, the irreparable nature of the threatened injury.

(d) The Attorney-General cannot obtain an injunction for the protection of interests vested in classes of people however extensive, as these are private rights. The court quotes with

[7] [1927] V.L.R. 22.
[8] [1894] A.C. 347.

approval the following statement of Isaacs J. in the *Union Label Case*:[9]

> ' If a public right is infringed, and the whole community is thereby affected, the Attorney-General may protect the public interests by appropriate action. He cannot intervene to protect a limited portion of the public which enjoy special rights. This does not mean that the actual wrong done or threatened must be detrimental in fact to more than a limited number of persons, nor, indeed, to any persons, but that the interest put in suit must be one enjoyed as of common right, and not one the title to the enjoyment of which consists of particular vestitive facts '.[1]

(e) The court admits that the Attorney-General has been successful in obtaining injunctions regarding for example the alignment of buildings on a street frontage; the uniformity in the width of a street,[2] the movable character of roads over a canal devoted to the public service,[3] and that the distinction between this type of interest and the general welfare which all these are intended to promote is not always easy. The court concludes, however, that the law which results from the exercise of the statutory power by a municipal council to prohibit commercial buildings in a certain residential area operates for the general advantage of the public at large not for the benefit of a class of persons cr a fraction of the public.

(f) This should lead to the conclusion that, in the case before the court, the Attorney-General and none other can sue; but surprisingly the court reaches the further conclusion that this public interest does not take the form of a ' positive interest susceptible of enjoyment by His Majesty's subjects as of common right '. Nothing analogous to an interest is created by the by-law, therefore equity cannot intervene.

Thus the Attorney-General can only intervene for the protection of the public as distinct from a proprietary or quasi-proprietary interest. But as public interests are not of a proprietary or quasi-proprietary character such as equity could protect the Attorney-General cannot sue. This leaves only

---

[9] (1908) 6 C.L.R. 469 at p. 557.
[1] *Per* Dixon A.J.
[2] *Attorney-General* v. *Wimbledon House Estate Co.* [1904] 2 Ch. 34.
[3] *Attorney-General* v. *North Eastern Railway* [1915] 1 Ch. 905.

a very limited class of cases for possible intervention by the Attorney-General. According to Dixon J. it would be confined to cases where the wrongful acts restrained tended ' to deprive the King's subjects of some definite positive advantage capable of specific enjoyment on the part of any of them '.[4] This would include such matters as the condition of the currency as an instrument of commerce, or the freedom of highways and waterways from the nuisance of obstruction, but not the interest of a resident in the observance of a local by-law. Even if one accepts this limitation, it is difficult to trace the borderline between ' positive advantages capable of specific enjoyment '—which admit of intervention by the Attorney-General, and ' interests vested in classes of people, however extensive ' which apparently are private rights and neither admit nor require such intervention.

The High Court of Australia, in *Ramsay* v. *Aberfoyle Manufacturing Company*,[5] came to similar conclusions though for rather different reasons. The judgment of Latham C.J. is mainly based on the reasoning that the statute in question— a by-law prohibiting the erection of a factory—was subject to statutory penalties, that it was not the function of the court of equity to enforce the law, that it was a function of the legislature and not of a court to decide on the proper sanction for breaches of the laws, and that the insufficiency of the statutory remedies to restrain a law-breaker was a matter for the legislature not for the court. Latham C.J., without openly dissenting, also criticised the decision of the Court of Appeal in *Attorney-General* v. *Sharp*:

' It appears to me that those principles are given a new application when a court decides that a penalty imposed by a statute is inadequate because it has not proved to be a deterrent in a particular case, with the result that an injunction is granted so that a further breach of the law will involve a contempt of court with consequent imprisonment. However, as I have said, the specific provisions for enforcement of this particular by-law distinguish it from such a provision as that which was under consideration in *Sharp's Case*, and in *Attorney-General* v. *Premier Line* '.[6]

---

[4] [1927] V.L.R. at p. 32.
[5] (1935) 54 C.L.R. 230.
[6] [1932] 1 Ch. 303.

A not very convincing distinction is drawn between the case before the court and the decisions in *Sharp's Case* and the *Premier Line Case*, in so far as the latter two dealt with statutes prescribing only a pecuniary penalty while in *Ramsay's Case* the council had the additional power to pull down or remove the offending building after due notice had been given. The main reason for the judgment of the Chief Justice is, however, revealed in the following passage:

'Upon this principle a court of equity would, in cases where the Attorney-General is a party, have a most extensive and hitherto unprecedented field of authority in securing observance of the law. Obedience to any ordinary public statute is a matter of concern to the public, but in my opinion the general interest of the public in the observance of the law is not in itself sufficient to justify the court in granting an injunction at the suit of the Attorney-General. I am not aware of any other authority which supports such a proposition stated in the general terms which have been quoted. *Prima facie* it is for Parliament to see that the remedies for breach of a statute are adequate to secure observance of the law, and it is not for any court of law or of equity to assume a general supervision, even at the suit of the Attorney-General, for the purpose of remedying what it regards as the defective machinery of a statute'.

The other majority judgments follow similar lines. The New South Wales decision in *Danglade's Case* [7] is distinguished though not openly dissented from; but a completely different note is struck in the dissenting judgment of Starke J. A survey of the English and Australian decisions leads Starke J. to the conclusion that:

The principle on which the equitable jurisdiction of English courts is exerted by way of injunction in the field of public law is ill-defined and difficult of statement.

But the decisions which have granted an injunction reveal, in the opinion of the learned judge, that the conditions stipulated in *Gill's Case* namely, the proprietary character or a positive interest susceptible of enjoyment as of common right are not necessary conditions of the remedy. The essential test, in the view of Starke J. is a 'provision enacted for the benefit of or in the interests of the public generally', such as provisions for

[7] (1929) 29 S.R. (N.S.W.) 118.

the public health or safety, or for the orderly arrangement of cities or towns, or for keeping public corporations created for particular purposes within the ambit of their powers. Led by these considerations Starke J. concludes that it is legitimate for the Attorney-General to decide that the statutory protection of the public law has proved insufficient and that he shall therefore invoke the protection of equity against the invasion of a public right.

While the majority judgments in *Ramsay's Case* and the decision of the Supreme Court of Victoria in *Gill's Case* strongly dissent from Starke J. in this wider though tentative interpretation of the ' notion of public interest ', the High Court has been much closer to the conception of Starke J. in the field of constitutional law. It makes liberal use of the notion of public interest for the purpose of admitting suits for declaratory judgments against proposed legislation. In a series of decisions, of which the *Potato Case*[8] and the *Pharmaceutical Benefits Case*[9] are representative, the court has consistently used the declaratory judgment to test the constitutional validity of federal legislation in regard to established individual rights. In the *Potato Case*, one Australian State sued another, but in the *Pharmaceutical Benefits Case*, the Attorney-General for Victoria intervened at the relation of a number of individual doctors, and successfully challenged the power of the Commonwealth to pass a Pharmaceutical Benefits Act. The admissibility of this action was not based upon the federal character of the constitution, that is to say, upon a conflict between State and federal legislation ' but upon the right, in some instances of the individual, and in other instances of the public or a section of the public, to restrain a public body clothed with statutory powers exceeding those powers ' (*per* Williams J.). The action is expressly linked with *Dyson's Case*, and the right of the Attorney-General to intervene is derived from the public interest: ' If the relief or advantage claimed is of such a nature that it does not specially affect them as individuals but only as members of the general public, then the Attorney-General is a necessary party to the

---

[8] *Tasmania* v. *Victoria* (1935) 52 C.L.R. 157.
[9] *Attorney-General for Victoria* v. *Commonwealth* (1946) 71 C.L.R. 237.

action' (*per* Williams J.). Reference is made to a recent and
rather little known decision of the House of Lords. In *London
Passenger Transport Board* v. *Moscrop*,[1] the respondent, an
omnibus driver in the service of the appellants, a public authority,
claimed a declaration that he was entitled to be accompanied
by an official of his own trade union. He was a member of a
minority union and appearing before a divisional superintendent
on a charge of an alleged breach of discipline. The House of
Lords dismissed the action on the ground that there was no
common law right to be represented by an official at all and that
the right to be accompanied by an official of the majority union—
the Transport and General Workers Union—rested upon a
special agreement between that Union and the employers. The
appellant, therefore, had no private right, nor had he suffered
special damage which, according to the decision in *Boyce* v.
Paddington Borough Council[2] would entitle him to sue. There is
one single and almost casual statement in the judgment of
Lord Maugham—with which Lord Wright concurred—to the
effect that an individual who did not fulfil the condition of
Boyce's Case 'could not sue without joining the Attorney-
General'.[3] It is this sentence upon which Williams J. relied in
the *Pharmaceutical Benefits Case*. The dictum implies that the
Attorney-General may sue—presumably at the relation of an
individual or without it—where such general principles are
involved as the freedom of the individual to choose his
own union or presumably an objection to compulsory union
membership which may follow from 'closed shop agreements'. The question whether the Attorney-General, as
guardian of the public interest, can intervene for the protection
of general freedoms which in Great Britain have no specific
legal or constitutional sanction is one of quite outstanding
importance. It deserves more than just a casual sentence which,
in *Moscrop's Case*, was only in the nature of a dictum. It is
true that Lord Maugham's judgment mentions the imaginary
case of a person residing in the parish asking for a declaration

---

[1] [1942] A.C. 332.
[2] [1903] 1 Ch. 109.
[3] [1942] A.C. at p. 345.

that persons residing in an adjacent parish were not entitled to a right of way over a neighbouring forest and points out that in the absence of a personal right of way such action was not maintainable. It may appear from the context that in such a case the Attorney-General might be entitled to intervene. Further cases mentioned by Williams J. in the *Pharmaceutical Benefits Case* yield no further enlightenment on the question what type of public interest would entitle the Attorney-General to intervene.

Apart from the above quoted passage in the dissenting judgment of Starke J. in *Ramsay's Case*, this question, of vital importance to the effective development of public law, remains shrouded in obscurity. It is clear from the foregoing discussion that the sole basis of any general function of the Attorney-General to be made a party to proceedings for the protection of certain ' public interests ' still rests solely upon a somewhat vague equitable jurisdiction. This dormant jurisdiction was unearthed in *Dyson's Case* to allow a declaratory judgment against the Crown as owner of a legal estate. In this capacity the Attorney-General represents the Crown as defendant. It is through him that the Crown must descend into the forum for the protection of certain interests of citizens. In the relator actions for injunctions the Attorney-General appears on the other hand as sole or co-plaintiff. There is no reason why, in appropriate circumstances, he should not sue for declaratory judgments as well. This is certainly implied in the judgment of Lord Maugham in *Moscrop's Case* (*supra*). In the above mentioned Australian constitutional cases, the Attorneys-General of States or the Commonwealth appear in fact as both plaintiffs and defendants. At this point, however, there is a decisive divergence in the interpretation of this type of remedy as between the English and Australian courts. The Court of Appeal, notably in *Sharp's* and the *Premier Line Cases*, has definitely abandoned the historical association of the injunction, as an equitable remedy, with the protection of property, and has invested it with the additional character of an ' ancillary remedy which is necessary to enforce public rights '.[4] The Australian cases, notably *Gill's Case*, limit the remedy to the protection of property or quasi-proprietary interests. As pointed out earlier, this practically eliminates the use of the remedy by the Attorney-General, either because of the logical dilemma of *Gill's Case*—the Attorney-General should only enforce public rights but he cannot enforce these because equity protects private property—or because of the tendency to regard statutory sanctions as exclusive. An entirely different attitude is taken by the Australian courts only where legislation with constitutional implications is concerned. In such cases they will entertain declaratory actions even to restrain legislation not yet in operation. English courts would not consider such actions, partly because of the different constitutional position of Parliament, and partly because of a different conception of the public interest.

But the question remains unsolved: ' What is a public interest? ' The overpowering effect of the common law tradition and the absence of a proper system of public law actions and administrative tribunals has retarded the proper elaboration of such a concept. The examples given by Starke J.[5] include firstly a variety of functions such as the maintenance of safety, sanitary or food regulations, the despoiling of public recreation grounds, or the infringement of by-laws.

---

[4] This development has gone somewhat further in American law. The Federal Declaratory Judgments Act (adopted in 1934, and revised in 1948) makes the declaratory judgment a general remedy available before any court of the United States, in a case of actual controversy within its jurisdiction. Some decisions have, however, limited the width of this statutory provision, by holding that the Act merely provides a new form of procedure for the adjudication of rights in conformity to known principles: *Colegrove* v. *Green*, 328 U.S. 552 (1946). The injunction, on the other hand, ' as a means of reviewing administrative action, is gradually moving away from its historical foundations in equity and is becoming a general utility remedy for use whenever no other form of review proceeding is clearly indicated ': Davis, 'Forms of Proceeding for Judicial Review of Administrative Action ' (1949) 44 Ill.L.R. 565. The injunction has, in the Federal courts, almost completely displaced certiorari as a means of reviewing administrative action. This is mainly attributed to the decision in *Degge* v. *Hitchcock* (229 U.S. 162 (1913)) which refused certiorari as a remedy for reviewing a fraud order issued by the Postmaster-General, as it was clearly an administrative action. The use of the injunction has reduced the importance of the vexed problem of ' quasi-judicial ' decisions. Unfortunately, the same has not happened in regard to the writ of Prohibition. (Cf. Davis, *loc. cit.*, p. 621).

[5] (1935) 54 C.L.R. 249, cf. above, p. 226.

The restraint of public corporations points to a second type of function which is indicated by some of the leading decisions in this field. In *London County Council* v. *Attorney-General*[6] the Attorney-General sued a public transport authority successfully at the relation of private competitors.

Again, in the *Pharmaceutical Benefits Case* the Attorney-General was the mouthpiece of the organised medical profession fighting social service legislation.

The interests of an organised group, such as doctors or bus operators, should not as such be described as a public interest, yet it is just and proper that in certain cases, the Attorney-General should intervene, either at their relation or without, in order to ascertain the limits of statutory powers of public authorities. In the mixed economy of both Britain and Australia, where public corporations and private enterprise operate side by side, their functions may easily overlap. A public airways corporation may wish to operate ancillary shipping lines. The Commonwealth-owned T.A.A. may consider a purely intra-State air service as 'incidental' to the proper establishment of inter-State services. Commercial broadcasting stations may challenge the exercise of the powers of the Australian Broadcasting Board. It is doubtful how far private interests could sue for declaratory judgments, injunctions or damages in these cases. The Attorney-General, in such situations, may be the proper authority to appear as a guardian of public policy at large to ascertain the respective legal spheres of public and private enterprise.

Finally, an even wider conception of the public interest is adumbrated by the above quoted decision of the House of Lords in *London Passenger Transport Board* v. *Moscrop*.[7] A workman or employee who loses the opportunity of employment because he refuses to join a union will find it difficult to bring a private action. If a collective agreement stipulates the closed shop, he has no contractual right to employment, nor will it be easy for him to establish a legally protected interest in the freedom of labour. Neither British nor Australian law embodies such specific guarantees. But freedom of trade is an established

[6] [1902] A.C. 165.
[7] [1942] A.C. 332.

principle of public policy, and it may well be that the casual observations in *Moscrop's Case* could be developed so as to constitute the Attorney-General as the guardian of vital freedoms, against monopoly practices by employers or employees' organisations, or against interference with other basic freedoms. It is only in the use of the injunction and, perhaps, the declaration, at the hands of the Attorney-General, that we can detect the development of a specific public law remedy in situations where a private person could not entertain any action. At the suit of a private person, an injunction will be granted only as an equitable aid to the common law; in other words, the plaintiff must have a legal claim or he will not get an injunction. He must be able to claim damages either for breach of contract, in tort, or for breach of a statutory duty owed to him. It is true that in *Leeds Industrial Co-operative* v. *Slack* [8] a divided House of Lords held that under Lord Cairns' Act the Court of Chancery had power to grant damages in lieu of an injunction even in a case where damage was only apprehended and could not therefore be given at common law. But this slight extravagance does not detract from the principle. If, for example, private airlines complain that a government airline has exceeded its powers by operating certain services, they will obtain an injunction only if they can prove that the statute in question created duties for their protection. This will be exceedingly difficult in the light of the decided authorities and the nature of the statutes, nor can there be any question of a breach of contract or a common law tort. It is possible that private citizens may, in such cases, obtain a declaratory judgment but *Moscrop's Case* makes it clear that even for a declaration they have to prove a special legal interest: it is only the Attorney-General as protector of the public interest who might claim an injunction.

CONCLUSIONS

The cautious extension of existing legal and equitable remedies for the purposes of public law is proceeding in a fashion characteristic of so much of English law. Instead of a systematic and scientific development of administrative law, there is a

[8] [1924] A.C. 851.

gradual and haphazard adoption of old remedies to new purposes. The present position may be summed up as follows:—

1. Public law usually provides for a penal sanction in the form of statutory fines for the violation of certain public law duties. This is often an inadequate protection.

2. Common law actions for damages and injunctions are increasingly available both for and against public authorities according to principles developed by the common law. This is limited however by the legal immunities and privileges of the Crown in so far as these still survive. A more general and fundamental indirect limitation is the scope of administrative discretion which will reduce the number of cases in which breach of legal duty by a public authority can be proved. This problem is illustrated in particular by *Kent* v. *East Suffolk River Catchment Board.* [9]

3. A declaratory judgment may serve to restrain public authorities including the Crown (represented by the Attorney-General) from transgressing the law. There is no reason in principle why the Attorney-General, as guardian of the public interest, should not act as plaintiff in such actions in order to elucidate certain legal problems of public interest, such as the extent of the powers of a public corporation. The Australian Attorneys-General have in fact repeatedly exercised this function in order to test the constitutional validity of certain statutes. This is to some extent the result of the Federal character of Australia. There is no reason, however, why an Attorney-General, whether in Britain or in Australia, should not bring a declaratory action, in addition to or in lieu of an injunction.

4. The injunction is developing into a powerful weapon in the hands of the Attorney-General as guardian of the public interest, in situations in which it would not be available to anybody else. But the extent to which it may thus develop is still very uncertain because of the obscurity which surrounds the notion of ' public interest '.

5. A more general use of declaratory judgment and injunction as public law remedies would also make it possible in most cases to dispense with certiorari and prohibition and thus reduce the

[9] [1941] A.C. 501. Cf. above, p. 175.

importance of one of the most vexed and disturbing problems
of modern administrative law, the need to define 'quasi-judicial'
as distinct from ' administrative ' actions of a public authority.

PART THREE

STATUTE LAW AND THE SOCIAL WELFARE STATE

CHAPTER 11

STATUTE LAW AND ITS INTERPRETATION
IN THE MODERN STATE

THE GROWING IMPORTANCE OF STATUTE LAW

A JUDGE as conscious of the interaction between legal and social developments as Lord Wright said, in a lecture delivered in 1937, that the bulk of ' the statutory portion of law . . . is now great and is growing, but such law is for the specialist and has little interest for the student of law save in so far as it illustrates principles of construction or save in so far as it indicates trends of social thought and policy, which may have repercussions on the attitude of judges when they deal with common law questions of kindred character '.[1]

Underlying this attitude is a lingering conception of the distinction between ' lawyers' law ' and ' political law '. The latter, both in the training and the outlook of the average lawyer, is remote and not infrequently suspect. The former is regarded as particularly the lawyers' concern. Can we agree with Lord Wright that the bulk of statutory law does not concern the student of law? There are two main reasons for doubt. In the first place, a glance at any modern law report shows that an increasing and, in many cases, an overwhelming proportion of decided cases is concerned with statute law, and notably with such pieces of legislation as Workmen's Compensation Acts, Rent Restriction Acts and taxation statutes. Mr. Justice Frankfurter, in a recent address,[2] said that the number of cases coming before the Supreme Court not resting on statutes was now ' reduced almost to zero '.

But there is a second factor of even greater importance. The assumption which has persisted in English legal thinking until recently, that the only law relevant to the ordinary lawyer

[1] *Legal Essays and Addresses*, p. 397.
[2] *Some Reflections on the Reading of Statutes*, Association of the Bar of the City of New York, vol. 2, No. 6 (1947).

is what comes before the ordinary law courts, is now more than ripe for relegation to the scrap heap. It is a legacy both of Dicey's identification of the rule of law with the common law courts, and of the definition of law as rules laid down by the law courts, put forward by Gray, Salmond and other leaders of the analytical school. Is it still possible seriously to argue that such Acts as the National Insurance Act, the Education Act, the National Assistance Act are not worthy of attention by the student of law, because they are operated by a mixture of administrative authorities and special administrative tribunals? The importance to the average citizen of this type of law, which is almost entirely statutory, is overwhelming.

The relative importance of statutory law has been further and vastly increased by the nationalisation of basic industries and the consequent embodiment in statutes of vast spheres of corporate economic and social activities. Today only the archaic concentration of legal training on such branches of the law, where statutes are at best consolidations or glosses on the common law, can make the gross neglect of a systematic study of statutory law and its interpretation explicable though not excusable.

Communities which live under a written constitution, such as the United States, Australia or Canada, should have a different attitude; for they live under the domination of a statute of the most general and sweeping character, far more powerful in its effect upon the life of the citizen than the codifications under which Continental States have lived for many years. Yet the experience of interpreting a constitution does not appear to have made any notable impact on the common law approach to ordinary statute law in these countries.

The distinction between lawyers' law and political law is becoming increasingly meaningless. Breaches of statutory obligations imposed by a multitude of social statutes may form the basis of common law actions. The operation of the acts governing nationalised industries may come before special administrative tribunals or—by way of applications for prerogative orders, or actions for damages or injunctions—before the ordinary courts. The distinction between the two types of

law has little more meaning than the distinction between
' legitimate ' and other spheres of State activity which still affects
so many modern legal decisions.[3]

The problem of the judicial interpretation of statute law is
by no means confined to common law countries. It has been
one of the favourite topics of juristic discussion on the Continent
for many years. There is only one notable difference. If it is
true, as has been attested by careful observers,[4] that English
judges have often tended to interpret statutes ' on the theory
that Parliament generally changes the law for the worse and
that the business of the judges is to keep the mischief of its
interference within the narrowest possible bounds ',[5] such an
attitude is not natural to judges whose work overwhelmingly
consists in the interpretation of codes. Apart from this difference
of approach, the problem is super-national and determined by
trends of legal thought and public policy rather than national
legal particularities.

THREE APPROACHES TO STATUTORY INTERPRETATION

Three types of legal approach to the interpretation of statutes
may conveniently be distinguished, both in Continental and
Anglo-American jurisprudence.[6]

The Pseudo-logical or Textbook Approach

The first is the analytical and pseudo-logical approach. It is
paramount in the current textbooks on the interpretation of
statutes.[7] In English jurisprudence the three main pillars of the
traditional interpretation of statutes are the literal rule, the
golden rule, and the mischief rule.[8] The literal rule says that,

---

[3] Cf. above, p. 210 ff.
[4] *E.g.*, Sir William Graham Harrison in (1935) *Journal of Society of Public Teachers of Law*, 34 *et seq.*
[5] Pollock, *Essays in Jurisprudence and Ethics*, p. 85.
[6] It is not intended here to give a summary of current maxims of statutory interpretation. For a most instructive combination of survey and criticism see Willis ' Statute Interpretation in a Nutshell' (1938) 16 Can. Bar Rev. 1. See also Allen, *Law in the Making* (3rd ed.), Excursus B, and Stone, *Province and Function of Law*, pp. 149–159, 193–201.
[7] *E.g.*, Maxwell, *Interpretation of Statutes* (9th ed., 1946); Odgers, *The Construction of Deeds and Statutes* (2nd ed., 1946).
[8] For a concise commentary on the operation of these rules see Willis, 16 Can. Bar Rev. 1.

if the meaning of a section is plain, it must be applied regardless of the result. The golden rule says that where the ordinary sense of the words would lead to some absurdity or inconsistency, the literal interpretation must be modified accordingly. The mischief rule expresses both the oldest and the most modern approach. Derived from *Heydon's Case* decided in 1587, it directs the interpretation of a statute in accordance with its general policy and the evil which it was intended to remedy. The social purpose of the statute must be found out in the light of the previous law, the specific defect unprovided for by that law, the specific remedy decided on by Parliament, and the true reason of the reform.

Even without the abundant illustration of contradictory judicial approaches to the interpretation of statutes, it is patent that these three rules cancel each other out. By emphasising either the one or the other, the judges can adopt a broad or a narrow approach, a reformist or a conservative attitude. The position is further confused by a number of apparently technical rules. The rule against the use of the history of a statute, which still prevails in the British legal systems, though not on the Continent and in the United States, is almost impossible to reconcile with the mischief rules of *Heydon's Case*; for it excludes the use of the main sources of reference for the evil which the legislature intended to cure. Another type of rule has a fallacious logic made more impressive by the use of a Latin formula. The use of *expressio unius est exclusio alterius* or, in the form more current in Continental jurisprudence, *argumentum e contrario*, gives a delusive comfort of logic. [9] An interesting illustration is afforded by a well-known Australian decision. In *Marks* v. *Forest Commission* [1] the schedule to a statute regulating the status of the Victorian Forest Commission laid down the conditions under which a contract was binding upon the commission. Lowe J., concerned with the question whether the commission was liable in tort for an injury caused by the negligence of one of its drivers applied the argument

---

[9] For some scathing comments on its fallacy, see Radin (1930) 43 Harv.L.R. 863, at pp. 873–874.
[1] [1937] V.L.R. 344.

of *expressio unius est exclusio alterius*. He argued that the deliberate regulation of the conditions under which the commission was liable in contract implied a legislative intention to exclude tortious liability. The conclusion may or may not be correct but it certainly does not flow from any compelling logical deduction. The use either of analogy or of the *argumentum e contrario* does not exclude the element of choice. It was possible to argue with equal logical force—and it is submitted with more justification—that the regulation of the conditions under which a public corporate body could enter into binding contracts in no way affected the question of tort. A contract means a deliberate commitment. Liability in tort flows from an unforeseen incident. A well-drafted statute on the status and functions of a public authority must lay down rules on the form and procedure of contractual commitments, but it is neither usual nor necessary to do the same for tortious liability. In other words, the deduction was correct only on the questionable assumption that the schedule intended to deal with both contract and tort.

Another type of guide to statutory interpretation, used extensively in current textbooks, elevates a particular social or political preconception into an absolute rule. The most important rule of this type is the presumption against encroachment on private rights. The rule is that statutes should be interpreted if possible so as to respect private rights, that doubtful sections should be construed in favour of the freedom of the individual and that proprietary rights should not be held to be taken away by Parliament without provision for compensation unless the legislature has so provided in clear terms.

'It is presumed, where the objects of the Act do not obviously imply such an intention, that the legislature does not desire to confiscate the property or to encroach upon the right of persons, and it is therefore expected that, if such be its intention, it will manifest it plainly, if not in express words, at least by clear implication and beyond reasonable doubt.' [2]

This kind of rule has aptly been described by Willis as 'a sort of fourteenth amendment', [3] corresponding to the elevation of

---

[2] *Maxwell* (9th ed.), p. 290.
[3] 16 Can.Bar Rev. at p. 23. Willis divides this presumption into four aspects: taking away a common law right, taking away property without

the 5th and 14th amendments in the American Constitution into absolute guarantees of private property against any encroachments of social legislation. In the absence of a written constitution similar tendencies in English law are very much weaker. It depends largely on the view of the court whether an intention of the legislature to interfere with private rights can be reasonably implied or not. The choice between different interpretations is merely shifted from one level to another. In many of the authorities quoted in support of the proposition it appears mainly as a rhetorical formula without influencing the decision itself.[4] In other cases the judges have made their choice using either one or the other part of the formula. Thus in *Colonial Sugar Refining Co.* v. *Melbourne Harbour Trust Commissioners*[5] the Privy Council applied the presumption in favour of non-encroachment on private property to exclude certain land from that presumed to have been acquired by a public authority.[5a] On the other hand in *Edgington* v. *Swindon Corporation*[6] the power of a local authority to construct street shelters was held to imply an intention of the legislature to restrict the adjacent property owner's right to a free frontage.

The related principle that statutes which impose pecuniary burdens are subject to strict construction in favour of the private citizen is of far greater practical importance. It has been responsible for a long judicial tradition of interpreting taxation acts against public authority, and in condoning attempts by taxpayers to use all conceivable loopholes in order to avoid taxation. The most famous statement of this judicial attitude is by Lord Sumner in *Levene* v. *Inland Revenue Commissioners*:

' They [*i.e.*, the taxpayers] incur no legal penalties and, strictly speaking, no moral censure if, having considered the lines drawn by the legislature for the imposition of taxes, they make it their business to walk outside them '.[7]

This is the expression of an ' inarticulate major premise ' to the effect that, in any conflict between private property and the

---

compensation, barring the subject from the courts, and interference with personal liberty (*loc. cit.*, pp. 20–23).
[4] *E.g.*, *Re Bowman* [1932] 2 K.B. 621, at p. 633.
[5] [1927] A.C. 343.
[5a] Cf. also the decision of the Supreme Court of Canada in the *Wheat Board Case*, discussed below, p. 258.   [6] [1939] 1 K.B. 86   [7] [1928] A.C. 217.

public interests secured by taxation, the former is valued more highly. The change of social conscience and the acceptance of a different conception of State functions has recently led to a decisive shift in judicial opinion. In *Latilla* v. *Inland Revenue*[8] the Lord Chancellor (Lord Simon) said:

' My Lords, of recent years, much ingenuity has been expended in certain quarters in attempting to devise methods of disposition of income by which those who were prepared to adopt them might enjoy the benefits of residence in this country while receiving the equivalent of such income, without sharing in the appropriate burden of British taxation. Judicial *dicta* may be cited which point out that, however elaborate and artificial such methods may be, those who adopted them are " entitled " to do so. There is, of course, no doubt that they are within their legal rights, but that is no reason why their efforts, or those of the professional gentlemen who assist them in the matter, should be regarded as a commendable exercise of ingenuity or as a discharge of the duties of good citizenship.'

Even more forceful is the language of Lord Greene M.R.:

' For years a battle of manœuvre has been waged between the legislature and those who are minded to throw the burden of taxation off their own shoulders on to those of their fellow subjects. . . . It would not shock us in the least to find that the legislature has determined to put an end to the struggle by imposing the severest of penalties. It scarcely lies in the mouth of the taxpayer who plays with fire to complain of burnt fingers '.[9]

More recently still, the Court of Appeal has twice given emphatic support to the avowed purpose of recent Finance Acts of fighting tax evasion.[1] On the other hand, the House of Lords, in a composition very different from that in *Latilla's Case*, regarded what was patently a tax evasion by the constitution of a trust abroad, as legal, on a technical construction of the terms, arrangement, ' settlement ', and ' beneficial enjoyment ' in the Finance Acts of 1936 and 1938. *Vestey's (Lord) Executors* v. *I.R.C.*, [1949] 1 All E.R. 1108.

These illustrations should be sufficient to show that the canons of statutory interpretation consist of a number of guides

[8] [1943] 1 All E.R. 265.
[9] *Howard de Walden* v. *Inland Revenue Commissioners* (1942) 25 Tax Cas. 121, at p. 134.
[1] *Congreve* v. *Inland Revenue Commissioners* [1947] 1 All E.R. 168, confirmed by House of Lords in [1948] 1 All E.R. 948, and in *Holt* v. *Inland Revenue Commissioners* [1947] 1 All E.R. 148.

which largely cancel each other out, of learned formulas giving a deceptive appearance of logic which only serves to conceal the choice between opposing conclusions of equal logical validity, and of inarticulate ideological premises which depend on personal predilections and on changing trends of public and social policy.

Current textbooks do little more than to mix these various recipes without any serious attempt at reconciling them. The following formulation in the last edition of the leading textbook on the subject speaks for itself:

' The tendency of modern decisions, upon the whole, is to narrow materially the difference between what is called a strict and a beneficial construction. All statutes are now construed with a more attentive regard to the language, and criminal statutes with a more rational regard to the aim and intention of the legislature, than formerly. It is unquestionably right that the distinction should not be altogether erased from the judicial mind, for it is required by the spirit of our free institutions that the interpretation of all statutes should be favourable to personal liberty, and this tendency is still evinced in a certain reluctance to supply the defects of language, or to eke out the meaning of an obscure passage by strained or doubtful influences. The effect of the rule of strict construction might almost be summed up in the remark that, where an equivocal word or ambiguous sentence leaves a reasonable doubt of its meaning which the canons of interpretation fail to solve, the benefit of the doubt should be given to the subject and against the legislature which has failed to explain itself. But it yields to the paramount rule that every statute is to be expounded according to its expressed or manifest intention and that all cases within the mischiefs aimed at are, if the language permits, to be held to fall within its remedial influence '.[2]

The first part of this statement tends to emphasise the ' liberal ' or ' beneficial ' as against the ' strict ' interpretation, leaving open the question of whose benefit is to be fostered by the interpretation. The middle part seems to answer this question by interpreting ' beneficial ', in all statutes other than penal statutes, as ' beneficial to the subject ' without differentiating between various types and purposes of statutes. This tendency is, however, qualified and possibly nullified by the conclusion that ' manifest intention ' and the mischief rule is to prevail ' if the language permits '.

---

[2] Maxwell, *Interpretation of Statutes* (9th ed., 1946), pp. 288–9.

This confusion and vacillation is fully reflected in many recent judgments. Some famous judges, like Sir George Jessel[3] or Lord Wright,[4] have tended to interpret the judicial function as one of active assistance in the progressive development of the law. They have therefore leaned against the prevalence of linguistic over policy arguments. This goes together with a disinclination to apply the strict doctrine of precedent to the judicial interpretation of statutes. On the other hand such judges as Lord Halsbury or Lord Sterndale have consistently expressed scepticism about the ' policy ' approach.[5] A practical expression of the strict approach is the oft-quoted decision of the House of Lords in *Ellerman Lines* v. *Murray*[6] where the House found itself compelled to interpret a British Act, adopted in implementation of an International Labour Convention, in defiance of the obvious purpose of the convention because the language of the Act did not permit the two to be reconciled. It should be noted however that the result was in this case beneficial to the ' under dog '. It was not dictated by socially reactionary views. Where the International Convention meant to guarantee to wrecked seamen two months' wages as compensation for unemployment caused through shipwreck, the decision gave them the right to obtain two months' wages from the date of the termination of their service even where the contract would normally have terminated a few days after the shipwreck. The opposite approach is apparent in a judgment interpreting another Act passed in implementation of an International Convention, the Maritime Conventions Act, 1911. The judgment of Scott L.J. in *The Eurymedon*,[7] apportioning damages in a case of ship collision, is specifically supported by the desire to maintain international unity in the interpretation of an Act implementing an international rule. A considerable number of modern decisions have adopted the social policy rule in interpreting a statutory rule containing phrases of general

---

[3] *E.g.*, in *River Wear Commissioners* v. *Adamson* (1876) 1 Q.B. 546.
[4] *E.g.*, in *Rose* v. *Ford* [1937] A.C. 826, at p. 846.
[5] Cf., *Hilder* v. *Dexter* [1902] A.C. 474, and *Scranton's Trustees* v. *Pearse* [1922] 2 Ch. 87, at p. 123.
[6] [1931] A.C. 126.
[7] [1938] P. 61.

social significance. Thus the House of Lords in *Summers* v. *Salford Corporation*[8] held that a house, protected by the Housing Act, 1936, in which one of the two windows had a broken sash cord was not ' fit for human habitation '. Yet a few years earlier Lawrence L.J. in *Morgan* v. *Liverpool Corporation*[9] had, in an identical case, declared such a view to be ' fantastic '. Occasionally, prejudice or expediency has driven the House of Lords to interpretations which distort the plain or ordinary meaning of the statutory clause in question. Two such cases have become famous for different reasons. In *Roberts* v. *Hopwood*[1] a statutory power given to local authorities to pay ' such salaries or wages as they . . . may think fit ' was interpreted by the House to mean ' may reasonably think '. By this judicial interpolation, the interpretation of reasonableness passed to the court which gave it a starkly biassed meaning, holding forth in no uncertain terms against the reasonableness of a minimum wage above the average, and even more against the equality of wages for male and female employees. Again history will probably regard the decision of the majority in *Liversidge* v. *Anderson*[2] as a concession to war emergencies.[3] In this case the majority did exactly the reverse of *Hopwood's Case*. It interpreted a clause in the Defence Regulation by which the Home Secretary had power to detain certain persons which he had ' reasonable cause to believe ' were of enemy origin or hostile associations, as meaning ' reasonable in the opinion of the Home Secretary '.

The Social Policy Approach

It is the vacillation between one type of interpretation and another, as applied to the increased tempo and urgency of modern social legislation, which has exasperated many legal critics. Dr. Jennings has given an illustration of the disastrous result to which these judicial vacillations rather than social prejudice have led in the case of public health legislation.[4] No

[8] [1943] A.C. 283.
[9] [1927] 2 K.B. 131.
[1] [1925] A.C. 578.
[2] [1942] A.C. 206.
[3] Cf., the recent decision of the Privy Council in *Nakkuda Ali* v. *Jayaratne*, discussed above, p. 159.
[4] Judicial Process at its Worst (1938) 1 M.L.R. 111.

less unfortunate has been the frequent obstruction of urgent
and unobjectionable housing improvement schemes, through the
judicial construction of the relevant orders and improvement
schemes as ' quasi-judicial ' even where the schemes were subject
to approval by higher authorities.[5] This has led a number of
modern critics to suggest an alternative principle of interpretation
which may be called the ' social objective ' principle. It has
been advocated among others by Laski,[6] Jennings[7] and Llewelyn
Davis.[8] Two arguments are adduced in support. Firstly, the
critics say that the prevailing rules of statutory interpretation
allow for diversity, vacillation and confusion. This is
undoubtedly correct. Secondly, they allege that the prevailing
tendency of courts is one of hostility to modern social reform
legislation. This contention is more doubtful.

As distinct from the history of the United States Supreme
Court, the cases in which British courts have used their judicial
power deliberately to frustrate a social purpose are not frequent.
Roberts v. *Hopwood* is probably the outstanding example. The
recent tendency of British courts has undoubtedly been one of
greater sympathy towards the social objectives of a statute.
Outstanding examples are the interpretation of the Road Traffic
Act, 1930, in favour of the third party whose compulsory
insurance was the intention of the Act,[9] a recent decision of the
Court of Appeal[1] which, refusing to surcharge Birmingham
City Councillors for a wartime children's allowance scheme,
expressed principles starkly contrasting with those of *Roberts*
v. *Hopwood*, the protection of the minimum standards to which
an indigent tenant must be held entitled in modern Britain,[2]
the many recent refusals of the House of Lords and the
Court of Appeal to hamper housing or town-planning policy

---

[5] Cf., in particular, *R.* v. *Electricity Commissioners* [1924] 1 K.B. 171, and
Estate and Trust Agencies v. *Singapore Improvement Trust* [1937] A.C.
898. Recent decisions show a sharp reversal of this attitude; cf., above
p. 170.

[6] Annexe 5 to Report of Committee on Ministers' Powers, 1932.

[7] ' Courts and Administrative Law ' (1936) 49 Harv.L.R. 426.

[8] (1935) 35 Col.L.R. 519.

[9] *Monk* v. *Warbey* [1935] 1 K.B. 75.

[1] *Re Decision of Walker* [1944] K.B. 644.

[2] *Summers* v. *Salford Corporation* [1943] A.C. 283.

by construing a ministerial decision as ' quasi-judicial ',[3] or the interpretation of the Statute of Westminster against the broad political purpose of granting full constitutional and political autonomy to the Dominions.[4]

Secondly, liberal as against social policy interpretation has not always been reactionary, as shown by the already quoted case of *Ellerman Lines* v. *Murray*.

Thirdly, the social objective policy sometimes has to be balanced against other legal or constitutional principles. The much-debated decision, for example, by which the House of Lords in *Minister of Health* v. *Yaffé*[5] held that a clause in the Housing Act under which ' the order of the Minister when made shall have effect as if enacted in this Act ' did not preclude the power of the court to hold the Minister's order to be *ultra vires*, was, in some of the judgments, coupled with a bias in favour of the house-owner as against public authority.[6] But the predominant concern of the House was with the constitutional problem of delegated legislation.

Fourthly, there are numerous statutory clauses which have no apparent or obvious social objective, but may nevertheless in a concrete case give rise to profound differences of social and political philosophy. Such a case is *Nokes* v. *Doncaster Amalgamated Collieries*.[7] The section of the Company Act which gives the court power to transfer, by statutory amalgamation, all the property and liabilities of one company to another and which defines property as including ' property rights and powers of every description ' is on the face of it of a highly technical character, and has no obvious policy behind it. Yet the section gave rise to one of the most important modern public policy decisions in English law when the House of Lords had to decide whether ' property ' included the services of miners and other employees. By a majority of four it held that the principle of

---

[3] Cf., in particular, *Johnson* v. *Minister of Health* [1947] 2 All E.R. 395, and *Franklin* v. *Minister of Town and Country Planning* [1948] A.C. 87.
[4] *British Coal Corporation* v. *The King* [1935] A.C. 500, and *Att.-Gen. for Alberta* v. *Att.-Gen. for Canada* [1947] A.C. 503.
[5] [1931] A.C. 494.
[6] Cf. the judgment of Scrutton L.J. in the Court of Appea land the dissenting judgment of Lord Russell in the House of Lords.
[7] [1940] A.C. 1014.

personal freedom of labour did not permit the compulsory transfer of employee's contracts in the course of amalgamation. Lord Romer, in his dissenting judgment, pointed out that it was futile to protect employees and workers in the relatively rare cases of amalgamation of companies while they were powerless in the far more frequent cases of changes of management or policy control through the acquisition of a controlling interest in a company, without change of legal identity.

Lastly, there are statutes with clauses so general and comprehensive that the definition of their policy is itself subject to the fluctuations of time and public opinion. This applies in particular to written constitutions, the problem of whose judicial interpretation in a democratic society—where the judiciary is neither compelled nor necessarily inclined to adjust its attitude to that of the current legislative or executive policy—has become increasingly complex and problematical, as shown by the history of the United States, Canada and Australia. The ' policy ' of a constitution designed to govern the life of a State, usually a Federal State, for many decades or even centuries, is itself a flexible conception. This gives rise to special problems of interpretation. [8]

It follows that the ' social policy ' interpretation, while an essential corrective to the pseudo-analytical interpretation, can at best only give a partial answer to our problem.

The ' Free Intuition ' Approach

A third school, despairing of any reliable objective rules to guide the judge in the interpretation of codes and statutes, advocates the use of free and creative intuition by the judge. In some ways this line of thought represents a more radical development of the social objective theory. It arose from the same revolt—initiated on the Continent by Ihering and Gény —against *Buchstabenjurisprudenz*, the exaggerated reverence for literal interpretation which usually goes hand in hand with a conservative philosophy. But this theory does not necessarily stop there. Its extreme exponents advocate the power of the judge to alter a statute where the results of literal interpretation

[8] Cf., further below, p. 253.

would be absurd or grossly unjust. Apart from Ehrlich, who advocated this approach as early as 1903, this school of thought found its most forceful exponents in Germany after the First World War, when a reactionary judiciary often enough defeated the purposes of republican legislation. [9] Some theoretical justification is lent to this view by the theory of the Vienna School of Jurisprudence which describes the judicial process as inherently creative, as being concerned with the making as well as the application of law. In American jurisprudence a counterpart is found in the views of some of the more extreme realists who discount legal principle and logical deductions altogether and see the solution in the free and creative handling of the concrete situations by adult and mature lawyers. [1]

The free intuition approach can however lead to very different results. In the hands of the Nazi regime it became a convenient way to dispense with legislative reform, while judges schooled in Nazi thinking or subject to rigid political pressure could distort existing statutes in the name of ' healthy instincts of the people '. There are obvious theoretical weaknesses in this approach. To admit that legal problems are infinite, that no codification or statutory regulation can preclude the element of choice or the weighing of social values and interests in the judicial process, does not mean that legal logic and rules are valueless. They are an important enough guide in the vast majority of routine cases. Jerome Frank has persistently argued [2] that the study of the law from the reports of the higher courts gives a completely misleading picture. But legal practice shows not only the importance of fact-evaluation but also the routine application of well-established precedents on such matters as maintenance, desertion, injury arising out of employment, warranty of authority, etc. They do not enter the law reports either, because

---

[9] Cf., Friedmann, *Legal Theory* (2nd ed.), pp. 235 ff.

[1] Mr. Justice Holmes, regarded by many realists as the personification of such a lawyer, was himself far from such an unorthodoxy except for certain over-popularised statements not borne out by his own judicial record. Radin seems close to the way of thinking described in the text when, despairing of the many delusive rules, he says that ' the sound sense of many judges will frequently penetrate this smoke screen and reach results that seem satisfactory, but it is often done half-consciously and almost surreptitiously ' (1930) 43 Harv.L.R. at p. 882.

[2] Cf., in particular, 'A Plea for Lawyer-Schools ' (1947) 56 Yale L.J. 1303.

they are applied as a matter of course. It is the marginal case and the novel situation in which judicial choice and uncertainty are decisive factors.

Comparative Evaluation of the Three Approaches

None of the three approaches just outlined can give the whole answer. The pseudo-logical approach is useful enough for the routine case. Such rules as the principles of literal and grammatical construction, the reading of a clause in the context of a whole statute, the *eiusdem generis* rule and others are convenient guides to the solution of the vast majority of routine and non-controversial problems, but they break down where there is a gap, where an apparently neutral clause necessitates a choice between values, or where the statutory term itself is so wide as to allow for the most divergent interpretations.

The social policy interpretation is an important corrective, increasingly so as social legislation grows in quantity and quality. But not all legislation is dictated by an easily definable social purpose. Modern Housing Acts have the definite purpose of improving housing standards and generally raising the standard of living of the poorer classes of the community. Law Reform Acts have the purpose of reforming a particular part of the law, such as the legal status of married women, or the rules on contributory negligence. An Act passed to implement an International Labour or Maritime Convention has the purpose of adapting national law to the international rule. In all these cases it is obviously right that the social purpose of the Act should be brought out and not defeated by the judiciary. But a vast number of statutes leave a choice of different social purposes. The clause of the Companies Act which was under discussion in *Nokes' Case* had no obvious relation to the principle of freedom of labour. The recent Nationalisation Acts in Britain, comprehensive as they are, give no indication as to whether public enterprise should be generally favoured at the expense of private enterprise or whether their functions should be interpreted restrictively. This depends on extraneous considerations. Most important of all, the written constitutions of the United States, Australia and Canada have obvious political and social purposes, but their content and direction change with succeeding generations and conditions, and with them the meaning of words changes too. The protection of persons against deprivation of life, liberty or property ' without due process ' (5th and 14th Amendments to the United States Constitution), the absolute freedom of interstate trade and commerce (section 92 of the Australian Constitution) had entirely different contexts in 1848, 1900 and 1950. Hence the importance of ' implications '.[3] Are federal constitutions to be read subject to the implication that the autonomy of States must be substantially preserved as against the encroachments of federal government ? Is the implication of the formal ' freedom of trade ' a constitutional protection against the restriction of the volume of trade between States, or is it a barrier against Socialism or State regulation ? Is ' due process ' a guarantee of fair trial and fair procedure or a protection of ' inalienable rights ' ? If a federal power to tax has, in 1950, economic, political and social implications entirely different from those conceived at the making of the constitution, must this power be subjected to an implied limitation ? If so, is the main guide to be the historical meaning given to the clause when it was enacted—or is the meaning to be gauged from contemporary trends and implications ? None of these questions has been conclusively resolved in any of the three constitutions mentioned. Nor can any help be derived from the textbook rules of statutory construction.

There is thus room for the free creative choice postulated by the free law theorists and the realists. It has found open though limited recognition in such clauses as section 2 of the Swiss Civil Code of 1907, which enjoins the judge to decide as if he were a legislator where he finds a gap in the statute before him. But absolute freedom of judicial choice would mean a surrender either to personal intuition or to purely political interpretations.

THE NEED FOR DIFFERENTIATION

In a free society, there is no master solution which could resolve the judicial dilemma. Totalitarian societies direct the judge to

[3] See Sawer (1948) 4 *Res Judicatae* 15, ss. 9.

decide in accordance with political principles laid down by his government, and they ensure his obedience by political and disciplinary pressure. The free judge has no such easy way out. His independence of changing legislative and executive trends is one of the few permanent essentials of democracy, yet he cannot isolate himself from the broad trend of political and social developments. Where judges have done so, as the majority of the United States Supreme Court have done between the middle of the 19th century and the early 1930's, the results have been socially disastrous.

The adult judge will have no illusions about the uncertainty of the situation and the frequent conflict of guiding principles. He must resolve such problems from case to case, yet a somewhat more differentiated guide and approach should be possible than has hitherto been assumed. The weakness of most theories of statutory interpretation lies in the assumption that all statutes are of the same type. A certain move towards differentiation has been made by Willis [4] in his distinction between social reform, penal and taxation statutes. It should however be carried further. The following is a preliminary and tentative attempt in this direction.

Differentiation of Statutes for Purposes of Interpretation
Constitutional statutes

In interpreting the British North America Act of 1867 Lord Jowitt L.C. in *A.G. Ontario* v. *A.G. Canada*,[5] like Lord Sankey in the earlier case of *British Coal Corporation* v. *The King*,[6] stressed the political character of the statute under consideration:

Giving full weight to the circumstances of the Union and to the determination shown by the provinces as late as the Imperial Conferences, which led to the Statute of Westminster, that their rights should be unimpaired, nevertheless, it appears to their Lordships that it is not consistent with the political conception which is embodied in the British Commonwealth of Nations that one member of that Commonwealth should be precluded from setting up, if it so desires, a Supreme Court of Appeal having a jurisdiction both ultimate and

[4] *Loc. cit.* above, p. 241, n. 3.
[5] [1947] A.C. 127, at p. 153.
[6] [1935] A.C. 500.

exclusive of any other member. . . . It is, as their Lordships think, irrelevant that the question is one that might have seemed unreal at the date of the British North America Act. To such an organic statute the flexible interpretation must be given which changing circumstances require, and it would be alien to the spirit, with which the preamble to the Statute of Westminster is instinct, to concede anything less than the widest amplitude of power to the Dominion legislature under s. 101 of the [British North America] Act.

The special character of constitutional documents has long been recognised. In the decision of the High Court of Australia on the legality of bank nationalisation,[7] Dixon J. quoted various well-known passages to that effect. Story said in his Commentaries: ' We should never forget that it is an instrument of government that we are to construe '. O'Connor J. in the *Jumbunna Case*[8] said: ' It must always be remembered that we are interpreting a Constitution, broad and general in its terms, intended to apply to the varying conditions which the development of our community must involve '.

The difference, for purposes of interpretation, between a Constitution and a Real Property or Trustee Act should be obvious. But what principles are to guide the flexible and dynamic interpretation of a constitution ? One alternative is the use of the parliamentary history of the constitution or any political statute to ascertain its meaning. It is however excluded from judicial consideration according to current canons of construction.[9] This has been attacked by many modern British jurists for it reduces a judge to a rough guess at what a study of the parliamentary history could tell him accurately.[1] But there is wisdom in the rule that the main meaning of a statute must be derived from its expressed content rather than from that indicated by parliament. Otherwise it would be impossible to use the parliamentary history—as is done widely on the Continent as well as in the United States—without tying the judge to a static and purely historical interpretation. Would

---

[7] [1948] A.L.R. p. 89.

[8] 6 C.L.R. 637.

[9] Cf. Maxwell *op cit.*, pp. 27 *et seq.*

[1] The different judgments in *Liversidge* v. *Anderson* [1942] A.C. 206, provide an excellent illustration of a thinly disguised reference to parliamentary history.

such an interpretation be desirable ? It may be said that the judge can never be more than a half-way reformer and that to bring out the inadequacies of an antiquated statute would serve to hasten legislative reform, which is the only method of legal reform appropriate to a democratic system. It would moreover be hasty to assume that a dynamic and flexible interpretation of a constitution is necessarily progressive while a static and historic interpretation is reactionary. The ' due process ' clauses of the 5th and 14th Amendments of the American Constitution assumed a dangerous and reactionary aspect only when the Supreme Court, from the middle of the 19th century onwards, proceeded to convert these clauses from guarantees against arbitrary procedure into constitutional guarantees of private property and private enterprise. Again, the Australian High Court, by means of a flexible interpretation, has given an increasingly widening meaning to the enumerated legislative powers of the Commonwealth, for example on taxation, defence and industrial arbitration, but it has largely cancelled the effects of this interpretation by the elevation of section 92 of the Constitution, which guarantees absolute freedom of trade, commerce and intercourse among the States, into something approaching a ' natural right ' guaranteeing freedom from State regulation of trade and commerce.[2] Finally, dynamic interpretation may lead to conflicting results. In the recent *Saratoga Springs Case*[3] the majority affirmed the federal power to tax State enterprises. The minority denied that power in the name of the principle of State sovereignty, but both majority and minority judgments agreed on the expanding functions of government and discarded the older conception that only traditional functions of the State are ' legitimate '.

Neither the historical nor the dynamic approach to a constitution will therefore necessarily solve the problem of interpretation of constitutions. On balance, however, a strictly static and historical interpretation is the greater evil.

[2] Cf. *James* v. *Commonwealth* (1936) 55 C.L.R. 1. And the *Bank Nationalisation Case* [1948] A.L.R. vol. 2, pp. 89.
[3] 326 U.S. 572 (1946). Cf. above, p. 211.

Where a constitution is fairly easy to amend, or where the validity of a statute is not strictly subject to a written constitution —as is the case for example in Switzerland—this approach might be commendable. In fact, however, Constitutions, especially federal Constitutions which matter most in this connection, are exceedingly difficult to amend, as shown by the history of both the American and Australian Constitutions and of the British North America Act. The petrifaction of the meaning of such a term as ' freedom of trade ' or ' banking ' or ' commerce ' is therefore apt to lead to very serious situations and to be repugnant to all but the most rigid and conservative judicial minds. A predominantly political document must be interpreted flexibly and general terms used in it must be understood in the light of changing social and political developments. The constitution sets into motion as it were a ' creative evolution ' (Bergson). ' Commerce ' in 1951 is not what the fathers may have meant in 1778 but what it means today.[4] ' Defence ', as the courts both of Australia and the United States have recognized, must be understood in terms not of 18th century but of 20th century war.[5] Obvious limits are set to a dynamic interpretation. A federal constitution, such as the Australian Constitution, which enumerates specific federal legislative powers cannot be stretched, even by the most flexible and ' dynamic ' judicial interpretation, so as to legalise the nationalisation of all industry, which in Great Britain would be a matter of a simple statute. It would be all the more regrettable if judges interpreting a constitution should be held to a strict historical interpretation. Despite notable exceptions, the vast majority of judges have no wish to live a century behind the times. A rule which would compel them to interpret a constitution so as to vitiate necessary social and economic changes would discourage many of the finest lawyers and citizens from judicial activity. Whatever a court called upon to interpret a written constitution may do,

---

[4] Cf., *Bank of New South Wales* v. *Commonwealth* (*Bank Nationalisation Case*) [1948] 2 A.L.R. 89, 157.

[5] Cf., *Korematsu* v. *U.S.* (1944) 323 U.S. 214, affirming the power of Congress to legislate for the removal of all persons of Japanese ancestry from a certain area in California; *Reid* v. *Sinderberg* (1944) 68 C.L.R. 504, affirming the validity of manpower control as an exercise of Commonwealth Defence Power.

it will be exposed to criticism either from the Left, for being reactionary and perpetuating out-of-date ideologies, or to criticism from the Right for being subservient to the government of the day. The Supreme Court of the United States has, for the better part of a century, successfully retarded elementary social legislation. During the last ten years its policy has been radically reversed. It now takes a more elastic view of the functions and purposes of government, and it is therefore suspect to a strongly conservative Congress as well as to the advocates of racial and religious discrimination. No magic formula can give a way out of this dilemma, but the tension can be more easily reduced by a flexible than by a static interpretation.

Social purpose legislation

A steadily growing proportion of modern legislation consists of statutes passed for a specific social purpose. Among recent British statutes, the National Insurance Act, 1946, the National Health Service Act, 1946, the Education Act, 1944, and the National Assistance Act, 1948, are obvious examples. The nature and direction of the social purpose can be easily ascertained by a variety of means. An application of the principle of *Heydon's Case*, supplemented where necessary by a study of the parliamentary history of the statute, will usually show the mischief against which the Act is directed. This is often reinforced by a brief description of the scope of the Act in the title,[6] occasionally by preambles or—more frequently in modern statutes—by specific ' purpose ' clauses in the Act itself, as well as by statutory definitions and authoritative interpretations which narrow the scope of judicial freedom.

Thus the Education Act in section 1 directs the Education Minister ' to promote the education of the people of England and Wales and the progressive development of institutions devoted to that purpose, and to secure the effective execution by local authorities (a), under his control and direction (b), of the national policy for providing a varied and comprehensive

---

[6] Writing from long practical experience, a former first Parliamentary Counsel to the Treasury, Sir W. Graham Harrison, has recommended reference to the title of an Act as a legitimate and desirable aid to judicial construction: [1935] J.S.P.T.L. 9 *et seq.*

educational service in every area '. The National Health Service Act (section 1) similarly directs the Minister of Health ' to promote the establishment in England and Wales of a comprehensive health service designed to secure improvement in the physical and mental health of the people of England and Wales and the prevention, diagnosis and treatment of illness, and for that purpose to provide or secure the effective provision of services in accordance with the following provisions of this Act '. The National Assistance Act (section 2 (2)) directs the National Assistance Board to exercise its functions ' in such manner as shall best promote the welfare of persons affected by the exercise thereof'. Statutory interpretations define the meaning of such terms as ' dependant ', ' disabled persons ', ' hospital', ' contract of service '. The series of Acts nationalising basic industries in Britain still show certain inconsistencies in drafting which are difficult to justify, but on the whole the use of standard terms, of identical formulas for identical conceptions, goes far to ensure a greater uniformity of legislative technique and to reduce the haphazardness of legislative terms.[7]

Such guides help the judge to arrive at interpretations such as that adopted by the House of Lords in *Summers* v. *Salford Corporation*.[8] In Acts of this type the presumption in favour of protection of private rights should be entirely and mercilessly scrapped. They fulfil State functions completely at variance with these earlier and vague presumptions. Interference with private rights is an avowed and unavoidable purpose of this legislation, and where the words leave any doubt its interpretation should not be hampered by extraneous presumptions.

Failure to appreciate such factors is responsible for the decision of the Supreme Court of Canada in the *Canadian Wheat Board Case*.[9]

The issue was the constitutionality of a post-war Order-in-Council which aimed at letting the nation rather than individual

---

[7] For an interesting and important example see the definition of control of a body corporate by another body corporate in all the recent Acts, *e.g.* Sched. 13 to Transport Act, 1947. This is a problem of great practical and theoretical importance.   [8] [1943] A.C. 283.

[9] *Canadian Wheat Board* v. *Hallet & Carey*; *Att.-Gen. of Canada* v. *Nolan* [1951] 1 D.L.R. 466.

dealers reap the large profits resulting from the difference between the controlled war-price and the decontrolled post-war prices for barley, by vesting in the Wheat Board all barley in the hands of commercial dealers at a certain date and directing the Board to pay the dealers the old controlled price. The Order was based on the National Emergency Transitional Powers Act, 1946, which gave the Governor in Council power to ' make from time to time such . . . regulations as he may, by reason of the continued existence of the national emergency arising out of the war against Germany and Japan, deem necessary or advisable for the purpose of

(c) maintaining, controlling and regulating . . . prices; or
(e) continuing or discontinuing in an orderly manner, as the emergency permits, measures adopted during and by reason of the war '.

The War Measures Act, which this Act succeeded, had given an express power to make regulations as to the appropriation, control, forfeiture and disposal of ' property '. From the absence of any such specific provision in the National Emergency Transitional Powers Act, the majority deduced a difference in substance, and lack of power to expropriate. The arguments of the majority are instinct with the assumption that this, like any other legislation, must be interpreted in favour of the integrity of private property. Both majority and minority were able to throw technical rules of statutory construction into the battle. The conflict was one of approach, of principles rather than technicalities of interpretation.[1]

Specific reform statutes

Where a statute sets out to reform a particular branch of the law, interpretation should be relatively simple, and where it has not been so it has generally been the fault of the judges. *Hyams* v. *Stuart King*[1a] is a deplorable example of judicial frustration of the obvious purpose of an Act. The majority

---

[1] This was fully brought out in the subsequent discussion of the case. Cf. Willis (1951) 29 Can. Bar Rev., 296–304, 580–585; Kent Power and Fillmore (1951) 29 Can. Bar Rev. 572–578.
[1a] [1908] 2 K.B. 696. This decision is now overruled by *Hill* v. *William Hill (Park Lane) Ltd.* [1949] A.C. 530.

judgment of the Court of Appeal held that a promise by the loser of a wager—unenforceable under the Gaming Act, 1845—to pay in consideration of the winner not denouncing him publicly was enforceable. The decision—from which Fletcher Moulton L.J. dissented in a powerful judgment—is not even justifiable by any of the traditional rules of construction. The various Law Reform Acts, passed in recent years in implementation of recommendations by the Law Revision Committee, afford good illustrations. The proper judicial approach to statutes of this type was formulated by Lord Wright in *Rose* v. *Ford*,[2] where he criticised the Court of Appeal for a tendency common in construing an Act which changes the law, that is to minimise or neutralise its operation by introducing notions taken from or inspired by the old law, which the words of the Act were intended to abrogate and did abrogate. The object of these Acts is generally clearly defined against the background of previous statutes or common law. Thus the Law Reform (Contributory Negligence) Act, 1945, obviously aims at the abolition of the common law rule which did not allow for apportionment of damage between two negligent parties.[2a] The British Crown Proceedings Act, 1947, is designed to put the Crown in principle on the same legal footing as any other legal person ' where any person has a claim against the Crown '. This is apparent from an examination of the previous state of the law, from the parliamentary history of the statute, and from its obvious context. The Act expresses this principle, first by substituting a claim as of right for a Petition of Right; and, secondly, by subjecting the Crown ' to all those liabilities in tort to which if it were a private person of full age and capacity, it would be subject ' (in respect of three broad categories of tort). The question might well arise as to the availability of a remedy in quasi-contract which in English law is not properly provided for. An earlier case[3] denied a Petition of Right to a plaintiff suing the Crown

---

[2] [1937] A.C. 826. The conclusion in the concrete instance, *viz.*, the award of damages for the loss of expectation of life or happiness, is more doubtful.

[2a] A note in (1948) 64 L.Q.R. 308 on *Almeroth* v. *Chivers Ltd.* [1948] 1 All E.R. 53, discusses the dictum in a recent decision by the Court of Appeal which would defeat this very object.

[3] *Brocklebank* v. *R.* [1925] 1 K.B. 52.

for recovery of money wrongfully obtained by a servant of the Crown. Whether or not this view has been implicity repealed by the House of Lords in a later decision[4] is doubtful. As the Act aims at the abolition of the privileges of the Crown in litigation—subject to specified exceptions—future decisions should have little difficulty in holding that a quasi-contractual claim, although not strictly provided for by the sections of the Act dealing with contract and tort, is enforceable as a matter of right.

Acts implementing International Conventions

This is a closely related category. The general objective in the interpretation of such Acts has been clearly stated by Scott L.J. in *The Eurymedon*.[5] As Sir W. Graham Harrison has urged, there is no reason why the text of the International Convention, if reproduced in the schedule, should not be resorted to in aid of interpretation. Where the clear wording of an Act deviates from the apparent purpose of an Act designed to implement an International Convention, it is, however, difficult to avoid the conclusion reached by the House of Lords in the *Ellerman Lines Case*, unless the application of the golden rule should be justified.

Penal statutes

The theory is still that penal laws should be construed strictly in favour of the subject. As pointed out in *Maxwell*[6] the rule has lost much of its force since the times when the cutting down of a cherry tree or begging by a soldier was punishable by death. The most important aspect of the rule is the presumption in favour of *mens rea* as a condition of criminal liability. A steadily increasing proportion of modern penal legislation is administrative in character. It imposes fines or other penalties which increasingly affect corporate bodies rather than individuals, as a means of ensuring, for example, the maintenance of certain standards of food, sanitation, safety provisions in factories. Such legislation is essentially of a social service character, and it is

[4] *United Australia Ltd.* v. *Barclays Bank* [1941] A.C. 1; cf. Street in (1948) 11 M.L.R. at p. 132.
[5] See above, p. 245.
[6] *Interpretation of Statutes*, 9th ed., p. 267.

penal in a sense very different from that of the common law offences. Moreover the presumption is doubtful in its application even in common law cases, as shown by the conflicting decisions on bigamy where the accused reasonably believed in the death of the first spouse.[7] The presumption is still justified in the case of common law crimes, whether consolidated by statute or not, but it should be discarded in the case of modern statutory offences unless they clearly require *mens rea* and are, at bottom, public law remedies, sanctions for the enforcement of administrative law.[8] In a very recent decision, the Court of Appeal[9] in interpreting the Finance Act, 1943, enabling the Crown retrospectively to levy an excess profits tax on certain types of extremely objectionable tax evasions, emphatically repudiated the suggestion that, in an Act of this type, *mens rea* had to be proved by the Crown. In other words, in the case of penal laws, as of other categories of legislation, there are statutes and statutes.

Taxation Acts

In English law at any rate, the presumption that taxation Acts should be construed in favour of the taxpayer is now very doubtful, as shown by much recent judicial authority.[1] Taxation Acts too are now regarded as social purpose Acts of a special type. Taxation has ceased to be regarded by most courts[2] as an impertinent intrusion into the sacred rights of private property and it is now rightly regarded as a vital instrument of State policy in securing a proper balance between the citizen's claim to the enjoyment of his property and the social purpose of assisting the provision of essential social services, through the equitable distribution of burdens in the community. This does not, of course, mean that courts should invariably assist the State against the taxpayer. A vast number of taxation problems turn on technical points, on the interpretation of such

---

[7] Cf. Willis, *loc. cit.*, pp. 424–5.
[8] Cf. above, p. 106 ff.
[9] *Holt* v. *Inland Revenue Commissioners* [1947] 1 All E.R. 148.
[1] Cf. above, pp. 242–43.
[2] But see *Vestey's Case* (above p. 243) for a recent reaffirmation of the former approach by the House of Lords.

terms as ' excess profits ' or ' income from investments ', which are determined mainly by technical, legal, financial and economic considerations. The courts have, however, now often adopted an approach similar to that laid down in the German Fundamental Tax Law of 1919, which directs the courts to bear in mind the purpose and economic significance of the tax statute and to frustrate attempts to avoid tax liability by the abuse of legal powers and constructions.[1] Avoidance of tax is now seen as an improper advantage gained by an individual taxpayer at the expense of the community. Modern Finance Acts often state the specific purpose of frustrating a certain type of tax evasion made possible by the earlier state of the law. In the interpretation of these Acts, the courts apply the principles of *Heydon's Case*. The mischief and the defect of the former law as ascertained and the reason for the remedy applied by the legislature are examined.

Predominantly technical statutes

For the multitude of statutes, or of statutory clauses which have a predominantly technical meaning, the technical rules of interpretation will generally suffice. A perusal of any recent volume of law reports will show that cases which require an interpretation of predominantly technical terms and which are not concerned with ideologies or social purposes prevail. Recent cases have for instance turned on the interpretation of ' act of bankruptcy ' and ' carrying on business ' under the Bankruptcy Act of 1914; the inclusion of an electric tram car among the vehicles subject to certain penal provisions under the State Carriages Act, 1832; the meaning of ' assurance ' for the purposes of section 87 of the Education Act, 1944; the definition of right of action which accrued to a wife before marriage as a ' thing in action ' under the Married Women's Property Act, 1882; the meaning of ' possessed of or entitled to ' for the purposes of the Administration of Estates Act, 1935; the meaning of ' income

---

[1] A close legislative parallel is sec. 126, Canadian Income Tax Act, 1948: ' When the Treasury Board has decided that one of the main purposes for a transaction . . . was improper avoidance of income tax, the Treasury Board may give such directions as it considers appropriate to counteract the avoidance '.

from an investment' for the purposes of the Finance (No. 2) Act, 1939. But as shown in the case of *Nokes* v. *Doncaster Collieries*, an apparently technical section may give rise to deep social or political issues. The judge is then faced with the general problem of the judicial function. The problem here is not different from that of the creative development of precedent.[2]

CONCLUSIONS

1. The steadily growing predominance of statute law in the legal life of modern communities is still insufficiently appreciated in the judicial approach to statute law as well as in legal education. A more systematic study of the principles of statutory construction is of vital importance.

2. The traditional rules of statutory interpretation as discussed in the current textbooks disguise the wide element of judicial discretion inherent in the non-logical choice between the many different and contradictory rules.

3. Broadly, there are three types of approach to the interpretation and construction of statutes. Firstly, the pseudo-logical or analytical approach represented in current textbooks; secondly, the 'social purpose' approach favoured by modern critics of the judicial attitude towards modern social legislation; thirdly, the 'creative intuition' approach favoured by critics who despair of the possibility of rational rules of construction and see the only hope in a free and creative judicial intuition.

4. None of these approaches is in itself sufficient. The analytical approach provides useful guides for the routine case but fails entirely in the solution of new situations or marginal problems which are quantitatively limited but qualitatively all important. The social policy approach offers reasonably clear guidance only for the construction of those statutes which have a clear and definite social objective. The free intuition approach opens the way to uncertainty, prejudice and 'inarticulate major premises'.

[2] On this complex problem, see the classical studies of Cardozo, *The Nature of the Judicial Process* (1921); Pound, 'The Theory of Judicial Decision' (1923) 36 Harv.L.R. at p. 958. For recent discussions see Stone, *Province and Function of Law*, chap. VII; Friedmann, *Legal Theory* (2nd ed.), chap. 24.

5. While there is no magic guide to the proper interpretation of statutes, a differentiation between various types of statutes should greatly assist an intelligent and rational approach to statutory construction. The main categories of statutes which ought to be distinguished for this purpose are: firstly, constitutional statutes; secondly, statutes implementing a specific social objective; thirdly, statutes carrying out specific legal reforms; fourthly, acts implementing international conventions; fifthly, penal statutes; sixthly, taxation statutes. This leaves a large proportion of predominantly technical acts in the interpretation of which a judge must be guided by the same principles as in the creative development of precedent.

CHAPTER 12

STATUTE LAW AND THE PRIVILEGES
OF THE CROWN

Is there any reason for the continued exemption of the State—
i.e., of governmental departments and of incorporated public
authorities which are covered by the ' shield of the Crown '[1]—
from the binding force of statutes of general application ? The
desire to extend equality before the law as far as compatible
with the necessary minimum of governmental and administrative
discretion should, one might have thought, have led the courts
to the utmost restriction of this privilege of the Crown except
where overriding interests of public policy demanded its
preservation. But it is not without irony that the English and
Australian law courts, which have shown great sensitiveness
to the growth of administrative power, and which have sometimes,
in the desire to restrict it by the prerogative jurisdiction of the
High Court, extended the notion of ' quasi-judicial ' to very
dangerous lengths,[2] should have moved in entirely the opposite
direction on the question of the binding effect of statutes on the
Crown.

THE CONFLICT OF TEXTBOOK RULES

The textbook rules on this matter are conflicting.[3] One rule
says that

' It is presumed that the legislature does not intend to deprive
the Crown of any prerogative, right or property, unless it expresses
its intention to do so in explicit terms, or makes the inference
irresistible '.

This rule, deriving as it does from the supremacy of the King
in the pre-democratic age, is of respectable antiquity.[4] But the

---

[1] On this problem see my articles ' Legal Status of Incorporated Public
Authorities ', 22 A.L.J. 7, and ' The Shield of the Crown ', 25 A.L.J.,
also above, p. 209 ff.
[2] As, for example, in *R.* v. *Electricity Commissioners* [1924] 1 K.B. 171,
cf. above, p. 169.
[3] Cf. Maxwell, *Interpretation of Statutes,* (9th ed.), p. 141.
[4] *Willon* v. *Berkeley* (1562) Plowden 236.

other rule is hardly less respectable: the rule that the King is not bound unless he is specially named, or must be included by necessary implication, does not apply

' when the Act is made for the public good, the advancement of religion and justice, the prevention of fraud, or the suppression of injury and wrong; " for religion, justice, and truth are the sure supporters of the crowns and diadems of kings " '.[5]

With the development of legislative activities the exception was either bound to swallow the rule, or the meaning of the exception had to be whittled down. Except for the dwindling number of private Acts, hardly any modern statute could fail to come under one or the other of the categories mentioned in the rule of the *Ecclesiastical Persons Case*. The last war, with its numerous defence or national security regulations, in particular those giving protection to tenants, brought the problem repeatedly before the courts. Instead of welcoming this opportunity of eliminating or at least reducing the scope of an inequality between governors and governed, perhaps even more objectionable than the now abolished privileges of the Crown in common law, the courts did the reverse. In *Att.-Gen.* v. *Hancock*,[6] Wrottesley J. held that the Crown was not bound by the Courts (Emergency Powers) Act, 1939, under which execution of judgments was not permitted without the leave of the court. He surveyed a number of previous decisions, the majority of which had declared the Crown exempt under comparable statutes. Although the learned judge, at the beginning of his judgment, clearly said that the original reason for the exemption of the King hardly applied to modern conditions, he was content to give as the main reason for his decision that ' this Act of 1939 is an Act which, if applied to the Crown, would clearly divest it of or diminish in some way, the Crown's property, interests, or rights '. If, in *Hancock's Case*, it could at least be said that the recovery of income tax arrears was a public interest, weighing more heavily than the war-time protection of debtors, such considerations do not apply to the later decisions. In *Re Hutley's*

[5] *Case of the Ecclesiastical Persons* (1601) 5 Rep. 14a; *Magdalen College Case* (1616) 11 Rep. 70b, 73a; *R.* v. *Armagh* (*Archbp.*) (1722) Stra. 516; Bac.Ab. Prerogative (E) 5.
[6] [1940] 1 K.B. 427.

Legal Charge,[7] recovery of possession of mortgaged farm land by the Public Works Loan Commissioners was the issue. In *Minister of Works (W. A.)* v. *Gulson*,[8] the Australian High Court was concerned with the ejectment of a tenant, a sergeant of police, from premises held on a weekly tenancy, and let to him by the Minister of Works under the Public Works Act. By a majority, the court held that the National Security (Landlord and Tenant) Regulations did not bind the Crown.[9] It is, however, the most authoritative of the recent decisions on this point which is also the most objectionable. In *Province of Bombay* v. *Municipal Corporation of Bombay*,[1] the Privy Council held that an Act of the City of Bombay which gave it power to carry municipal drains through certain streets, roads, and land, did not bind the Province of Bombay, then a part of the Crown. The judgment, which was delivered by Lord du Parcq, had little more to say in support of its decision than ' that to interpret the principle '—*i.e.*, that the Crown cannot be held to be bound by statutes enacted for the public—' in the sense put on it by the High Court would be to whittle it down, and they could not find any authority which gives support to such an interpretation '.

PUBLIC POLICY AND JUDICIAL INTERPRETATIONS

When faced with conflicting or ambiguous rules, the courts have frequently recourse to considerations of public policy or general justice, sometimes in situations far more dubious than the present one.[2] It is difficult to understand why they have so conspicuously missed an opportunity of moulding the law in accordance with principles of legal policy which are above party controversy.[3] Socialists may regard the reduction of Crown immunities and prerogatives as a price to be paid for the socialisation of industries

---

[7] [1941] Ch. 369.
[8] [1944] Argus L.R. 349.
[9] Similar decisions have been given under the English Rent Acts: see, *e.g.*, *London County Territorial and Auxiliary Forces Association* v. *Nichols* [1949] 1 K.B. 35.   [1] [1947] A.C. 58.
[2] For a survey of decisions and developments see Friedmann, *Legal Theory* (2nd ed.), chap. 23, especially pp. 285–305. Stone, *Province and Function of Law*, pp. 494–504.
[3] The Crown Proceedings Act, 1947, for example, was supported by all parties.

and other extensions of governmental activity in the planned State; Conservatives may regard it as a necessary safeguard for the citizen against the arbitrary encroachments of bureaucracy, and as a guarantee for fair competition between public and private enterprise. But both philosophies arrive at the same conclusion. Why should a government department which owns land be exempt from an obligation to lay drains which serve agricultural or sanitary purposes ? Why should a State housing commission be exempt from the building regulations of a local authority ?[4] The ordinary citizen is bound to feel resentment against such differentiations. Thanks to the line taken by the courts, he may come to regard the State as landlord with particular apprehension. Again, it is hardly encouraging for local authorities to watch government departments, or any other public authorities protected by the ' shield of the Crown ', flouting the standards or obstructing the services which the local authorities are developing within their sphere. Nor are the decisions based on any contrary legal philosophy or policy. They are distinguished by the absence of any guiding principles. Such a guiding principle may well be derived from a version of the traditional rule as adopted in *Craies on Statutes* [5] from various older sources and repeatedly used by Australian courts.[6] It says that the King cannot be stripped by a statute, which does not specifically name him, ' of any part of his ancient prerogative, or of those rights which are incommunicable and are appropriated to him as essential

---

[4] Such was the decision of the Supreme Court of N.S.W. in *N. Sydney Council* v. *Housing Commission* (1948) 48 S.R. (N.S.W.) 282. The decision followed the *Bombay Case*. On the other hand, the Victorian Supreme Court, in *Victorian Railway Commissioners* v. *Herbert* [1949] Argus L.R. 440, held railways commissioners bound by the Landlord and Tenant Act, 1948 (Victoria), on the ground that, in so far as they owned and let property, they were not exercising a governmental function, and thus were not ' under the shield of the Crown ': cf. *Tamlin* v. *Hannaford* [1949] 2 All E.R. 327. This decision would not help, however, where a government department is a defendant.

[5] (3rd. ed.), p. 356.

[6] The High Court in *Sydney Harbour Trust Commissioners* v. *Ryan*, 13 C.L.R. 358, used it to hold the New South Wales Government bound by the Employers' Liability Act; the Supreme Court of Victoria, in *R.* v. *Hay* [1924] V.L.R. 97, used it to hold the Crown bound by the Statute of Frauds. Unfortunately, the majority of the High Court took a more narrow view in the recent case of *Minister of Works* (*W.A.*) v. *Gulson* [1944] Argus.L.R. 349, where Williams J. was content to say that the principle of Crown immunity clearly applied to all property vested in the Crown.

to his regal capacity '. On the other hand, a statute may, without naming him, deprive him ' of such inferior rights as belong indifferently to the King or to a subject, such as the title to an advowson or a landed estate '. Translated into modern terms, this means that the presumption should be against a statute binding the Crown where it would interfere with the governmental functions outlined by the prerogatives (notably Military Affairs, Foreign Affairs, Treaty-making Power) but that the presumption should be the other way where the statute concerns activities which put the Crown on the level of other individuals, that is to say, industrial, commercial and managerial activities. Such a rule would combine historical continuity with an intelligent interpretation of the many new activities of the State. It would constitute an acceptable compromise—for the guidance of Parliament as well as of the courts—between the preservation of governmental freedom of action in certain spheres and the submission of the State to the rule of law, where it is compatible with and indeed demanded by the public interest.

The problem discussed here points to the need for a more articulate theory of State. The historic continuity of the development from the absolute monarchy to modern constitutional democracy, as well as the disinclination of British jurisprudence to formulate general theories of law, has been in the way of such a development. But as with the problem of administrative justice, the absence of articulate thinking now threatens the proper functioning of the machinery of justice.

THE STATE AS SOVEREIGN AND FISCUS

Continental theory has long known the dual aspect of the State, as sovereign and as fiscus. It has been compelled to think about the problem mainly because of the need to adjust the jurisdictions of the civil courts and the administrative tribunals. Continental legal theory and practice is by no means unanimous as to the proper solution. The French distinction, for example, between *gestion publique* and *gestion privée*, attempts to make the nature of the service the distinguishing test. It is of course never easy to draw an exact borderline between predominatingly administrative and predominatingly civil functions and activities

of public authority. However, French jurisdiction has worked
out reasonably satisfactory practical tests. The adoption of
familiar civil law institutions, for example, of employment
or transport contracts in the common form, points to a *gestion
privée* rather than a *gestion publique*, and consequently indicates
civil instead of administrative jurisdiction.[7] In view of the
high competence and legal independence of administrative
tribunals, which in many cases have given more protection
to the citizen than the civil courts,[8] the citizen is not greatly
affected by the distinction. A nearer analogy to the problems
of the common law systems may be found in the doctrine of
State immunity in international law. The increasing commercial activities of States have made the traditional principle
of immunity of ships owned by foreign States under their own
jurisdiction out of date and unjust in its application.
Characteristically, most Continental courts have attempted to
restrict the immunity of States by distinguishing between the
different types of State activities. But British and American
courts have refused to modify traditional principles, though
hardly out of any particular sympathy with socialism or State
interference in commercial matters. The Continental courts
have experimented with three different solutions[9]: the first
makes the *form* of the transaction decide; Belgian and Italian
courts in particular hold the State liable when it concludes a
contract, for example, when Army authorities buy shoes, or
bullets. Requisitions, on the other hand, are held to be acts
of sovereignty and immune from jurisdiction. This test is
satisfactory enough for most cases, but it does not solve situations
such as that discussed in the case of *Rederiaktiebolaget*

---

[7] Cf. Waline, *Manuel Elementaire de Droit Administratif* (4th ed., 1946)
pp. 54–58. Above, pp. 60–62, 178.

[8] A prominent example is the doctrine of ' imprévision ', through which the
French administrative courts have developed principles of revising and
adjusting contracts in the light of changed circumstances. The French
civil courts still refuse to adopt this doctrine, but it has had great influence
on the doctrine of frustration of contract in modern German, Swiss and
Greek law. Cf. David, Cohn and Deschenaux in *Journal of Comparative
Legislation and International Law*, Vol. 27, pp. 11–25, and Vol. 30, pp.
55–56; Zepos (1948) 11 M.L.R. 36–47.

[9] Cf. in detail Allen, *The Position of Foreign States before National Courts*
(1933); Niboyet, (1936) 43 *Revue générale de droit international public* 525.

Amphitrite v. *R.* [1] where the promise of the British Government
to release a Swedish ship when she had entered a British port,
was held not to be of a contractual nature. Nor does the test
provide a solution where the government may be liable for
negligence or other torts. The second solution distinguishes
between sovereign and non-sovereign, or public and non-public,
functions of the State. This is very close to the distinction between
' governmental ' and ' non-governmental ' functions, which is
responsible for so much confusion in British and American
law, and which should now be abandoned as bad in theory
and unworkable in practice, for it is impossible to achieve any
generally acceptable line of demarcation between ' proper '
and ' improper ' activities of modern governments, without
adopting a specific political theory. [2]

There remains the functional test. Whether or not a State is
immune from jurisdiction and liability should depend on the
nature of the particular activity. This is a test adopted by the
nine nations which signed the Brussels Convention of 1926 [3]
concerning immunities of government vessels. State-owned
vessels carrying cargoes and passengers were declared subject to
the same rules of jurisdiction and liability as private vessels, with
the exception of certain specified categories comprising warships,
hospital ships, and other non-commercial vessels. A parallel
development is the increasing subjection of commercial inter-State
transactions to private law and municipal jurisdiction. [4] In a
recent discussion of the borderlines between public law and
private law transactions between States, Dr. Mann concludes [5]
that no single test has been evolved to distinguish the two
categories. The nature of the transaction, the capacity in which
the parties acted, the wording and contents of the agreement,
have been relied upon to determine its character. Commercial
or industrial purposes, coupled with the adoption of contractual
forms, will normally imply the adoption of private law and
municipal jurisdiction. Recent developments in Britain and the
Dominions reinforce this trend of the law. Government

[1] [1921] 3 K.B. 500.   [2] Cf. above, p. 210.   (1948) 22 A.L.J. 7.
[3] Britain signed but did not ratify the Convention.
[4] Cf. in particular *R.* v. *International Trustee* [1937] A.C. 500.
[5] *Brit. Y.B. of Int. Law* (1944), p. 27.

undertakings predominantly concerned with the conduct of industrial or business enterprise, or a comprehensive social service, have been incorporated and thus become subject to the rights and liabilities of private legal persons.[6] But as the cases discussed in this article show, numerous government activities remain which it is not practicable to incorporate but which may nevertheless create acute problems of liabilities and immunities. The functional test appears to be the only possible guide. Where a government department concludes a contract for the purchase of stores; where it runs a factory operating machinery, employing clerical and technical staff; where it builds houses or treats patients in hospitals—it should be as nearly as possible in the same position as private legal individuals. To maintain that the operation of an ammunition factory, a national health service, or a railway is not the exercise of a proper government function would mean the adoption of a theory of government now rejected in the practice of every modern State. It would be little better to single out certain traditional functions, such as defence, foreign affairs, police, as being necessary aspects of sovereignty. The running of ammunition factories is an aspect of defence, but its operation is a managerial enterprise, which involves contracts of purchase and employment, and the observance of numerous statutory obligations. The broad guiding principle should be that where the industrial, commercial, or managerial aspects of a government activity are involved, the presumption should be in favour of the application of the general law. As shown here,[7] this should include statutory obligations and penal liabilities, subject to the limitations which have been indicated. There will, of course, always be difficult borderline cases. But such difficulties occur in all branches of the law, and a problem analogous to the one under discussion here has occupied Continental jurisdiction for many years.

CONCLUSIONS

The conclusions reached in this chapter may be summed up as follows: first, it is now increasingly necessary to abandon the

---

[6] For details about Britain see (1947) 10 M.L.R. 233, 377; about Australia, 22 A.L.J. 7.
[7] Cf. also above, Ch. 9

lingering fiction of a legally indivisible State, and of a feudal conception of the Crown, and to substitute for it the principle of legal liability where the State, either direct or through incorporated public authorities, engages in activities of a commercial, industrial or managerial character. The proper test is not an impracticable distinction between governmental and non-governmental functions, but the nature and form of the activity in question. Secondly, the rule that the Crown is not bound by statute except when specifically mentioned or by necessary implication, is socially and politically objectionable, nor is it legally compelling. It is the exception to the rule which should be developed by the courts, not the rule itself. The application of the rule should be limited to such cases where an overwhelming public interest demands that the Crown should be exempt.

Lastly, all these problems underline the necessity of a more articulate theory of State in modern British law.

PART FOUR

THE WELFARE STATE
AND THE RULE OF LAW

CHAPTER 13

THE PLANNED STATE AND THE
RULE OF LAW

WHETHER it is possible to preserve in a planned State the essential principles of law of a free democratic society is one of the most important problems facing the surviving democratic societies of our day. There are many who would reconcile themselves to the necessities of planning if they were not convinced that it could only be done by sacrificing the rule of law. Yet there has been surprisingly little serious investigation of the more fundamental aspects of the problem. What there is has mainly come from non-lawyers.[1] The notions both of ' planning ' and of the ' rule of law ' provoke violent emotions of attraction and repulsion, which tend to obscure cool and objective investigation. The first task is a reasonably clear definition of these two ideas.

THE WELFARE STATE AND THE ROLE OF THE LAWYER

Legal analysis is not primarily concerned with the desirability of a particular social or political trend. The judge—interpreting the law on behalf of the community—cannot, in a democratic society, base his decisions on his personal predilections for planning or *laissez faire*. But the illusion that, because of his politically neutral function in the community, the judge, and the lawyer in general, can pretend to ignore social and political trends, is no less fallacious and dangerous than open ideological prejudice. The Swiss Code enjoins the judge to decide ' according

---

[1] Cf. in particular the controversy between Hayek, *Road to Serfdom*, chap. 6, and Finer, *Road to Reaction, passim.* For constitutional law, Sir Ivor Jennings' *Law and the Constitution* has uncovered the ideological assumptions in Dicey's conception of the rule of law. Professor Stone's *Province and Function of Law* has some critical observations on the identification of laissez-faire and the rule of law. Lord Justice Denning, *Freedom under the Law*, has observed on the impact of new functions of government on the problem of ' Justice between Man and the State '. Though published in 1930, Mr. Justice Frankfurter's *The Public and Its Government* is probably still the best general assessment of the impact of new social demands on law, government and democracy.

to the rule which he would make as a legislator ', where neither the statute nor customary law provides an answer for a particular situation.   Mr. Justice Cardozo came to substantially similar conclusions[2]: 'Logic and history and custom and utility of the accepted standards of right conduct, are the forces which singly or in combination shape the progress of the law. Which of these forces dominate in any case, must depend generally upon the comparative importance or social value of the interests which will thereby be promoted or impaired '.

The modern judge would not give an unpolitical but simply a bad decision, if, in deciding a conspiracy case, he did not recognise collective bargaining and group action, for the pursuit of better conditions of work, as an accepted principle of modern British law.   In deciding whether to give the rule of common employment an extensive or a restrictive interpretation, British courts have in recent years been largely guided by the evolution of legal policy, which rejects the rule as repugnant to modern conditions of industrial society, as well as to contemporary ideas of social justice.   In estimating the trend of public policy, the judge cannot, of course, choose that of one party or opinion in preference to another, which may be equally widely accepted. He can follow the evolution of social thought only with some caution, absorbing in the interpretation of such legal problems as involve elements of public policy, ' the accepted standards of right conduct '.   These considerations apply particularly to a modern analysis of the rule of law.   An analysis which would preserve Dicey's suppositions about a liberal, essentially negative State would not be controversial, it would be a bad analysis and poor jurisprudence.   For although platform controversy and political polemics still argue in terms of Liberalism against Socialism, or Private Enterprise against Planning, the Social Welfare State is now a basic reality of modern Western life, accepted to a lesser or greater extent in every Western democracy.   There are three major causes for such a development.   The first is the industrialisation and urban-isation of Western society.   The sheer physical and technical conditions of life increase the need for control.

[2] *The Nature of the Judicial Process* (1921), p. 112.

One of the best known of modern anti-planners, Professor Hayek, illustrates the difference between a planned State and a State governed by the rule of law by saying that the former ' commands people which road to take, whereas the latter only provides sign-posts '.[3] But in modern industrial society vast masses live together in close physical and economic inter-dependence. The traffic is so dense that many more policemen, beacons, and sign-posts are necessary to avoid chaos. The traffic of London requires more regulation than that of Much-Binding-in-the Marsh.

The second reason is an evolution of social philosophy. In the last generation, a decisive shift has taken place in public opinion, and the legislative policy of all major parties. Conservatives, Liberals, as well as Socialists and Communists, all reject unmitigated economic individualism. They hold the State responsible for creating conditions of stable and full employment; they accept the responsibility of the community for minimum standards of living, housing, labour conditions, and social insurance. The Beveridge Report put these demands in picturesque language, when it spoke of ' the giants of idleness, disease, squalor, and want '. There is controversy on the degree of public controls, and the socialisation of industries and public utilities. But some degree of socialisation and public operation of industries is recognised by all major parties. The nationalisation of the British coal industry was accepted by all parties as necessary in the circumstances. In Britain, as in Australia or Canada, a number of important public utilities, such as electricity, forestry, and transport services, are run by the State, or by public corporations. Nor is there more than a difference of degree between British and American developments. The Federal government and other public authorities control a vast proportion of the United States electrical power generation. Public housing programmes and social insurances, farm support, and other subsidy schemes, have been enacted to an increasing extent. The responsibility of the Federal and State governments to cope with unemployment has not yet been severely tested, because of the post-war

[3] *Road to Serfdom*, p. 54.

boom conditions, and the re-armament drive which followed it almost immediately, but the machinery exists, and neither political party would today disclaim responsibility for full employment.

The third cause of this transformation of the social pattern is the state of mobilisation or semi-mobilisation, now unfortunately too permanent a feature of modern Western society to be regarded as a passing emergency. For the last 35 years the conduct or aftermath of war has alternated with preparations for new wars, or, as at present, a state of high military and industrial mobilisation, which may or may not avert war, but certainly leaves its impact on society. It entails an increasing measure of State control over the nation's manpower and resources, over scientific research and the location of industries, over priorities in employment, and a multitude of other activities implied in the preparation for modern war.

Such a transformation on society cannot but have a profound —though still largely unnoticed—effect on legal concepts and relations. The notion of a government which concerns itself exclusively with military defence, foreign affairs, police and legal justice, is now a matter of the past. Modern government, whatever its political complexion, must discharge certain social protective functions, through factory and health legislation, and other legal measures of labour protection, through social insurance provisions which may range from elementary unemployment assistance to the comprehensiveness of the British National Insurance Act of 1946. It must further concern itself with the conservation of vital national assets, such as forests or water-ways or roads. Every State has to exercise a varying degree of control over scarce resources, both raw materials and consumer goods, and to ensure their equitable distribution, through rationing, price control, or other means. Moreover, control of certain national resources is often required for the fulfilment of international obligations, of which the European Recovery Programme and the International Wheat Agreement provide recent examples. Such control often means active measures of State supervision, as for example the prescription of agricultural minimum standards and the powers of dispossession of bad farmers under the British

Agriculture Act of 1947. Further, the control of investments and employment, in order to mitigate violent fluctuations between boom and depression, implies credit control, public works and other regulative measures. Finally, public corporations control and manage such vital industries as coal, transport, electricity, and gas.

All these functions entail the making of public contracts, the interpolation of compulsory conditions in private contracts, the imposition of statutory duties, restrictions on property use, and a host of acts of interference by public authorities with the free and unrestricted exercise of private rights.

The sum total of these different State activities is sufficient to transform the free economic society in which the State is a glorified policeman, but otherwise a disinterested spectator, into a controlled society in which the State is an active participant in the economic and social life of the citizen.

To take all these factors into account in a redefinition of the rule of law, is not only permissible but indispensable. Lawyers are frequently under the illusion that the continued acceptance of definitions and rules formulated a century ago means being ' non-political '. In truth, it means the intrusion of yesterday's politics into today's law. Living as we do in a planned society, we have to accept it for purposes of legal analysis, and in particular, for the redefinition of the rule of law.

THREE MEANINGS OF THE ' RULE OF LAW '

In the first sense, the rule of law simply means the ' existence of public order '.[4] It means organised government, operating through the various instruments and channels of legal command. In this sense, all modern societies live under the rule of law, fascist as well as socialist and liberal States. Time and again futile attempts have been made to deny the character of law to rules of a certain political flavour. It is tempting indeed to say that a State which forbids marriages between Jews and non-Jews, or one which regulates the mass deportation or even murder of innocent people, has no law. But it is impossible to establish a criterion of distinction between ' law ' and ' non-law ', without colouring it with a particular political ideology. This is often

---

[4] Jennings, *Law and the Constitution* (3rd. ed.), p. 42.

cloaked by such phrases as ' natural justice ', ' laws of humanity ', ' sentiment of right '. But no meaning can be attached to such formulas other than in terms of specific religious, political or social values. It is both more honest and more fruitful to distinguish between the formal ordering of government, for which, for better or worse, the term law had become usual, and specific ideals of justice associated with a particular conception of society.

Usually, the term ' rule of law ' is given an ideological connotation. It is identified with a specific ideal of justice. In democratic society, most people understand by ' rule of law ' a state of affairs in which there are legal barriers to governmental arbitrariness, and legal safeguards for the protection of the individual. This political conception of the rule of law applies to what we may broadly call ' democratic ' society. It differs from Fascist or Communist, or Catholic ideas of justice. It is with this specific idea of justice in a democratic society that the following analysis will be concerned.

A democratic ideal of justice must rest on the three foundations of equality, liberty and ultimate control of government by the people. It is, however, far from easy to give these concepts a specific meaning. Democracy is certainly based on the ideal of equality, but no democratic State has seriously attempted to translate this ideal into the absolute equality of all. There are numerous inevitable inequalities of function and status, between adults and infants, between sane persons and lunatics, between civilians and military, between private citizens and officials. We can still not formulate the principle of equality in more specific terms than Aristotle who said that justice meant the equal treatment of those who are equal before the law. We can give to this apparent tautology a more concrete meaning by saying that a democratic ideal of justice demands that inequalities shall be inequalities of function and service but shall not be derived from arbitrary distinctions based on race, religion or other personal attributes. In a society governed by international law we should add that inequalities must not be based on nationality. But in a society still dominated by national sovereignty this is no more than a pious aspiration.

The meaning of ' liberty ' is hardly more easy to define. In terms of a democratic ideal of justice, liberty means certain rights of personal freedom which must be secure from interference by government. They include the legal protection from arbitrary arrest, freedom of opinion and association, of contract, labour and many others.[5] Briefly they may be subsumed under the two broad categories of the freedom of the person and the freedom of the mind. But there is perhaps only one legal and constitutional maxim of general validity which can be deduced from this principle: that in so far as an individual is granted specific rights they should be secure from arbitrary interference. This means that a judiciary as independent from interference by the executive as is possible, given the interlocking of State functions and the human factor in the judicial function, is an essential of the democratic ideal of justice. But it is impossible to lay down a generally accepted rule either as to the substance of these rights or as to the manner of their protection. The Declaration of Rights recently debated by the United Nations is vastly different from the Bill of Rights embodied in the American Constitution. The Australian Constitution contains no individual rights other than the guarantee of religious freedom and perhaps— though this is still very much open to doubt—a protection of the individual from the restriction of free inter-State trade by State regulation (s. 92). A similar position exists in Canada owing to the interpretation given by the Privy Council to the ' property and civil rights ' clause of the British-North America Act. British law knows of no guarantees of individual rights other than the limited guarantee of personal freedom in the Bill of Rights of 1689 and the Habeas Corpus Acts. This leads to a more fundamental difference between two types of democratic constitution. In one type of democracy, a written constitution, which it is normally very difficult to alter, formulates and at the same time petrifies the meaning of the rule of law in a manner binding upon legislative and executive alike. Under these systems, a law court acquires the decisive function of an authoritative interpreter of the meaning of the rule of law, within the framework of the constitution. It is difficult to exaggerate the difference

[5] For a survey, see Friedmann, *Legal Theory* (2nd ed.), chap. 32.

between this system of ultimate judicial control, which gives way to political control only in the rare cases of constitutional amendment by referendum, and the purely political control which prevails in a country such as Great Britain. There the rule of law is whatever parliament as the supreme law-giver makes it, and the judge has the much more limited function of interpreting statutes, in so far as they come before him. If his interpretation differs too much from that of prevailing public opinion, a simple statute will alter the law. The difference between these two types of democratic systems is far more fundamental than that between English and Continental ideals of justice which Dicey exaggerated so much.

Lastly, the principle of control by the people means that law must ultimately be the responsibility of the elected representatives of the people. This is indeed a vital principle but it can say little about the technique by which the modern legislator can discharge this function.

This analysis of the rule of law has so far ignored the social service State. It has presupposed a State confined to purely protective functions. Some have deduced the social welfare functions of a modern democratic State from the very principles of equality and liberty. This is inherent in the utilitarian ideal of the greatest happiness for the greatest number. T. H. Green contrasted the formal freedom of contract described by Maine as a vital aspect of modern progressive society with the lack of real freedom resulting from the inequality between property owners and others. This of course has been carried to much greater length by Marxist analysis. Similarly, all sorts of social reforms, from social insurance and factory legislation to the national ownership of industries, have been deduced from the need to give actual social and economic equality, as distinct from the purely political equality of voting rights. It has been shown earlier that this social philosophy is now generally accepted in modern democratic society. Whatever the justification, the realisation of social justice must today be added to the basic values of a democratic society, and it is precisely the question how far this modifies or negatives the principles previously formulated which will occupy us here.

DICEY AND THE RULE OF LAW

In a third sense the rule of law has been identified with certain constitutional principles of nineteenth-century Britain. The ' rule of law ' as classically formulated by Dicey,[6] has three aspects. Firstly no man is punishable except for ' a distinct breach of law established in the ordinary legal manner before the ordinary courts of the land ', and therefore the rule of law is not consistent with arbitrary ' or even wide discretionary authority on the part of the government '. In the second place, the rule of law means equal subjection of all classes to the ordinary law of the land as administered by the ordinary law courts, and therefore a rejection of so-called administrative justice administered by special tribunals on the continental model. The third aspect of Dicey's rule of law means in essence an historic generalisation: in English law private individual rights derive from court precedents rather than from constitutional codes. This quite clearly applies only to Britain itself and would have no application to a State which, like Australia, is governed by a written constitution, let alone in the United States whose constitution embodies a comprehensive catalogue of individual rights.

Dicey's formulation of the rule of law has in recent years come in for much criticism, from such eminent contemporary constitutional lawyers as Jennings, Wade, Carr or Robson. It has been directed mainly against the inconsistencies of Dicey's own teaching, his overlooking of the privileges and immunities of the Crown, and of the many other inequalities in the English legal system of his own or even of our time, the unresolved contradiction between the principle of parliamentary supremacy and constitutional guarantees, and, above all, Dicey's misunderstanding of the nature of administrative justice.

It rests on his distinction between law and administration. To Dicey the former means a body of rules established or at least interpreted by the ordinary law courts. Administration is contrasted with law. Administration means discretion, and therefore any wide measure of discretion is incompatible with the rule of law. The evolution of modern government has made

---

[6] *Law of the Constitution* (9th ed. (Wade), 1939), chap. 4.

it increasingly clear that this antithesis between law and administration is false. In a recent instructive decision of the High Court of Australia an order of general application had been made by an administrative body set up during the war for the control of vegetable seeds. The classification of the rules of the committee, as either law-making or administrative, caused great difficulty to the court. In the words of Dixon J.:

> The power itself belongs to an administrative body or authority. It would, I think, be classified nowadays as an administrative power. If adherence to the old dichotomy of non-judicial governmental power into executive or legislative were obligatory and also significant, in the decision of the case, it would probably be necessary to dissect the power and allot some of its content to one head and some to the other. For the authority it gives of control and regulation by means of orders is exercisable either by the promulgation of a general rule to be observed by all or by the issue of specific directions with reference to a particular transaction.

In a more recent English decision,[7] the Court of Appeal was faced with a similar problem. It had to interpret the legal significance of circulars by which the Minister of Health had delegated to local authorities certain powers of requisitioning vacant houses. Prima facie, such internal administrative circulars, addressed from the superior to a number of inferior authorities, appeared to be plainly administrative. Yet the court, in particular Scott L.J., pointed out that these circulars ' were not mere executive directions, but delegated legislation with statutory force, conferring powers on the corporation, which they would not otherwise have possessed, and imposing on them duties for the reasonable protection of the individual houseowner '. The practical consequence was, that in the opinion of the court, certain rules of delegated legislation applied to this type of ' sub-delegated ' legislation.

Legislative and administrative aspects in a given action by a public authority are often inextricably mixed. This makes Dicey's antithesis of law and administration as being one between fixed rules and discretion highly unreal. Another reflection shows the fallacy of this distinction. Modern jurisprudence has increasingly found that in every judicial decision and indeed in every

[7] *Blackpool Corporation* v. *Locker* [1948] 1 K.B. 349.

application of legal principles to a given case, there is a larger or smaller degree of judicial discretion, expressed usually in terms of ' good faith, reasonableness, equity ' and so forth. As Jennings has observed, Dicey could gloss over this fact only because to him the rule of law meant really the rule of the judges.[8] The vast discretion exercised by magistrates in the scale of punishment, or by judges in the application of general equitable principles to a given case, did not worry him. Discretion was objectionable only when exercised by administrators. Yet as, among others, Dicey's great contemporary Maitland realised, even in 1885 a vast variety of public authorities possessed administrative discretion. Jennings quotes as examples the discretion of the Home Secretary in regard to nationalisation of aliens, the prerogative of the Crown in regard to private property in times of danger, the compulsory powers of public health authorities. To rule out administrative discretion would have meant an abandonment of the most elementary principles of social welfare even in Dicey's time.

The problem of delegated legislation is only a special aspect of this problem of administrative discretion. The necessity of delegating rule-making on the largest scale to administrative authorities is as much a basic fact of modern industrial society as the assumption by the State of certain obligations of social welfare. Nor is there any basic disagreement on this among modern students of the problem, or any reason to doubt that the administrator is less capable of exercising discretion than other sections of the community. In 1932, the Committee on Ministers' Powers emphasised the necessity and the inevitability of delegated legislation on the largest scale. As vigorous a critic of modern bureaucracy, planning and government by orders as C. K. Allen, writing in 1945, comes to the same conclusions.[9] Sir Cecil Carr[1] has formulated the problem as follows:

> We can trust a committee of judges and legal practitioners to make rules of court. We can trust some recognised organisation with proper academic and professional qualifications to say what is a dangerous poison or what is a safety lamp proper for coal miners

[8] *Law and the Constitution*, p. 290.
[9] *Law and Orders*, chap. 6.
[1] *Concerning English Administrative Law*, p. 35.

to use. We ought to be able to trust expert administrators, if the country in the persons of its elected representatives can in the long run control them through some vulnerable ministerial head or otherwise and if the Chadwicks do not get out of hand, to work out a policy which the legislature has adopted and prescribed.

It is futile to ask whether delegated legislation is necessary or not. The problem is how delegated legislation and administrative discretion in general can be confined and controlled in such a manner as to comply with the principles of justice valued by a democratic society.

To sum up this critical analysis of the liberal conception of the rule of law, only two principles remain as essential to democratic society: the safeguarding of protected individual rights by impartial judicial authority, though this need not necessarily be the ' ordinary '[2] law courts, and the principle of equality before the law of those who engage in comparable legal transactions and enterprises. The second principle is linked with the first; lack of equality impairs legal security. Both principles need reassessment in the light of two factors ignored or misunderstood by Dicey: the relativity of the distinction between law and administration, and the State's obligation to ensure minimum standards of social welfare. The fulfilment of these standards demands a far greater degree of administration and administrative discretion than Dicey would admit.

THE ROAD TO SERFDOM AND THE RULE OF LAW

Dicey himself clearly realised in later years the growth of the social service State and began to modify some of his conceptions.[3] It has been left to a modern economist to revive an uncompromising and radical version of Diceyism. According to Hayek, the

---

[2] As Jennings points out, Dicey's use of the term ' ordinary ' is deeply influenced by his aversion to administrative justice and assumes that only the common law courts can be called ordinary courts: *Law and the Constitution*, chap. 7.

[3] See especially his preface to the second edition of *Law and Public Opinion in England during the Nineteenth Century* (1914) and his article on ' The Development of Administrative Law in England ', in (1915) L.Q.R., pp. 148 *et seq.*

planned State is incompatible with the rule of law. Hayek's definition of the rule of law is summed up in one sentence.[4]

> Stripped of all technicalities this means that government in all its actions is bound by rules fixed and announced beforehand—rules which make it possible to foresee with fair certainty how the authority will use its coercive powers in given circumstances, and to plan one's individual affairs on the basis of this knowledge.

The rest of the chapter provides no more than an elaboration of this thesis, without any attempt to test it in the light of the mechanics of law. According to Hayek, the law should only give general orders but not particular directions. He regards the resort to such general formulas as fairness, equity, reasonableness, as evidence of the decline of the rule of law. Hayek's only reference to detail is his apparent approval of building regulations and factory laws. Beyond that he does not indicate the admissible limits of State action. The formula that the State should provide traffic signposts but not command people which road to take is of no practical value to the legislator, administrator or legal practitioner.

What is the lawyer's answer to Hayek's contention that the rule of law means predictability, that is the fixing of rules ' independently of the concrete circumstances which can neither be foreseen or taken into account beforehand ', while planning means absolute unpredictability ? [5]

Let us take four typical examples of the kind of interference which occurs daily in the modern government of Great Britain or other democracies of the common law system.

In the first place, the State interferes with the free and untrammelled conduct of individuals through a multitude of restrictive conditions. Price control by State regulation is the most familiar type of restriction of freedom of contract raised by scarcity of materials or State planning of economic priorities. Its violation may lead to sanctions of private as well as of public law (nullity of contract, and liability to fines[6]). The lawyer is

---

[4] *The Road to Serfdom*, p. 54.
[5] For a vigorous reply to Hayek's general thesis see Finer, *Road to Reaction* (1945).
[6] Cf., *e.g.*, for Australia, National Security (Prices) Regulations Nos. 29, 31 and G. Sawer, ' Price Control and the Validity of Contracts ', 22 A.L.J. 173.

most familiar with the legal consequences of statutory duties, the breach of which may lead to both fines and actions for damages, and the restriction of freedom of contract by compulsory terms. The Factory Act of 1937 or the Coal Mines Act of 1911 are full of regulations regarding the safety of machinery, and numerous actions have been brought in which the breach of such a duty has led to the award of damages to the injured individual. The need for such safety regulations is now an accepted part of the law, and no political part or other group of importance would now attack the legal policy underlying such regulations. There is of course no question of unpredictability in any of these cases. The rules are laid down in Acts and Regulations which are known and accessible to everybody concerned.

An interesting example of compulsory conditions of contract is provided in the Schedules and Regulations appended to the Agriculture Act of 1947. They standardise to a large extent the tenancy agreements for agricultural holdings by laying down rules about compensation for improvements, conversion of pasture to arable land, alteration of buildings and other important aspects of the landlord-tenant relationship. They are all designed to ensure the maximum degree of agricultural efficiency, in pursuit of the social and economic objective of reviving British agriculture. This objective is also a matter beyond party controversy, and the compulsory conditions of tenancy, far from destroying predictability, reinforce it and protect the numerous tenants who might otherwise agree to injurious, anti-social or inequitable terms of contract.

A second type of interference is the order by which, under the New Towns Act of 1946, the Housing Act, 1936, or the Town and Country Planning Act of 1947, the minister or a Public Corporation may compulsorily acquire land. The alternative is between a voluntary agreement for purchase or a compulsory order. Where the minister or a New Towns Development Corporation wants to acquire a particular area, a draft of the order with all details must be published in the *London Gazette* and in newspapers circulating in the locality. It must describe the area, state the details of the proposed order, and fix a place and time for an inquiry to be held with the local authority and all other interested parties in case any objection is raised. The minister is not bound to abide by the objection; but he is bound to hold an inquiry and to consider the objections, though it has been laid down by the House of Lords [7] that it is not for the law court but for Parliament to examine the manner in which the minister has exercised his discretion.

Certainly it is impossible for any private landowner today to predict whether, in three or five years' time, his particular land may be designated for new town developments and compulsory purchase. To this extent action is unpredictable, although the Minister of Town and Country Planning has published a general development plan for the outer area of Greater London, in accordance with the so-called Abercrombie Plan. There is a conflict of legal values, between the claim of the individual to enjoyment of his property and the social interest in the planned and balanced development of town and country, at a time when the congestion of the population, in such cities as London, is becoming a major social menace as well as a matter of grave concern to the military authorities. The conflict is, however, lessened by the respect paid by the expropriation legislation to the principle of private property. The compulsory acquisition of property is subject to a definite and regulated legal procedure, partly consolidated for Great Britain in the Acquisition of Land (Authorisation and Procedure) Act, 1946, and in the different Nationalisation Acts. All the Nationalisation Acts make compulsory purchase subject to compensation, and this compensation is assessed by an independent administrative tribunal.

There is, however, a deeper economic and sociological problem which Hayek ignores completely. Is the unpredictability of planned State action for defined and regulated social purposes, coupled with the obligation of adequate compensation, any greater than the uncertainty which faces the property owner under a system of free and unregulated economic competition ? The last century has witnessed the swallowing of thousands of small enterprises by greater ones, and the increasing substitution, for genuine free private competition, of combines, market and

---

[7] *Franklin* v. *Minister of Town and Country Plannning* [1948] A.C. 87.

production cartels, as well as the control of inventions and research by the dominating enterprise or group of enterprises in a particular field. The suppression of competitors by any means, short of physical violence or other methods specifically prohibited by law, was legally sanctioned by the famous decision of the House of Lords in the *Mogul Case*,[8] which considered systematic boycotting, under-cutting and pressure exercised upon third persons, as a legitimate means of competition. It is true that the neo-liberal school deplores the development of monopoly and that it wishes genuine competitive enterprise to be restored by State action. Some such action has been taken by the American Anti-Trust legislation, notably the Sherman and Clayton Anti-Trust Acts, with results that have not been altogether negligible, but which certainly have not broken the predominant power exercised at least in some vital industrial spheres by monopolistic or quasi-monopolistic corporations.[9] The Monopolies and Restrictive Practices Act, 1948, goes little further than to set up machinery for the investigation of monopolistic practices. But any restoration of genuine economic competition, as a substitute for planning, could only be undertaken by deliberate State action on a very considerable scale. Such State action might operate through the revision of patent law, public utility regulations, anti-trust and anti-monopoly legislation, and through other measures designed to restore the free market. But all this would require a degree of State interference which might possibly lead to an economically preferable situation but which would require a very substantial amount of State interference, that is, State planning.

In short, planning action by the modern democratic State of the type just described means an interference predictable in general outline but not in detail, according to a regulated procedure and subject to compensation, as compared with the hazards of economic competition which exposes the weaker to unpredictable action by the stronger, without compensation.

---

[8] [1892] A.C. 25.
[9] In 1947, 113 firms controlled 46% of the total capital assets of U.S. manufacturing corporations. (Report by U.S. Federal Trade Commission.) Since then, the rearmament drive had further stifled the efforts of the anti-trust division.

The transfer of such actions from the private to the public sphere does not weaken but strengthens the influence of law. It increases if anything the amount of protection for the individual. This does not mean that it is economically or socially preferable. It is a matter of political and economic controversy whether the assumption of such vast responsibilities creates too complex an administrative machinery and too big a financial burden for the State, outweighing the social and economic wants which prompt such planning legislation. What has to be noted here is that even in this field the antithesis of predictability and rule of law does not stand the test of close examination.

A third type of administrative interference, for the sake of broad social and cultural objectives, is the complicated network of grants, minimum standards and inspections provided by the Education Act of 1944. This Act, passed by the war-time coalition government in Britain, is designed to ensure minimum educational standards throughout the country and to diffuse free higher education throughout the population regardless of means. It does not, however, abolish independent and private schools. It is thus, in the field of education, a counterpart to the mixture of public and private economic enterprise which exists in Britain and to a lesser extent in Australia. The administration of this Act undoubtedly means a great deal of administrative discretion. Part of it resides in the local education authorities, part of it in the minister and the ministerial inspectors. Certainly the minister has many discretionary powers, including a number of semi-judicial functions. He may direct an authority to provide transport for the purpose of facilitating the attendance of pupils at school; he may decide to which school a particular child may go in case of a dispute between the education authority and the parent; he may determine a dispute between a local education authority and the managers of a school; he may veto an application for the post of Chief Education Officer; he may authorise the State payment of repairs to aided schools. Above all, he has the power to give or refuse grants to independent schools subject to certain conditions. Is this ' arbitrary discretion ' in the sense of Dicey, or ' unpredictable action ' in the sense of Hayek ? The standards required for State aid are laid down in a number of Ministry of Education circulars. Independent schools have been well able to ascertain their position by studying the Act, the regulations and the circulars. On the remaining points of doubt they have obtained information from the county education authority or from the Minister of Education. If there should nevertheless be a case of unjust discrimination, the local Member of Parliament can raise the matter in Parliament to which the minister is responsible. The minister has the important power to serve notice of complaint upon private schools which appear to him objectionable on specified grounds of unsuitability. The persons affected may appeal against such notice to an independent schools tribunal, with a legal chairman and two impartial assessors, and this tribunal has power either to strike the school off the register or annul the complaint.

We have then in this situation—which is typical of many similar administrative actions, in matters of health, housing, hospital services and so on—a mixture of administrative discretion, standards devised in Acts or regulations, and resort, in cases of special importance, to independent administrative tribunals. Can it seriously be argued that this is incompatible with the rule of law? Those who do so fall, it seems, under the spell of one of the most naive but also most persistent myths, which is particularly evident in Hayek's treatment of the ' rule of law ' as something abstract, objective and impersonal. Everybody with the slightest knowledge and experience of law knows that the independence of the judiciary does not eliminate the human or the discretionary element from the administration of law. Oliver Wendell Holmes wrote in 1897 that ' the prophecies of what the courts will do in fact and nothing more pretentious are what I mean by the law '. Jerome Frank has recently gone so far as to suggest that the teaching of legal principles should be largely abandoned in favour of ' legal clinics ' provided by the trial courts. He argues that all law resolves itself into multitudes of concrete actions taken in particular cases by trial judges. Most lawyers would regard this view as greatly exaggerated, but few will deny the vast amount of discretion and uncertainty following from the weighing of evidence and fact-finding, by magistrates, juries and trial judges.

Nor does the binding force of precedent provide more than a modicum of certainty. Every branch of the law supplies abundant illustrations of the conflicting decisions made possible by distinctions of fact or different interpretations of legal principle.[1] The federal systems of the United States, Canada, and Australia compel a court to determine daily the most intricate questions of economic and social policy. True, the judges are bound by a written document, the constitution, but as hundreds of judgments under both constitutions show, the general principles formulated in the constitution, regarding freedom of conscience, property and trade, police power, taxing power and so forth, leave a vast amount of doubt, discretion and choice between conflicting values. Chief Justice Taft of the U.S. Supreme Court once said: ' the constitution is what the judges say it is '. Had he followed, for example, the judicial interpretation of the clauses regulating federal competences in matters of commerce and trade in Australia, Canada and the U.S.A. over the last twenty-five years, Hayek would have known that the rule of law does not mean the rule of certainty. Modern legislation has deliberately strengthened the element of free judicial discretion as the best means to attain justice. Criminal law gives the judge a wide discretion of punishment, being content to lay down maximum and minimum penalties. With juvenile offenders, the discretion includes corrective measures, as an alternative to punishment. In private law, judicial apportionment of responsibility between joint tortfeasors or of damages in cases of contributory negligence, are examples of recent British and Australian legislation. One of the finest of modern civil codes, the Swiss Code of 1907, has given the judge a reserve power to decide as he would were he a legislator, when faced with a gap in the law. A distinguished Canadian lawyer has recently summed up the last twenty-five years of development, in a branch of law still overwhelmingly judge-made, as follows:

'The most important trend in the modern law of torts is the attempt to seek broad generalisations under which the facts of individual instances can be related, not with a view towards automatic solution, but rather with a view to the object or purpose to be attained '.[2]

[1] Cf. *Legal Theory*, (2nd. ed.) chaps. 23, 24.
[2] C. A. Wright (1948) 25 Can.Bar Rev. 75.

From Aristotle to Pound, legal philosophers, legislators and practitioners have seen the necessity for a wide measure of individualising discretion, the tempering of general law by individual equity, and that is a problem fundamentally similar for the judge and the administrator. It needs the courage—and the innocence—of Hayek to sweep all this away with the words that the extension of the use of ' equity ' and ' fairness ' formulas proves the decline of the rule of law. The independence of the judiciary from administrative interference is an eminently desirable and necessary principle in democratic society, but it is a fatal illusion to believe that the rule of law is something floating in space, isolated from social policy, public opinion and political theory.

There is, lastly, a type of planning interference which is of particular interest to the lawyer, though very little explored. Modern States, especially in times of war or other economic emergencies, conclude a multitide of contracts, for arms and other vital supplies, for bulk purchase, etc. Most of these public contracts are now made by public corporations constituted as separate legal personalities such as the National Coal Board or the Transport Commission in Great Britain, or the Forestry Commissioners, Railway Commissioners, Repatriation Commission, the Housing Commissions in Australia. The legal position of these public authorities creates some difficult problems. On the whole, however, it is clear that they are bound by the ordinary rules of the common law.[3] A more complex situation arises when government departments enter into contracts. Is it not the case that government departments, in making contracts, are in a position of superiority as towards the private contractor, that they can put the power of the State behind their transactions and violate the principle of equality ? How much substance is there in this contention ? The most typical instance is the so-called ' break ' clause in contracts between government departments and other parties. In the 1947 version of the Standard Conditions of Government Contracts for Stores Purchases, the following clause occurs:

---

[3] Cf. above, p. 206 ff.

' The Authority shall, in addition to his power under any other of these conditions, have power to determine the contract at any time by giving to the contractor written notice, to expire at the end of the period specified in the schedule, and upon the expiration of the notice the contract shall be determined without prejudice to the rights of the parties accrued to the date of determination but subject to the operation of the following provisions of this condition. . . . ' (S.56 (1).)

Subsequent clauses provide for fair compensation for unused material and indemnification against commitments entered into in connection with the contract.

Here, on the face of it, is a typical example of arbitrariness and unpredictability, of the inequality between an all-powerful government and a feeble private contractor. What does closer analysis show ? The contractor knows when signing the contract that the contract may be terminated unilaterally under certain circumstances. He calculates that risk in estimating his cost. He can weigh the risk of possible termination of the contract against the advantage of large scale supplies to a most important and solvent customer. But how big is the risk ? It is nothing more than the inability to obtain damages for loss of profit in case of termination. For if the contract is terminated, the contractor will obtain a fair and reasonable price for all unused materials and indemnification against commitments, liabilities or expenditures. Holmes' risk-theory of contract, according to which the object of contract is not performance but liability to damages for breach of contract,[4] is not undisputed. In some cases there may be an order for specific performance or an injunction. But it is broadly correct for the ordinary commercial supply contract. The standard government contract limits the amount of damages, as do thousands of private contracts, by fixing liquidated damages. Subject to certain exceptions disputes on the compensation payable are submitted to arbitration.[5]

Finally we cannot ignore some social and economic realities to estimate correctly the difference between this type of

---

[4] *The Common Law*, p. 298. Cf. above, p. 70.
[5] See above, p. 64. An exception open to criticism is the right of the authority (*i.e.*, a party to the contract) to determine finally and conclusively complaints on hardship arising from the break clause and referred to it by the contractor.

government contract and the ordinary private contract. The vast majority of modern contracts are standard contracts, concluded not between equal individuals but between an industrial or commercial firm which uses the standardised terms of its trade association, and another party who can, of course, choose to refuse to make the contract, that is if he can afford not to travel on railways or steamers, not to take a mortgage on his house or not to insure.[6]

It is too often forgotten that the textbook contract is no more than a theoretical pattern and that the most important modern commercial contracts are governed by standard conditions imposed upon the other party in everything but name.

To sum up, Hayek's sweeping generalisations collapse on closer investigation. It might be truer to say that planning means too much law, not too little.

FIVE LEGAL ASPECTS OF THE SOCIAL WELFARE STATE

Five different State functions call for analysis. They result from the activities of the State: Firstly, as Protector; secondly, as Dispenser of Social Services; thirdly, as Industrial Manager; fourthly, as Economic Controller; fifthly, as Arbitrator.

The State acts firstly as a protector. This is its traditional function, and classical liberal thought regards it as the only legitimate function of the State. Older British and American decisions reflect this conception in describing defence, foreign affairs, police and the administration of justice as the legitimate functions of the State.[7] To this may be added a limited taxing power confined to the efficient discharge of these functions. These are the traditional spheres of State sovereignty, and consequently it is in this field that the inequalities which detract from the rule of law in Dicey's sense are most evident, though Dicey consistently attempted to belittle them for the sake of his principle. The immunities and privileges of the Crown, in regard to litigation, taxing, submission to statutes, and other fields, are survivals of feudal sovereignty; the special law and jurisdiction for military forces are an aspect of the defence power. The

---

[6] Cf. above, pp. 45–48.
[7] Cf. *Ohio* v. *Helvering*, 292 U.S. 366. *Coomber* v. *Justices* (1883) 9 A.C. 61.

important prerogatives of the Executive lie in the fields of foreign affairs and defence. The emergency defence powers of the Executive in time of danger, the so-called acts of State, and other prerogatives which are above judicial scrutiny are all detractions from the principle of equality. They are bearable only as long as State functions are limited. As the activities of the State extend in the direction of industrial and commercial enterprise and of social services, the whole field of these privileges and immunities requires re-definition and limitation; otherwise it would gradually engulf a growing portion of the whole field of law. [8]

But three further and increasingly important functions of the modern State now look for adequate legal analysis. The first of these is the function of the State as dispenser of social services. Legally it expresses itself in two different ways. Many important social services are discharged through the imposition of compulsory duties and conditions on private relationships. A multitude of statutory duties affects both public and private law; their infringement leads to fines, as well as to remedies at the suit of persons protected by the statute. There is a parallel expansion of common law duties of employers towards employees through the assimilation of new principles of public policy by the law courts. [9] At the same time social minimum standards are enforced through compulsory conditions in contract. Service contracts are subject to many such compulsory terms. The Truck Acts invalidate provisions for payment in kind to defined categories of servants. Repatriation Acts compel the reinstatement of ex-servicemen. Agriculture Acts lay down compulsory terms of agricultural tenancies in the interests of agricultural efficiency. Every employment contract in Great Britain is now subject to compulsory national insurance terms.

The discharge of social service functions also requires a multitude of active administrative and managerial functions by government departments or independent public authorities. Public and private law are intermingled. Catchment boards, regional hospital boards, repatriation commissions, forest

---

[8] Cf. above, p. 209 ff., 266 ff.
[9] See in particular *Wilsons & Clyde Coal Co.* v. *English* [1938] A.C. 57.

commissions, discharge administrative functions of a social service character. In doing so they must make contracts, buy and sell large quantities of equipment and other goods, engage and dismiss staff, and undertake altogether a multitude of activities regulated by the law of property, tort and contract. The main legal problem here is the adjustment of administrative discretion and private law obligations. The discussion of this problem has shown a clear tendency to bring the legal duties of public authorities into line with the general law, except where this would impair the fulfilment of overriding public duties.[1]

A supplementary and generally more important safeguard for the proper exercise of administrative discretion is provided by administrative law, through general directives and standards. An example is given by the Ministry of Education circulars or by the many public service regulations. This raises the twin problems of delegated legislation and administrative jurisdiction. It is necessary that administrative actions affecting the community as a whole or groups of individuals should as far as possible follow general directives and that these directives should be subject to parliamentary scrutiny. The decision of the Court of Appeal in *Blackpool Corporation* v. *Locker*,[2] strongly criticised the practice of ministerial directions on the requisitioning of houses not being made available to the owners concerned. This criticism led to an administrative reform. Requisitioning powers are now delegated singly, and the instruments made available to the owner.[3] It is equally necessary that issues affecting important rights of the citizen should be subject to decision by an independent tribunal. The constitution of compensation tribunals to assess the compensation in the case of the nationalised industries, or of schools tribunals to decide on the closing down of independent schools, are important moves in this direction. But co-ordination and classification, is badly needed. In particular, a uniform system of publication of regulations, together with a co-ordination of the principles of judicial review of administrative actions with the principles

[1] Cf. above, p. 60 ff.
[2] [1948] 1 K.B. 349.
[3] Cf. *de Smith*, 12 M.L.R. 43.

governing administrative tribunals is long overdue. It would, for instance, be a great step forward if the multitude of different compensation tribunals could be combined in a single compensation court, which should have general competence and should form part of a co-ordinated system of administrative jurisdiction.[4] Lastly, the growing practical and theoretical importance of administrative law should be recognised by the publication and systematisation of the judgments of the hundreds of scattered administrative tribunals. This would greatly assist the development of public law principles, in which the administrative courts of the Continent have played an outstanding part.

Next, the modern State increasingly engages in the conduct of industrial and commercial activities. It does so either directly, through the State ownership of ships or railways or—increasingly —through independent corporate authorities, such as coal boards, transport commissions, or State trading corporations. Sometimes the State simply acquires a controlling interest in a company. The legal form of the enteprrise, which is, from a sociological and economic point of view, a matter of accident, should not determine legal rights and liabilities. While the Crown must be made fully liable in tort and in contract, commercial and industrial activities should as a rule be carried on by incorporated public authorities. The Crown will always enjoy certain privileges, for example freedom from taxation; but the incorporated public authority should be subject to the same rights and liabilities as any other legal person. It should be liable for taxes, rates and other charges and be bound by general statutes. This is the legal position of the newly nationalised industries in Britain.[5]

Subjection to ordinary legal liabilities need not prevent the fulfilment of economic, social and other planning functions. Both government departments and separate public authorities operate in the service of public interests or national plans, to which the legal principle of security of transactions must be

---

[4] In a Supreme Administrative Court of the continental type, one senate would normally deal with all compensation matters; this greatly helps the development of constant judicial principles.

[5] But see above, p. 209 ff, for the position in Australia.

adjusted. As we have seen, the break clauses in government contracts safeguard the power of the government to terminate contracts which have lost their purpose, such as war supplies, subject to fair compensation and indemnification. This is no worse, and in some cases compares favourably, with the standard terms contractually imposed by private industries on the other party. But the government should not be judge in its own cause. Disputes arising from such contracts should be justiciable, whether before the ordinary courts, an arbitration court or an administrative tribunal. To some extent public authorities must contract with each other as well as with private parties, and it is quite likely that a change of national production plans will entail the modification of contracts. All this can be done by the appropriate use of standard conditions. In the relations between public enterprises, it may mean the deliberate encouragement of one and the throttling of another industry. This is in essence part of a national economic policy. What is essential is that it should be subject to public and parliamentary scrutiny. The latter is provided for in the statutes which prescribe accounting, auditing and parliamentary debate of the annual reports of all the public corporations carrying on commercial or industrial activities, although a workable practical procedure can establish itself only by trial and error.[6]

An additional problem arises where public enterprise operates side by side with private enterprise. In Australia, for example, a recent decision of the High Court[7] has confirmed the constitutional power of the Commonwealth to establish a government-operated interstate airline, but has denied it the power to operate an interstate airlines monopoly. As a result, a government-controlled airline operates side by side with private airlines. Does the rule of law demand that the government should dispense its favours equally among its own instrumentality and the private operators? Is there anything objectionable, for example, in the government giving all air-mail contracts to the government enterprise or ordering civil servants

---

[6] See above, p. 192.
[7] *Australian National Airways* v. *Commonwealth* (1946) 71 C.L.R. 29.

to use no other air transport?[8]   It seems that to hold so would be an impossible legal fetter on policy decisions in a democratic community. The establishment of public enterprises is the result of a parliamentary decision and subject to parliamentary control. It is a perfectly legitimate objective for the government of the day to encourage a form of enterprise which it regards as preferable to private enterprise, within the limits set by a constitution or other positive legal restrictions. It would be absurd to expect a Labour government to allocate contracts equally among its own enterprise and private competitors if this is contrary to its avowed policy, and in the play of political forces it will be for any alternative government to reverse this policy if it wishes. For the sake of continuity, a wise government will act with moderation either way; but this is a matter of policy not of law.

The dual role of the State which both enters into the field of government and industrial commercial management and, at the same time, acts as the general controller over the allocation of economic resources for the nation, leads however to a further and more subtle problem. The State as economic controller allocates scarce resources among different industries and for different purposes. This function of the State is becoming increasingly important in a world dominated by scarcity due to the aftermath of a previous war or the fear of another. Economic necessity is mingled with social policy. In a social democracy like modern Britain essential industries are favoured as against luxury industries, exports at the expense of home consumption. This means not only the allocation of essential materials according to a priorities plan, but also the direction of labour. In this capacity the State can exercise a two-fold vital influence which is not immediately apparent in individual legal transactions but which regulates them by remote control. A State can thwart certain industries and encourage others. But it can also exercise a vital influence on the scope of individual liberties. Steel or coal are purely economic commodities; paper is not only an economic commodity which costs dollars but also the material basis without which mental and spiritual

---

[8] The latter but not the former is, at present, the case in Australia.

freedom is bound to wither. Again, the direction of labour threatens one of the most vital aspects of personal freedom, the right to choose one's job. It is true that both freedom of opinion and freedom of labour are severely restricted by existing social and economic conditions, by newspaper monopolies, economic compulsion and other factors. But the threat is no less great if it comes from the State itself. The problem does not exist in a totalitarian planned economy where any protection of individual freedoms is at best conditional and where such rights of private property and enterprise as remain are clearly subject to overriding State necessities. But it is acute in a planned economy of the democratic type which regards certain individual freedoms as essential and recognises the existence of a private economic sector along with public enterprise.

In a general sense it may be said that, in such a democratic society, the State is free to pursue its policies within the limits of constitutional power. It can socialise as far as a parliamentary majority authorises it to do so, and subject to overriding constitutional limitations. In the United States both the individual guarantees embodied in the first ten Amendments and the distribution of Federal and State competences impose restraints. In Australia only the latter check operates. In Great Britain neither limitation applies. Yet the directive principles are not vitally different. In so far as in Great Britain, for example, private industry operates side by side with public industry,[9] the government should be free to give government contracts to public rather than private enterprises if it so chooses. But it would be undemocratic and contrary to the spirit of the constitution to suffocate private enterprise indirectly by denying it essential materials for its operation rather than by the open constitutional device of socialisation. The borderline is a fine one. But recent British experience does not suggest that it cannot be found. The upholders of the traditional rule of law, who never tire of attacking the incompetence or even corruption

---

[9] This is not, at present, the case to any large extent. The newly nationalised industries (coal, electricity, gas, inland transport, airlines, iron and steel) are government monopolies. By contrast, a state-owned airline in Australia, and state-owned railways in Canada compete with private enterprises of similar scope.

of bureaucracy in the allocation of resources, are generally silent on the far more dangerous discrimination which is possible when the distribution of scarce resources is left to interested organisations themselves.[1]

The power of the government of the day to throttle criticism by its policy in allocating paper, or to curtail freedom of personal movement by direction of labour, certainly raises one of the gravest problems in modern planned democracy. Under the American Constitution, such action might result in complex legal controversies, about the interpretation of the first ten Amendments of the Constitution, in particular the First, Fifth and Fourteenth Amendments. In Great Britain this is a matter of purely political decision, for Parliament and public opinion. It has been suggested[2] that, on such matters as the allocation of paper resources between government departments and other applicants, twelve-men juries should be instituted to decide on the respective merits. On closer examination such a proposal seems impracticable. A similar claim might well be made out for the allocation of other scarce raw materials. Government policy would be made increasingly impossible by a series of twelve-men juries. The vigilance of Parliament and public opinion may in special cases justify the setting up of representative commissions to investigate problems of urgent concern.[3] But it would be unwise and impracticable to transfer vital government functions to juries of laymen not responsible to Parliament.

Finally the State functions as arbitrator between different groups in society. The term 'collectivist' State is often used loosely. A social service State need not be collectivist. It can be a parental or dictatorial State dispensing social welfare among the citizens while forbidding them to engage in any autonomous collectivist association, like Nazi Germany or Fascist Italy or Franco Spain. On the other hand, the State may take complete responsibility for all group activities going on within its borders,

---

[1] In Western Germany, for example, the Chambers of Industry and Commerce consisting of representatives of industry and business have wrested from the official authorities the power to allocate resources within different branches of industry: [1948] *Economist*, June 12.

[2] [1948] *Economist*, June 12.

[3] Such as discrimination in the allocation of paper, extent of newspaper monopolies, abuses of patents and so forth.

while regarding their quasi-autonomous organisation as convenient and necessary from an administrative and managerial point of view. This is the position in Soviet Russia where the managements of State-operated industries face trade unions. But the trade unions are not genuinely autonomous collective organisations. They represent group interests, within a well-defined national plan, and subject to overriding State policy ensured by the one-party system, political pressure and the many other sanctions at the disposal of the totalitarian State. In the modern democratic society, group associations are still permitted to develop freely in principle and to adjust their relations by mutual agreement, that is in the sphere of private law. English law, during the last century, has moved from original discrimination against trade unions to the full and equal recognition of trade and manufacturers' associations, employers' associations and trade unions, each entitled to foster and protect its interests by group action.[4] This purely passive function of the State is proving increasingly insufficient. As the moral and legal authority of employers' associations and trade unions increases, their agreements become more and more a matter of national concern. The vast majority of States are now in a condition of more or less permanent economic crisis. They cannot afford a prolonged standstill of production, or a rise of prices, profits and wages which paralyses the economic capacity of the nation. Hence the State must intervene, by wages boards, conciliation commissioners, compulsory awards, arbitration courts and other means designed to ensure industrial peace, as well as a certain amount of public influence on the formation of prices and wages. It is almost impossible to reconcile a compulsory national wages policy with the recognition of full freedom of organised groups and the consequent right of unimpeded collective bargaining. The most desirable solution is voluntary agreement and persuasion, but this leaves the legal dilemma unsolved. The most direct threat to the principle of equality is the increasing tendency of modern employers towards cartels, and of workers' associations towards the ' closed shop '. This operates to exclude the freedom of the individual to contract

[4] Cf. above, Ch. 6

on his own—unreal though this freedom is in the majority of cases—or to join another union. Freedom of association does not only mean freedom to associate but also freedom not to associate. It is true that increasingly agreements made between the major employers' and employees' associations are applied to the whole industry so that even non-members join in the benefits of such agreements. Graver, however, than this situation would be the recognition of a general principle of compulsory union membership as a condition of employment. This would transform democratic industrial society into that of the corporate State. The practical difference is small, for the trend is towards powerful unions which hardly need coercion. The freedom of the occasional dissenter makes a difference of principle out of proportion to its economic significance.

In short, the State as arbitrator in a democratic society has three tasks: the maintenance of a rough balance between contending organised groups and the usually unorganised consumer; the protection of the individual freedom of association; and the safeguarding of overriding State interests, such as the maintenance of export capacity.

CONCLUSION

The following is a summary of some of the ways by which the reconciliation of planning with democratic principles of justice might be achieved.

In the first place the privileges of the State as sovereign must be reduced to the absolute minimum. This means above all the abolition of the Crown's privileges and immunities in legal transactions affecting the citizen, and the limitation of the prerogatives, which have sometimes been unduly extended by the law courts in time of war.[5] The counterpart is judicial restraint in the application of prerogative orders to administrative action. If decisions like *Liversidge* v. *Anderson* [6] come dangerously close to a legitimation of administrative absolutism, a decision

---

[5] *R.* v. *Halliday, ex parte Zadig* [1915] A.C. 260. *Liversidge* v. *Anderson* [1942] A.C. 206. *Duncan* v. *Cammell Laird* [1942] A.C. 624. Contrast the Privy Council decision in the Australian case of *Robinson* v. *South Australia* [1931] A.C. 704.

[6] [1942] A.C. 206.

like *Roberts* v. *Hopwood*[7] oversteps the limits of judicial neutrality. But this has been rectified by recent English decisions,[8] and the refusal of the Australian High Court to investigate the reasonableness of delegated legislation.[9] In a federal system, these principles are however modified by the reference to judicial decision of many policy questions bearing on constitutional powers and rights.

The second, and possibly the greatest, of all problems is the proper control of administrative discretion. Three safeguards—which are increasingly applied in the modern legal practice of English-speaking democracies—are essential. First, general directives accessible to parliamentary scrutiny should to the largest possible extent lay down principles of administrative action in such fields as education, health, housing, State supervision of farming and other social services.

This needs, secondly, to be supplemented by the general principle of submitting disputes of major significance to independent tribunals. Whether a full system of administrative jurisdiction should be constituted by a hierarchy of special administrative courts or by a combination of administrative tribunals, with an appeal jurisdiction to the High Court, is a matter of relatively minor importance.

In the third place, the borderline between administrative discretion and the legal duties of public authorities must be clarified. The development should be along the lines indicated earlier in this book.

The third principle is that the State, as an industrial and commercial manager, must have equal rights and duties in equal situations. In other words, the Crown as well as separate public authorities must be subjected to the principles of common law, and this means the abolition not only of the privileges of the Crown in litigation but of a considerable number of other anomalies, survivals of a time when the State had far more

---

[7] [1925] A.C. 578. Above p. 164. And, for a similar tendency, *R.* v. *Paddington Rent Tribunal*, above pp. 161-62.

[8] *Re Decision of Walker* [1944] K.B. 644, *Franklin* v. *Minister of Town and Country Planning* [1948] A.C. 87. *Nakkuda Ali* v. *Jayaratne*, 66 T.L.R. 214, see above, pp. 165, 170.

[9] *Industrial Lighting Case* (1943) 67 C.L.R. 413.

limited functions. Among these are 'the shield of the Crown' which puts many public authorities in a legally privileged position,[1] or the continued presumption of Crown immunity from the binding force of statutes,[1a] or the limitation of the liability of local authorities for highway accidents to so-called acts of misfeasance.[2] Nor is there any reason why the Crown should be held immune from criminal liability where the penal sanctions ensure the observance of administrative and social duties.[3] Slowly, British law is moving towards a solution which, thanks to a more developed conception of public law, has long been accepted in Continental States, such as France or pre-Nazi Germany.

The State itself, as well as legally autonomous public enterprises, has, under these legal systems, long been legally responsible for unlawful interference with the protected rights of the citizen. Many problems have arisen with regard to the distribution of competences between 'ordinary' and administrative courts. But the tests suggested, such as the distinction between the public or private character of the transaction, between the State as sovereign or the State as Fiscus, between the use of command and the use of private legal instrumentalities, are of minor interest for our problem. Contrary to Dicey's view, Continental administrative courts have steadily extended the legal responsibility of public authority to the citizen. Compared with the position still obtaining in English law, it matters little whether a State tobacco monopoly is liable in negligence before a civil or administrative court. The main point is that, both under French and German law, a State department or a public corporation would be liable in tort, contract, or quasi-contract, like a private person.[4] The problem common to British, American and Continental law is that of the border-

---

[1] See in detail above, p. 209 ff.
[1a] See above, Ch. 12.
[2] See Salmond, *Law of Torts* (10th ed.) § 70; Friedmann, *Res Judicatae*, April, 1951.
[3] Cf. above, Ch. 5.
[4] For present-day French law, cf., *e.g.*, Waline, *Manuel Elémentaire de Droit Administratif* (4th ed., 1946) pp. 57 *et seq.*

line between administrative discretion and legal responsibility. For this is inherent in the nature of public administration.

In a democracy of the British type, the most important control over planning activities will, however, always be political control by the supreme legislative authority, *i.e.*, Parliament. The need for greater efficiency in the discharge of this control increases with the growth of State planning functions. The creation of the Parliamentary Committee of 1944 which scrutinises delegated legislation is an important step in the right direction. It must be supplemented by the creation of representative expert committees for the examination of the annual reports, accounts and audits of public enterprises. It is only by this method of expert decentralisation that parliamentary control, that is to say, ultimate government by the people, will avoid becoming a mere fiction.

There is a lot to be done in all these directions. But all these principles can be implemented and have at least partly been realised in the English-speaking democracies. It is for economists and politicians to debate the proper division between State planning and private initiative. But the lawyer can no longer ignore the fact that the accepted minimum of planning in a modern society is important enough to demand the reconsideration of legal principles. It would be unwise to expect too much of the law. No armoury of legal devices can imaginably solve such basic antinomies of political life as the tension between social planning and individual freedom. The strength of public opinion and political wisdom is ultimately more important than the most elaborate legal safeguards. The lawyer can, however, assert with confidence that the incompatibility of planning with the rule of law is a myth sustainable only by prejudice or ignorance. And once he has conquered his own articulate or inarticulate prejudices, once he has grasped and accepted the essentials of the social evolution of the last half century, the lawyer can make an important contribution to the problem of reconciling planning and freedom. Without its solution, democratic society cannot survive.

SUGGESTED READINGS

CHAPTER 2

Berle and Means	..	*The Modern Corporation and Private Property* (1932).
Renner	.. ..	*The Institution of Private Law and their Social Function* (1949) (Eng. ed. by Kahn-Freund).
Simpson and Stone		*Cases and Readings on law and Society*, Vol. 2, pp. 783–813; 1198–1219.
Arnold	.. ..	*The Folklore of Capitalism* (1938).
Gutteridge	.. ..	' Abuse of Rights ' (1933). 5 Camb.L.J. 22–45.
Kruse ..	.. ..	*The Right of Property* (Eng. ed. 1939).

CHAPTER 3

Holmes	.. ..	*The Common Law* (1881), Lecture VIII.
Maine	.. ..	*Ancient Law* (1906), Ed. by Pollock, Chap. 5.
Cohen, M.	.. ..	*Law and the Social Order* (1933), pp. 69–111.
Prausnitz	.. ..	*Standardisation of Commercial Contracts in English and Continental Law* (1937).
Teller	.. ..	*Labour Disputes and Collective Bargaining* (1940), 2 Vols.
Berman	.. ..	*Justice in Russia* (1950), Chap. 2.
Gsovski	.. ..	*Soviet Civil Law* (1948), Vol. 1, Chaps. 11–13.
Berman	.. ..	' Commercial Contracts in Soviet Law ' (1947), 35 Cal.L.R. 191.
Kahn-Freund..	..	' Collective Agreements under War Legislation ' (1943), 6 M.L.R. 112.
Cohn, Deschenaux and others		' Comparative Symposium on Frustration of Contract ' (*Journal of Comp. Legislation*, Vols. 28–30).
Zepos ..	.. ..	' Frustration of Contract in Comparative law and the new Greek Civil Code of 1946 ' 11 M.L.R. 36–46.

CHAPTER 4

Bohlen	.. ..	*Studies in the Law of Tort*, 126, pp. 334–440.
Isaacs ..	.. ..	' Fault and Liability ' 31 Harv.L.R. 954.
Wright	.. ..	' Law of Torts, 1923–1947,' 28 Can.Bar.Rev. 46.
Bohlen	.. ..	' Fifty Years of Tort ' 50 Harv.L.R. 725.
Holmes	.. ..	*The Common Law* (1881), Lectures III and IV.
Friedmann	.. ..	' Modern Trends in the Law of Torts ' (1937), 1 M.L.R. 34.
Lawson	.. ..	*Negligence in Civil Law* (1950).
Holdsworth	.. ..	*History of English Law* (1925), Vol. 8, pp. 446–482.

Ehrenzweig ..	..	*Negligence without Fault* (1951).
Paton	.. ..	'Evolution of Negligence,' 23 A.L.J. 158.
		Report by Departmental Committee on Alternative Remedies (1946 Cmd. 6860).

CHAPTER 5

Hall ..	.. ..	*General Principles of Criminal Law* (1947), Chaps. 5, 6, 10.
Sayre ..	.. ..	'Public Welfare Offences' (1933), 33 Col.L.R. 55.
Welsh ..	.. ..	'Criminal Liability of Corporations' (1946), 62 L.Q.R. 345.

CHAPTER 6

Dicey ..	.. ..	*Law and Public Opinion in England in the Nineteenth Century* (1914) (2nd. ed.).
Stone ..	.. ..	*Province and Function of Law* (1946), Chap. 23.
Simpson and Stone ..		*Cases and Readings on Law and Society* (1949), Vol. 2, pp. 1233–1274.
Lewis ..	.. ..	'Monopoly and the Law' (1943), 6 M.L.R. 97. *Monopolies and Restrictive Practices Commission* (*U.K.*), (First Report, Dec., 1950).

CHAPTER 7

Maitland	.. ..	*Selected Essays* (1936 ed.), Chaps. 3–5.
Lloyd ..	.. ..	*The Law Relating to Unincorporated Associations* (1938).
Lloyd ..	.. ..	'Disciplinary Powers of Professional Bodies' (1950), 13 M.L.R. 287.
Latcham	.. ..	'Private Charitable Foundations' (1950), 98 Penn. L.R. 98.
Note ..	.. ..	(1948), 34 Virg.L.R. 182–201.
Keeton	.. ..	'The Changing Conception of Trusteeship' (1950), 3 *Current Legal Problems* 14–29.

CHAPTER 8

Denning	.. ..	*Freedom under the Law* (1949), Chap. 3.
Robson	.. ..	*Justice and Administrative Law* (1951), (3rd ed.).
Wade, E. C. S.	..	'The Courts and the Administrative Process' (1947), 63 L.Q.R. 164.
Wade, H. W. R.	..	'Quasi-Judicial and its Background' (1949), 11 Camb.L.J. 239.
Mitchell	.. ..	'Limitations on the Contractual Liability of Public Authorities' (1950), 13 M.L.R. 318, 455.
Schmitthoff ..	..	'The Growing Ambit of the Common Law' (1951), 29 Can.Bar.Rev. 469.

CHAPTER 9

'Symposium on Nationalisation of British Industries' (1951), *Law and Contemporary Problems*, Autumn Issue.

Robson .. .. 'The Public Corporation in Great Britain Today' (1950), 63 Harv.L.R. 1321.

Robson .. .. 'Nationalised Industries in Britain and France' (1950), 44 Amer.Pol.Sc.Rev. 299–322.

Wade .. .. .. 'The Constitutional Aspect of the Public Corporation' (1949), 2 *Current Legal Problems* 172–182.

CHAPTER 10

Borchard .. .. *Declaratory Judgments* (1941), (2nd ed.), pp. 875–926.

Jennings .. .. 'Declaratory Judgments against Public Authorities in England' (1932), 41 Yale L.R. 407.

Davis .. .. .. 'Forms of Proceedings for Judicial Review of Administrative Actions' (1949), 44 Ill.L.R. 565.

CHAPTER 11

'Symposium on Statutory Construction' (1950), 3 Vanderbilt L.R. 365–596.

Read and MacDonald *Cases and Materials on Legislation* (1948), Chap. 7.

Allen .. .. .. *Law in the Making* (1939), (3rd ed.), Excursus B.

Willis .. .. .. 'Statutory Interpretation in a Nutshell' (1938), 18 Can.Bar.Rev. 1.

Radin .. .. .. 'Statutory Interpretation' (1931), 41 Harv.L.R. 863.

Stone .. .. .. *Province and Function of Law* (1946), Chap. 7.

CHAPTER 12

Friedmann .. .. 'The Shield of the Crown' (1950), 25 A.L.J. 275.

Williams .. .. *Crown Proceedings* (1947).

Mann .. .. .. 'The Law Governing State Contracts' (1944), 21 Brit.Y.B. of Int. Law 11–33.

CHAPTER 13

Dicey .. .. .. *The Law of the Constitution* (9th ed. by Wade), Chaps. 4, 12, and Introduction.

Jennings .. .. *The Law and the Constitution* (4th ed.), Chap. 2.

Wade and Phillips .. *Constitutional Law* (1950), (4th ed.), Chap. 3.

Hayek .. .. *The Road to Serfdom* (1944), Chap. 6.

Finer .. .. .. *The Road to Reaction* (1946).

Denning .. .. *Freedom under the Law* (1949), Chap. 3.

Stone .. .. .. *Province and Function of Law* (1947), Chap. 27.

INDEX

NOTE: Bold type indicates a major discussion of the subject. The index
of names is confined to those whose views or judgments are quoted
or discussed.

abuse of rights, 22-23
administrative discretion, **163-71;
178-83;** 299-301.
administrative law, 60-63
and see administrative discretion;
continental jurisprudence;
public Welfare offences;
public law
administrative tribunals, 60, 155-56,
164, 170-72, 300-2
agricultural land commission, 192,
200
Allen, C. K., 287
alternative remedies committee, 93
American law,
administrative law, 193, 230
anti-trust legislation, 17
constitutional law, 13, 20, 40-41,
242, 249, 252, 255, 256, 283, 295
criminal law, 107
declaratory judgments, 230
frustration of contract, 68
injunctions, 230
labour law, 52
patent law, 24-25
standardised contracts, 47-48
state functions of, in, 211
tort, trends in law of, 75-78, 80,
82-85, 88, 94
Anglo-American jurisprudence, 11-
13, 15, 134
animals, liability for, 83-84, 95-96, 99
Anstalt, 10, 62, 63, 133
Aristotle, 296
Atkin, Lord, 93, 158, 159, 169-70,
176
Atkinson, Lord, 164-5
Attorney-General, function of, in
public law, **217-234**
Australian law,
anti-communist legislation, 159
constitutional law, 13, 27-28,
179-80, 249, 252, 255, 256, 268,
283, 295, 302, 308
criminal law, 102-105
crown, legal position of, 102-5,
212-15

Australian law—*cont.*
declaratory judgments, 32, 217-21
industrial law, 20, 52-53, 117, 148
injunctions in public law, 221-31
law of associations, 145
public corporations, 188, 193, 212-
15, 279
restraint of trade, 125
statutory interpretation, 240-41,
269
air corporations, 191, 198, 199,
203-4

Bentham, J., 39, 109, 117, 120.
Berle, A. and Means, G., 14-16
Beveridge Report, 87, 88, 279
Birkenhead, Lord, 123
Blackburn, J., 210
boards, *see* public corporations
Bohlen, F., 80
Burnham, J., 16
British Electricity Authority, 191,
195, 196, 197, 199, 204
British Transport Commission, 191,
197, 200, 207, 208-9

Cahn, E., 71
Canadian law,
charitable foundations, 139
constitutional law, 13, 249, 253-54,
283, 295.
industrial law, 52
law of tort, 78, 100
public corporations, 188, 279
statutory interpretation, 258–59
capitalism, 9-11, 14, 33, 154
and see property, law of
Cardozo, J., 110, 128, 211, 277-78
Carr, Sir C., 285, 287-88
cartels, 111, **122-30**, 291–92
Central Land Board, 192, 207, 208
certiorari,43-144, 156, 162, 205-6, 230
charities—*see* foundations
Cheshire, G. C. and Fifoot, C. H. S.,
40
closed shop, 20, 132, 306-7, *see also*
collective bargaining

Cohen, M. R., 45, 70

common employment, doctrine of, 85, *and see* tort, law of

collective agreements,
and equality of bargaining, 44
and freedom of trade, 147
and status, 71
as alternative to individual contracts, 19-20, 306-7
in American law, 50-52
in Australian and New Zealand law, 52-53
in Canadian law, 59
in English law, 48-50
in Nazi law, 54
in Soviet law, 54
communism, 19, 101, 154-55, 279, 305-6
and see Soviet law

company law, 137-42, 204, 248

conspiracy, law of, 20, 42, **109-122**, 147

constitutional law, 238, 242, 251-52, 253-57, 305
see also American law; Australian law; Canadian law; judicial process; state, theory of; statutes, interpretation of

Continental jurisprudence,
abuse of rights, 22-23
administrative law, **60-62**, 107
alternatives to trust, 133-34
concepts of negligence, 91
developments in company control, 15
distinction of public and private law, **153-56**
interpretation of statutes, 238-40
legal definitions of property, 11-13
legal position of State and public authorities, **60-62**, 164, 178, 270-73
public contracts in, **60-62**, 64
theory of collective agreements, 50

contract,
compulsory, 55-59, 209
freedom of, 19, 21, **34-9**, 42-3, 45-8
public, **59-67**, 175-77, 181-83
distinction from private contract, 60-2
in continental law, 60-3
in English law, 62-4
in Soviet law, 65-6
and see collective agreements; frustration of contract

co-operatives, 123-25

corporate enterprise, 14-18

corporate personality, 31, 105-8, **137-42**, 206-9

Corwin, E., 41

Craies, 269

criminal law, 4, 98, **102-8**, 110, 217, 261-62
and see public welfare offences

Crown, legal position of,
abolition of litigation privileges, 35, 93, 218-19, 260-1, 301
contracts made by government departments, 296
criminal liability, **102-8**
discovery of documents, 158
relation to public corporations, **208-16**
immunity from statutes, **266-74**, 301, 307
liability for taxes, 301
liability in quasi-contract, 260-1
liability in tort, 93, 260, 381
prerogatives, 157, 307
privileges in patent law, 24

damages, juristic aspects of, 36-37, 70, 217, 233

Davis, K. C., 230

Davis, Ll., 247

declaratory judgments, **217-221**, 233

delegated legislation, **285-88**, 310
and rule of law, **285-88**, 310
and separation of powers, 168-71

democracy, legal principles of, 29, **282-310**, *and see* liberalism

Denning, L.J., 78, 146, 180–81, 192, 209, 277

development corporations, 192, 212
and continental jurisprudence, 153, 284
and equality before law, 116, 298
on administrative law, 153, 178
on collectivism, 3, 173
on rule of law, 163, 238, **285-88**

Dicey, A. V., 3, 5, 106, 113, 153, 163, 178, 238, 278, 284, 285-88, 298

Dixon, J., 103-104, 108, 212-213, 223-225, 254, 285

domaine public, 23

Douglas, J., 211

droit administratif, 60-61

due process. *See* American law; sub constitutional law

Duguit, L., 153, 155

du Parcq, Lord, 95, 268
duty of care, *see* negligence; tort

Ehrenzweig, A., 99
Ehrlich, E., 250
employers, legal duties of, to
    employees, 84-87
equality,
    and privileges of Crown, **209-216,**
    266-74, 308-9
    and rule of law, 283
    and standardisation of contract,
    45-48
    and basis of law of contract,
    36-37, **39-43**
    between Government and subject,
    177-86, 297, 308-9
equity,
    and equality in contract, 41-42
    as basis of public law remedies,
    218-34. *See also* declaratory
    judgments; injunctions
Esher, Lord, 113
Evatt, J., 110, 117

Farwell, J., 147
fascism, 19, 54, 155, 250, 281, 305
fault liability, **75-101,** *and see* tort,
    law of
federal constitutions, *see* judicial
    process
Finlay, Lord, 125, 127
foundations, charitable, 27, **138-42**
fiscus, 61, 178
Frank, J., 250, 294
Frankfurter, J., 211, 237, 277
freedom of contract—*see* contract
freedom of labour, 43
    and see closed shop; collective
    agreements
freedom of person, 157-58
freedom of Property, **22-33,** 160, *see*
    also property, law of
freedom of trade, 109-32, 147,
    159-60, 231-32
    and business competition, **112-17,**
    127-29, 292
    and labour organisations, **117-22**
    and trade associations, **122-28**
French law,
    abuse of rights, 22
    administrative law, **60-61,** 155,
    270-1
    administrative tribunals, 61, 176,
    270-72

French law—*cont.*
    concept of public property, 28
    definition of ownership, 1!
    frustration, doctrine of, 62, 68, 271
    public contracts, 61, 178
frustration of contracts, 58-59, 62,
    67-70, 72, 271
    as instrument of legal adjustment
    of economic upheavals, 69-70
    in English law, 58-59, 68-69
    in French administrative law, 62,
    67, 68
    in German law, 68
    in Greek law, 68, 271
fundamental rights, 12-13, 20, 29

gas board, 191, 195, 196
Gény, F., 211, 249
German law,
    abuse of rights, 22
    administrative contracts, 178
    cartel legislation, 17
    definition of ownership, 11
    forms of public enterprise, 28,
    187-88
    frustration, doctrine of, 67-68, 271
    legal treatment of charities, **133-37**
    unincorporated associations, **135-**
    37
Goddard, Lord, 162, 171
government, functions of,
    and arbitration in social conflicts,
    305-7
    and commercial activities, 211-12,
    214-15, 273, 280, **301-5**
    and economic control, 303-4
    and government immunity from
    penal sanctions, 102-8
    and interference with private con-
    tract, 55-59
    and legal liability of State, 179-81,
    184-85
    and privileges of Crown, **266-74**
    and shield of the Crown principle,
    209-216
    and supervision of private
    associations, **142-49**
    and social services, **192-93,** 212,
    299-300
Gray, J. C., 238
Greek law, 68, 271
Green, T. H., 284
Greene, Lord, 30, 84, 95, 163, 166,
    172-73, 202-3, 243
Gutteridge, H. C., 23

Hall, J., 97, 98, 107
Halsbury, Lord, 112, 245
Harrison, Sir W. J., 257, 261
Hayek, F. A., 278-79, 288-91, 294, 295, 296
Heok, F., 211
Holdsworth, W. S., 94
Holmes, O. W., 70, 73, 97, 101, 211, 250, 294, 296

Ihering, R., 249
imprévision, 62, 67, *and see* frustration of contract
independent contractors, 78-79, *and see* tort, law of
injunction as public law remedy, 205, **221-35**
international corporations, 188-89
Italian law, 271
interpretation, *see* statutes, interpretation of
Iron and Steel Board, 191, 196, 197

Jennings, Sir I., 218, 246, 247, 277, 281, 285, 287, 288
Jessel, Sir G., 245
Jowitt, Lord, 253-254
judicial process,
  and administrative process, 30-31, **163-71**, 308
  and business competition, **112-13, 116-17, 122-28, 292**
  and collective agreements, 48-55
  and control of corporate organisations, 129-30, 136-37, **142-49**
  and development of administrative law, **60-64**
  and development of public law remedies, **217-34**
  and evolution of law of tort, **75-87, 93-96**
  and federal constitutions, 13, 20, 249, 251-52, 295, 304, 308
  and freedom of contract, 42-43
  and freedom of trade, 42-43, **109-22**
  and law of conspiracy, **109-22**
  and legal privileges of Crown, **179-83**, 307-8
  and legal status of public authorities, **171-77, 209-16**
  and political ideologies, 29-30, 40
  and political statutes, **253-57**
  and principles of criminal liability, **102-6**, 108

judicial process—*cont.*
  and protection of private rights, 21, **29-32**, 40, **157-77**, 241-42
  and public interest, 38-39, 55-57, **157-63**, 231-32
  and public policy, 268-70
    see also public interest
  and social evolution, **277-81**
  and social legislation, **246-49, 257-59**
  and stability of contract, **67-70**
  and standardised contracts, **46-47**
  and statute law, **237-65**
    see also statutes, interpretation of
  and trade unionism, **114-22**
  and corporate personality, **142-49**
justice, interpretations of, 281-88
    see also rule of law

Kahn-Freund, O., 12, 26, 27, 48, 49, 201
Kant, I., 121
Keeton, G. W., 142
Kelsen, H., 153-54, 155

land law, 22-23, 26, 35, 58, 76, 290-91
  legal duties of landlords, 35, 76
  legal restrictions on use of land, 22-23, 26, 58
  private ownership and planning powers, 290-91
Laski, J., 247
Latham, C. J., 103, 104, 212, 225-226
lawyer's law, 237-39
Lawrence, L. J., 161, 246
liberalism, **113-116**, 130-32, 163, **277-81**, 285
  and administrative law, 163
  and laissez-faire, 276-78
  and modern corporate organisation, 130-32
  and rule of law, **285-99**
  as basis of judicial decisions on freedom of trade, 112-16
  eclipse of, **277-81**
  redefinition of legal ideals of, 287-304
    and see democracy
Lindley, Lord, 114
Lloyd, D., 130, 137, 147
Lowe, J., 240-41

McCardie, J., 129
MacDermott, Lord, 96
MacMillan, Lord, 94
MacNaghten, Lord, 202
Maine, Sir H., 19, 34, 284
managerial revolution, 14-16
Maitland, F. W., 5, 11-12, 125,
    133-38, 140, 142-44, 149, 287
mandamus, 156, 205-6
Mann, F. A., 272
manufacturers, liability of, 75-78
    and see tort, law of
Marx, K., 9, 16, 121, 131
Marxism, *see* Marx, K.
Maugham, Lord, 129, 228
mens rea, 106-108
Monopolies and Restrictive Practices
    Commission, 130
monopoly,
    and cartel agreements, **122-30**
    and right to work, 231-32
    in Britain, Germany, U.S.A., 17
    legislative measures against, 17-18
    private, as alternative to State
      planning, 291-92
Moulton, Lord, 80, 260

National Assistance Board, 207
National Coal Board, 190, 191, 194,
    195, 196, 197, 199, 203, 204,
    207, 212
Nazi law, *see* Fascism
negligence, **75-79**, **93-96**, **171-77**
    and see tort, law of
New Zealand law, 52-53, 148
nuisance, 79, 82
    and see tort, law of

occupiers, duties of, 82-83, 96
O'Connor, J., 254
ownership, *see* property

Parker, Lord, 125
Parmoor, Lord, 124, 125
Pashukanis, 154
patent law, 23-25
Paton, G. W., 76, 82
Pitney, J., 40
planning legislation, 30, 162-63
    see also welfare state
planned society, *see also* welfare
    state
political law, 237-39
Pollock, Sir F., 239

Porter, Lord, 90
Pound, R., 211, 296
prerogative jurisdiction 143, 148,
    156, 162, **167-71**, 205-206, 230,
    307-8
    and see certiorari
professional associations, **142-49**
prohibition, 156, 230
property, law of, 4, **9-33**
    and abuse of rights, 22-23
    and anti-monopoly legislation
      16-18
    and compulsory contracts, 26
    and credit control, 27-28
    and patent law, **23-25**
    and public ownership, 28-29
    and statutory duties, 25
    and taxation, 26-27
    and the judiciary, **29-32**
    Continental concepts, of 11-13
    English concept of, 11-13
    Marxist analysis of, 9-11, 14
    transformation of, in modern
      capitalist society, **14-16**
Prosser, W. M., 82
public authorities, **59-67**, **163-183**,
    202-203, **209-216**, 233, 309
    and see crown; public corpora-
      tions
    abuse of powers by, **202-6**
    and administrative discretion,
      177-86
    and law of contract, **60-67**
    and "shield of the Crown"
      principle, **209-16**
    judicial supervision of, **164-71**
    legal duties of, **171-77**, 233, 309
    legal position in Continental
      systems, **60-63**
    legal position of, in Soviet law,
      65-67
public contracts, *see* contracts
public corporations,
    advisory councils, **195-8**
    and collective bargaining, 49
    as agents of commercial State
      activities, 296
    as instruments of public ownership,
      28-29
    constitution, **193-95**
    general characteristics, **191-93**
    legal liabilities, 63
    legal powers, **198-206**
    legal status, **206-16**
    liability for criminal offences, 105
    place of, in national economy, 67

public corporations—*cont.*
powers of terminating and disclaiming contracts, 58-59
reasons for creation of, 48
types of, **189-91**
public law, 5, 30-32, 56-58, **60-67**, 71, **153-234**
and see administrative law; public corporations
and common law duties, **171-77**
and defence power, 157-58
and equality between governors and governed, 177-83
and judicial supervision of administrative authorities, **163-71**
and personal liberty, 157-58
and private property, **30-32, 160-62**
impact of, on law of contract, **56-59**
in Continental legal systems, **60-63, 153-56**
in English legal system, 63-64, 67, 71, 155-56
in Soviet law, **65-67**, 154-55
public ownership, **28-29**
and see public corporations
public policy, 55, 107, **122-32 146-49**, 268-70, *see also* judicial process (public interest)
Public Welfare Offences,
and criminal liability of Crown, **102-8**
and mens rea, 25, 98

quasi-judicial functions,
definition of, by English courts, 30-31, 148, **168-71**, 234, 247
of professional bodies with disciplinary powers, **143-44**

Radin, M., 250
regional hospital boards, 188, 192, 193, 194, 200, 207-8, 215
Reid, Lord, 96
Renner, K., 9-11, 14, 19, 22, 26, 32, 154
restraint of trade, 38-39, 42-43, 55
Robson, W. A., 285
Romer, Lord, 249
Roosevelt, F. D. R., 189
Rowlatt, J., 179
rule of law, **277-310**
and Dicey's theory, **285-88**
and equality between governors and governed, **296-98**

rule of law—*cont.*
and Hayek's theory, **288-98**
and democratic ideals of justice, 282-84
and legal certainty, **294-96**
and natural law, 281
and planning functions of modern government, **290-98**
and public order, 281-82
and welfare state, 298-306
reconciliation of, with modern government, **307-10**
Russell, Lord, 202, 248
Russia, *see* Soviet law
Rylands v. *Fletcher*, Rule in, 75, 80-81, 93-95

Salmond, J., 201, 238
Salter, J., 160
Sankey, Lord, 253
Scots law, 68
Scott, L.J., 46, 96, 168, 245, 261, 286
separation of powers, 155, **285-88**
Scrutton, L.J., 115, 123, 127, 248
shield of the Crown, *see* Crown, legal position of
Simon, Lord, 37, 119-20, 176, 243
Singleton, L.J., 166
Smith, A., 211
social insurance,
and equality of bargaining, 21
and redistribution of property, 27
and tort liability, *and see* tort, law of, 73, **87-92, 99-101**
in recent British legislation, 73-74
Socialism, 3, 16, 28-29, 33, 65-67, 268-69, 279
and Crown immunities, 268-69
and see public corporations
and law of property, **9-14**
and modern property restrictions, 33
and public ownership, 46
sanctions for breach of contract, **65-67**
Soviet law, 19, 23, 28, 54, **65-67**, 68, 101, 154-55, 187, 189
and collective bargaining, **54-55**
and right of property, 23
and socialisation of industry, 28
contracts between State enterprises, **65-67**
frustration of contract, 68
significance of public law, 154-55
State trusts, 186, 189
trade unions, 19

Spencer, H., 120, 211
Stammler, R., 120
standard contracts, **45-48**
Starke, J., 104, 226-227, 229
state, legal theory of, 104-108, 177-81, 270-74, 309-10
  and executive prerogatives, **179-81**
  as basis of science of public law, 178
  immunity from criminal prosecution, **104-8**
  sovereign and non-sovereign functions, **178-81**
  and see Government, functions of
status, 34-35
statutes, interpretation of, 160-63, **239-265**
  analytical approach, **239-46**, 251
  and private rights, 241
  and protection of private property, **241-44**
  constitutional statutes, 252, **253-57**
  housing legislation, 160-61
  international conventions, 261
  intuitive approach, 249-51
  liberal and strict approach, **244-46**
  penal statutes, 261
  reform statutes, **259-61**
  social policy approach, 246-49, 251, 257-59
  tax legislation, **242-43**, 262-63
  technical statutes, 263-64
statute law, significance of, 5, 30, 237-39
statutory duties, 21, 25, 56, 86-87, 299
  as compulsory terms of contract, 56
  as legal instrument of welfare state, 25, 86-87, 299
  interpretation of, 21
  of employers, 86
statutory powers, 171-77, 184
Sterndale, Lord, 245
Stiftung, 134
Stone, J., 277
Story, J., 254
strict liability, **75-87**
Sumner, Lord, 242
Sutherland, J., 211
Swiss law, 11, 22, 68, 252, 271
  abuse of rights, 22
  definition of ownership, 11
  doctrine of frustration, 68, 271
  judicial law-making, 252

Taft, C.J., 295
tax law, 26-27, 30, 139-42, 242-43, 262-63
  as instrument of redistribution of wealth, 267
  interpretation of tax legislation, 242-43, 262-63
  judicial approach to, 30
tort, law of, 26-27, 30, 139-42, 242-43, 262-63
  and alternative remedies, **87-92**
  and Beveridge Report, 88
  and social insurance, 73-4, **87-92**, **96-101**
  animals, liability for, 83-84
  Cavalier v. *Pope*, rule in, 35-77
  common employment, rule of, 85-86
  contributory negligence, 85
  controllers of property, duties of, 32, **75-84**
  dangerous things, liability for, **76-77**
  development of, and judicial process, **75-87**, **93-96**
  Donoghue v. *Stevenson*, rule in, **75-78**
  employers, duties of, 84-87
  independent contractors, liability for, 78-79
  invitees, duties to, 78, 82-83
  licencees, duties to, 82-83
  nuisance, liability in, 79-80
  res ipsa loquitur, 77
  Rylands v. *Fletcher*, rule in, 80-81
  statutory duties, 86
  strict liability, 80-82
  and see negligence
totalitarianism, 19, 54-55, 304
  see also Communism; Fascism
Tennessee Valley Authority, 188, 189, 211
trade associations, 115-17, **122-32**
  and cartel agreements, 122-28
  blacklisting by, 115, 128
  monopoly tendencies of, 115-16
trade unions, 19-20, 42, 49, **114-22**, 143, 147, 305-6
  and enforceability of collective contracts, 49-50
  and equality of bargaining, 19-20
  and judicial supervision, **143-49**
  and liability for conspiracy, 42, **114-22**
  in Soviet Russia, 19, 306
  and closed shop, 306-7

trust, 5, 11, **133-37**, 149
   and charitable foundations, **138-42**
   and divided ownership, 11
   social function of, in English law, **133-37**, 149
   trust corporations, 142

ultra vires, 201-6
   and see public corporations,
unincorporated associations, **135-37**

Verein, 133, 134, 135-37

Wade, E. C. S., 285
Watson, Lord, 112
Welfare State,
   and comparative law, 13
   and managerial functions of government, 275
   and planning powers, 163

Welfare State—*cont.*
   tax policies of, and charitable foundations, 138
   and restrictions on private property, **25-28**
   and rule of law, **275-310**
   and social insurance legislation. **87-92**
   and transformation of law of contract, 44, **55-59**
   impact on English legal system, 3-6
   and see rule of law; Government functions of; State, theory of
Welsh, R. S., 106, 108
Williams, G. E., 192
Williams, J., 104, 227, 228, 229
Willis, J., 30, 241-42, 253
Wright, C. A., 82, 295
Wright, Lord, 77, 93, 111, 121, 161, 237, 245, 260
Wrottesley, J., 267

DATE DUE